INTERNATIONAL SECURITY

INTERNATIONAL SECURITY
PROBLEMS AND SOLUTIONS

Patrick M. Morgan
University of California, Irvine

CQ PRESS

A Division of Congressional Quarterly Inc.
Washington, D.C.

CQ Press
1255 22nd Street, NW, Suite 400
Washington, DC 20037

Phone: 202-729-1900; toll-free, 1-866-427-7737 (1-866-4CQ-PRESS)

Web: www.cqpress.com

Cover and text design: Auburn Associates, Inc.

Cover credits: Top photo, AP Photo/Rodrigo Abd; Bottom photo, Reuters/Mike Segar

⊛ The paper used in this publication exceeds the requirements of the American
National Standard for Information Sciences—Permanence of Paper for Printed Library
Materials, ANSI Z39.48-1992.

Printed and bound in the United States of America

10   09   08   07   06   1   2   3   4   5

Library of Congress Cataloging-in-Publication Data

Morgan, Patrick M.
   International security : problems and solutions / Patrick M. Morgan.
      p. cm.
   Includes bibliographical references and index.
   ISBN 1-56802-587-4 (alk. paper)
1. Security, International.   I. Title.

JZ5588.M67 2006
355'.033—dc22

                                                                    2006002953

To Marilyn

CONTENTS

Part IV
Conclusion

For people intrigued by the title of this book, here is an overview of the contents. It grows out of my experiences teaching a course on war in international politics. I use security as the lens to narrow the focus on that vast subject. The point is not to study war comprehensively but to view it as a source of insecurity with which governments and their leaders must grapple. I describe war as a problem because of how it affects security, in posing direct threats of harm to governments, societies, and individuals and in raising more indirect threats to the international system, nations, and societies. *Security* is defined as physical safety from harm that others might inflict by military means. This is a relatively traditional conception, used here because it is still highly relevant. Other conceptions of security are now widely employed, but for nearly everyone physical safety still takes precedence. The subject is therefore how people operating in international politics have tried to enhance security by reducing the threat, incidence, and consequences of war.

The book begins by explaining the nature of security in international politics and then turns to examining why and how war erodes security and is therefore a problem, something more complicated than it might seem. The largest part examines how scholars, officials, military officers, and others think about preventing or controlling (and even sometimes using) warfare to enhance security, and the kinds of steps that thinking has led to. These steps are discussed as *strategies* for dealing with the problem of war—such as the distribution of power, deterrence, collective security, and multilateralist management—and working *tactical* efforts within any systemic arrangement—such as negotiation and mediation, peacekeeping, peace enforcement, and peacebuilding. The central concern is with efforts to deal with war *without abandoning international politics*. Governments and peoples will not soon want international politics to disappear, to be replaced by, for example, a world government that displaces their sovereignty. So long as that is the case it is not worthwhile studying how to handle war by erasing international politics.

Wars and threats of them arise both in relations *among governments*, in international politics as normally defined, and *inside* the societies they govern. Security studies in international politics, actually the field of international politics itself, developed out of an urgent need to better understand and control warfare among governments. Some analysts have even argued that the core element of international politics is war and therefore insecurity. Approaching international politics, war, and security in this way meant that at one time warfare within societies received limited attention. Although the two kinds of warfare are related in that international politics often plays a role in wars inside states and those wars often affect international politics, it seemed that, for the most part, wars among governments could be studied and dealt with independently, and that they were the most important and most dangerous.

In recent decades wars in societies have come to look much more important, so they receive significant attention here as well. Such warfare is now important in and of itself. Wars inside societies are much more numerous than wars between governments. In a typical year, they kill or maim far more people, produce far more refugees, damage more of people's livelihoods. This has led to increased pressures to attend to them. Saying such warfare is not a regular part of international politics leads to responses that it ought to be, that it deserves to be part of the agenda in relations among governments. Also, warfare inside societies is increasingly seen as related in important ways to relations between governments; it affects international politics whether someone puts it on the agenda or not. The implication is that security studies must attend to wars inside societies too.

There was another division in the study of international politics pertaining to warfare. The study of war was often tied to analysis of the use of force and threats as a tool in foreign policy. Alongside that was an effort to study war primarily to do away with it, an effort generally referred to as *peace studies*. The distinction is roughly what would exist between fields that study the development and impact of disease as part of understanding how people and societies function, and fields that study disease primarily to treat or eliminate it.

These subfields of security studies should not be approached separately. Students should have a chance to explore them in combination in their coursework. However, pulling together readings, concepts, findings, and cases from different academic bastions can result in students feeling that they are studying two different subjects, taking two different courses at once. I discovered that the sort of book that would help me get around this problem did not exist, so I have written one.

This book offers a framework that embraces the traditional way of thinking about security studies with its focus on intergovernmental wars, and the rising concern about wars inside societies, plus major elements of the peace studies perspective. It includes a three-level conception of security: physical safety from harm at (1) the level of the international system, (2) the level of governments, and (3) the level of societies. Wars have harmful effects, especially in promoting insecurity, at all three levels. In fact, they sometimes have harmful effects on all three levels simultaneously.

That framework is used to assess remedies for warfare by seeing how they work and evaluating their impact on each level. This includes demonstrating that what looks successful and appealing on one level may have limited and even harmful effects at another, thus posing dilemmas, problems, and difficulties. The overall picture is somewhat pessimistic with regard to how much has been accomplished because wars have certainly not disappeared. On the other hand, it is relatively optimistic in that warfare and the scale of its harmful effects have been declining. Warfare is down and security is up at every level. That's nice, though how permanent it is remains uncertain, and there is still a long way to go.

An important part of the framework is that it presents security in international politics through relevant theoretical views. The emphasis is not on abstract analytical aspects, for the most part, but on how such views are expressed and used in policy making, public discussions, and other debates about what to do, where, and when. The objective is to help students spot and understand the underlying ideas, assumptions, and patterns of analysis that are at work in seemingly complicated, jumbled ways.

The book cites and discusses numerous historical examples and contemporary situations, wars and conflicts pertinent to the subject. Because history is rarely the strong point of students, "Cases and Context" boxes describe important historical cases or current conflicts in more detail, separate from the running discussion in the book. A number of important terms and concepts—state, sovereignty, security dilemma, hegemonic stability, terrorism, human rights, and so on—are laid out in the text, but some receive further elaboration in "Terms and Concepts" boxes. A glossary offers additional information on important terms, highlighted in boldface in the text.

Each chapter ends with a short bibliographical essay that briefly cover further readings that could be consulted. I hope this is more useful than long bibliographical lists of sources under topic headings or elaborate footnotes about sources, since the essays contain some indication as to why these works are relevant.

A final note on the writing. Many subjects can be dull or numbing in complexity, including aspects of international politics, and little can be done to avoid this. Writing a textbook offers an important opportunity to try to demystify and uncomplicate things, hopefully without being dull. So I have tried to talk about the subject with a bit of levity, in a more relaxed and breezy way, but without oversimplifying.

There you have it. This is what I hope to have accomplished in the book, and what I hope can be accomplished in using it either as the central textbook in a course on security and war or as an additional textbook in broader courses in international politics. However, claiming this is all my doing would expose me as a fraud and a humbug. I have had a great deal of help. My students have given me useful and candid reactions and advice. I have benefited from a number of reviewers who provided feedback and comments on various drafts of the manuscript and book proposal. They include Risa Brooks, Northwestern University; Earl Conteh-Morgan, University of South Florida; Torbjørn L. Knutsen, Norwegian University of Science and Technology; Ranan D. Kuperman, University of Haifa; Laura Neack, Miami University; J. David Singer, University of Michigan; Richard J. Stoll, Rice University; Michael P. Sullivan, University of Arizona; and other anonymous reviewers. Charisse Kiino, chief acquisitions editor for the College division at CQ Press, did much to convince me that this could be a useful book and was patient and supportive during my poky progress. Michael Kerns, development editor, has effectively steered its intellectual content and the writing at crucial points, so much so that he deserves another vacation in Italy. Thanks as well are due to production editor Kerry Kern, who was unfazed by last-minute changes, and Steve Pazdan, the managing editor.

Patrick M. Morgan
University of California, Irvine

INTERNATIONAL SECURITY

CHAPTER 1

An Introduction to Security in International Politics

In considering the problem of security in international politics, the place to start is with war. War is a concern in international politics because war, or even the possibility of it, can destroy security. Security is a fundamental value for just about everyone. It is the quality of being and feeling safe from harm. Being safe from harm is important in itself, as is feeling safe. People prefer to live without being highly anxious over their safety. Furthermore, significant insecurity can interfere with the pursuit of everything else that people value and desire. When people, and many of the things they cherish, appear to be threatened, they are likely to put aside what they are doing to attend to the threat as best they can. If security is lost, other things they prize may be lost, too.

In international politics, security has been a constant topic of debate and a frequent concern, primarily because often too little of it has been available. Even for the most powerful governments, security has been the central preoccupation in their foreign policies, imposing great expense and often either serious harm or a real risk of it. Weaker governments have frequently had to face the threat of wars that could (sometimes would) drive them to extinction. Koreans, for example, attribute their perennial insecurity to their country being "a shrimp among whales," the whales now being the United States, Russia, Japan, and China. Some whales love to eat shrimp.

Imagine what it meant for Poland and its people when World War II broke out in 1939. Poland was invaded, first by the Germans and shortly thereafter by the Russians. They divided the country between them, and later in the war Poland was again invaded by the Russians. It disappeared for years as a country and a state. Millions of Poles became refugees, leaving everything behind. Many millions more, especially Jews, were deliberately killed or died from starvation, exhaustion, overwork, and other mistreatment in being used as slave labor. Hundreds of thousands were killed or allowed to die to clear the way for the new rulers, German or Russian. The fighting physically destroyed much of the country. Dominated by the Union of Soviet Socialist Republics after the war, Poles did not have a government that was fully theirs for another fifty years. This is an example of how war and insecurity can go hand in hand. The combination of these two things is the focus of this book.

In recent years, particularly after the end of the Cold War, the concept of security has been reexamined, with governments, journalists, scholars, and citizens debating what security means. This has occurred because clearly the threat or outbreak of war is not the only important kind of insecurity. Frequent references are now made to economic security and threats to it, environmental security, and security in terms of human rights and national cultures. I will talk more about this toward the end of this chapter and again later, particularly in Chapter 12, in terms of how broader conceptions of security pertain to war, the threat of war, or its elimination. For now I turn to security from physical threats of harm.

THE REALIST PERSPECTIVE

To begin to understand security and the threat of war requires grasping the main assumptions behind the traditional view of international politics, **realism**. The core of the realist perspective is several hundred years old and has had many trimmings added in the last fifty years or so. This is a perspective with roots in the writings of the ancient Greek historian Thucydides and great Renaissance and Enlightenment philosophers such as Nicolo Machiavelli, Thomas Hobbes, and Jean Jacques Rousseau, all of whom tried in their writings to capture how states behave. Other important perspectives will be discussed later in this book. But it is necessary to start with the realist view because it offers what was the most influential theory of, and in, international politics over the centuries and is still widely employed today. As its name suggests, it claims to harbor no illusions about the nature of that realm. In the realist view, international politics is inherently dangerous and insecure for everyone involved, for several reasons.

To begin with, the international system is **anarchical**, which means that international politics as a whole has no ruler or authority, nothing running it that is comparable to the way a government runs a country. A government is therefore **sovereign**, meaning it is a state in charge of its territory and ruled by no one higher (see the *Terms and Concepts* box, "Some Basics"). **States** are the most powerful actors in international politics, and they have **autonomy**—meaning they do not have to take orders from someone higher. As a result governments of states are free to do as they please in international affairs unless and until other governments stop them. Of course, elements of international law and order have developed over time, such as the United Nations (UN) Security Council and numerous international agreements between governments, that can deal with peace and security by limiting governments' behavior. But in the realist view these elements are weak in practice; they largely depend on states keeping themselves in compliance. If states do not want to comply, getting them to do so is very difficult.

This anarchical situation is unfortunate for achieving security. At times highly dissatisfied and ambitious rulers and governments, such as Adolf Hitler in Germany in the 1930s and Napoleonic France in the late eighteenth and early nineteenth centuries, grasp for more: more territory, more power, and more wealth. Furthermore, governments and peoples with deep-seated grievances against others often will fight for what they think is their due, such as the Palestinians against the Israelis. Often such actors are ready to make trouble in a violent fashion such as engaging in terrorism or initiating a war to gain recognition or power. And in an anarchical system—little law and no available international police—there may be no force to turn to for help in stopping them.

Terms and Concepts: Some Basics

A **state** in international politics is a political and administrative entity that controls some extensive territory and the people living there. In addition, it is now emphasized, it exists as an actor in international politics when recognized by other states as a state. For example, Taiwan is a political and administrative entity just like a state but not widely recognized by others as such, that is, as a member of the community of states. A state and its territory constitute a country, a term used for all such entities and no others. In the modern world, countries have clear territorial boundaries. A **nation** is a large cluster of individuals who feel strongly that they are alike in important ways and who form a group, a **people**, to which they are deeply attached. Typically they feel alike because they have a common culture, language, history, and territory. When a nation has a state drawn from it and which in turn governs it, this is called a **nation-state**. The term is somewhat misleading because few states encompass and govern just one nation or people. It is used for many states that have a dominant nation plus others within their borders, and even for states that have no clearly dominant nation. A state is then specifically run by a government, and when it is a **sovereign** government it is the supreme decision-making authority in that country. As such it has **autonomy**, which means it is not subject to any other government.

Nationalism is the deep attachment of a people to itself as a whole and its members. This deep attachment has often been expressed, in part, in a desire to have itself represented and governed by its own state and having that state recognized by others as its own, legitimate, state. Nationalist feelings usually include a strong sense that a certain territory belongs to that nation and should be governed by its state, that the nation is unique or distinctive (different from other peoples) and perhaps that the nation is in some fashion superior to others.

In international politics the distinctions between state, nation, people, government, and country are understood, but it is common to use "state," "government," "country," and sometimes "nation" to mean roughly the same thing or to label an entity in the same way (such as using Germany to refer to the state, its government, and the country). Thus they are used almost interchangeably, as they are in this book. States, nations, peoples, governments, and countries are also often referred to as **actors** in international politics, which can be confusing because other actors operate in international politics as well, such as international organizations, nongovernmental international organizations, the Catholic Church, and so on.

Security is also threatened by the nasty impact of **scarcity**. Leaders, governments, and nations want more of what people and governments deeply value—power, wealth, security, status, territory, and so on. They may be selfish or greedy, but even if they are not, these things do not exist in enough abundance to satisfy legitimate needs and desires (and certainly not enough for illegitimate ones). So strife and struggle is inevitable. In settled societies, the tools of politics and government are used to help determine who gets how much, but there is no government to reliably and authoritatively do this in international politics.

Finally, although states do not face conflicts and threats all the time, they know that those contingencies could arise. States and some other actors in international politics always have the power to attack, so wars will occur. Thus the fear of war flourishes, too. Actors worry about being safe even when they face no real threats. As a result they try to take out insurance against real or possible threats, such as by arming themselves or entering into alliances. These actions, however, can appear threatening to others. Imagine your neighbors see you lugging several big guns into the house, then pointing them out the windows in various directions "just in case," you tell them, someone tries to attack you. They will not think kindly of this and will wonder about your intentions as well as your sanity. If they take the same precautions in response, you may feel that you had a right to worry—the neighbors may be up to no good. In short, a spiral of perceptions (or misperceptions) and actions may produce or reinforce the insecurity governments feel. The efforts to be safe can make everyone feel less safe and, in the end, this could help lead to war. This **security dilemma** arises in a world with no supreme government. Because these difficult conditions cannot be avoided, proposals to achieve greater peace and security such as disarmament, negotiations, conciliation, and better understanding can make things worse. If people and governments take them seriously, they will be too optimistic about sustaining peace and security and not take necessary steps to protect themselves for fear of making things worse. Thus they will fail to do the tough things needed to keep safe.

As a result, in the realist view, security is very important, a constant preoccupation. It is what international politics has always been about. No wonder governments fight wars occasionally and fear war all the time. They have to plan for that possibility, building forces to try to deter attacks. They may even attack in a preventive or preemptive way because they anticipate a future attack, as the United States did to Iraq in 2003. No wonder some classic analysts described international politics as a continual state of war.

The realist approach is not the only one, and some of its components are more influential than others. Treating international politics as anarchical and anarchy as breeding insecurity and warfare have been its most well known and most widely used contributions. Later discussion will focus on other perspectives that are less pessimistic.

PROBLEMS IN COOPERATION

The same conditions—anarchy, scarcity, continual threats, and the security dilemma—also work to keep governments from cooperating sufficiently with each other to make them all safe. With preserving their autonomy and the burden of scarcity in mind, they frequently disagree about who is to get what—in territory, wealth, power, and so forth—and who should give way to resolve the disputes. The more important and valuable the stakes the less likely they are to agree about how to end the conflicts, and so the less likely they are to cooperate enough to resolve them, especially the most dangerous ones. States with strong conflicts cannot just promise not to harm each other because they cannot fully trust each other. After all, there is no easy way to enforce such a promise. If the rewards look high enough a government may break its promise and use force to get what it wants. Governments do cooperate to form alliances, but alliances tend to be temporary and are sometimes unreliable. If the costs look too high, allies might abandon you when the time comes for them to help you. That happened to Czechoslovakia in 1938. In the run-up to World War II, Hitler threatened to seize part of the country so the Czech government turned to its allies, France and Great Britain. They replied, in effect: "Give him what he wants." So the Czech government gave in and in less than a year Hitler swallowed the whole country.

States will not cooperate to set up a powerful regional or world government or greatly strengthen international law because they love autonomy too much. It is an integral part of their sense of security, one of the things they most want to protect. They also worry that if they did surrender a good deal of their autonomy to international organizations and agreed to disarm they would still not be safe. The temptation for a government to defect from cooperation by secretly retaining or redeveloping its arms would be huge, given that possession of even modest forces and weapons could make a government the most powerful one in the system. (As the saying goes, "In the kingdom of the blind, the one-eyed man is king.") In addition, international organizations can fall under the control or influence of powerful blocs or individual states pursuing their own interests, so governments also fear that an international body will be dominated by unfriendly elements and used against them.

Realist analysts also stress that whenever significant cooperation is found among a group of states the door is open to another form of cheating—much like the temptation to defect—called **free riding**. Free riders seek to get the benefits of cooperation without doing their share of it. People practice free riding when they want the government to provide police, schools, and roads but try to cheat on paying taxes. If states agree to cooperate by helping any state that is attacked, leaders are likely to try to get other governments to pay most of the costs. Small states will try to leave the fighting to great powers; each great power will try to leave it to the others. As a result security will be underprovided because too little is done to maintain it. Thus in the late 1930s when war with Germany approached, the British and French were prepared to fight but each maneuvered to get the other to bear the brunt of it. They wanted the United States and the Soviet Union to help. The United States was sympathetic but Americans preferred to leave the fighting to the Europeans, while Moscow was happy to see Britain and France keep Germany busy fighting so Germany would be willing to divide Poland with the Soviet Union.

In another form of free riding, if a group of states cooperates because they are eager to avoid war, a state can exploit this by being obstinate and threatening about getting its way. Such a stance puts cooperation in general at risk and plays on the strong desire of the other governments to be conciliatory to prevent their cooperation arrangements from dissolving. The obstinate party lets the others carry the burden of keeping those arrangements going. In the 1930s Hitler did this repeatedly with great success—Czechoslovakia was one of the victims of it.

Because wars have been frequent and efforts to create and maintain peace have so often failed, the realist view has been highly influential in international politics over the centuries, almost universally held at times, and it does not paint a pretty picture. Fortunately, as discussed later, it is incomplete.

LEVELS OF SECURITY

In considering war and the desire for security, numerous analysts have concluded that security concerns arise on or pertain to different levels. The three considered most important are the systemic (international system), the state, and the societal. Each approach to or strategy for maintaining security discussed in this book will be evaluated as to how it affects all three levels. Understanding each level of security is important because solutions for insecurity and war can be attractive at one level but much less so at another.

Systemic Security

Most people want to live in a world, or at least their part of it, that is safe; and most governments would agree. If the international system is not intrinsically safe and can lead to harm from warfare both directly and indirectly, this can easily stoke anxiety. People would like a safe world just like they want a safe neighborhood, city, or country. Thus, people want the international system to be stable and orderly without constant threats arising in one place or another and hampering activity, such as, for example, trade investment and tourism. This can best be termed **systemic security**, the security of living in a world run in such a way that war, and the threat of it, is limited or even eliminated.

Getting rid of war entirely is a tall order and not likely to be achieved soon. Fortunately, systemic security can exist short of completely eradicating war, in at least two broad forms. First, it can be high if war among states has become rare, no large war involving some or all of the strongest states is likely, and wars inside states rarely threaten to spread and disrupt the international system. These conditions normally mean that the international system is stable, secure, and unlikely to be torn apart by violence. A good deal of progress has been made on this type of systemic security, and how various approaches to the problem of war have contributed to this success will be assessed.

Second, if people live in a dangerous neighborhood, they do not feel safe even if their society as a whole is doing well. In the same way, systemic security can seem good or bad for nations depending on what their regional part of the system is like. Many nations live in safe neighborhoods, but more than a few do not, and they have no way to move out. Why some regions are much safer than others needs to be explored. The question is, How can large regional chunks of the international system be made safe? The successes offer clues about how best to try to do better elsewhere.

State Security

The international system is made up of actors at the state level, thus security for states is a concern as well. The starting point of **state security** for a state is its survival. It does not want to be driven out of existence by war, internal or external, and it does not want to have to use war to avoid being driven out of existence by something else, such as an economic collapse. For many states and their governments today, as in the past, the main threat to their survival comes from inside the country—from a possible coup, a guerrilla war, a potential revolution, a breakdown of law and order, a secession movement, domestic terrorism, or some combination of these. A few unfortunate, or badly run, states face serious threats from outside and inside (a subject considered in more detail in Chapters 9–11).

Nothing, it seems, is fixed and permanent, including states' preoccupation with survival. In a few cases states have willingly gone out of business instead of fighting to survive. Czechoslovakia did it twice, once in 1938 and again in 1993, and the Soviet Union did it in 1991. Czechoslovakia also did not resist when it was invaded in 1968 by Soviet-led forces that ousted the government. But such an occurrence is rare.

Apart from survival, the next most important value for states, under most circumstances, is autonomy. Autonomy offers perhaps the ultimate appeal of power. At one time or another everyone hates taking orders. Political systems are permeated with efforts by people to become or remain independent of control by others. That is much of what politics is always about, and states have consistently behaved this way in international politics, too. Other important elements of state-level security include being physically safe from attack even if survival is not at stake and being able to promote the state's power and status, such as by national development, which often strengthens the state domestically, provides greater military resources to draw on if necessary, and offers numerous other benefits. Thus states also want to avoid or repel threats to core values such as these as well. These things collectively constitute state security.

Societal Security

Societal security has to do with people—their physical safety and the preservation of their personal autonomy, the ability to do what they want to do. This personal and social dimension is what is normally meant by security—that people can protect themselves (their families, communities) or their prosperity and way of life, or that all these things can be protected by others on their behalf so that if jeopardy arises they can be confident help will come and all will turn out well. People want to be safe not just from a military attack but also from terrorism or economic hardship deliberately imposed on them by outsiders or through outside interference in their political system. People also want to be safe from a collapse of the political system, a breakdown of law and order, civil war, economic disaster, and other internal calamities.

Even if things turn out well for the nation in fighting a war or because of its strong military efforts to prevent one, the resulting strains on people's lives can be immense because of such things as heavy casualties, huge economic burdens, and strong state security measures that cut deeply into citizens' autonomy. Often particularly frightful is an internal war, in which one part of society is fighting another. Civil wars can devastate citizens' lives, property, jobs, education, health, and welfare. Conditions such as these are the opposite of security, and they are experienced by millions of people every day around the world.

Tensions among the Three Levels

The three levels of security overlap somewhat and each can reinforce tendencies toward peace and security displayed in the others. They can complement each other in important ways. For instance, often the best way to maintain societal security is to sustain and expand prosperity, which can be much easier to achieve in a stable and peaceful international environment—systemic security—in which the costs of arming, arms racing, and fighting are low. Currently, China's national strategy rests on this notion. It is working hard to keep systemic security, particularly in its part of the world, in a healthy condition so that it can put its greatest efforts into national development. The reverse is also sometimes true. Major revolutions, particularly in highly significant countries, usually affect societal and state security deeply—that is, after all, what a revolution is essentially about. However, major revolutions can seriously disrupt, damage, or even transform systemic security as well. Examples usually cited include the French Revolution and the Russian Revolution, but the point applies to others, too.

Another example of how the levels of security complement each other is displayed in one fundamental premise of American foreign policy today: A well-established democracy is more likely to run a peaceful society, to exist in a state that is safe from domestic threats, and to behave peacefully toward others, especially other democracies, thus helping to create a stable and peaceful international system.

However, the three levels are not facets of a single large phenomenon. They are distinctive in their characteristics and status. As a result, systemic, state, and societal security often contradict each other in terms of what happens when a step is taken to enhance security. What makes for security at one level can mean considerable insecurity at another.

SYSTEMIC VERSUS STATE SECURITY

Systemic security can be, and often is, at odds with state security. A safe and orderly system may require—is normally assumed to require—seriously curbing the autonomy of states, which means damaging those aspects of their security related to their having a good deal of freedom to do as they please. For instance, many analysts and governments believe that the international system will be much less safe if nuclear weapons spread to more countries. They promote international arrangements to suppress nuclear proliferation. This clashes with the desire of various states to be free to develop, or maybe even buy, nuclear weapons if they feel doing so is vital. As long as states put a great emphasis on autonomy, it is extremely difficult to fully reconcile state security and systemic security.

As another example, states have often insisted that autonomy includes the right to use force for what each particular state considers legitimate reasons. That used to mean that a state could attack another just because it wanted to. Today, there is more insistence in international politics that states should not attack each other, that they should use force only to defend themselves. But states like to insist that they are the ones entitled to decide when they have been attacked. In 1991 Iraqi leader Saddam Hussein accused Kuwait of having attacked Iraq by stealing some of its oil underground and conspiring with others to keep oil prices so low that Iraq could not make enough from selling its oil to grow and prosper (see the

Cases and Context box, "The Wars of Iraq"). Saddam's reaction was to seize Kuwait. The rest of the world thought that was not justified and Iraq's freedom to do what it pleased was rejected. Twelve years later, the George W. Bush administration insisted on attacking Iraq to prevent being harmed by Iraq's alleged plans to have nuclear weapons in the future, regardless of what the rest of the world thought.

Thus states often value state security, including the freedom to do what they want, more than systemic security. They realize that it can be difficult to reconcile the two, that a trade-off between them is unavoidable, and they prefer to make that trade-off in favor of autonomy or other elements of state security. Observers who see systemic security as crucial have often said that states would "rather be free than safe." To the states, however, this is a foolish way to look at things because losing autonomy sacrifices the essence of their security—state safety begins with autonomy.

States will often insist that their autonomy is vital for the security of their societies, too. This may be a self-serving rationalization, but not always. Often a society identifies closely with its state so that the state's security is seen as an extension of its own. The political core of nationalism is typically that people feel safer only if, and when, they have their own state—when they are governed by people like themselves. If that state does not exist, or is not autonomous and safe, then they do not feel secure either. This is how most Iraqis reacted to the U.S. occupation of their country after the 2003 invasion. No matter how happy they were to have Saddam Hussein gone, they felt unsafe because outsiders were running their country. The capacity for peoples to identify that closely with their states has been the most powerful force in the history of international politics, and it has often clashed with efforts to make the international system less violent or unstable.

SOCIETAL VERSUS STATE SECURITY

In contrast, state security is sometimes seen by leaders as independent of, and more important than, societal security. They insist that their personal survival, or the survival of the regime or the state, is far more important than any citizen concerns or citizen welfare. They readily sacrifice citizens, strip them of freedom and prosperity, or drive them harshly to do whatever else is needed to serve the state's goals. They may claim that national security requires repressive measures even when there are no signs of impending attacks by other nations.

Thus societal security can sometimes require steps to make society safe from the state, from threats the state or the government that controls it pose to the society, and not just from threats posed by outsiders. Thinking along these lines did much to create the American Revolution and its Declaration of Independence. A government may be a real threat to its society by inhibiting development, practicing vast corruption, exploiting or enslaving the people, imposing frightful bur-

Cases and Context: *The Wars of Iraq*

Saddam Hussein came to power in Iraq in 1979. When revolution broke out in Iran that same year, weakening that country and cutting it off from its major patron—the United States—Saddam launched a war on Iran over past border disputes and in hopes of permanently weakening a regional rival. Events did not go as he planned. The war ground on until 1988 and led to perhaps 1.5 million casualties, enormous expense, and the devastation of certain areas, leaving the nation in bad shape. Seeking national recovery Saddam began complaining that the price of exported oil, Iraq's main revenue, was too low, set purposely so by Kuwait and Saudi Arabia to keep Iraq weak. When he moved troops to the Kuwaiti border in 1990, many governments and analysts saw this as a bargaining ploy. It came as a shock when they then seized an essentially defenseless Kuwait.

The United States and others were concerned that Saddam could soon control the Persian Gulf, perhaps invade Saudi Arabia, and dominate world oil exports and the Organization of Petroleum Exporting Countries (OPEC). President George Bush mobilized a large coalition force through the United Nations (UN) Security Council and in 1991 easily drove Iraqi forces out of Kuwait. Saddam's efforts to threaten to use weapons of mass destruction to deter the UN forces, and to rally the Arab world behind him by attacking Israel with missiles to bring it into the war, failed.

Following the war, Iraq had to submit to inspections designed to rid it of weapons of mass destruction and ballistic missiles. When it did not fully cooperate it was subjected to years of containment, sanctions, harassment, and some bombing, mainly by the United States and Great Britain, leaving the government unable to rule a good portion of the country. Many expected that Saddam could not survive in power. However, he managed to retain his control, only to become the target of the U.S.-led invasion of Iraq in 2003 that easily overran the entire country. The justifications offered for this war were that Iraq still had chemical and biological weapons and a recessed program to develop nuclear weapons, had links to terrorists, and was run by a highly dangerous and vicious regime at great cost to its citizens.

As the occupation by the United States and allied forces began, there was severe internal turmoil—looting, assassinations, a sharp rise in violent crime, collapse of the economy. Gradually a substantial, organized insurgency emerged; that is, a low-level civil war that brought high-level insecurity in many parts of the country. This handicapped efforts to get the country up and running again. Iraq now has been living with war and the grievous aftermath of war for more than twenty-five years.

dens on them, or killing them in large numbers because of their ethnicity, religion, or political views or because in some other way they are deemed threats to national security. While the state can embody its citizens—when it is safe, so are they—sometimes they are safe even when the state is not; they may even be safe only if the state is not. Societal security of this sort encompasses individuals, groups, and the society as a whole and can be evaluated on that basis. Various international organizations and the U.S. State Department evaluate countries every year in terms of human rights progress or abuses. Other organizations evaluate societies in terms of corruption or the degree of freedom of the media or the available rights for women.

Leaders may pursue objectives abroad, claiming they are vital for state security, in ways that lead to wasting the lives of their citizens in war, wasting the society's resources through high taxes for wars and related policies, and risking societal security by plunging into risky foreign operations. For the sake of his ambitions and his state, Saddam Hussein crushed domestic opponents, slaughtered thousands of citizens, and made decisions that led to hundreds of thousands of others being killed. He left Iraq exhausted by attacking Iran in a long and futile war, then by attacking Kuwait in a failed effort to seize it, then by refusing to bow fully to the demands of the UN Security Council so that his people suffered deeply from UN economic sanctions, and finally by choosing not to surrender his rule when faced with an American invasion.

The same pattern was evident in Nazi Germany and Imperial Japan from the 1930s to 1945 and in Napoleon's France in the late eighteenth and early nineteenth centuries. Libertarians in America subscribe to the view that as their nation's leaders pursue international ambitions, either from lofty conceptions of the U.S. role in the world or for less noble reasons, they ignore societal security, which is greatly damaged by the huge burdens placed on citizens as a result of their policies.

Thus citizens in various countries may be unattached to the survival of their government; they may see it as the most threatening thing in their lives. They may be opposed to the survival of the state itself because it is not seen as theirs. Normally citizens who feel this way are members of an ethnic or religious group, and the state is run by another group hostile to them. So it is not their state; they want to secede from it and build their own instead. In the Soviet Union many Ukrainians felt this way. When Germany invaded in 1941 and overran much of the country they greeted German forces as liberators. When the opportunity to be free of control from Moscow came again, in 1990 as the Cold War ended and the Soviet Union began to dissolve, Ukrainians seized it and created a nation-state.

Systemic versus Societal Security

Can systemic and societal security be in conflict, so that a stable and orderly system—one that even curbs the harm states do to their societies—is seen as threatening by the members of a society? Sure. Imagine that an international system is stable and orderly, but the members of a particular society feel it is fundamentally unfair or exploitative and needs to be either sharply changed or eliminated. Many critics of the current international system feel like this, particularly in poor societies. They believe the rich countries try to keep the international system stable and orderly mainly so that those countries and their governments can run it for their benefit and still be safe from all the poor societies that are being exploited. When the Organization of Petroleum Exporting Countries (OPEC) first seized control of world oil markets in 1973, the members imposed huge charges for oil on the rich developed countries. Even though the rest of the world also had to pay the additional costs, people in poor countries often cheered this attack on the power of the rich.

In turn, advocates of a stable, secure international system have often insisted that some societal security has to be sacrificed for that purpose. Efforts to insist on family planning, to force countries to promote it even if their citizens are strongly opposed, are ultimately assertions that the international system cannot indefinitely stand the strain on food, resources, and wealth, and thus unchecked population growth and societal preferences to the contrary must give way. In the same way, international arrangements to save the world environment are designed to prevent people from continuing to do what many of them like to, or feel they must, do, such as cutting down tropical forests or dynamiting coral reefs to capture fish or developing economically via forms of energy production and consumption that damage the ozone layer.

SECURITY DILEMMAS AND THE
DILEMMAS OF PURSUING SECURITY

The underlying lesson in these examples of security at one level being at odds with security at another is this: There is more than one kind of security dilemma. Remember that in a security dilemma steps taken to ease security for one party can reduce the security of others. That is just what all these examples display. While security dilemmas are not impossible to escape, they are always difficult, complicated, and frustrating. Security dilemmas are at the heart of certain standard, repeated difficulties that must be dealt with in international politics. I will return to those difficulties in evaluating the various ways people and their governments have devised to effectively pursue security by containing conflict and war.

There are many ways to harm states and societies, or the international system, besides military actions and wars. Nonmilitary developments and conditions such as epidemics, global warming, economic crises, terrorism, and international crime do harm, too. The same security dilemmas often apply to handling these problems too. To deal with terrorists often leads a state or an international agency to demand something another state rejects as a threat to its sovereignty. To combat global warming it may be necessary to sharply restrict states, corporations, and others in making many economic policy decisions.

Finally, it is important to supplement the emphasis I have placed on security dilemmas by pointing out that problems exist with pursuing security in the first place. There is more to life, including life in international politics, than security. People, officials, and governments have often been willing to trade some security for other things, sometimes just for the chance to try to gain other things. As individuals, or together as a society, people frequently feel that up to a point insecurity is good for them. Risk of failure and unemployment keeps companies, businesses, and workers on their toes, to be more alert and more productive. Having to take chances through competition keeps schools, firms, and political parties vigorous and efficient. It is also good for keeping governments in touch with their constituents (lest they lose the next election). Americans feel that dispersing power is good for keeping the powerful under control—and less secure—because those who try to use power excessively risk rousing strong opposition, failure, and loss of their power. In the study of international politics some analysts contend that it was the insecurity and frequent warfare of international politics from 1500 into the twentieth century that drove Western states to develop so much faster and more powerfully than other states and societies, so that the West came to dominate nearly the entire world and continues to do so.

Thus people want to do something about insecurity, about conflict, and certainly about war. But they could have second thoughts about eliminating all conflicts, rivalries, and struggles, even if such a thing were possible and scarcity could be eliminated. A part of being human is a willingness to sometimes be unsafe for a while if that is a necessary part of striving hard to achieve something deeply desired.

CONCLUSION

In this chapter I have introduced the problem of security in international politics. However, the book is particularly concerned with war as the source of much of the world's insecurity. That is the subject of Chapter 2, which lays out the nature of the problem that war poses for and in international politics. Once war has been given some careful consideration, it will be possible to turn in the ensuing chapters to examining various ways worked out over the history of international politics to cope with the problem of war. Part I (Chapters 3–8) discusses traditional solutions to the problem, ones rooted in some aspects of the basic nature of international politics, starting with those with the longest history of use. I call these "strategies" for dealing with war. I begin with strategies used by individual governments acting largely on their own. Then come strategies that are more collective in nature; they involve more cooperation among governments. Strategies in which cooperation becomes progressively more extensive are taken up one after another. Part II (Chapters 9–12) examines ways to cope with war that attempt to develop enough cooperation to shift the nature of international politics significantly. This involves modern, decidedly nontraditional, methods that have a more tactical character. They put emphasis on helpful techniques and much more specific agendas for action in dealing with warfare. They also pertain much more to contemporary internal wars than the approaches discussed ahead of them in the book.

In covering these strategies and tactics the chapters to come will return often to the concepts introduced here and the points made about the three levels of security, using them as the analytical framework that drives the chapters' conclusions. In particular, I will evaluate each approach in terms of how well it seems to work at each level of security and how each deals with various security dilemmas.

SOURCES AND OTHER USEFUL READINGS

A somewhat similar design to this one for a book on managing international politics is employed in Bruce Cronin, *Community under Anarchy.* To explore how the concept of security has been broadened in recent years, see Barry Buzan's *People, States, and Fear,* Barry Buzan, Ole Waever, and Japp de Wilde's *Security,* or Terry Tarriff, Stuart Croft, Luch James, and Patrick M. Morgan's *Security Studies Today.* Major exponents of the realist perspective include Kenneth N. Waltz, who wrote *Theory of International Politics,* and John J. Mearsheimer in *The Tragedy of Great Power Politics.* The perspective is comprehensively reviewed in several chapters of James F. Dougherty and Robert L. Pfaltzgraff Jr., *Contending Theories of International Relations* and elaborated upon in Michael Brown, Sean M. Lynn-Jones, and Steven E. Miller, *The Perils of Anarchy.* The classic concept of the security dilemma is reviewed and applied to internal conflicts in Jack Snyder and Robert Jervis, "Civil War and the Security Dilemma." Inhibitions on cooperation among governments and overcoming them is the topic of Kenneth A. Oye's *Cooperation Under Anarchy.* Other relevant works on that subject include Stephen D. Krasner, *International Regimes;* Robert O. Keohane, *After Hegemony;* and Michael Doyle, *Ways of War and Peace.*

The three levels of security, and sometimes others, are cited, described, and used for analysis in a classic book—Kenneth N. Waltz's *Man, the State, and War*—and a classic article by J. David Singer, "The Levels of Analysis Problem in International Relations." The three levels are often discussed or used in other works such as the Buzan books mentioned above, or the article by Jack L. Levy, "Theories of Interstate and Intrastate War." To consider how revolutions can disrupt systemic security, see Stephen M. Walt, *Revolution and War.*

Most of the terms listed in the *Terms and Concepts* box are defined and discussed in all works introducing theories of international politics, including the Dougherty and Pfaltzgraff book above; Paul R. Viotti and Mark V. Kaupi,

International Relations Theory; and Lawrence Ziring, Jack C. Plano, and Roy Alton, *International Relations: A Political Dictionary.*

On Iraq's wars there are numerous works including Anthony H. Cordesman's *The Iran-Iraq War and Western Security* and his *The Iraq War,* as well as Lawrence Freedman and Efraim Karsh, *The Gulf Conflict 1990–1991.*

CHAPTER 2

The Problem of War in International Politics

This book deals with security in international politics, but it focuses on a particular threat to security, namely, war both between and within nations. Special attention is paid to wars among the most powerful members of the international system. The focus is on war because it is directly and deeply harmful to security. It causes or helps bring about economic, medical, and other disasters, and it eats up vast resources that could otherwise be used to help resolve other threats and problems. The question thus is: Why, and how, is war a problem in international politics? The answer is found in examining how war has developed throughout the history of the international system and how war appears to individuals or groups in a society (at the societal level), to states (at the state level), and to someone looking at the international system as a whole (at the systemic level).

War is organized military conflict between clearly identifiable groups, particularly groups with a cohesive structure and recognized leadership. What sets war apart from other forms of group violence, such as a mob, is that the pursuit of violence is undertaken with some degree of order, discipline, direction, and planning. What distinguishes it from many forms of group violence that are disciplined, directed, and planned, such as beatings or burning or bombing empty buildings to intimidate, is that the intent is to kill at least to the extent that seems necessary to achieve perceived objectives and maybe more. Finally, in war the killing is on a significant scale. Thus, the most well-known academic compilation of wars, the Correlates of War Project, defines a war as involving at least one thousand battle deaths. Other war studies use similar sorts of measures to categorize wars differently from small border clashes, various kinds of terrorism, or demonstrations that turn into riots that provoke a tough response with killings on each side. Thus war can occur between an international organization and a state, between states, between a states and a portion of its society, and between different parts of a society. It can involve the use of weapons of mass destruction (nuclear, chemical, and biological), professional military forces (conventional wars), irregular and often small nonprofessional forces (guerrilla wars), and terrorist attacks employing all sorts of people.

CAUSES OF WAR

Normally, the best way to solve a problem is to start with a good grasp of what causes it. However, designing a solution to deal with the causes of a problem has not worked well as an approach to thwarting war in international politics. Innumerable studies have been conducted on the causes of war, but no broad agreement has emerged on what those causes are. War is a label assigned to a wide number of somewhat different events and processes. War is a phenomenon that can be caused by numerous things; and, therefore, the causes of war vary from one war to another. On war, no explanation fits all. Analysts and officials, governments and international institutions, have had to come up with antidotes to war on some other basis.

If this seems odd, consider the long struggle doctors and researchers have had with cancer. It is not a single disease but a set of numerous similar medical conditions. Cancer is caused by many things working together in many ways. As a result, a variety of explanations has been put forth for what causes cancer but no consensus has been reached on which are the best. So the solutions—cures—for cancer have been developed and applied without knowing for sure what causes the conditions they are supposed to fix. Just as with war, solutions work unevenly and inconsistently, but some progress has been made nevertheless. People can often do much about a problem even if its ultimate cause remains a mystery.

What is some of the thinking on the causes of war? As discussed in Chapter 1, analysts in international politics have often traced wars, at least in part, to an absence of effective government. At the systemic level the culprit is anarchy. In domestic affairs it is weak or collapsing governments or a government that arouses both wide and deep opposition, because then control and order begin to erode. At either level, war results at least partly because little constrains familiar human impulses that can lead to it. Thus international politics is a realm of serious insecurity, according to realist analysts, and so are domestic societies when they become similarly anarchical—violence can too easily result.

Another argument claims that war is typically caused by aggressive, greedy expansionists. Here war is akin to violent crime. Most governments, leaders, and peoples can and do live peacefully together most of the time. Within societies most people most of the time do not commit organized violence against each other. But a few always do, and it does not take many to bring on feelings of insecurity, including fear, suspicion, and uncertainty. Security dilemmas often emerge out of the ensuing reactions to insecurity.

Along different lines, other explanations refer to specific things wars seem to be about as the causes. War is said to be caused by the preoccupation of peoples, societies, and states with maintaining or adding to their lands and territories.

Historically, disputes over territory most commonly incite wars. Others claim struggles to control the prerequisites for subsistence and survival or for development, wealth, and power precipitate war. After all, disputes over territory are often really about control over resources, population, markets, food sources, and so on.

An attractive explanation recently emerging in security studies is that most wars in the last two centuries were caused in regional international systems by gaps between the number of states that exist and the number of people who think of themselves as nations that should have their own states. Sometimes a region has too few states, and a number of peoples want to secede from one or more of them and create new ones. For example, in the Balkans in the early 1990s, Bosnians, Croats, Kosovars, Macedonians, and Slovenians wanted to secede from Yugoslavia. Sometimes a region has too many states, and elements of a people spread across several states seek to combine into one. Periodic efforts have been made to unite Arabs into a single state for an "Arab nation." Sometimes the state for one people seeks to add similar members of its ethnic group and their territories to itself, as was the case with Adolf Hitler's Germany in the 1930s. Existing governments usually will strongly resist secession. They also resist mergers, except for the government expecting to rule the newly created or enlarged country. After fighting occurs to settle those matters, more fighting will often arise over how borders will be drawn and what, and who, will fall within them.

Several popular explanations emphasize the nature of political and socioeconomic systems. Wars are said to be caused by advanced capitalist systems, which eventually develop into rapacious imperialists. This was Vladimir I. Lenin's explanation of World War I, which, because of the Russian Revolution he led, gained wide currency not only in communist countries but in many others as well. Fascist systems were said to glorify war as the way to triumph over others in what they saw as a struggle to determine which nations, peoples, and systems were best suited to survive. Another popular explanation points to undemocratic political systems and leaders as causing wars. They lead or manipulate their citizens into wars for power and glory, for wealth and status of the leader or ruling elites, or to hide the leader's inadequacies at home and suppress resentment over them. A recent version of this is that undemocratic leaders, systems, even societies hate democracies because they are proponents of freedom. Many observers think that societies with immense poverty, corruption, and malnutrition are breeding grounds for violence within them.

Still other analyses cite fundamental human tendencies toward and capacities for intense group loyalty. Outsiders as a result can become aliens, strange and threatening. Wars can stoke such perceptions and bury them deep in group psyches. Alternatively, some analyses focus on the human capacity for aggression, or frustration over living in pitiful circumstances, to fuel violence. Another category of explanations stresses misperception, such as the argument that no war would occur if the parties agreed on how it would turn out. The certain loser(s) would have no incentive to fight. Thus a war must occur because all parties expect to come out better than their opponent(s) and one or more are wrong.

The catalog of causes could continue. What has been done in international politics to deal with war is only unevenly related to what supposedly causes war. The efforts to contain or end warfare described in this book rest on the assumption that, whatever those causes are, something useful can be done.

War is commonly seen as a serious problem because of the destruction and loss of life it inflicts—the consequences. This perspective and the cry that something must be done "to stop all that killing" usually have a powerful appeal. But in international politics this way of looking at war has been relatively unimportant and ineffective because it oversimplifies the problem.

If the great problem with war is that it brings widespread death and destruction, and thus serious insecurity, then people probably would have done something highly effective about it by now. Of the classic scourges in human history—war, plague, pestilence, famine, flood—war is the one on which the least progress has been made. There is a reason for this. War has often been seen by governments and other organized groups as useful, necessary, and perhaps even unavoidable. Sometimes people or groups like war because it inflicts death and destruction on a hated enemy, and particularly if inflicted only or mainly on the enemy and not themselves. People, governments, and leaders are not normally pacifists. They typically think that things worth fighting for are also worth doing great harm to others to gain or maintain.

PERCEPTION OF WAR AT THE THREE LEVELS

A standard practice throughout most of the history of international politics was for governments of states to insist that they had a right to make war. One implication of this view was that, to them, war was not inherently a problem. If governments insisted on the right to make war, then it could hardly be said that they saw war as the source of insecurity. War was a tool for governments. The fact that it occurred was not the problem; the problem was that one might lose or might win but at too high a cost. If you won, and won cheaply enough, war was not a problem. The real difficulty for a state was that it might get into a war when it did not want to, under circumstances when war was not the right tool to use, and pay a high price as a result.

Of course, citizens could have felt that war was awful and that they wanted no part of it. When the opinions of citizens mattered, that could have made war a problem after all. However, throughout history in many societies and countries, people have at times supported, have even been eager to support, a war and been ready to participate in it. That is, they approved of a particular war. So it is not true that from a state perspective war has always been a problem. It has often been seen instead as a frequently problematic and dangerous tool, but a useful tool nonetheless.

The same applies to how war has been seen from the systemic viewpoint for most of the history of international politics. From the onset of nation-states, and hence of international politics, governments and leaders expected to achieve and maintain a stable and orderly international system, and thus increase their security at least temporarily, mainly via the pursuit of a balance of power. This concept is examined in Chapter 3. Maintaining the proper balance of power, in the way that it worked and that governments tried to sustain and use it, required regularly making war or issuing threats of war. The essence of security was not the absence of war, because sometimes war was required to sustain the continuation of the proper sort of international system to keep its members secure. This was so for individual states and for the international system—a system with a suitable distribution of power, maintained in part by war, would be sufficiently stable and orderly. War was a tool in the search for security, even though it could also contribute to insecurity. As such, it was an ambiguous phenomenon.

This conception of war as sometimes valuable for the international system has not disappeared, though it is much less in vogue. War is still used to promote security at times. That was the intent when the United Nations (UN) coalition went to war to drive Iraqi leader Saddam Hussein's forces out of Kuwait in 1991. But it is less popular than it used to be among governments, analysts, and others. War developed over the history of international politics as steadily more dangerous and destructive. As a result, its impact as a source of insecurity became greater and more compelling. It was less ambiguous in its effects and more likely to generate insecurity than security. This has been especially true of great-power wars, those that involve one or more of the great powers on each side. Describing how this happened is important because it has been largely responsible for a number of efforts to deal with war that are discussed in this book.

In the history of international politics great powers have participated in many more wars, and larger wars, than other states. Nothing provides a sense of how true this is like visiting the great national war museums in France, Great Britain, and Spain and the expansive graveyards from the two world wars that are scattered around the globe. While the great powers have had many wars against all sorts of opponents, their most significant and sometimes most frequent wars have been among themselves. Their fighting occurred partially because war was a tool they used in regulating or managing their relations with each other. War was one way in which the balance of power among the great powers operated. If a particular great power was getting steadily more powerful relative to the others and began to expand its territory and resources, other great powers might make war on it to halt its expansion and the growth of its power. Thus in the middle of the nineteenth century when the kingdom of Prussia pulled most of the Germans in Europe together into a much larger and more powerful state, Imperial Germany, the balance of power in Europe was upset and the leaders of France began to plan a war with Prussia to contain and reduce its power (see the *Cases and Context* box, "Nineteenth-Century Prussian Wars"). The effort, however, failed, because France was too weak to do the job and lost the war. In other words, war—and especially the threat of war—was used to limit the aspirations, expansionist tendencies, and influence of each great power. Meanwhile, war was one of the main ways individual states tried to evade, overturn, or defeat containment of their power and expansion by others. As is apparent, war was a standard move in the game of international politics.

During the same time period, operating international politics in this fashion began to be more difficult to tolerate. A number of important developments, in tandem, contributed to this. One was that governments became better at extracting resources and support from their societies, which meant that they could conduct warfare when necessary on a larger scale than before. They could mount larger armies, with more weapons, to conduct wars over wider areas. Governments could command more support from society in large part because of the appearance and growth of modern nationalism. Nationalism is a profound emotional commitment of the members of a large group of people to each other and, if one exists, to the state that embodies and represents them. The emergence of nationalism is usually traced back to the French Revolution, which broke out in 1789, but it had begun emerging well before this. Once nationalism had blossomed in France it soon began doing so in other areas of Europe, in part because of the wars revolutionary France and then Napoleon's government fought across the continent. That series of conflicts convulsed Europe until 1815.

Nationalism made it possible to attract men into armed forces in far greater numbers, leading to forces that were larger, followed orders better, and fought with more intensity. Before then armies and navies often were constructed by emptying out the prisons or were made up of men rounded up off the street or in raids on villages. Nationalism also made it possible to generate more public support for those armed forces and any war that they fought. Governments worked hard to cultivate national sentiment for just this reason. In fact, if they did not do so, they were unlikely to survive wars with those that did.

The effect was a profound change in the nature of warfare. In the eighteenth century, wars had often been slow and orderly. Armies were relatively small and often had little willingness to fight—desertion was a major problem. Warfare was

Cases and Context: *Nineteenth-Century Prussian Wars*

A major turning point in international politics, with consequences evident for well over a hundred years since, was the effective use of war by Prussia from 1862 to 1871. Prior to that time the Germans in Europe lived in dozens of different states and lesser entities, the two largest being Austria and Prussia. The Prussian government set out to bring almost all those states under its rule, in service to not only its own power and status but also the powerful pressure of German nationalism for a new unified Germany. The Prussian chancellor, Otto von Bismarck, provoked a war with Denmark in 1862 to force it to give up certain German entities and bring them under Prussian control. Then he maneuvered Austria into a war after diplomatically isolating it from assistance. Through its quick defeat, other territories came under Prussian control and Austria dropped out as a competitor among the Germans. That left France determined to prevent the complete collapse of the European balance of power. Bismarck found it easy to maneuver France into a war in 1870–1871 after, like the others, isolating it diplomatically. Prussia then absorbed the rest of the German states except Austria.

The consequences? The new Germany became the dominant power in Europe. The combination of its military prowess, the largest and strongest economy, the largest population except for the Russian empire, a strong nationalism, and its strategically central location made Germany the natural leader, and thus a serious potential threat to the other great powers. The relationship between Germany and the others was the greatest problem in the international system, often referred to as "the German problem." It took two world wars and a cold war to arrive at a general agreement among Germany and the other great powers on Germany's most suitable role in the international system. In various ways resolving the problem of Germany was the major reason for the development of European integration.

therefore fought by maneuver as much as by fighting battles, by siege as much as attack. Napoleon changed all that. He burst onto the scene during the French Revolution and soon set about seizing much of Europe. A large coalition of other great powers and some smaller ones was necessary to take it back from him, by defeating French forces and exiling Napoleon to an island in the South Atlantic. Backed by French nationalism he fielded huge armies, which he moved swiftly, nearly always to attack. He was able to smash other armies and defeat their governments for years, so everyone else had to adapt to his way of fighting. From that point on warfare as practiced by major states developed in a more professional direction, often backed by a carefully cultivated mass support. One of the most impressive displays of how war was changing in all these ways was the American Civil War (1861–1865). Equally impressive and much more influential were the Prussian victories at roughly the same time.

Governments also became much more capable bureaucratically in the course of the nineteenth century. They were becoming better at extracting taxes and other resources from their societies. They kept better records and thus, for example, could devise elaborate systems to draft men into the armed forces. They became capable of more elaborate and detailed planning. A huge bureaucratic improvement involved the appearance of the concept of a general staff, a bureaucratic structure that could integrate the efforts of a nation's armed forces and all the things that went into using them, such as transportation, communications, and supplies, within an overall strategy. Introduced by the Prussians, their general staff was eventually widely copied. In all of this governments also were helped by nationalism, which pulled their nations more solidly together behind the armed forces in a greater readiness to pay taxes or buy bonds to support war efforts. In addition, citizens displayed more willingness to be called into military service to fight wars. Governments could better promote and then exploit nationalism because of the development of more modern communications, beginning with the telegraph, which facilitated mobilizing the nation behind a war and then managing the huge forces from national headquarters.

And there were more resources for governments to extract. European states, the United States, and some others grew prodigiously in the nineteenth and twentieth centuries through the emergence of the industrial revolution. Economic development meant more resources could be tapped to pay for military establishments and wars. Development provided important technological improvements in transportation (shipping, railroads, cars and trucks, and planes) and communications (telegraph, telephone, and radio) for building and deploying ever larger and more powerful forces. National development brought women and the elderly into the workforce to perform more jobs and, in a war, allow more men to be sent to fight. It made the notion of women fighting in wars much more feasible as well.

Together, these developments allowed another important change. Building on the innovations introduced by Napoleon and with much greater resources, governments could aim to fight huge battles for smashing victories that would defeat an opponent through just one or two huge blows. Now even a great power had to face the possibility that it could be overwhelmed in a single huge battle, maybe at the beginning of a war, and that as a result the state itself might quickly collapse and disappear.

Thinking along these lines about how to fight wars was stimulated by an ongoing revolution in battlefield firepower as a result of technological change. It was a revolution that had taken a long time in coming to fruition, as it could be traced back to the introduction of gunpowder centuries before. However, it blossomed in the nineteenth century through a cluster of interlocking changes. The great improvements in artillery and naval guns meant more rapid fire over greater distances, with the use of larger shells that landed with increasing accuracy. Similarly, the rifles that replaced muskets in the middle of the century were far more accurate at a much greater distance and could be fired much faster, while machine guns were even more lethal. The improvements in these and other weapons continued in the twentieth century. Weapons were put on tanks, trucks, railroad cars, and then planes and missiles to make them more mobile. States got better at killing, at wholesale slaughter if necessary. Mounting huge armies to fight devastating battles as the way to win wars became even more attractive. Governments began to anticipate and then experience, particularly in the twentieth century, wars of unprecedented death and destruction. They covered such vast areas that they were called world wars.

Equally unfortunate was that the expanded range of weapons and mobility of forces was accompanied by a parallel growth in the possible scope of major wars, in the extent to which nations could be affected by them. In the late eighteenth and early nineteenth centuries, using blockades as a weapon became more feasible to bottle up not just a seaport or a city but also an entire country—even a large one. A blockade could exploit the vulnerability associated with a slowly growing reliance of states and societies on trade, particularly in food and vital materials. But a blockade would be a relatively indiscriminate weapon, affecting nearly everyone in the enemy nation, including those far from the battlefield or the front lines. Wars then could be, and were, brought home to the enemy's civilian population. For example, in the American Civil War, the Union used blockades to starve the South of food and vital supplies.

The scope of war was also enlarged by the greater reach of military forces when they exploited the development of the railroads. For example, General William Tecumseh Sherman, in his march to the sea through the heart of the confederacy late in the Civil War, struck at the civilian sector of the South, burning farms, towns, and cities and destroying bridges, roads, railroads, and dams to break down the South's resistance and finally end the war. Vast technological changes in the twentieth century put civilians more directly and immediately at risk in wars. Exceedingly long-range artillery was first used during World War I. Then planes carried bombs to enemy homelands at a modest rate in World War I. Finally, strategic bombing in World War II culminated in great fire raids and other destruction that burned out or razed cities such as Dresden, Hamburg, and Tokyo and inflicted nuclear obliteration on much of Hiroshima and Nagasaki. After 1945 nations expanded the range of planes by thousands of miles and their ability to do even more damage, while eventually developing ballistic missiles that could deliver hydrogen bombs five thousand miles or more away in roughly half an hour.

It was not just that weapons could reach much farther that put civilians at greater risk. In a modern war, national armed forces came to depend on a massive level of support from civilians, who then were treated as a legitimate target by the other side. The same reasoning led to Sherman's march to the sea. People who fight wars have always found it tempting to prey on civilians, and often armies were expected to live off the countryside as they moved. However, the laws of war, such as they were in international politics, had long emphasized that civilians should be spared, that they should be rejected as deliberate targets, and that only military installations and forces should be attacked instead. But by 1939 and the start of World War II, strategies had emerged, or soon developed under the pressures of the fighting, for winning wars by attacking the whole society—the workers, the war industries and other factories, communications and transportation facilities, the government installations, power plants, and eventually housing and other elements of everyday life. The enemy economy was a major concern and, to the extent that it could be disrupted or destroyed, ordinary citizens suffered greatly. However, citizens were also targeted more directly in an effort to undermine national morale in hopes that the enemy war effort would be weakened. Citizens had become strategic targets, and the harm that was done to them while the fighting occurred, whether their national forces were winning or not, grew steadily. By the 1960s, vast numbers of nuclear weapons mounted on ballistic missiles or long-range bombers had put virtually everyone on the planet potentially at risk.

These developments were not confined to the great powers. In some cases, as with the United States, they did much to create a new great power out of what had been a weaker nation. In many cases one or more of these developments were adopted by smaller states to pursue national expansion or deal with hostile neighbors. Israel built modern armed forces and a sizable nuclear weapons arsenal, and its neighbors replied by seeking nuclear weapons and developing stockpiles of chemical and biological weapons. Many governments, including some with limited resources, invested in large numbers of tanks and planes, and to date some thirty have either bought or developed ballistic missiles. But for the most part these developments in national capabilities, weapons, and warfare, especially when considered as a whole, applied particularly to the great powers of the world, and they had their greatest impact when the great powers went to war with each other. Thus the most exhausting, lethal, and destructive conflicts were World War I (1914–1918) and World War II (1939–1945). The preparations during the Cold War for a possible third world war consumed many dollars, approximately five trillion in the United States alone. If a third world war, fought with nuclear weapons, ever occurred, it might eliminate most or all of the life on the planet.

THE IMPACT ON STATE AND SOCIETAL SECURITY

How did the changes in warfare shape state and societal security over the past 150 years? The effect was paradoxical. On the one hand, the great powers came to be highly vulnerable—in principle—to a crushing defeat, in which the state and even the nation might not survive. They became as vulnerable to that as smaller states had always been. When Adolf Hitler attacked the Soviet Union in 1941, he planned to do away with that country as a great power by breaking it into pieces and turning much of it into an expanded Germany or German colonies. The impact on Soviet citizens would have been catastrophic because Hitler envisioned letting many of them die to make room for German settlers. The Soviet Union had a larger Jewish population, and Hitler wanted to have those that fell into German hands killed. When Germany and Japan lost World War II they temporarily disappeared as states and were ruled by the victorious Allies. They were better off than the state of Austria-Hungary after World War I because with its defeat it disappeared forever. Imagine the damage done to societal security in Germany and Japan—destitution from the war, so many lives lost in losing causes, chaos from collapse of their governments, millions turned into domestic refugees, money of no value, people forced to sell or barter anything they had for food, and some women turning to prostitution to survive. The ultimate in vulnerability for the great powers came during the Cold War when enough nuclear weapons were available to their opponents to wipe them off the face of the earth—not exactly a high point in their national security.

On the other hand, the greater national cohesiveness, the ability to draw the entire population into fighting or supporting a war, and the ability to tap much greater resources meant that if a state was not defeated at the outset or obliterated by nuclear weapons, it might be almost impossible to defeat it so as to force an end to the fighting. Furthermore, if it was defeated, the eventual victory might be terribly costly. This came to be true not only of great states but of some smaller states, too. France's Napoleon discovered the costs of protracted war when trying to defeat the guerrilla warfare mounted by his opponents in Spain and in his futile invasion of Russia. World Wars I and II lasted a long time and brought about unprecedented levels of death and destruction even to the winners because the staying power of great states had grown so markedly. This made many states far less attractive to attack, thereby enhancing their security.

As will be discussed in Chapter 5, the arrival of nuclear weapons also allowed their possessors to do such drastic harm even if they were defeated or eliminated that the idea of attacking them, particularly in any large way, became less attractive. This contributed to the absence of anything like another world war or smaller wars among the great powers during the Cold War, a pleasing development for citizens of these countries that has continued to the present. It was another enhancement of the security of these states and their inhabitants.

Thus great states (and some others) became simultaneously more vulnerable and less vulnerable. It was possible to envision a kind of war in which they could disappear, a particularly disturbing concern for a great power such as the United

States not used to living with such a threat. But in most sorts of conflicts they could offer a daunting challenge to even a combination of opponents.

THE IMPACT ON SYSTEMIC SECURITY

Outbreaks of widespread warfare among the great powers have always aroused fears about the future of international politics and the international system. With regard to systemic security, all the developments outlined above combined to provoke repeated and rising concern about how dreadful general great-power warfare—simultaneous fighting among all the great powers, usually over a long period of time—could become. Such conflicts are often referred to as **systemic** (or systemwide) **wars**. The first example of a systemwide war in Europe was the Thirty Years War in the early seventeenth century. Instead of being one war, it was a series of wars that raged off and on for, as the name suggests, roughly three decades and had damaging results. Much of the fighting was between protestant and catholic religious camps and the killing was particularly vicious. (Participants felt service to God demanded nothing less.)

The Thirty Years War was so disruptive and destructive in its impact on the international system that, when the fighting ended, states moved to adopt a number of reforms that have deeply affected international politics ever since. First, the principle of sovereignty was widely adopted after the war. Much of the fighting had been about some governments objecting to the religion adopted by the governments of other states and enforced on their citizens. To prevent future wars over such issues, sovereignty was taken to mean that a state was entitled to do what it wanted domestically—on religion and in other areas—without external interference. While states continued to interfere in each other's internal affairs in various ways, recognition of sovereignty had a major impact on how far and for what purpose states would engage in such interference thereafter. Wars of religion largely disappeared among Western states.

Second, states settled into ways of fighting for about 150 years that, until Napoleon came along, were much more restrained and orderly. The emphasis was often on winning engagements and wars by maneuver so as to avoid large and costly battles. Wars were fought for limited aims, and as a result they were less intense. Codes of conduct helped limit the methods used on the battlefield and thus contain some of their destructiveness.

Third, codes of conduct contributed to the continuing development of international law, particularly on war, which had been greatly stimulated by the Thirty Years War. While it was only marginally effective in many wars, international law came to emphasize that wars should be fought only for legitimate objectives and in ways that would minimize the killing of civilians, curb unnecessary damage to civilian sectors, and confine the use of force to what was necessary to gain the objective. In short, after the Thirty Years War states were so devastated that their governments attempted to get war under some control. It was not until the twentieth century that states turned again to weapons and wars that were often designed to greatly expand, at times even maximize, the killing of civilians.

The next instance of systemic war was the set of wars that grew out of the French Revolution and dominated the Napoleonic era. The seemingly interminable fighting from 1792 to 1815 all across Europe was so disruptive for the international system that the great powers put a cooperative management arrangement in place as a result (see Chapter 6). They agreed to meet when necessary to prevent major wars from breaking out, manage crises, and keep other conflicts under control. Historians claim that this arrangement helped to contain warfare for a number of decades. Over the next one hundred years, international law also developed further, including the law on war. The first steps toward what is now called arms control were taken during this period, culminating in the Hague Conferences in 1899 and 1906, which were the first modern attempts to curb arms races and outlaw ugly new weapons systems (such as submarines).

The twentieth century saw more of the same—brutal conflict and then a reaction to it. Each of the world wars was followed by renewed efforts to enhance the management of international politics so as to alleviate the problem of war's devastation. The World War I peace conference, with the Treaty of Versailles, culminated in the creation of a League of Nations to curb international conflicts so another such war would never occur and to bring smaller wars under control as well. After World War II a similar effort resulted in the development of the United Nations for the same purpose, replacing the failed League. The post–Cold War era has been no different. The end of that long conflict, which had kept people deeply fearful of another world war and had generated or exacerbated numerous smaller wars, was followed by efforts to use existing international institutions, and create new ones, to better restrain political conflicts and prevent wars.

Clearly the international system has been thrown into complete disarray a number of times by systemwide war. Also, on many occasions, smaller wars between states put a considerable strain on systemic security by intensifying rivalries and arousing fears. A good example from the Cold War era was the Korean War (1950–1953). Like Germany, Korea had been divided when the victorious World War II allies, in this case the United States and the Union of Soviet Socialist Republics, could not agree on the formation of a new Korean government. When North Korea invaded South Korea to unify the country under its rule and the United States organized an international effort to drive North Korea out and, eventually, to unify Korea by invading North Korea, the international consequences were immense. China intervened to save North Korea, putting the United

States (and its UN allies) at war with China for several years. As a result, the United States suspended any dealings with China for nearly twenty years; made China a target of containment to limit its development, power, and influence; and declared that it would defend Taiwan. Sino-American tensions lasted for many years thereafter and their dispute over Taiwan remains the most plausible source of a great-power war now. As part of containing China, the United States would eventually intervene in Vietnam's civil war politically and then militarily, creating the American version of that conflict during its involvement from 1965 to 1975. (The Vietnamese were often at war from 1946 to 1975 against the French, each other, and the Americans.)

In another reaction to the outbreak of the Korean War, the United States and its European allies decided to sharply increase their defense budgets and to strongly enlarge their military forces in Europe, with the United States sending six divisions and thousands of nuclear weapons there and admitting West Germany to the North Atlantic Treaty Organization (NATO) and allowing it to rearm. In response, the Soviet Union formed the Warsaw Pact and all the members—including East Germany—greatly increased their forces. The Korean War also contributed to a sharp escalation in the nuclear arms race. As is often said, the Korean War did much to militarize the Cold War, to sharply escalate the fear of war on each side and the preparations for it. Thus the aftereffects of the Korean War reverberated through the international system in ways that sharply decreased systemic security.

Sometimes the disturbing smaller wars have been internal wars, wars inside states. Individual wars of this sort have been very disruptive in the international system on numerous occasions, and they began to be particularly threatening to systemic security in the first decades after World War II. Many of the same developments cited above were at work—nationalism, better communications, deadlier and more plentiful weapons, the ability to field and wield larger forces, the need to tap the support of civilians and thus to target enemy (or even neutral) civilians—and with the same results. Internal wars experienced a significant increase in the potential and actual destructiveness and homicide involved. Eventually internal wars around the world were to produce collectively, and sometimes individually, millions of casualties, more millions of refugees, and frequently the near destruction of normal society in the countries that were the battlefields. In recent decades it has become rare to have a large interstate war, but many civil wars are being fought around the world today. In the Sudan, for example, war between the Arab north and the Black African south went on for decades and produced more than two million deaths.

Internal wars have stimulated rising attention and concern over time, in part out of systemic security considerations. With their often mindless violence and near anarchy, atrocities that have included genocide, side effects in terms of disease, starvation, economic decay, and refugees, intrastate wars have slowly come to also seem intolerable in a world experiencing rising interdependence. This has given rise to more energetic efforts to do something about such wars, efforts reviewed in the last section of this book. The UN may have been created to curb international conflicts and wars, but today its main concern is with internal conflicts and wars.

Thus it has been clear for a long time to governments, leaders, and analysts that something has to be done about the problems of great-power wars, smaller wars among states, and internal wars. This is in view of problems of war's devastating effects on society and civilians, its potential to eliminate a nation or state, the cost a war imposes on governments, and the ripple effect of insecurity spreading from one part of a system to another or from inside a state to its surrounding neighborhood. As a result, a substantial amount of experience has been accumulated in trying to manage conflict—enough to write a book about.

CONCLUSION

By now you should better understand the problem of war. War is organized military conflict between clearly identifiable groups that have a cohesive structure and recognized leadership. In the view of many governments or observers, particularly the great powers, the problem is that general great-power wars are intolerable in terms of their costs and their consequences. Such wars are not impossible, unfortunately, just intolerable—the loss of life, the destruction, the economic costs, and the disruption of the international system are too vast to ignore. In fact, a systemwide war among the great powers had become too awful even by 1815, but the actors in international politics have been slow to figure out what to do about it. Systemwide war became potentially more deadly over the next one hundred years and then lived up to that potential in World War I. The actual and potential consequences of a systemwide war then became even worse over the rest of the twentieth century. Thus neither the problem nor the efforts to develop solutions are new. It is a sad fact that the development of war has consistently outrun the development of solutions in the past.

This problem has come to apply to other wars as well. If a general great-power war was intolerable, then any war between two or more great powers could also be considered so dangerous as to be intolerable, because it could easily become a large and devastating struggle, and because other great powers might readily be drawn in—creating a systemwide war. Military technology spreads, as all major technologies do, when smaller countries imitated the great powers. When other changes discussed above affect those countries, wars among other less powerful states also began to look less tolerable. They could now do immense damage. As noted in Chapter 1, the Iran-Iraq war in the 1980s was responsible for more than one million deaths, plenty of destruction, and the use of chemical weapons. Such "small" wars sometimes threatened to sharply disrupt and damage the international system, for example, by drawing in some of the great powers and escalating to a higher level. In the Arab-Israeli wars in 1956, 1967, and 1973 quarrels arose between great powers over what to do, raising the threat that they might intervene against each other. The 1973 war brought a serious disruption of the world economy through an Arab oil embargo and a huge jump in oil prices.

From 1945 on, internal wars became common—wars of national liberation against colonial rule, wars of attempted secession, wars of revolution against existing governments. These wars, too, have often seriously disrupted the international system. They have sometimes attracted fierce outside interventions, such as that of the Americans into the Vietnam War or the Soviet Union into the war in Afghanistan.

Hence the essence of the problem for governments is that a traditional recourse of major states in international politics, one regularly used by the great powers in their relations with each other and as a key element in their overall management of the international system, and one often also used by lesser states and by movements within states, had become too deadly. A main tool of statecraft has turned on the statesman. Domestic warfare or seemingly small interstate wars could do great damage and could evolve into great-power wars, which might turn into systemwide wars.

This may seem like an unusual way of characterizing the problem. People often say the problem with war is war itself. But in international politics war was, for a long time, normal. Not a constant phenomenon by any means, it was hardly unusual and it was not illegitimate. It was a tool. The same had long been true for settling serious internal political, religious, and ethnic disputes. War was an accepted recourse. So the problem now is not war itself, but the plausible scale of war and its possible consequences.

People often talk about security in terms of the safety of their nation. This book defines the security problem more broadly, in terms of three levels related to international politics as a whole, depicting the problem as it confronts all states in some fashion. The rest of the book explores what has been tried to solve the problem within international politics. Many people have suggested dealing with it by doing away with international politics, creating potent institutions that displace anarchy to run the world. That might or might not be a good thing to do, but it is highly debatable, very hard to achieve, and unlikely to happen in most of the world any time soon. So the book proceeds by trying to see what works and what does not within international politics. People are going to be living in international politics for the foreseeable future, often in nation-states that are of questionable stability and legitimacy, and vulnerable to civil wars that can badly disrupt international politics. Wars can be lethal far beyond their original scope. If people fail to get an increasing grip on the problem of war and keep it under control, international politics could even be the death of everyone.

SOURCES AND OTHER USEFUL READINGS

Distinguishing wars from other violent conflicts is discussed in Lotta Harbom, *States in Armed Conflict 2003*. Continually updated statistical information on wars, armed conflicts, and other violence can be found in the *States in Armed Conflict* series published annually by the Uppsala University Department of Peace and Conflict Research and the *SIPRI Yearbooks* of the Stockholm International Peace Research Institute, which come out annually. The "Armed Conflict Database" is a regularly updated source of information on individual violent conflicts around the world, prepared by the International Institute for Strategic Studies (IISS) and can be found at its Web site (www.iiss.org). For a number of years, the annual publication of IISS, *The Military Balance,* has included a large, pull-out map of violent conflicts in the world.

Other broad discussions of violent conflicts and wars include Peter Wallensteen's *Understanding Conflict Resolution;* his fine textbook *Preventing Violent Conflicts;* Ted Robert Gurr's book on ethnic conflicts, *People versus States;* J. David Singer and Melvin Small's *The Wages of War* and *Resort to Arms,* both of which describe the Correlates of War Project, which pioneered modern data collection on wars; John A. Vasquez's *The War Puzzle;* and Kalevi J. Holsti's *Peace and War.*

The literature on the causes of war is vast. Overviews are provided in several chapters of James E. Dougherty and Robert L. Pfaltzgraff Jr.'s *Contending Theories of International Relations* and Jack S. Levy's articles "War and Peace" and "The Causes of War and the Conditions of Peace." Descriptions of war in excerpts from classics appear in Richard K. Betts, *Conflict after the Cold War.* For analysis of causes of contemporary wars, see Daniel Byman and Stephen Van Evera, "Why They Fight"; Holsti, *Peace and War;* and Vasquez, *The War Puzzle,* which report that disputes over territory are the most common ones in wars. The discussion in Louis Kriesberg, *Constructive Conflicts,* on the causes of conflict surveys a wide range of theories that are applicable to explaining warfare. A source describing war as the result of gaps between the number of states and the number of nations in a region is Benjamin Miller, "Between Hot War and Cold Peace." Vladimir I. Lenin's explanation for World War I is laid out in his *Imperialism,* first published in 1916. An easy-to-comprehend review of theories of war is William M. Evan, *War and Peace in an Age of Terrorism*. War as seen from a peace activist and peace analyst point of view is discussed in Johan Galtung, *Peace by Peaceful Means*.

A number of histories of international warfare in world politics have been written. Those of Michael Howard are almost universally admired, such as his *War in European History*. A study that fits well with my book is David Kaiser, *Politics and War*, which focuses on explaining systemwide wars such as World War I and World War II. To get a flavor of what made World War I intolerable, see Joseph E. Persico, *Eleventh Month, Eleventh Day, Eleventh Hour;* and for the arms buildup that led to it, see, for example, David G. Herrmann, *The Arming of Europe and the Making of the First World War*.

The most credible estimate of the costs of nuclear weapons for the United States during the Cold War is Stephen I. Schwartz, *Atomic Audit*.

CHAPTER 3

The Appropriate Distribution of Power

The next six chapters examine the most fundamental attempts that governments have devised and, in some fashion, put into practice to solve the security problems associated with war in international politics. The results have not been consistently rewarding. The record is not one of governments at their best. In part this is because these efforts reflect the fact that states have been unwilling to abandon core elements, specified in the realist perspective, of classic international politics such as national sovereignty and anarchy. States and their citizens remain deeply attached to national autonomy. They resist developing any strong version of a global or regional government. Even in Europe, resistance to carrying integration to this point, particularly in foreign policy and security matters, has been substantial and durable. The situation is similar to the difficulty in establishing order in the United States' Wild West. In Western towns, especially those in which cowboys drove cattle to the railheads, there was initially no law and order and men largely did as they pleased. Just as western movies depict it, when the sheriff or marshal was serious about running a safe place he ordered everyone to deposit their guns at his office until they left town. Men enjoyed carrying guns in those days; carrying a gun meant that maybe no one (even the sheriff) could tell you what to do. Men were often reluctant to give up their guns. But the sheriff ordered that they do so because having many people armed was dangerous for everyone. With the gambling, drinking, and general hell-raising in those towns, plus the usual quarrels found anywhere, homicide rates were often extraordinarily high. So, the sheriff started by ordering that men stop carrying guns in town; later he wanted everyone to behave better so as to cut down on instances of violence; eventually he and others wanted real law and order with fairly elaborate constraints on people's behavior. Autonomy was steadily cut back. Something of real value had to be exchanged for enhanced security.

Later in this book efforts will be considered that reflect a different conception of international politics, which I term "liberalist." In this perspective, many ways exist to modify anarchy and sovereignty without eliminating them, so that governments can get to be less dangerous to each other without having to take a much more radical step. They would place international politics in between being what it has been and becoming something else entirely. But many governments are uncomfortable even with that. They fear things will go as they did in the Wild West, with something of real value lost as more autonomy is traded for rising regional or global government. It is probably correct to see such liberalist steps as producing an unstable variant of international politics, and people and their governments will have to choose between staying in international politics and abandoning it.

States love autonomy, including the right to be armed and dangerous. So they have wanted to retain an international political environment with few restraints from some higher legal or political authority. As of now they have no plans to do away with international politics, so they must find other ways to cope with the fact that interstate warfare, especially among great powers, has become counterproductive. They started trying in serious ways to get war under control a long time ago and have been at it ever since.

STRATEGIES FOR PEACE AND SECURITY

In reading the discussions in this book about the different solutions to the security problem that war generates, you should keep several things in mind. First, each solution, as a strategy for peace and security, involves a conscious effort to bring about a general state of affairs that will be safer, including steps to avoid, neutralize, or defeat resistance to it. The underlying view is that security via an end to fighting will not just happen; it has to be arranged. Thus the working assumption is that international politics is not beyond control. Various things can be done to contain and manage international politics, deliberately and according to a plan for making it safer either as a whole or for at least some members.

Second, the strategies are, for the most part, not mutually exclusive. Often a number are pursued simultaneously. Some are employed in only part of the international system, alongside others used in other parts of that system. Some are employed by states together. Furthermore, strategies overlap somewhat. Often they involve some similar steps. Though each strategy is discussed individually to keep the discussion clear and orderly, that is not how the strategies play out in the real world.

Third, inside any government, and its society, debates take place about which strategy to pursue and how to implement it. Sometimes getting a consensus behind any one strategy is so difficult that several are followed at the same time, including ones that are contradictory, as a way of satisfying enough people to maintain broad support for the government and its policy. Or, different strategies are taken up simultaneously because knowing what to do is unclear. The advantage is that an unworkable strategy can more easily be abandoned in favor of another. For instance, some cite the old saying "If you want peace, prepare for war," which is an argument for being ready to fight as the best way to get the other side to negotiate for peace while taking out insurance in case a war breaks out anyway. Pursuing either negotiations or a military buildup alone might be too con-troversial, while doing both can satisfy many critics. The danger is that building more military strength may make the other side doubt the seriousness of the negotiations effort and that your side sincerely wants peace, which is the security dilemma at work (see Chapter 1). If both sides build up their military strength, negotiations can become impossible or unproductive, as each side thinks the other is not serious. Also important is that strategies can shift, such as after a major change in the leaders or political orientation of the government or when leaders change their minds. Governments must not ignore this. The pursuit of peace and security was conducted differently during President Ronald Reagan's second term, for example, than in his first term.

Finally, the strategies are part of normal international politics. Ever since inter-national politics first emerged, proposals have been made for a world government, or at least regional governments, to control warfare through interventions, by force if necessary, in interstate conflicts. Because governments have not been inter-ested in this idea, I ignore most of the proposals because they have not had much impact. The major exception is integration in Europe (see Chapter 8). Many pro-posals have been put forth for effective international law and a strong world court. While the international tribunals on war crimes in the Balkans were an important step, not much other progress has been made. Governments, not international courts and law, have the last word as to what governments do, so international courts and law receive little discussion here.

THE STRATEGY OF ARRANGING AN APPROPRIATE DISTRIBUTION OF POWER

In thinking about the problem of war, states, statesmen, and observers have often put their greatest emphasis on the distribution of power in the international sys-tem. This is referred to as a balance of power approach, but the term is mislead-ing. When people refer to a balance, they often do not mean a roughly equal dis-tribution of power among states. Instead, they are usually referring to the distribution of power among a group of states no matter how unequal it is. Thus discussions of whether the balance of power is shifting or not in the Middle East or East Asia or South Asia are common, even though, strictly speaking, a balance cannot shift. If a balance shifts, it disappears. I mention the term only because it is commonly used so it is valuable to be familiar with it and to understand that it should not be taken literally. Maintaining peace is often sought through an appro-priate distribution of power instead.

Power is also a troublesome term. In the broadest sense power is the ability to make happen what one wants to have happen, to be the cause of it happening. Just having those things happen is not enough, because luck or someone else's efforts may be involved. Power enables something to happen because you set out to make it happen and without your effort it would not have occurred. Thought of in this way, power is exceedingly complex, and I can only scratch the surface of it here. However, it is important to keep in mind that there are numerous ways to make things happen, so there are numerous kinds of power—economic, political, cultural, ideological, and so forth. The power that comes from having prestige, respect, political and cultural influence, legitimacy, and attractive ideas is real and is often referred to as **soft power**. In international politics people understand this, but they frequently simplify things by emphasizing a particular kind of **hard power**—the power to coerce, hurt, and destroy, particularly with force and weapons. Thus, a powerful country is one with great ability to hurt and destroy using military means. The view is particularly associated with the realist tradition (see Chapter 1). In this view, national power lies mainly in military might and the additional things needed to create, maintain, and use it effectively—the necessary wealth and economic strength, good leadership, a suitable population, strong public support, and so on. The United States is constantly cited today as the world's most powerful country, and what is meant by that, more than anything else, is its unequaled military might.

When I discuss distributions of power, the power involved is predominantly military. The strategy for dealing with the problem of war is achieving an appropriate distribution of military power. The core assumption is that power is central in international politics and that, when it comes to peace and security, the most important factor is the power to hurt. War is the deliberate application of just that. The way to achieve peace is to keep the power to hurt contained.

This is a familiar way of thinking about power for most Americans as well as people in many other political systems. The American political system rests on the idea that power is dangerous, especially the ability to hurt. Therefore, power should be dispersed, not concentrated in a few hands and a few places, so that those with considerable power offset each other to some degree. That is, they check and balance each other. Americans operate their political system amidst almost endless checks and balances in federalism; the separation of executive, legislative, and judicial powers at each level of government; constitutional limitations on power delineated, for example, in the Bill of Rights; multiple and overlapping military and police forces; citizens having their own weapons; and decentralized legislatures and political parties.

In international politics states have power, and they worry about each other's power and how it might be used or abused. Almost instinctively, governments and leaders think about the distribution of power in the system, particularly military might and related capabilities, as an important factor shaping whether and when wars occur. The point at which this becomes a strategy is when the belief takes hold that the distribution of power among the major states has much to do with whether major warfare will occur. (See the *Terms and Concepts* box, "Is This a Strategy?") Similarly, the distribution of power between any two states is believed to have much to do with whether war will break out between them. Governments presumably are basically rational and will normally not choose to go to war unless they enjoy military superiority and thus are likely to win. To prevent war, therefore, the distribution of power must be arranged so that it is unfavorable for those who would otherwise choose to go to war, presumably because they want something so strongly they are ready to fight for it. Such governments are unhappy with the status quo, with things as they are or the direction in which they are developing. They want more of something for the future—power, wealth, status, territory, people, democracy—and they feel they are unlikely to get it unless they fight and they are willing to do that.

Governments try to maintain or adjust the distribution of power in international politics in a number of ways. A government can form alliances either to pool its strength with others against someone they all fear, in hopes of avoiding war, or to gain the superior power needed to win the war they want to fight. Given

Terms and Concepts: Is This a Strategy?

Some analysts argue that governments work to maximize their power and the distribution of power is what results. They do not work to shape it into what they want it to be. Therefore a suitable distribution of power is not a strategy, just one possible result. The distribution of power is a condition under which states operate, like a traffic pattern for drivers. A government mainly adjusts to this condition, tries to take advantage of favorable shifts in it, and reacts when it looks full of danger.

While there is something to this view, it is not correct. It applies to weaker states, which most states are, in their relationship to the distribution of power in the international system as a whole or a regional system. But when it comes to how a government will react to specific foes, a state is likely to make an effort to keep the power ratio it has with a threatening government at an appropriate level or try to adjust it in that direction. And powerful states can, and at times do, try to adjust the distribution of power in the system as a whole.

As for maximizing their power, states have better things to do than spend all their time, effort, and resources in seeking to be as powerful as they can be. This is in part because if they have some success it may be offset by adjustments to counter it that other states make. Thus they put up with power relationships that are good enough, and that they can never do much about. And they try to adjust power relationships they think are dangerous and that they might be able to change, particularly if conditions seem favorable for doing so.

that war can be a tool, alliances can be made for preventing a war or for initiating one. In addition to alliances, a state can build up its own military power: buy arms, spend more on military training, or put its forces on higher alert. If it fears another state, it might take steps to help strengthen a third state that the leaders of the second state are worried about so that that government feels more pressure and has more threats to worry about. The general idea is plain enough—more power in the right places and the right hands to offset the power of those who seem threatening or to guard against hypothetical future threats

Many analyses have been conducted of how a balance of power works. For example, during the Cold War the view that gained the most prominence came to be referred to as **structural realism**. It indicated that peace and security—including curbing the incidence of any grave wars—depended on the structure of the international system. In turn, structure was defined as the way power was distributed among the most important states in the system.

Peace by Preponderance

What is the appropriate distribution of power, the best structure for the international system, to discourage attacks? There is much disagreement about this. First, governments always disagree about which of them are dangerous, that is, are threats to go to war. No government wants to think of itself as the problem. Thus governments disagree about what distribution of power among themselves is most appropriate. For years the United States has clearly been the most powerful country, particularly since the end of the Cold War. Since the end of that half-century conflict, the American government has been officially committed to keeping things that way, to staying ahead of any potential military competitor or cluster of competitors through its defense spending, weapons, military research and development, and training and deployment of forces. It believes that American predominance is good for world peace, not just for U.S. security, because the United States has goals many others endorse, because it protects numerous allies, and because its military might keeps large parts of the international system (East Asia, Europe, the Americas, the Middle East) more stable and peaceful than they otherwise would be. However, numerous governments think the United States has too much power, is too dominant, and is too likely to attack other states—that it is not a status quo government and society. Even in Europe public opinion polls often list the United States as the world's most dangerous country. Many governments also think it would be more appropriate if the United States was less powerful so they would be more powerful.

Such disagreements about what is best in the entire international system, in relations among small groups of states or in relations between just two states, are normal. The disagreements concern not only current but also future distributions of power. The United States is far more powerful than China today. The Chinese government dislikes this situation because the United States might pressure or even attack China over a serious conflict down the road. While the United States can feel safe now, in relation to China, numerous American analysts and officials fear that when China gains on the United States even modestly in military power it will make grave trouble over issues such as the political status of Taiwan and might even provoke a war. Thus even when U.S.-China relations are good and U.S.-China economic relations are flourishing, which is the case now, each country is concerned about the other and thus real disagreement arises between and within the two countries over what an appropriate distribution of power between them is.

On top of this, analysts and officials do not agree as to what power distribution is best for preventing wars. This leads to different versions of the strategy. The first version calls for confronting a state that might use war to make gains for itself with a highly unfavorable distribution of power. It would be kept inferior in military and related kinds of power to the states fearful of it. When the leading states in the international system, or in a regional system, are involved, an arrangement is created and maintained in which one state or a cluster of states has far more power than any other state or cluster that would use force to change things. That state or group is called the **hegemon**. Peace is sustained by having a clear imbalance of power, often referred to as peace by preponderance. The United States today is often referred to as a hegemon.

How is such an imbalance created and then maintained? One possibility is that it arises automatically out of a major war among the great powers. If a clear winning state or coalition emerges, it is, in effect, a hegemon—much stronger than any competitor. Maintaining the imbalance for as long as possible is attractive to the state or coalition, because being on top is nice. It is also appealing because otherwise the loser(s) will probably seek to attack at some future date to get back what was lost and create a more favorable distribution of power. The winner can stay on top, for a while at least, if it can limit the loser's armaments directly, its involvement in alliances, its arms purchases from abroad, or its dominion over territory and resources. Doing so can be done through provisions of the peace treaty that ends the war, or they may be negotiated separately. Furthermore, the hegemonic state or coalition can outspend rivals or potential rivals on defense or negotiate a freeze on changes in armaments while it is ahead.

Some examples will illustrate all this. In the 1860s Prussia maneuvered its way into a series of wars that made it the most powerful state on the continent of Europe. It became the first version of what is now Germany (see the *Cases and Concepts* box in Chapter 2). The Prussian chancellor, Otto von Bismarck, sustained the peace in Europe for over two decades by maintaining a Prussian-dominated hegemonic power distribution. His main concern was France. The key war in achieving Prussia's dominance had been its victory, in 1870–1871, over France. Bismarck feared that sooner or later France would want to return the favor so as to avenge its defeat, slash German power, and restore its former preeminence.

Bismarck's solution had two elements. The first was to consistently emphasize that Imperial Germany was satisfied with the status quo. That is, it was not interested in expanding its power or territory at others' expense. The second element was to exploit this image by signing alliances with Austria-Hungary and Russia and by keeping on good terms with Great Britain (which was never eager to be drawn into a war in Europe). This left France with no other great powers as its allies and thus no way to build a powerful coalition against Prussia. Bismarck's coalition was too powerful to attack, hence Germany was safe.

Another example is the situation in Europe after World War I. With the end of the war in 1918, Germany was defeated and exhausted, and its allies—Austria-Hungary and Turkey—were in even worse shape (the Austro-Hungarian and Ottoman empires broke up into little states and disappeared). U.S. troops had gone home, and the Russian state collapsed into revolution, chaos, and civil war. The most powerful countries remaining in Europe were Britain and France, and they tried to keep it that way. First, they continued to cooperate on many matters. Individually neither was overwhelmingly powerful but together they were formidable. In addition, France maintained alliances with numerous smaller countries around Germany to contain German power. Second, in the peace treaties they insisted that Germany eliminate significant border defenses, maintain only a small army and navy, and abandon its big defense industries. Its colonies and some of its territory were taken away, and important areas in Germany were run under French occupation for years to help keep Germany weak. Britain and France feared Germany would otherwise rebuild its military and economic preeminence and then seek to defeat them in another war. Hegemony was a way of keeping the peace and remaining safe.

A third example is taken from the Cold War. By the early 1970s the power of the Soviet Union seemed to be rising rapidly. It had the world's largest armed forces, a huge nuclear arsenal, a steadily rising defense budget, a rapidly expanding and modernizing navy, and plenty of friends and allies. Most important, it sought—and often quarreled with the other major powers to get—more influence in world affairs. What emerged in reaction was an informal coalition. Washington and Beijing moved to patch up the severe political conflict between them, starting with President Richard M. Nixon's visit to China in 1972. Then the United States, the main states in Western Europe, Japan, and China began to cooperate, which was a big change because China had not been closely associated with any of the others for years. They all boosted their defense spending; some Western countries sold military equipment to China; the United States began sharing intelligence information with China about the Soviet Union; and China began applauding increases in European, Japanese, and U.S. defense spending, something it had previously condemned. All this created a power imbalance against the Soviet Union, designed to prevent it from attacking any coalition members or being too adventurous elsewhere in the world.

Here is a recent example. When the Cold War ended in 1990, the Soviet bloc began to dissolve. Even the Soviet Union dissolved into numerous weak states. The largest, Russia, went into a tailspin militarily, economically, and politically. The United States was left as the only superpower, a hegemon. The United States has decided that this is a good thing. It has more useable military power than the other great powers combined and would like to keep things that way. It spends more on defense than those other states, particularly on military research and development. It retains all its alliances, which include the next most powerful countries in the world— Britain, France, Germany, and Japan. It still keeps military forces all over the globe to help project its military power, if necessary. Critics in Russia and China claim it deliberately tries to cripple their nations' development so they pose no threat in the foreseeable future. The United States tries to remain the most powerful country in European affairs, in Middle East affairs (by crippling Iraq and Iran), in East Asia, and in the Americas. This is a strategy of hegemonic stability—keep yourself and your friends so much stronger than anyone else that no one wants to make trouble and thus peace and security are maintained.

Peace by Balance

The second variant of the strategy is to seek a roughly equal distribution of power among conflicting or competitive states instead of a clear imbalance. While examples to the contrary can be cited, this solution to the problem of war usually is adopted out of necessity, not by choice. Most states would prefer a clear imbalance in their favor, but often this is not feasible. The State of Blue aims to keep up with Green, Orange, and Red militarily because it does not want them to be too powerful. However, trying to outdistance them is not reasonable because such an attempt would provoke them to take steps to keep Blue from getting too powerful. As a result, the states choose to live with a relatively equitable power distribution.

If a roughly equal distribution of power exists between the two most powerful states or groups of states in a regional or global system and they are far more powerful than any other members of their system, a bipolar power distribution results. The term was invented during the Cold War. The two dominant states were so much more powerful than others that they came to be called superpowers. Each formed a pole of power with supporting states attached. (Power is concentrated in two poles and blocs, thus it is bipolar). If there are more than two major poles of power, especially if there are more than three, a multipolar power distribution results. There is no hegemonic state or coalition.

As noted earlier, a state may enhance its power to achieve this balance in various ways—by undertaking arms buildups or improvements, joining an alliance, or helping others (terrorists, guerrillas, third-party states) hostile to a government considered too powerful. The principle at work is "the enemy of my enemy is my friend." A state can also fight to weaken other states, using war to redistribute power.

Another possibility for maintaining a fairly even power distribution in a multipolar system is to have a balancer. For example, if two states (or coalitions) are vying to attain a dominant position and one gets close to achieving superiority, an important third party moves to support the weaker side to preserve the balance. If the weaker party becomes much more powerful, then the balancer returns to being neutral or, if that party is now a threat to become dominant, joins the other side. In that way no state or coalition becomes powerful enough to dominate everyone else.

There are numerous examples of this approach. Chancellor Bismarck's arrangements to keep Germany in the driver's seat in Europe were abandoned around 1890. Bismarck was sent into retirement, and the government moved both to expand German power and territory and to let its alliance with Russia languish and eventually expire. This set off moves to adjust the distribution of power among those who now feared Germany's power. No longer allied with Germany, the Russian empire entered an alliance with France to balance (even outweigh) the Germans, who responded by strengthening ties with the Austro-Hungarian empire and eventually reaching an alliance with Turkey. Concerned that Germany was getting too powerful, particularly at sea, the British edged steadily closer to an alliance with France, which therefore made Britain an ally of the Russians, too. Both sides tried to entice Italy into joining them, but Italy joined Britain, France, and Russia only after World War I was well under way. The two coalitions engaged in a huge arms race for over two decades, and other countries concerned about these developments also built up their military strength. The result was a rough balance between the coalitions in military and economic power.

Another example arose in 1938–1939. By then the superior English-French coalition from the years after World War I had lost much ground. Germany had fully recovered from World War I and, in shaking off the limits imposed on it after that war, had become more powerful than ever. Its rising strength was augmented by alliances with Italy and Japan. By the mid-1930s arms buildups were getting under way in all of these countries and the Soviet Union (the successor to tsarist

Russia). Britain and France were concerned, correctly, that they were lagging behind Germany in military strength and that Germany might start another great war. Therefore they sought an alliance with the Soviet Union. They were looking to create an imbalance in their favor and thus discourage Adolf Hitler from going to war. They were too late. Hitler offered the Soviet Union a deal if it would not engage in a war with Germany: half of Poland (which Hitler planned to conquer shortly) and three Baltic states—Estonia, Latvia, and Lithuania—which had been part of the Russian empire until 1918. A greedy Joseph Stalin, the Soviet leader, took the deal. He believed Germany and Italy were roughly a match for Britain and France, but because Germany had come close to winning World War I all by itself in 1918, he should have known better. That left Hitler free to go to war. Within a week he did, confident that his was the superior side.

During a brief period after World War II, the winners—Britain, France, the Soviet Union, and the United States—tried to maintain the coalition they built to win the war, but it soon deteriorated into a bipolar power distribution. The United States and Soviet Union gathered friends and allies into eastern and western blocs. Some states disliked the alliances and hoped to see a multipolar situation emerge, but that never happened. The Cold War thus became an outstanding example of peace pursued via a bipolar power distribution. While each side was willing to try to become dominant and predicted that eventually it would be, far greater effort was put into not becoming inferior to the other side—to staying at least roughly equal. Both sides did not feel it was vital to achieve hegemony because they felt safe enough under **bipolarity**. Because they were deeply fearful of what could happen if the other side ever became dominant and knew the other side felt the same way, it became less stressful to live with bipolarity and not aggressively seek hegemony.

CREATING AN APPROPRIATE POWER DISTRIBUTION INSIDE STATES

On maintaining peace and security inside states, the use of a proper distribution of military power strategy is rarely discussed. Terms such as *hegemony, bipolarity,* and *multipolarity* are not normally used. However, this strategy is highly relevant and is often pursued inside states, and the effects on international politics, and vice versa, can be substantial.

Preponderance

The transition from feudalism to the modern world in Europe, especially in the sixteenth and early seventeenth centuries, involved the achievement by royal rulers of consolidated control over their realms into what are now called states, along with the emergence of what is now called international politics among those states (there could be no international before there were nations), which eventually claimed to be sovereign entities. Prior to that time military power in Europe had been largely dispersed. Concentrations of it were held by the feudal nobility and other regional leaders and groups. The ruler of the country was more like the first among equals. Typically a good deal of fighting took place among the many clusters of power or between some of them and the ruler. Peace and security was usually in short supply. The modern state was created in various places by rulers generating a hegemonic distribution of power in their favor. Part of their ability to do so was that hegemony came to be considered vital for peace and security. As they developed further, states got to the point of claiming, and insisting, that they have a monopoly (not just hegemony) on the legitimate use of force inside their territories. The philosopher Thomas Hobbes referred to such a state as the **leviathan** and insisted it was crucial for ending domestic warfare. European states were relatively successful in pursuing this goal. Max Weber's definition of a state as the entity that exercises a monopoly on the use of force within its territory is now often cited, and it is taken as one of the major characteristics of a viable state. This is peace by preponderance carried to an unusual degree. If a state today does not have this monopoly, it usually is thought of as being in serious trouble.

With preponderance carried to this degree, any concern about the state having too much power had to be dealt with by some means other than creating different distributions of power than hegemony, such as placing significant limitations on the state's use of power against its citizens. The United States is an example of a state founded by people who took a dim view of entrusting the national government with a monopoly on the use of force. The Constitution provided for defense of the country via a militia—armed citizens coming to its defense—instead of relying on a large standing army and for defense at sea by having the government officially turn private ships into warships instead of just maintaining the U.S. navy. But over time the United States came to look like other modern states. The use of organized violence is entirely the business of the state, and other means are used to control how that power is used.

Balance

In many countries today the national government is too weak to even be a hegemon, much less to effectively claim a monopoly on the use of force. In some cases, the state has never fully consolidated its rule over the country. Such political systems resemble feudalism. They are roughly on a par with England in the time of Richard the III (who ruled from 1483 to 1485), about whom Shakespeare wrote so powerfully. In Afghanistan, throughout its existence as a country, regional warlords have been quite powerful, battling among themselves and resisting the emergence of a strong central government. The government has usually had no monopoly on the use of force and only tenuous control, at best, over the country. That remains true of Afghanistan today.

In other cases a state has lost its ability to maintain a monopoly on the use of force. This can occur for any number of reasons. No reliable sources of income or excessive corruption in disposing of it, strong political disagreements within the ruling elite, or exhaustion from fighting with outsiders, for example, can leave the government a basket case politically and economically. A history of abusing the citizens or running the country into the ground can bring a widespread loss of support that weakens the government. In short, the government no longer has the capacity to sustain a monopoly on the use of force. The door then is opened for criminal groups, dissatisfied ethnic or religious groups, regional political leaders, or others to build their own military strength to replace the state in providing peace and security, often because they see a need or think they will be at least as well off. A similar scenario played out in the Soviet Union in the last years before it dissolved. Even if such a state does not dissolve, however, it is likely to lack a monopoly on using force. This has been true in the Congo and a number of other African states. Normally states that never had, or have largely lost, the capacity to monopolize the use of force are now referred to as weak states or **failed states**.

Another kind of failed state is one that loses its monopoly because a part of the country is willing to fight either to achieve a high level of autonomy or to set itself up as a separate state and the government cannot readily suppress the rebellion. Just such a situation has existed for several decades in the Sudan, during which an inconclusive civil war took, by usual estimates, more than a million lives. The United States was on the verge of becoming such a failed state in 1860 when it was not clear that the Union could win the civil war that was about to break out.

A different sort of situation is when a state loses its monopoly on force not intrinsically but for temporary political reasons. For example, sharp disagreement arises over who should be running the government, and the people and groups involved are willing to fight to decide this. What results is a coup attempt or a rebellion, which seeks to forcibly replace the government with another one. The state loses its monopoly to the extent that the government is vulnerable to being attacked. However, monopoly may be reestablished if one side wins a clear victory. This has been true periodically in countries such as Iran, Iraq, and Pakistan.

In all these sorts of cases at least some of the parties will prefer a balance—a bipolar or multipolar distribution of power—as best for their security. Afghani warlords want a multipolar distribution to retain their autonomy. Only a warlord seeking to seize control of the entire country would want otherwise. Those who want to secede prefer a distribution of power close enough to, or the equivalent of, bipolarity or even superiority so they can break away successfully, maybe with little real fighting. When East Pakistan declared its independence from Pakistan in

1971 it lacked the military power to achieve such a condition and suffered greatly in the ensuing civil war with the central government. However, when India declared war on Pakistan also, the balance shifted markedly in East Pakistan's favor militarily and it then successfully seceded as Bangladesh.

Steps taken to alter the distribution of power are also similar to those employed in international politics. In seeking to maintain its monopoly, a state tries to keep actual or potential opponents disarmed, or weak economically and in other ways. Meanwhile, opponents seek to expand their power. Both build up armaments, improve the readiness and training of their forces, and seek alliances with insiders and outsiders for aid, arms, and recruits for their forces. Lebanon was for decades a country with a precarious multipolar distribution of power among a variety of well-armed groups. Outside governments aided various factions in the struggles over who would run the country, seeking to help determine the winner or to act as balancers to prevent anyone from completely controlling the state, both when the struggles were peaceful and when they took the form of a nasty and destructive civil war. In 1990 Syria succeeded in suppressing the fighting and promoting factions it supported into achieving control of the government, a situation it maintained until 2005 by keeping forces in Lebanon.

DOES THE DISTRIBUTION OF POWER STRATEGY WORK?

The thinking and behavior behind the distribution of power strategy are as old as international politics and were displayed in other systems of autonomous states in the past. Two variants—preponderance and equality—can be assessed along two lines of inquiry. First, is either variant particularly useful for avoiding wars? Second, how does each variant seems to affect systemic, state, and societal security?

In interstate relations, the debate about avoiding wars has been immense and inconclusive when carried on in governments, their political systems, and analytical studies. You will have to settle for a brief summary here. Those who believe in preponderance make various claims. They have to reject the traditional view that a dominant state will go on expanding its power and territory—swallowing others like Rome did to its neighbors around the Mediterranean. Instead, they argue that preponderance in the hands of a relatively satisfied state or coalition has often led to a long period of peace and stability. After all, the hegemon is apt to like things as they are and want to keep them orderly with minimal effort and expense. What fun is hegemony if you cannot enjoy it? Being clearly inferior to the hegemon, unsatisfied and ambitious states lay low and avoid provoking or starting a war. It is when the hegemon begins to decline, or when it is perceived to be declining, that those states seriously seek more power, by force if necessary, sharply raising the chances of war. Various historical examples of this scenario playing out can be cited, such as the Bismarck system and its decline. The broad name for the most well developed analysis along these lines is the theory of hegemonic stability. It is relatively popular in the United States today, and some U.S. (and Chinese) analysts are busy calculating when China's rise in power and America's decline will make a great-power war plausible again.

Proponents of the theory of hegemonic stability also argue that, as happened with Stalin, leaders can make mistakes in calculating the distribution of power so it is best if the uneven distribution is glaring, that is, almost impossible to misread by even an obtuse government. In a multipolar system, they say, life is much more complicated and mistakes are much easier to make. They also say that peace is promoted because under a hegemon other governments are more ready to cooperate in all sorts of ways. They live in a stable system that the hegemon keeps safe so cooperation with others is less risky. Rising cooperation in turn makes conflict less likely or less severe, and thus war anywhere in the system becomes less likely.

A belief in power preponderance is one element behind the long American opposition to nuclear proliferation. While reluctant to contemplate giving up nuclear weapons itself, the United States never supported its allies developing them, much less its opponents, and it remains intensely opposed to new additions to the nuclear club today. A major justification for the 2003 U.S. war on Iraq was to resist nuclear proliferation. The ongoing U.S. pressure on North Korea is focused on thwarting its nuclear ambitions.

Those who believe in power parity can espouse either **bipolarity** (between two states or coalitions) or **multipolarity** (among more than two significant actors). During the last part of the Cold War era the dominant view was that bipolarity is best, with the Cold War cited as the main example. It was said that bipolarity makes things simple. Two dominant states or coalitions focus mainly on each other as threats, such as the Soviet Union and the United States did. They know clearly who their main enemy is and when they are beginning to fall behind and need to make an effort to catch up. But they are too powerful to be easily defeated so they realize that an all-out war would be disastrous. Each is so strong it can suffer losses, the defection of allies, or serious domestic difficulties, without falling too far behind the other. As a result, they take such difficulties in stride instead of hitting the panic button and rushing into war before the other side gets too strong. Thus in the Cold War China started out on the U.S. side, shifted to the Soviet side, then shifted back toward the United States, each time without setting off a panic in Washington or Moscow.

Next, when the bipolar situation stabilizes the two sides may be able to work out some accommodations, rules of the game, and other practices to make life more tolerable, such as arms control, other limits on competition, or a modest level of trade. Such steps reinforce stability, and the parties to the conflict become more satisfied with the status quo. A bipolar relationship or bipolarity-dominated system was considered simple enough that even slow-witted governments could understand it and thus avoid major miscalculations.

As for **multipolarity**, its champions during the Cold War relied mainly on the argument that governments in a bipolar situation can become too single-minded, too intensely focused on a conflict and trying to win it. The enemy is too obvious, too powerful, and too threatening. Everything seems at stake so the conflict remains intense. Ancient Rome was so preoccupied with Carthage that it would accept nothing short of its complete defeat and the destruction of the entire city—stone by stone. The India-Pakistan dispute has frequently seemed likely to end up the same way once both countries acquired nuclear weapons. Much better, advocates of multipolarity say, to have multiple governments competing, and cooperating, to keep each other in check. Maneuvering takes the place of intense rivalry, and various coalitions form and reform. Another argument in favor of multipolarity points to the danger in trusting any one state or coalition or even two states or coalitions to always be rational, to be supportive of the status quo. Strange and ambitious leaders (Hitler) may emerge, or states may experience domestic upheavals or come to be dominated by extreme nationalism (Napoleonic France) or achieve technical breakthroughs and quickly gain a surprising military superiority (the United States in the 1990s). Much better to have power dispersed so that no single government can suddenly upset the system.

As with the other views, proponents of multipolarity cite historical examples of periods with little or no bipolarity or hegemony and when wars were limited in scale, the favorite being Europe from about 1650 to 1790. Today some add an important argument, namely, that multipolarity is inevitable. Too many states are unhappy with hegemony or bipolarity because they are second-class players. Eventually they will succeed in catching up. Multipolarity is popular with governments and analysts in places such as China, Cuba, France, and Russia. These governments dislike living under the dominance of the United States or the West, fearing that their relative weakness will always be exploited. They see the dominant governments as too arrogant, too intrusive, and too inclined to run everything for their own benefit. They take comfort in the view that, over time, other governments always imitate those who are dominant, always catch up in power and influence, and hegemonic or bipolar arrangements always turn into multipolar ones. They cite a long list of dominant states and coalitions in international politics that rose and eventually fell.

And what does the evidence show? The three views of appropriate power distribution continue to flourish because the evidence is inconclusive. The theory of hegemonic stability rests on the hegemon being relatively satisfied and acceptable enough to others. But in the past some potentially hegemonic states aroused huge fears. Imagine how rapacious a hegemonic Nazi Germany, or the German-led Axis as a hegemonic coalition, would have been upon winning World War II. Such a hegemonic system is likely to be unstable, with unrest and continual fighting, because it is so unpopular

In addition, preponderance, even when tolerated, is no guarantee of safety. Numerous examples exist of wars started or not avoided by the weaker parties in serious disputes, even when they knew they were weaker. Spain had no good reason to go to war with the United States in 1898, and Japanese leaders knew they were taking a terrific gamble in going to war with the United States in 1941. North Vietnam began killing American soldiers in South Vietnam and kept on doing so even though the United States could have reacted by easily killing every person in North Vietnam. In 1973 Egypt crossed the Suez Canal to attack a much more powerful Israel. The attack organized by Osama bin Laden on the World Trade Center and the Pentagon in 2001 is just the latest example of the weak attacking the strong.

As for a more equal distribution, the bipolarity of the Cold War era had several moments, such as the Cuban Missile Crisis, when a few missteps could have produced a cataclysm. Sometimes bipolar rivalries have operated like the one in ancient Greece between the Athenians and Spartans, with decades of war until Athens collapsed instead of peace and stability. Many multipolar situations have displayed high levels of recurring warfare frequently used in struggles to maintain an appropriate power distribution. It was this repeated warfare that led many people to conclude after World War I that multipolarity was inadequate because it produced, or at least failed to prevent, that horrible war.

Statistical analyses seeking to determine, from studying many cases, the probabilities of war under each of the three power distributions come to somewhat conflicting conclusions as well. While the distribution of power has some effect on whether wars occur, many other factors play a role. For instance, power is constantly shifting, so analysts fear that a leader or government may see itself as gaining a temporary advantage and seek to exploit it by going to war to consolidate its superiority. Or a government might think (as Japan did in 1941) that it can gain an advantage through a surprise attack, which it can then consolidate. Or a dominant state or coalition that is steadily losing ground to a rival might launch a **preventive war** to hit the enemy before it gets too strong and can attack whenever it wants to. In short, it is not just the distribution of power but also what leaders and governments think about it that counts.

Do nuclear weapons make any difference? Perhaps, but not consistently. Most analysts think that what constitutes a real balance in power looks different among nuclear armed states than it does among those without nuclear weapons. The claim is that what needs to be in rough balance is an ability to destroy the other side or to do it so much harm, such unacceptable damage, that no war is considered worthwhile. If one state can do this with one hundred nuclear weapons that will survive to retaliate after any attack, and its rival can do the same with one hundred nuclear weapons as well but has an extra three hundred in its stockpile, the extra three hundred do not matter. If both states have sufficient ability to inflict unacceptable harm, then peace will be maintained even though numerically they are not equal in power. This kind of reasoning is behind the efforts of various countries to obtain nuclear weapons or other weapons of mass destruction. They are seen as a shortcut to being sufficiently equal to be safe from attack. And it is on this basis that some analysts see nuclear proliferation as a good thing. If India and Pakistan have enough nuclear weapons, then they will stop going to war periodically.

The ultimate example of a fierce conflict kept peaceful by nuclear weapons is the Cold War. While not everyone agrees, the general view is that this appropriate power distribution—each side able to completely destroy the other—did much to keep the Cold War from ever becoming hot. Only small wars in which East and West supported opposing sides occurred, while the central Cold War remained peaceful. However, analysts are also inclined to believe that a power imbalance resting only on nuclear weapons is probably no good for keeping the peace in serious conflicts. On numerous occasions states without nuclear weapons either have attacked states with nuclear weapons directly or have attacked the allies of those states. Israel has been attacked several times since it developed its nuclear weapons, most recently by Palestinian terrorists and, in the 1991 Persian Gulf War, by Iraqi missiles. India and Pakistan engaged in low-level warfare—artillery barrages and terrorist attacks—for years after they both had nuclear weapons. At one point so did the Soviet Union and China. There are a number of other examples, and in each case the party attacking counted on the nuclear power being unable to bring itself to use its nuclear weapons and was always right.

Why doesn't the distribution of power, either as predominance or some kind of parity, determine whether wars occur? In part it is because mistakes are made in reading the distribution of power. One of the major arguments for a hegemonic arrangement is that mistakes about the power distribution are less likely. Still, mistakes occur for a number of reasons. The most obvious is that power is notoriously difficult to measure. Just the military components are hard to assess, because the true test of military power is the ability to win a war and wars are not common. For instance, one side—or each side—may read the current distribution incorrectly and think it is superior when it is not, behave with more confidence or assertiveness than it should, and thus provoke a war. As noted, Stalin did a terrible job assessing the power distribution in Europe in 1939. He made that mistake partly because

Germany was about to try out a new way of making war (see Chapter 4). Germany did not look all that strong in World War I terms, so many experts in Europe agreed with Stalin that Germany could be offset by Britain and France. Instead, Germany's new approach made mincemeat of everyone's forces in Europe, including Stalin's at first, when Germany invaded the Soviet Union in 1941.

Power is difficult to measure in part because it is relative. How much you have depends on what you want to do with it. The military power needed to defeat great states can be far less effective against terrorists. How much power you have also depends on how powerful the others are against which you will be using it. Having easily overrun most of the rest of Europe in 1939–1941, Germany invaded the Soviet Union expecting to win easily and at first had great success. In the end, however, the Germans could not compel the Soviet Union to quit fighting, became bogged down, and were overwhelmed. And it can be difficult to know in advance who you will be using your power against. What if the opponent attracts help from others? In 1991 Iraqi leader Saddam Hussein believed that Arab governments would not actively join a coalition organized by non-Arabs against his Arab state, or would not participate if the coalition attacked Iraq, or would not stay within it if he could spread the war to Israel. Instead, Arab governments joined the U.S.-led coalition, and some sent troops to attack Iraq's forces in Kuwait. Furthermore, none defected from the coalition when Saddam attacked Israel with his missiles. He was consistently wrong about whom he would be fighting.

Because power is so difficult to measure, another reason it is assessed incorrectly is that subjective feelings play a role. For instance, a state or coalition that is growing in relative strength may become cocky, overconfident, and too ready to run risks. Meanwhile, a state or coalition that seems to be declining in power might decide to launch a preventive war to maintain its position. The result could be a war precipitated by different subjective estimates that converge on the conclusion that it is a good time for one. Another subjective element is wishful thinking. Governments may need to risk or fight a war so badly that they are strongly biased toward the view that the power distribution is in their favor. Because they need it, they convince themselves it will work. Many outsiders expected Saddam Hussein's Iraq, facing a huge coalition in 1991, to prefer retreat to defeat. But Iraq convinced itself that it could hurt the United Nations (UN) coalition enough in a war—produce so many casualties—that the coalition either would not attack or would break up before it could win. Instead, the fighting destroyed Iraq's ground forces in about a week and the UN coalition suffered only a few hundred casualties.

In intrastate relations, the use of the variants of the distribution of power strategy is similarly uneven and the best approach is not clear. States prefer hegemony or a complete monopoly on the use of force. In many cases they have been able to generate this and go on to establish or reestablish peaceful and secure conditions that are durable. However, in trying to defeat everyone who is or might be a threat, a government can overreach itself, on the one hand, and inflame opposition, on the other. This has happened with a number of third-world governments, such as Indonesia, which might have been better off settling for less dominant military control in favor of more accommodative behavior toward its opponents, such as granting some regions a greater degree of auton-omy. In other cases, the creation of stable and secure conditions is ephemeral, usually because the underlying conflicts are not effectively dealt with, and sooner or later a violent conflict erupts again.

Trying for a stable balance is often unsuccessful over the long run. An agree-ment may be reached to create a bipolar or multipolar situation to avoid a civil war or halt one, but all too often when the power distribution shifts, or the parties think that it has, the agreement begins to fray. As discussed in Chapter 12, out-siders often suggest that it is better to get the parties to disarm and then to estab-lish a new national military force in which all the parties participate. A new gov-ernment can be developed that seeks a monopoly on the use of force but is subject to constraints on how it is used.

CONCLUSION

How can the appropriate distribution of power strategy be evaluated in terms of systemic, state, and societal security?

Systemic Security

In international politics, the strategy has most often been evaluated as a contri-bution to systemic security. To the present-day analysts have contended that get-ting the right power distribution is the key to having a stable and peaceful sys-tem. What they disagree about is what the right distribution is and how to get it and then maintain it. Two major difficulties arise. First, the power distribution that looks most effective for systemic security is probably hegemony; it has a somewhat better record of sustaining a peaceful and stable international system than bipolarity or multipolarity. However, analysts of hegemony always say that, if the hegemon declines in power, the chances of disorder, conflict, and war rise steeply. Then they add that hegemons always decline. That is not reassuring for the long run. Furthermore, many analysts believe that international politics can-not sustain peace and order indefinitely. If the potential destructiveness of war-fare is too high and warfare in the future is plausible, this is not a solution that offers much comfort.

Second, war is considered a central mechanism for achieving and then main-taining the right distribution of power. In discussing how governments can try to adjust the distribution of power in the system, I purposefully underemphasized one of their tools: war itself. If a government does not like the distribution of power, it can go to war and defeat others so that it rises in power. If a government does not like some other state getting steadily more powerful, it can go to war to cut that state down to size, as France hoped to do to Prussia in 1870. A striking feature of past multipolar international systems has been the use of war to adjust the distribution of power. If the problem is that war undermines peace and security, a solution that rests in part on using war is apt to be unattractive. That was the conclusion President Woodrow Wilson and others reached by 1918, the end of World War I. He said that, if a more effective solution to the problem of war than power distribution was not found, another great war would be fought someday. That turned out to be true.

Broadly speaking, arranging the right distribution of power has been the most durable strategy in seeking a peaceful international system. But international politics has a long history of war and high levels of insecurity based on fears of war. Not only has the strategy not solved the problem, but it also is often blamed for sustaining the problem or making it worse.

Out of fear about how internal wars can damage the peace and security of the international system, governments generally favor having stable states that are powerful and effective enough to keep peace at home. They depart from this preference only when they strongly dislike a government because of its foreign policy, when its domestic behavior is deplorable (it massacres many of its citizens or terribly mistreats them in other ways), or when its domestic behavior is believed likely to bring about a catastrophe with effects that spread beyond its borders. Governments today generally oppose secession and would like to see any civil wars for whatever purpose stopped through effective agreements. They rarely endorse a power balance among armed factions, suspecting that such an arrangement will be unstable over the long run. The preference is a monopoly of force in the hands of the state, used wisely.

State Security

If the strategy does not have a good record in international politics, why has it persisted? At least one reason is that it has a better impact on state security. States suffer from wars and from the insecurity that fear of wars brings. Particular wars have often been devastating for governments, leading to their disappearance and sometimes to the dissolution of the states they ruled, which represents about the worst sort of insecurity. Having to prepare for possible wars has often been ruinously expensive, threatening the staying power of states. This happened during the last two decades of the Soviet Union when extremely high military expenditures contributed to the economic decline and political collapse of the country and the government. In short, the problem of war leaves some states constantly at risk and others potentially at risk. Seeking the right distribution of power often does not do away with those risks.

However, the strategy has its attractions. First, it leaves states highly autonomous, it does not erode their freedom to do what they want. This is deeply appealing. Of course, states are not free to do just anything. They are constrained in part by the power of other states. But they are free to choose—how to respond to those constraints, how to try to change them if they wish, how best to try to keep themselves safe.

Second, states sometimes want to make war for their own purposes. A strategy for doing away with war that does not strip states of their power to use force to achieve what they want is appealing. States have often seen war as good for their security, in gaining wealth, territory, and population, in weakening competing states, and even in shoring up domestic political support. They dislike the thought of having to give up that option completely.

The third attraction is more subtle. Whether a state gains from a particular war, and states often do not, states as a whole have benefited in numerous ways from the constant possibility and frequent occurrence of wars. Wars and the preparation for them historically had a great deal to do with making states—with the buildup of their ability to control their populations, extract wealth from their societies, organize their citizens, and attract powerful political support from them. States justify their existence and all the things necessary to sustain it in part by citing the threats they face and emphasizing how they offer protection that their citizens need. In many instances, the threats are real. In other cases, the threats are just potential or are invented to help sustain the state. Either way, the state benefits. Dealing with the problem of war by securing the right distribution of power fits well with keeping or enhancing the power of the state domestically.

With regard to internal conflicts, states are interested only in being highly dominant with regard to the use of force, and that is considered very helpful in maintaining state autonomy. In facing external threats, governments are concerned that they not have any violent internal conflicts. Those conflicts might be exploited by external opponents. Even if they are not, they will sap resources and attention, possibly making the state less able to defend itself abroad. Thus only one kind of distribution of power internally is to their liking.

Societal Security

The chief benefit to people in society of a power distribution approach comes from their identification with the autonomy of their state and their nation. For some people this is the most important aspect of security, so a strategy that does not heavily encroach on state security is beneficial. For example, people in many societies would reject the concept of a world government to keep the peace because of the loss of sovereignty their nations would suffer.

The next benefit to people in society is that when the strategy works they are spared most of the potentially awful costs and burdens of warfare. Peace and security are maintained. This is partly offset by the fact that the strategy does not work all the time—attacks and wars occur—and that sometimes carrying out the strategy involves fighting wars, such as to maintain the right distribution of power.

The approach has drawbacks for societies. The strategy has been the most widely practiced one and the history of international politics is littered with wars. Societies have often suffered a great deal in the past as a result, in casualties, financial costs, destruction of property, lives being upended, economic disruptions, and social upheavals. Even when the state remains relatively safe in fighting a war and because it fights the war, the damage done to its people may be severe, undermining their security directly and indirectly. Societies also bear the costs of having to prepare for possible wars in peacetime—men (and sometimes women) being drafted to serve for years in the armed forces, the taxes to pay for those forces, and so on.

Societies must also bear the costs that come from the way the threat of war has helped make states that are more dominating, more controlling, more intrusive, and thus often more oppressive. People value their personal autonomy and the autonomy of their local groups, and this strategy does not help much in maintaining it. The most obvious, and all too frequent, example is when military forces built to jockey for power in international politics are used by political leaders to oppress the citizens or by military leaders to seize control of the political system. In many countries, particularly in developing countries, the armed forces do not exist primarily to defend the nation or advance its other interests against outsiders. Instead, they are largely engaged in extortion, forcing their societies to yield them all sorts of benefits.

Little incentive exists for pursuing the right sort of power distribution in international politics in an effort to do much about stopping internal wars. They often do not pose enough of a threat. In fact, a state may help incite or sustain an internal war to keep the government of that country weaker than it otherwise would be. Little intrinsic incentive exists for doing something potent about a state's dreadful mistreatment of its citizens. Amid the maneuvering in the international system, the safety of people where they live can fall by the wayside.

Final Assessment

The distribution of power strategy seems best used as a last resort because it is a burden for many governments and societies and too often has not worked. Paying attention to the power distribution in international politics makes sense when the international system seems full of conflicts so serious that they could result in war or when individual states' opposition to other specific states could lead to war. The power distribution might then be important in determining whether a war occurs and will be important in determining how a war will turn out. But it does not work consistently in preventing wars and may sometimes promote them. If there is a primary solution to the problem of war, it must be something else.

SOURCES AND OTHER USEFUL READINGS

The pursuit of peace and security via arranging the distribution of power is characteristic of realists, though they disagree about what sort of distribution is best. Thus analysts associated with the realist tradition are the best place to start: John J. Mearsheimer, Hans J. Morgenthau, Kenneth N. Waltz, and a number of the authors in *The Perils of Anarchy,* edited by Michael Brown, Sean M. Lynn-Jones, and Steven E. Miller. A fine overview of realist thinking can be found in James E. Dougherty and Robert L. Pfaltzgraff Jr., *Contending Theories of International Relations.*

The concept of soft power is most closely associated with Joseph S. Nye Jr. in such works as *Bound to Lead* and "Soft Power and Conflict Management in the Information Age." Efforts by governments to manage the distribution of power are carefully laid out in John J. Mearsheimer, *The Tragedy of Great Power Politics.* The chief analyst associated with structural realism is Kenneth N. Waltz, especially in his *Theory of International Politics.* A good example of anticipating a war with China in the United States is Robert Kagan, "How We Will Fight China."

Advocacy of bipolarity as the best solution is associated particularly with the books in the bibliography by Kenneth Waltz and John Mearsheimer. Recent analyses of balancing power can be found in *Balance of Power,* edited by T. V. Paul, James J. Wirtz, and Michael Fortmann. Those associated with the utility of predominance and often referred to as theorists of hegemonic stability include Robert Gilpin, *War and Change in World Politics;* A. F. K. Organski and Jacek Kugler, *The War Ledger;* George Modelski, "Long Cycles of World Leadership" and "Long Cycles and Global War"; and William C. Wohlforth, "The Stability of a Unipolar World."

Defenders of multipolarity are discussed, and doubts expressed about it, in Charles Kegley and Gregory Raymond, *A Multipolar Peace.* On the inevitability of multipolarity, see Christopher Layne, "The Unipolar Illusion." Statistical studies include Jacek Kugler and Douglas Lemke, *Parity and War;* and John A. Vasquez, *The War Puzzle.*

On how nuclear weapons seem to have helped keep the peace but had their limitations, see Patrick Morgan, *Deterrence Now;* and John Lewis Gaddis, "Great

Illusions, the Long Peace, and the Future of the International System." The role of war in building states is most associated with Charles Tilly. See his *Coercion, Capital, and European States* and "War Making and State Making as Organized Crime." Another discussion along those lines is Karen A. Rasler and William R. Thompson, *War and State Making.*

CHAPTER 4

Seeking Cheap Victories

The second broad strategy for dealing with the security problems that war creates is for states to look for cheap victories, solutions to win conflicts easily and with few costs. Seldom identified as a security strategy, as a way of coping with the problem of war, the strategy does not come up in studies about dealing with war in international politics. However, historically it has been an important way of managing that problem, especially with regard to great-power wars, by serving as one of the most attractive and influential strategies employed over the past two centuries. Because it involves narrow, self-interested behavior, the strategy is very much in line with traditional international politics.

War may be getting too awful to accept but the cheap victory strategy, instead of pursuing cooperative steps to give it up, has been used by states to keep it available as a tool by making violent conflicts tolerable. The strategy began to emerge and have a serious impact not long after the realization that great-power war was getting to be too costly in human lives (see Chapter 2). Analysts and activists took this to mean that war would no longer be a deliberate choice of policy makers, but states either knew better or suspected that wars would still occur. The prospect of war as dreadful helped lead a number of states to develop the strategy in response. The desire was not simply to fight cheaply, which is present in most approaches to fighting a war. Instead, a conscious and deliberate response is made to the prospect that war can be devastating by developing a way to keep it cheap. The strategy turned out to be so appealing, attractive, and at times successful that several other strategies discussed later in the book were developed, at least in part, to try to nullify it.

States employ some version of a cheap victory strategy when they figure out a way to conduct wars that they hope will allow them to fight (and win) cheaply. The steps involved are relatively clear. A government, particularly in a great power, starts with the realization that it might have to fight a potentially devastating war. After all, it might be attacked by an aggressive opponent. Or the national leaders may be pursuing objectives that they believe will require that they attack someone else. Then those leaders decide that they would be much happier if the war was devastating only for the other side. Thus the war would not be intolerable. They try to achieve such an outcome not by avoiding the war but by manipulating the way it is fought.

A war can turn out to be so intolerable that national leaders must worry about it in four ways. First, a nation could lose the war and suffer greatly in doing so. Second, the war could be a stalemate so costs and losses mount with little or nothing gained, instead of the war ending in a suitable fashion with an acceptable result. Third, a nation might win but at such a great cost that it is ruined or exhausted, that is, the victory is not worth the effect. Finally, the war might attract the participation of others, particularly great powers, so that it becomes something else, for example, a much different conflict to have to fight that has greatly increased costs and damage as a result. The last of these four is particularly worrisome. In a larger great-power war the consequences can be appalling not only for one's own nation but also the entire international system. Various states can collapse, the international economy can be gravely disrupted, and the loss of life and destruction can be magnified dramatically.

ELEMENTS OF A CHEAP VICTORY STRATEGY

States facing the possibility of a war would always want to achieve a cheap victory. That is just good sense. But achieving it is normally difficult against a well-equipped, determined enemy. States will certainly do their utmost not to lose. Thus the hunt for a cheap victory strategy is particularly important when it is pursued in opposition to the general view at the time that no such strategy is available. If nearly everyone thinks that such a strategy does not exist but State A comes up with one, then it has a huge advantage if, in fact, it works. For one thing, everyone will conclude that State A will probably not go to war if it is not likely to win. However, if State A has a cheap victory strategy, it can decide on war and catch others by surprise, which may be a key reason the strategy works. This is particularly valuable if State A is facing an opponent seemingly far more able to bear the burdens of war because it is richer or more powerful. The strategy is better than a great equalizer because it reverses each side's prospects. Having a cheap victory strategy is also attractive when your opponent wants a war; that is, you do not want a war but are going to be attacked anyway, so it is nice to know how to fight it cheaply.

Of course, everything is relative when it comes to being cheap. How cheap something is always depends on how it compares with the value of what is to be gained. It can also depend on what the available alternatives are. Paying a large amount to succeed at something that is vital can seem cheap if the alternative is failure. Thus a cheap victory strategy is a clever way to fight the war in an unexpectedly inexpensive way, even if the costs to be paid are not, in the normal sense of the term, cheap. Below are examples in which the strategy was expected to involve thousands of deaths, much destruction, and huge financial costs. Cheap is relative.

Great Military Superiority under Any Circumstances

How does a government shape a cheap victory strategy? One option that may be open, particularly to an unusually powerful state, is to carefully construct an overwhelming military capability. Being much better prepared to fight any prospective war may lead to a cheap victory. This is currently a basic objective of U.S. military planning and the continued improvement of its military forces—that is, a military capability greater than any conceivable combination of opposing governments. While a government can have the best military forces for fighting in an expensive way, so that victory is likely, it usually will not be cheap. That is how the North defeated the South in the Civil War. Thus whether one has military superiority or not, other things usually must be used to win cheaply.

Strategic Surprise

One of the oldest ways of fighting of any sort, and certainly of fighting wars, is to catch the opponent by surprise. Seeking to surprise the other side is always a good tactic for winning a particular engagement. However, a **strategic surprise** is a way to fight the enemy that has a powerful overall, perhaps decisive, impact. It so disrupts the opponent's plans that it either ends the war or does much to determine the eventual outcome, that is, dictating who wins. When one party's strategic surprise ends the war successfully before the costs get too high, then that party has devised a cheap victory strategy. The surprising step or steps that produce this result could be any number of things, alone or in combination. Imagine that you are the leader responsible for coming up with such a plan. What might you propose? You might introduce an unusual or brand-new weapon or devise some highly innovative military operations to which your opponent cannot respond effectively. Or you might attack in an unexpected and strategically important place, winning a crucial victory and determining how the war ends. Or you might attack at an unexpected time, catching the opponent unprepared, and win that way. Surprise is, in fact, fairly easy to achieve and often occurs in war. However, strategic surprise, which may determine the outcome of the war, is much more difficult to pull off.

Rapid Mobilization and Use of Force

Another way to try to win cheaply is to overwhelm the opponent by mobilizing forces faster than it does and moving those forces into battle more massively and rapidly—the idea is to "get there first with the most." Victory in battle often goes to those who succeed in doing this. If it can be done in a crucial battle or crucial series of battles, the opponent may surrender or collapse, producing victory without a longer war and all the costs associated with it. This is like getting a one-punch knockout at the start of a fight. In 2003 the United States and its allies launched the war against Iraq with a precise cruise missile attack on a building in Baghdad where it believed the Iraqi leaders were meeting. The hope was that killing those leaders in the first blow would cause the Iraqi resistance to collapse—a cheap victory.

Isolate the Opponent

Still another way to seek a cheap victory is to try to isolate an opponent politically, diplomatically, and militarily. If an opponent has no powerful friends who will come to its assistance with money or arms, who will fight alongside it, and who will try to build international pressure in its support, then it may be unable to put up much of a fight. Without friends elsewhere, it may lack advanced weapons, replacements for the weapons it loses, or money and other resources to keep fighting for long. How can such isolation be achieved? Those who might be of help to an opponent can be wooed diplomatically to stay neutral, or encouraged to be neutral by offerings of political favors or potential spoils, or threatened with harm if they consider helping the opponent.

Establish a Solid Defense

A final way governments can seek a cheap victory is to devise and install such a magnificent defense that an attacking opponent will wear itself out while inflicting little or no serious harm. Once an opponent is badly weakened by launching attacks that are costly but have little effect, it can be attacked and defeated relatively easily or will just give up. What makes this particularly appealing is that in warfare often it is less costly in casualties and money to fight on the defensive than on the offense, that is, to be attacking. This approach seeks to maximize that effect.

CHEAP VICTORY STRATEGIES IN THE TWENTIETH CENTURY

Various cases of attempted cheap victories were adopted by the great powers over the past two centuries, some successful and some not. The following are cases since 1900 in which the use of cheap victory strategies was particularly prominent.

World War I

The search for a cheap victory dominated many of the national plans for what became World War I (1914–1918). Prior to the onset of the war it was widely believed that such a war was coming and would determine the mastery of Europe and much of the world. For more than two decades governments engaged in a massive arms race and made elaborate preparations for a large-scale war. Military analysts pondered what the war would be like and how it should be fought. Many analysts anticipated that once it broke out the opening battles might be crucial in dictating the outcome, so nations were expected to bring huge armies to the battlefield. Because of modern firepower, those battles would produce enormous casualties, and therefore the battles would not be sustainable for long because not enough men would be available to fight. Nearly all of the troops would be called into battle right at the start, and the grim casualty figures would shrink their numbers and damage morale, eventually eroding public support for the war. With the men at the front, factories would be idle and crops left unharvested. National economies would quickly slow down, and the huge costs of fighting the early battles would soon bankrupt governments and their societies. Finally, with such sacrifices demanded of them, ordinary citizens would begin to insist on having more say in running the country. Thus the war could not go on long without provoking political upheavals—undermining autocratic rulers, ousting old political elites, and destroying capitalist systems.

Clearly, therefore, the war would have to be short—or so strategists thought. Government leaders and the general staffs in their armed forces decided that the best strategy had to bring victory quickly, before the nation's military efforts began to collapse from casualties and national exhaustion began to set in. For this purpose offensive operations were best, that is, smash the opponent quickly. Sitting in defensive positions waiting to be attacked would do nothing to end the war fast enough; after all, those defenses would be mauled by modern firepower. So all major states in Europe, and some smaller ones, drew up elaborate plans for going on the offensive if a war broke out. The reserves would be called up rapidly to build the huge armies that would be needed. Then those armies would be moved to the battlefield very fast so as to arrive before the opponent was fully prepared, enabling them to overwhelm the enemy in the initial battles, and to destroy its forces so it would have to quit. The planned result was a victorious end to the war in just a few weeks.

The most famous of the cheap victory strategies was the Schlieffen Plan, named for the head (Alfred Graf von Schlieffen) of the German General Staff and drawn up in the late nineteenth century. Germany's greatest strategic problem in the much anticipated great war was that it probably would have to fight on two fronts simultaneously—against France in the West and tsarist Russia to the East. Neither country was as strong as Germany but together they could probably defeat Germany if they attacked at the same time or outlast it if the war dragged on very long. The Schlieffen Plan called for Germany to mobilize much faster than Russia, an undeveloped country in many ways. While Russia was slowly mobilizing, Germany would concentrate nearly all its main forces in the West to deal with France, the stronger of the two allies. But the forces would not be used to attack

France directly in large battles. Instead, most of the forces would make a surprise sweep through Belgium so as to go around and then behind the French lines along the Franco-German border and outflank the French armies. They could be surrounded and forced to quit. An additional complication was that Great Britain had moved to become an official ally of France so the sweep had to be successfully carried out before much help for France could arrive from the British. Once Paris had been seized, the French armies overwhelmed, and France defeated—in only a few weeks—any further fighting by the British in France would be useless and they would withdraw. Meanwhile, Germany would shift its major forces to the East to defeat the much weaker Russians. This would provide a cheap victory by rapidly defeating the two great opponents and their British allies, one at a time.

France, meanwhile, was committed to what it called the doctrine of the offensive, as were the Russians in their own way. The plans in France called for rapid mobilization to generate huge armies and then mount a major offensive against Germany as soon as possible after the war started. This would be in conjunction with an offensive by the Russians so that German forces would be too thin in one place or the other, or both, and would be quickly smashed. In the east, the Russians planned to mobilize huge forces—easily the largest in Europe—as quickly as they could and attack Germany, both to begin destroying German forces and to keep Germany pinned down so it could not defeat France first and then attack Russia. Together France and Russia would win, and cheaply (relatively speaking), while fighting Germany alone each would lose.

Britain was thinking along the same lines about such a great war. It planned to mobilize and send troops to Europe as soon as possible to attack Germans and keep France from being overwhelmed. Britain's other major responsibility was to confront the Germans at sea, defeating the German fleet in a great opening battle so Britain would control the seas and could then cut Germany off from the rest of the world on water, just as France and Russia would cut it off from much of the rest of the world on land.

Notice that three approaches to a cheap victory strategy were at work. All the major powers sought to use rapid mobilization for a big and early triumph so the enemy would collapse and the war would be over. The Germans also prepared a strategic surprise. While the French were ready to fight along the border with Germany, the German forces would be racing through Belgium and into an undefended part of France so they could seize Paris and surround the French forces from the rear—a giant encirclement. After a defeat on that scale France's ability to fight would be over. Britain, France, and Russia also planned to isolate Germany (and its weak allies) early on so that it would soon run short of raw materials, food, money, and the like.

The history books have nothing to say about a short and, for someone, victorious World War I, because all these strategies did not work. The German sweep through Belgium came close to seizing Paris and maybe bringing a French collapse, but it was stopped just short of Paris. The Schlieffen Plan did help throw the French offensive out of kilter and it did not work either. The Russian armies lurched into Germany but were no match for the quicker, better organized, and more mobile German forces and were badly defeated. The British and German navies never fought that great sea battle. It seemed too dangerous for either side to risk control of the seas on one battle. The Allies achieved and maintained a blockade relatively cheaply in an unexpected way, but it was not decisive for the war. World War I lasted until late 1918. It was a war of attrition that gravely weakened or exhausted nearly all the participants.

World War II

A broad cheap victory strategy guided Germany's initial approach to what became World War II. Adolf Hitler wanted to go to war but specifically planned to avoid creating another world war. First, he moved to prevent any great coalition against Germany. He built an alliance with Italy; created associations with Hungary, Romania, Spain, and Turkey; and signed a nonaggression treaty with the Soviet Union under which neither would go to war against the other and the Soviet Union would provide assistance to Germany (food, raw materials) if it was involved in a war (see Chapter 3). Then he planned to defeat Poland so fast in the fall of 1939 that its allies, Britain and France, would have no time to help. Once he gobbled up Poland he would offer peace to Britain and France. Why would they want to go on fighting for a country that had disappeared? Surely they would agree and the war would be over, at little cost to Germany

Everything went as Hitler had planned at first, and Poland disappeared in a few weeks. But Britain and France scorned his peace offers and insisted on continuing the war. Hitler then came up with a second plan for a cheap victory. By now the British and French were well armed and entrenched along France's border with Germany and its border with Belgium, too, ready to confront direct German attacks on France and to rush into Belgium if Hitler tried another Schlieffen Plan end run. The German plan involved faking a sweep through Belgium so British and French forces would go into that country, then making a lightning attack through the Ardennes—a mountainous, and heavily forested area not considered suitable for an attack and not well defended—which was the hinge between the forces in Belgium and the French forces along the border with Germany. The attack also would involve an innovative approach to war called blitzkrieg (lightning war)—making a major attack at some weak point and then pouring forces through the gap to fan out in all directions behind the lines. The emphasis after the breakthrough was on constant movement, steady disruption of the enemy by using tanks supported by dive bombers. As planned and then carried out in the spring of 1940, German forces poured through the Ardennes and then raced out to the English Channel to cut off the Allied forces in Belgium. German units also went south to Paris and beyond to trap the French forces on the border with Germany (remember the approach of the German forces to Paris early in the classic movie *Casablanca*). As in World War I, the idea was to win the initial great battles so the enemy would be forced to quit and the war would be short.

The strategy did give the Germans a cheap victory. The French war effort collapsed in a few weeks even though prior to the war some observers considered France the strongest military power in the world. However, Hitler expected the British to accept a peaceful settlement once their major ally had been defeated, but they refused to quit and Hitler never found a way to defeat Britain cheaply. He also was unable to prevent the war from spreading and growing in scale, eventually becoming a true world war.

These examples have involved offensive approaches. What about trying to gain a cheap victory by fighting in a predominantly defensive way? Here are two examples from World War II. When Germany attacked France in 1940 it was able to exploit France's commitment to a deeply defensive strategy. France was counting on the Maginot Line, an elaborate set of massive defenses along the Franco-German border. World War I had convinced the French and many others that direct attacks on a well-prepared enemy would be terribly costly in lives and probably not lead to many gains, so they wanted Germany to attack deeply entrenched forces along the border or in Belgium in any future war. Once the attacks failed with great loss of life, Germany would be gravely weakened, easy pickings for the Allied armies that would then launch attacks into Germany. So the worst costs of a war would be avoided—no mass attacks on defense positions such as those the French and British had mounted in World War I that led to great slaughter of their forces, and no great loss of French territory to the Germans. This meant that French forces were stationary, and when the German forces rushed through the Ardennes, they were able to easily come around behind the defensive positions France had built.

Another example of a defensive approach involved, strangely enough, Japan's attack on Pearl Harbor in the U.S. territory of Hawaii. Japan's strategy called for combining fierce offensive efforts with a massive defense. In 1941 Japan attacked seemingly everywhere in the Pacific. It used strategic surprise against the United States in attacking the Pacific Fleet at Pearl Harbor and in invading the British colony of Malaya (now part of Malaysia). It rapidly built up large forces to overwhelm the opponents and seize Guam, Hong Kong, Indochina, the Philippines, and chunks of the Dutch East Indies (now Indonesia). The idea was getting there first with the most to win crushing victories. However, the Japanese leaders knew that the United States, in particular, and probably others such as Britain would not just accept these defeats and let their war efforts die out. So the underlying strategy was as follows. The initial attacks were to add vast new territories to the Japanese empire, territories rich in food, raw materials, and oil. With these additional resources in its grasp Japan was to go on the defensive, putting up a fight at the frontiers of its empire, in islands and territories far from Japan. Its defenses were to be so stout, taking advantage of the fact that it was usually cheaper to be on defense, that eventually the United States and its allies would tire of the war and agree to a peace treaty. This would leave Japan in charge of an empire with up to one-quarter of the world's population, gained without the war ever having reached Japan itself.

The Cold War and Post–Cold War Eras

Still another example of a cheap victory, mercifully one never put into practice, was the American plan for an all-out war with the Soviet Union in the 1950s drawn up by the Strategic Air Command (SAC). Nuclear weapons delivered by each side would have been catastrophically destructive, so the goal was to make sure the United States would not suffer that fate. The United States had thousands of strategic nuclear weapons and hundreds of bombers, eventually about two thousand, poised all around the Soviet bloc. The SAC plan called for detecting the initial steps toward the outbreak of war and quickly launching an all-out nuclear blow that would catch the Soviet bombers before they were launched. This would destroy all Soviet economic and other capabilities for war, all Soviet military power, and all Soviet ability to continue the war. The anticipated casualties for the Soviet bloc from the attack were at one point estimated to be as high as 500 million. If successful, the United States and its allies would have won without suffering Soviet retaliation, that is, would have won cheaply. The other side would have paid all the costs.

The Cold War era offers another example involving both offensive and defensive efforts. During the 1980s the Reagan administration proposed the Strategic Defense Initiative (SDI or "star wars") program, which would develop a national defense against missile attacks from the communist world. The announced goal was to provide protection against an accidental nuclear attack or a limited nuclear attack by the Soviet Union by shooting down the missiles carrying nuclear weapons before they reached the United States. The missile defense alone clearly could not protect the United States from a larger, more serious Soviet missile attack, so SDI was not designed to provide a cheap victory by itself. But as the Russians liked to point out, some people in Washington thought that if the antiballistic missile technology was effective enough, when it appeared that a war was about to break out the United States could launch a severe attack on Soviet nuclear forces. The missile defense system would have to shoot down only the rest, a far smaller number. Combining an initial, destructive attack with a missile defense system might have allowed the United States to come through a nuclear war largely unscathed. If fully prepared, that would have been a true cheap victory strategy. Given what would have been riding on it, it is a good thing it never had to be put to the test.

Since the end of the Cold War in 1990 the United States has been developing applications of what is often called the **Revolution in Military Affairs** (RMA). Using new technologies and suitable training of its forces, the United States now fights wars by using very accurate weapons, often fired from long distance, to attack targets very efficiently. The targets can be precisely located, even if they are moving fast, and information about their location can be fed rapidly to American forces and their weapons systems. The plan is to find (by satellites, advance patrols, drones, or sensors), then aim (with the help of computers and other rapid information processing technology), and nullify or destroy. At peak effectiveness the strategy inflicts a defeat while leaving the opponent with little chance to inflict casualties and destruction. In all, the result is a war that is fought with much smaller forces, fewer weapons, less time, and few casualties—a cheap victory.

This way of making war was first displayed in the Persian Gulf War in 1991, which Iraqi forces lost in roughly four days of ground fighting to U.S.-led United Nations forces. Another version was the North Atlantic Treaty Organization (NATO) war with Yugoslavia in 1998, brought on by the opposition to Yugoslav actions in Kosovo. Precise weapons were used to attack specific targets that disrupted the Yugoslav systems and weakened Yugoslav forces. While the bombing had to be conducted much longer than expected, threats of further escalation eventually led the government to quit. The attacking forces suffered virtually no casualties.

In the 2003 war with Iraq a cheap victory was achieved as the coalition had relatively few casualties while defeating and occupying Iraq, which took roughly two weeks. However, the techniques and technology of this kind of warfare have not yet been fully designed for combating insurgencies, and the postwar fighting in Iraq by U.S. occupying forces had to be conducted without a cheap victory strategy. Analysts debate whether full application of the RMA in the future to irregular warfare (guerrillas, urban terrorism, ambushes) will also produce cheap victories, but it remains a possibility. Also unclear is how widely an RMA approach to war will spread. It is expensive and the training and organization of forces to use it effectively is complex. The United States is much further down this road than anyone else, but success breeds imitation and that could turn out to be the model other countries pursue as well.

THE APPEAL OF A CHEAP VICTORY STRATEGY

Understanding why developing a cheap victory strategy grew to be so attractive is easy. Great-power warfare expanded in potential destructiveness during the nineteenth and twentieth centuries, and no major state believed it could avoid such wars forever. With the rising lethality of modern war, cheap victory plans became increasingly attractive to great-power governments and military leaders. Some smaller states have resorted to cheap victory strategies, too. For example, Israel looked for a cheap victory approach in planning for wars with its Arab neighbors. The Israeli leaders felt that Israel was too small to endure a long destructive war with the much larger Arab world. In 1956, 1967, and 1973 Israel fought successful wars that were short, less than a month each in the basic fighting, by combining blitzkrieg with deceptive attacks and modern air power with, at times, preemptive attacks.

In fact, if war is potentially very destructive it is the responsibility of political and military leaders to seek such a strategy. They have a duty to secure the survival and flourishing of their society under all circumstances, including war, and a cheap victory strategy might be the only way to achieve that. As long as war is a realistic possibility, if a government fails to look hard for such a strategy, its political opponents are likely to charge that it is soft on defense, guilty of exposing the nation to possible disaster. While such criticisms are particularly likely in a democratic country because the public will insist that the nation's casualties and destruction be as limited as possible, it can happen in an authoritarian political system, too. As an example of the former, the American government came up with a way to end a terrible war cheaply in 1945 when it developed nuclear weapons. While the United States was getting ready to invade and conquer Japan to end the war, expecting that might produce as many casualties as it had suffered in the war to date, atomic bombs were used to destroy two Japanese cities. The Japanese government promptly surrendered, so all potential American casualties were avoided. In the secret debate inside the U.S. government about whether to use the weapons, a key argument was that, if it did not, the public reaction after the war to the American lives lost by having to defeat Japan in another costly way would be crushing. The first use of atomic bombs was tremendously popular because American lives were saved. Authoritarian governments often can ignore their citizens' concerns in such situations, but not always. In planning the initial German attack on French and British forces in World War II, Hitler was dismayed when his generals came up with a warmed-over version of the Schlieffen Plan, which no one expected to bring a quick victory. Determined to avoid a long and exhausting war, knowing what it had done to Germany the last time, he seized on the plans by lower level officers for blitzkrieg war instead.

Other incentives exist for seeking a cheap victory strategy. Especially when it is built around going on the offensive, such a strategy holds many attractions for military leaders. Modern military subcultures in many societies emphasize winning a war by vigorously destroying the enemy or its will to fight. This idea of how best to conduct a war is associated with the famous nineteenth-century analyst Karl von Clausewitz, the most influential military thinker in Western history, and is widely taught. The fact that fighting in this way justifies having large forces at a high state of readiness, hence bigger military budgets, is not lost on military leaders either. They also know that a clever offensive strategy to win easily is apt to require giving the armed forces great autonomy, which they strongly support, to fight in the best way possible because so much depends on winning in an overwhelming way.

Perhaps the greatest appeal this sort of strategy has held for military leaders in recent decades is relevance. A standard view of modern war conducted with all the power of modern states is that it is so destructive it is no longer a rational instrument of policy. This is particularly said of nuclear weapons and nuclear war, but many also hold it to be true for large conventional wars. That would make the military profession largely irrelevant, more like a threat to the national interest than a servant of it. Military officers naturally dislike any such notion and have looked hard for a way around it. Governments also do not like the idea that war may not be a sensible tool of foreign policy. If a cheap victory strategy allows them to make war successfully at low cost, and even achieve victory while doing only limited harm to the enemy, then the relevance of war as a tool is restored.

There are other attractions to cheap victory strategies. Such a strategy can restore a government's sense of autonomy, its feeling that it is in charge of its affairs, and is free to do what it needs to in pursuing the national interest. It can be used not only to cope with a war a government does not want but also to make wars safer that it does want. Hitler wanted to save Germany from another great war through fighting that did not exhaust the nation as it secured a vast empire.

Finally, governments can never be certain they can avoid a major war and that makes them think about how to survive one. During the Cold War the United States relied on threatening to destroy the Soviet Union in retaliation for starting another great war. But this meant destroying the Soviet Union only after it had already done terrible harm to the allies of the United States or the United States itself. So government officials sought ways to not have to rely on threats of retaliation, to win before the Soviet Union could wreak death and destruction. Critics charged this was dangerous—being able to win could lead the United States to start a war, not just try to prevent it. But one secretary of defense, when challenged because he sought ways to fight and win a nuclear war, said, in effect, "What do you expect me to do? Plan to lose?"

CONCLUSION

On balance, cheap victory plans sometimes work and at other times have come close to working, so they are not inherently silly. Prussia built modern Germany in the 1860s through three wars won with cheap victory strategies. Germany defeated France in 1940 with stunning ease. Israel has had several valuable victories in this way. The U.S.-led UN coalition used a cheap victory strategy to tear through Iraq's forces in 1991. So, such plans are tempting.

But the overall record of this approach is dreadful. Where great-power war is concerned it has usually failed, producing wars so vast and vicious they were intolerable. The cheap victory plans in 1914 did not work, and the bones of young men who disappeared in the mud on the western front still come up every spring on old World War I battlefields. Hitler did not get his short war. World War II was responsible for as many as sixty million dead. Japan lost with its cheap victory strategy and was pulverized by the great fire raids on Tokyo and other cities and in the atomic bombing of Hiroshima and Nagasaki.

In terms of systemic security, the failures of cheap victory plans have led to the worst wars ever fought, wars that threw the international system into upheaval, turmoil, and disruption. At times it has seemed like the international system would not survive those wars. During the Cold War this was widely expected to be the case in another world war with nuclear weapons. Some of the strategies for dealing with the problem of war discussed in coming chapters are therefore designed to negate cheap victory strategies because they are so harmful.

However, what if there are ways to fight wars that lead to far less harm to both sides? The further development of the Revolution in Military Affairs has revived the idea, which classic "just war" theory endorsed, that a war should involve only military targets, should do little harm to civilians, and should inflict only the casualties needed to win. Recent wars using the elements of the RMA have been much closer to that ideal. Extending this, a good deal of research has been conducted into developing nonlethal weapons for use in many situations. If a war is needed at times to uphold peace and stability in the international system, it would certainly be nice if it was victorious while being cheap in its effects for everyone involved—on both sides of the conflict. Several analysts have argued that systemic security may be more readily maintained in the future than in the past as a result.

Many states are now uneasy because the United States has made even sizable wars look cheap and easy. They fear that the United States alone, or with its allies, will be too ready to use force to get its way. In effect, war would become too useful and thus too tempting. Equally disturbing is the fear that one obvious response is to develop weapons of mass destruction (WMDs). States such as Iran and North Korea are interested in developing such weapons precisely so they can keep the Americans from attacking them whenever they feel like it. A related fear is that enemies of the United States, perhaps of the entire West, will turn to terrorism on a large scale, possibly with nuclear or other WMD, for the same reason. All of these developments—an overly aggressive United States, a rise in WMD proliferation, and the spreading of terrorism—would be hard on systemic security.

As for national security, states seem better off proceeding as if major wars are going to be awful. They should go to extreme lengths to avoid them, using a cheap victory strategy only as a last resort instead of as a tool for making war to get what they want tolerable. When such a plan fails, it usually fails big and the state itself may be destroyed. This happened to the Russian empire and, eventually, the German empire in World War I and to the states of Germany and Japan in World War II. As for smaller states they may find that cheap victories in their wars will, in the long run, bring the wrath of large and powerful states down on them. This is what happened to Iraq in 1991.

Still, the appeal of cheap victory strategies is unlikely to go away for states when faced with serious threats to their security. If war could destroy your country, you would want to do more than just wring your hands in dismay at the prospect. For a number of governments in recent years it has seemed necessary to at least seriously explore developing weapons of mass destruction so as not to fall victim to others' cheap victory strategies. This is a good example of state security clashing with systemic security in a security dilemma.

Regarding societal security, if war cannot be eliminated, it perhaps can be made far less lethal and destructive, particularly for those not involved in the fighting. This would reverse the trend in wars, interstate and internal, in the twentieth century. The result would be a great improvement over the wars fought throughout most of the history of international politics. It could be the most important long-term implication of the Revolution in Military Affairs.

However, to this point the effects of cheap victory plans have often been harsh on people with governments that have used them, and especially when those plans failed. Some of the greatest suffering from the failure of Hitler's efforts to gain cheap victories was inflicted on his own people. The same was true for the German and Russian peoples in World War I, who perished by the millions. Because a cheap victory approach to the problem of war has so often been tried with terrible consequences, international politics has been deeply effected. People still live today with the aftereffects of huge wars that resulted when cheap victory strategies failed. Thus a number of the other strategies for coping with the problem of great-power warfare were specifically developed to nullify the cheap victory approach because it has been so dangerous. The next chapter reviews the most significant one.

SOURCES AND OTHER USEFUL READINGS

Strategic surprise attacks have been studied for many years, mostly to try to find ways to explain why it occurs and how to prevent it. A book such as *Strategic Military Surprise,* written by Klaus Knorr and Patrick M. Morgan, contains a good deal of information on both, although not about the most recent examples. The most readable book on the cheap victory strategies of the great powers going into World War I is still Barbara Tuchman's *The Guns of August.* A good study on the same subject is Jack L. Snyder's *The Ideology of the Offensive,* as is Barry R. Posen's *The Sources of Military Doctrine.* Debates about the origins of World War I cheap victory strategies are presented in *Military Strategy and the Origins of the First World War,* edited by Steven E. Miller. Joseph E. Persico's book on World War I (*Eleventh Month, Eleventh, Day, Eleventh Hour*) is also helpful in explaining strategies used on the western front. A book long forgotten, recently available again, lays out the thinking behind the expectation that World War I would be short: Ivan Bloch, *The Future of War,* published in 1899. Any number of studies have been made of Hitler's approach and blitzkrieg warfare; they are easy to find. A great many histories have been written of both world wars. John Toland's *The Rising Sun* is a very readable discussion of Japan in World War II.

Among the many studies already available on the Persian Gulf War are the books by Thomas A. Keaney and Eliot A. Cohen (*Gulf War Air Power Survey Summary Report*); Anthony H. Cordesman (*The Iran-Iraq War and Western Security*); Benjamin S. Lambeth (*NATO's Air War for Kosovo*); and Lawrence Freedman and Efraim Karsh (*The Gulf Conflict 1990–1991*). On nonlethal military technologies, see Richard Garwin, *Nonlethal Technologies.* On the war in Kosovo, see David Halberstam, *War in a Time of Peace*; or Ivo H. Daalder and Michael E. O'Hanlon *Winning Ugly.* The war against Iraq that began in 2003 is described in Anthony H. Cordesman, *The Iraq War.*

CHAPTER 5

Deterrence and Arms Control

The essence of deterrence is threatening a harmful response to keep someone else from doing something you do not want done. As such, deterrence is almost as familiar in everyday life as dust on your shoes. Threats of punishment are used to train animals, raise children, manage traffic, and control crime. Employed in many cultures, it is no stranger. Deterrence is also a venerable practice in international politics. To prevent being attacked by others, governments threaten to fight hard if they are. Deterrence and related threats have often been used for other purposes, too. To prevent someone from taking a step that is unacceptable (such as joining an alliance, seizing a piece of territory, or buying arms) a government may issue a threat to attack or impose some other punishment. This was part of the traditional strategy of trying to maintain an acceptable distribution of power among states (see Chapter 3). Deterrence has been pursued by individual states, alliances, even international organizations. Threats of harm have often been associated with negotiations, bribes, concessions, and other tools of statecraft. They are woven into the warp of foreign policy. Thus deterrence is one aspect of what is called **coercive diplomacy** in which a government uses force or threats to get what it wants.

This way of practicing deterrence was characteristic of relations among nations, particularly great powers, for centuries. Used by the great powers especially from about 1890 to 1914, it came back into prominence in the late 1930s. But after World War II the practice of deterrence changed in important ways. Deterrence among the leading states soon came to rest primarily on nuclear weapons, which can do incredible damage. They turned to nuclear deterrence in large part because the Cold War was a political conflict so profound that it seemed capable of bringing on another great war at almost any time. Deterrence thus became more important than anything else for the great powers in trying to survive and keep safe. It became a broad security strategy in its own right, not just a standard tactic. Great states and societies bet their lives on it—for decades. In fact, they bet the lives of everyone on the planet. As a result, the nuclear deterrence practiced by each great power on its own gradually became a partially cooperative, partially competitive management of security for the entire international system. All this was unexpected and unplanned and not always well understood. It is amazing that the nations involved lived to tell about it.

THE MAIN ELEMENTS OF DETERRENCE

In security affairs, deterrence means preventing someone from attacking you by threatening to hurt them badly if they do. You might do this by putting up a strong defense. Or you might lash out ("I cannot keep you from stealing my cow, but if you do I will kill your bull and maybe your pig, too"), which is a threat of retaliation. Or you might do both. The object is to not have to do any of these things, because you mount such an effective threat that the other side decides not to attack in the first place.

Normally, states have chosen defense as the best way to keep safe. But in the twentieth century that became steadily harder to count on because bombers became so hard to defend against. Bombers could not do much damage at first, and in World War II societies demonstrated that they could put up with a good deal of damage from bombing. Therefore, a weak defense against bombers was not fatal. But late in the war, when the bomber fleets had become vast, some countries began to suffer staggering damage. In fire raids over Tokyo and some German cities, hundreds of bombers dropped incendiaries to start thousands of fires. Once those fires got going simultaneously, they created firestorms that burned huge sections of these cities. They sucked in oxygen, which created high winds that fanned the flames (much like a forest fire does) and generated the conditions of a giant outdoor blast furnace—melting most structures, suffocating people who were hiding in shelters or lakes and rivers, and killing as many as 100,000 people at a time.

In 1945 the United States demonstrated it could produce the same results and much worse with just one atomic bomb. The bomb used on Hiroshima not only created a firestorm but also flattened the entire center of the city and spread so much radioactivity and radioactive debris that it killed people miles away. Perhaps 100,000 people died, maybe more. No one knows. Many were vaporized and disappeared without a trace.

In the face of atomic bombs, conventional defenses looked useless because only a few bombs delivered on their targets could be devastating. But atomic bombs dropped on Japan were puny. The Hiroshima bomb delivered about twelve thousand to fourteen thousand tons of dynamite in its explosive power. Once hydrogen bombs appeared in the early 1950s, a bomb could be the equivalent of a million tons (a megaton) of dynamite, or five megatons, or ten. For years U.S. B-52 bombers routinely carried four twenty-million-ton-equivalent bombs per plane. Once the Soviet Union had these weapons, too, every country in the world faced the fact that at least one other country could destroy it. No country could count on being able to successfully defend itself. That led the great powers to think hard about deterrence. Because it seemed they could not survive a massive attack via their defenses, they would have to deter it, mainly by threats of retaliation, not threats to defend. After all, facing a sizable bomber attack the country might easily be destroyed if just half the incoming bombers got through, or even a third. In the late 1950s defenses began to get more flimsy because of the appearance of long-range missiles. Bombers could be shot down, but nobody could reliably shoot down a missile warhead delivered by a long-range missile. This is still true today, though that may change in the next decade or two. The best that could be done was to threaten retaliation—"If attacked, I will do so much damage that having attacked will not be worth it to you." All the great powers built nuclear arsenals with atomic and hydrogen bombs; all had bombers and eventually missiles. A handful of other states built nuclear weapons, too (India, Israel, North Korea, and Pakistan). (South Africa secretly built a small number of nuclear weapons but later decided to dismantle them—also secretly.)

In the midst of the Cold War little chance existed of having successful negotiations resolve the big political issues. During that intense conflict little engagement took place between the two sides to help bridge the gap. But a war would have been dreadful. So the only thing left to count on was deterrence. Each side in the Cold War felt that its survival depended on deterrence, especially nuclear deterrence.

The fundamental elements of the deterrence approach to security begin with the idea that some enemy government, for example, the Union of Soviet Socialist Republics (USSR) or the United States, was strongly motivated to launch an attack, strongly enough that it would probably do so if it thought it could get away with it. During the Cold War each side depicted the other as poised to attack if a chance arose. To combat this threat the basic approach to deterrence assumed that the opponent was, to some extent, rational. In the opponent's set of goals, avoiding defeat and continuing to survive would be a high priority. In looking at the options available for achieving the country's goals and calculating the costs and benefits, the risks, and chances of success, it would pick the one that seemed likely to bring the best payoff, the best outcome.

Deterrence worked by making a war look unrewarding by threatening the opponent with unacceptable damage in retaliation for starting it. Nuclear weapons made this easy. A small nuclear arsenal could do immense damage in retaliation (see the *Terms and Concepts* box, "Deterrence and Arms Control"). A deterrence threat might be issued to protect the deterrer from attack, **direct deterrence**, or to protect a third party, **extended deterrence**. However, the threat would be no good unless the deterrer could suffer a terrible initial attack and still respond. If the deterrer could not do this, then the other side would win with what would amount to a one-punch knockout in a fight. But if the deterrer could retaliate, and the opponent knew that, then the opponent would not attack because it

Terms and Concepts: *Deterrence and Arms Control*

The term unacceptable damage comes from the idea that a person will not do something if the consequences are unacceptable. To deter someone from doing something you do not want done, you have to threaten damage in retaliation that is regarded as unacceptable. Threatening anything less might not do the trick. Determining the threshold of unacceptable damage might be difficult, but nuclear weapons made that easy because they promised devastation.

Direct deterrence is the use of threats of harm in retaliation to prevent a direct attack on the deterrer. Extended deterrence involves threats of harm to prevent an attack on a third party, such as an ally. A first-strike capability is the capacity to attack with such effect that the opponent is not able to retaliate in any serious way. To deter, a government must be able to retaliate at an unacceptable level of damage after it has been attacked. It must take steps to deny the opponent a first-strike capability. If it does this, then it is said to have a second-strike capability, which is the ability to be attacked and still strike back effectively. A first-strike capability is also called a preemptive attack capability, the ability to strip the enemy of the ability to respond effectively to an attack and thus of its deterrence.

The stability-instability paradox says that, if deterrence can prevent some conflicting states from escalating a conflict to a level in which they would suffer unacceptable damage, each may then feel free to fight at a lower level. Stability—the absence of nuclear war, for instance, because of deterrence—could lead the parties to carry on their conflict by fighting a large conventional war. Deterrence thus would be unstable at the conventional level. The Strategic Arms Limitation Talks (SALT) focused on the most powerful and long-range weapons that the two superpowers had. The objective was to limit such weapons so that each side had a second-strike capability and could do unacceptable damage in retaliation. The goal was to make deterrence more stable, particularly in a crisis, by taking away any incentive to try to pull off a successful preemptive attack. Thus effective ballistic missile defenses were outlawed.

Vertical proliferation refers to the enlargement of an existing arsenal, that is, the pile of weapons gets bigger. Horizontal proliferation refers to an increase in the number of actors that have the weapons of concern. Since the end of the Cold War the great powers have mostly been doing the reverse of vertical proliferation of weapons of mass destruction (WMDs), and a strong effort has been made to try to prevent any further horizontal proliferation of WMDs.

would suffer unacceptable costs. In calculating the costs and benefits, other options would look better than attacking. Nuclear weapons made this very likely. Almost anything would look better than that level of destruction. During the Cold War the result sought via deterrence was a stalemate with each side persuading the other not to attack by holding the other hostage for its good behavior.

Despite this nicely worked out explanation as to how deterrence worked, during the Cold War people worried about it constantly. The two great powers eventually had many thousands of nuclear weapons. The Soviet Union alone had more than thirty thousand. Thus it looked like little would be left after the next great war. Deterrence had to work all the time or else, yet it was easy to think of ways that deterrence might fail. These worries eventually dictated how nuclear deterrence was practiced.

THE CREDIBILITY PROBLEM

Nuclear deterrence had, and still has, an inherent credibility problem. When a government threatens to use nuclear weapons, it is unlikely to be believed. Early in the Cold War the United States issued some nuclear threats, but the Soviet Union seems to have ignored them. In leading the United Nations (UN) fight against North Korea, and eventually Communist China in the Korean War, the United States had nuclear weapons and its opponents did not. The Soviet Union, ally of China and North Korea, had tested a nuclear device but had no nuclear weapon and no way to deliver one against the United States. When the president hinted that the United States might consider using nuclear weapons, he scared America's allies. The British prime minister flew to Washington to gain assurances that the United States would do no such thing. The United States did not use nuclear weapons, suffering close to forty thousand lives lost in combat instead. Why? Using nuclear weapons would have been like taking a sledgehammer to swat flies. The method was disproportionate to the problem. More important, the United States and others feared that using those weapons would suggest they were too much like other weapons, easy to use. What they wanted was to have it understood that nuclear weapons could be used only as a last resort.

The same thing happened to the United States in Vietnam in 1962–1975. It fought a nasty war and lost, but still it could not bring itself to use such awful weapons. The Soviets in 1969 engaged in serious border fighting with China and floated the idea in international circles of using some nuclear weapons. They got no support. Nothing came of the idea, and China did not tone down its criticism of the Soviet Union. During the war in Afghanistan in the 1980s, Soviet forces were defeated without resorting to nuclear weapons. When the Falkland Islands were seized by Argentina in 1982, the resulting war between a nuclear power and a non-nuclear power saw no use of nuclear weapons. The point is clear: Deciding to use nuclear weapons is hard and, as a result, making believable threats to do so is difficult, too.

The situation is further complicated when the other side also has nuclear weapons. Deterrence rests on threatening unacceptable damage. But, if the other side has nuclear weapons, it could threaten unacceptable damage back—and thus deter the deterrer. This would mean a stalemate with no one ready to use nuclear weapons, leaving the opponent free to attack. Suppose I want to protect State A and you want to attack it. I threaten you with harsh retaliation, but you do the same to me. If you attack State A and I am rational, I should decide to do nothing because attacking you could mean my country suffers greatly. So my threat is not believed and deterrence fails.

Logically, this problem also applies to deterrence at lower levels too. If I face the prospect of unacceptable damage for retaliating against the attacker, the attacker should have no reason to believe my threat. The problem is at its worst in cases, such as in this example, of extended deterrence. Unacceptable damage may be low for me when I was not the one who was attacked but someone else was.

Many steps were taken to try to ease the credibility problem, particularly by the United States and others in the West. There was great interest in the notion that, when it comes to credibility, commitments are interdependent. How you behave on one commitment affects the credibility of all your others. If you do not want a reputation as a liar, you better tell the truth all the time. Telling just a few lies reduces the likelihood people will believe you in the future, as in the story of the boy who cried "wolf." This idea had a major impact on American foreign policy. When the Korean War broke out in 1950, some American officials called for U.S. intervention because, they said, if the United States did not help South Korea, neither the Soviets nor U.S. allies would believe the U.S. promises made to the North Atlantic Treaty Organization (NATO) alliance the year before. When the United States was considering whether to send troops to help South Vietnam, a key reason it did so was that otherwise the communists would be emboldened to challenge American commitments elsewhere.

Efforts also were made to reduce the West's reliance on nuclear weapons. The argument was: "Who will believe us when we threaten to use nuclear weapons to respond to a limited attack on an ally? This sort of deterrence lacks credibility so it is likely to fail. We must be ready to fight at the level of the attack and win, without using nuclear weapons. Then when we say we will respond to some provocation everyone will believe us." This doctrine of **flexible response** was debated for years and influenced American and NATO forces and military doctrines.

Both sides in the Cold War tried to figure out how to win even a large nuclear war via a cheap victory strategy. One argument was that if you thought you could win a nuclear war and suffer only modest damage, then your threat to use nuclear weapons would carry more credibility. It was also thought that many things could affect credibility such as spending large amounts on new weapons systems. Why would a country do that if it was not ready to use them? Similarly, heavy defense spending was justified in part by asserting that it conveyed national resolve. At times officials even opposed summit conferences, arms control talks, and the like because to participate might convey an image of being nervous or afraid. Looking weak was bad for credibility, it was said.

Ultimately analysts decided that some credibility was inherent in nuclear weapons. This was done by relaxing the assumption of rationality. Even if I have nuclear weapons, it might be irrational to ever use them. But if I am attacked, who says I will be rational? I might be enraged, confused, or scared and use them anyway. If I did this, and then the enemy would be destroyed, why would the enemy take that risk? So deterrence works.

This became the dominant view about deterrence during the Cold War, and it was the heart of the strategy known as **mutual assured destruction** (MAD). If the United States and Soviet Union could destroy each other and each other's allies, and no guarantee could be made that they would not, no matter how irrational that might be, then everyone would behave with great caution and avoid rash moves. MAD was influential in shaping U.S. views and forces from the early 1960s to 1980. The Soviet version was that, if a significant war broke out between East and West, the Soviet government would assume it would quickly escalate to the nuclear level. The implication was that it would therefore start the escalation. MAD also became the basis for NATO's strategic posture. NATO's European members refused to build the forces supposedly needed to defeat a Soviet bloc attack at the conventional level, despite heavy U.S. pressure for this. Why? They felt that the best deterrent was the possibility that a Soviet attack would soon escalate to all-out war, and the best way to make it look like this could happen would be to

- Have NATO forces in Europe known to be too weak to defeat the Soviet forces so that NATO would feel forced to escalate to nuclear weapons;

- Have NATO doctrine promise an early escalation to nuclear weapons; and

- Have Europeans possess nuclear weapons that they might use to trigger the escalation.

Did these steps solve the credibility problem? Not really. The United States, for instance, could fight hard in Korea but then decide not to fight hard elsewhere if it thought a direct attack on the United States could occur as a result. Commitments might not automatically be treated the same way so they were not fully interdependent. Having the ability to fight hard at a lower level could even be taken as evidence of a strong desire to never escalate. Fighting hard in Vietnam to bolster U.S. credibility destroyed political support in the United States, at least temporarily, for fighting anywhere else, so its commitments became less credible. Finally, MAD was always an uncomfortable proposition. It said that deterrence was credible because governments could be irrational or could lose control. It was hardly comforting that possibly irrational governments, with thousands of nuclear weapons at their disposal, could periodically be involved in wars.

The credibility problem had other effects. The superpowers worried about political credibility, about how reliable and successful they looked around the world. The fear was that if you failed to press hard on defending your friends politically, or if they were not doing well compared with the other side's friends, others (friends, neutrals, the opposing side) could come to believe that history was not on your side, because your side was losing. Thus a loss anywhere is a loss everywhere. For instance, your allies would begin to rethink their support, maybe try to cut deals with the enemy. Neutral countries would lean toward the opponent, too. And the enemy would be emboldened, more inclined to mount challenges. Thinking like this meant that the superpowers had to care about almost everywhere and not let the other side gain an edge without a fight even in seemingly unimportant places. Thus they had to be ready to intervene, if necessary, in Angola and Afghanistan, Grenada and Ethiopia, Laos and the Congo. It turned out deterrence had hidden costs and burdens.

THE STABILITY PROBLEM

Equally important for the development of nuclear deterrence in practice was the stability problem. Here "stability" referred to deterrence successful in preventing the outbreak of a major war, particularly a nuclear war. The widespread feeling was that deterrence stood in the way of another great war. But was deterrence stable? Could it maintain peace indefinitely?

Initially, the greatest concern had to do with crises. Analysts suggested that under some circumstances the arrangements made to deter might, in a crisis, provoke an attack instead. They cited 1914 as an example. The cheap victory strategies of the time rested on rapid mobilization, to get to the battlefield better prepared than the enemy. When a deep crisis arose and war looked likely, military leaders were afraid to be the last to mobilize and attack because they thought this guaranteed a crushing defeat. When it was most important that deterrence work, the military arrangements for deterrence were pushing military leaders to press their governments to mobilize, which is what all governments regard as a virtual declaration of war. Analysts realized that nuclear weapons offered an ideal route to a cheap victory strategy: Attack hard and the opponent would disappear. Any military action on an enemy's part might be precluded, hence the term **preemptive attack** was used to describe this strategy. The ability to mount such an attack came to be called a **first-strike capability**, with the first strike winning the war. In a crisis if one side had that capability it could attack and emerge virtually unscathed, so chances were good it would do just that. What frightened analysts was that if both sides had a first-strike capability each would be desperate to attack first in a crisis. The military arrangements for keeping the peace would make a war inevitable.

The first response by the governments facing this problem was to try to ensure that an enemy knew its forces for retaliation could not be destroyed in a surprise attack. The only way to do this was to keep a large portion of the forces in question on constant alert, ready to go on almost a moment's notice at the first warning of an attack. Eventually, governments took steps to make their nuclear forces hard to destroy in a surprise attack: hiding them on missiles aboard submarines in the ocean, moving them around constantly on land, and burying them in concrete silos underground. However, some forces would always be on high alert. Even now a good many nuclear armed missiles around the world are still ready to be fired in as little as two minutes.

Governments had to avoid developing first-strike capabilities. But how? Any military establishment facing a possible nuclear war would be eager to have a first-strike capability as the only way to guarantee the nation's survival. Any government involved in a ferocious political conflict like the Cold War would expect the enemy to be seeking to develop a first-strike capability and then attack. The answer was both to unilaterally avoid a first-strike capability and to seek an agreement with the enemy to forbid development of ideal first-strike weapons and military postures, that is, an agreement with the enemy to cooperate. The answer became the foundation of modern **arms control**, in theory and practice.

The heart of Cold War arms control efforts was negotiating to limit dangerous strategic weapons. Major agreements limited each side's offensive weapons somewhat. Strategic defensive weapons, systems to shoot down ballistic missiles, were also sharply limited, so that one side could not attack and destroy most of the other side's weapons and then use its defenses to shoot down the rest. The goal was to maintain mutual vulnerability to destruction. Each side was always to be hostage to the other.

In a way, dealing with the stability problem the Cold War displayed international politics at its most absurd—and its most tragic. A bunch of adults, high officials in leading governments, seemed able to maintain security only by arranging that all of their peoples were constantly vulnerable to destruction. If they could agree to that, why couldn't they agree to do away with nuclear weapons and conduct their political conflict peacefully? International politics involves governments constantly afraid their opponents will cheat, and secretly strive to achieve military domination, so sensible agreements can become politically impossible to reach. That was true in the Cold War.

Many other arms control steps were taken to deal with the stability problem. For instance, deterrence might fail because of miscommunication or misperception in a crisis. As a result, the great powers developed **hot lines**, direct communications links open all the time so top officials could talk to each other instantly. (Some smaller states eventually developed similar arrangements.) Or deterrence might fail because of the unauthorized use of a nuclear weapon. For example, a nuclear missile could be fired by a launch crew gone crazy, or a bomber crashes in a sensitive area and one of the nuclear weapons on board goes off and the other side thinks this is the start of an attack so it launches its weapons. Such fears led to mental health screenings for people who handled nuclear weapons and elaborate systems for arming weapons that required two people to take steps (turn keys) at the same time some distance apart. Special codes were created for arming weapons (sent only by the national government at the right time) that would break down and be unusable if the wrong code was entered, and weapons were made that could survive a plane crash or sit in a jet fuel fire without going off.

The stability problem also helped turn nuclear deterrence into a **global security management system**. There was fear that deterrence would be unstable because of **escalation**. Some small conflict would gradually build into an all-out disaster (for example, World War I). Concern arose about possible escalation of a conflict between the United States and the USSR or NATO and the Warsaw Pact. A crisis leads to border fighting, emotions and tensions rise, and heavier fighting results, leading to putting more nuclear weapons on alert. Then, a weapon gets used or a serious misperception is created that an attack is coming, and one side fires off its weapons. Living with terrifying weapons always on a hair trigger made the great powers go to elaborate lengths to control their interactions around the globe. For example, the superpowers tried not to be seen directly killing each other's citizens except under very unusual circumstances. In the Cuban Missile Crisis the United States decided not to bomb the missile sites partly because doing so would kill some Russians and maybe escalate the conflict. The superpower intelligence agencies, the Central Intelligence Agency (CIA) and the KGB (Komitet gosudarstvennoi bezopasnosti, State Security Committee), avoided killing each other's operatives. Only in direct overflights for intelligence was this arrangement violated. Western planes flying over communist territory to take pictures or monitor radars were sometimes shot down.

Because deterrence might be unstable if a crisis got out of hand, the United States and USSR signed several agreements to head off crises. They also tried to prevent their friends and allies from instigating crises in the first place. At times this led the superpowers to jump into conflicts around the world to try to prevent them from becoming worse. They did not want to be drawn into being face to face in a tense situation.

The superpowers made strenuous efforts to prevent **nuclear proliferation**— the emergence of more nuclear armed states. The Americans tried to discourage the British and French nuclear weapons programs; the Russians did this with the Chinese program. Both pressed for a broad treaty on nonproliferation and leaned on their allies to sign it. The United States forced Taiwan and South Korea to halt fledgling nuclear weapons programs, and the United States and Soviet Union jointly tried to stop Iraq, North Korea, South Africa, and Pakistan from developing nuclear weapons. These efforts were reinforced by (unevenly practiced) controls on transfers of the technologies useful for making nuclear weapons.

Critics said this was the "haves" trying to retain their special status by keeping the "have-nots" out of the nuclear club. There is something to this, because great states are seldom models of altruism. But the superpowers had a point. Whatever utility nuclear deterrence had in keeping a deeply divided world safe could only be eroded by increasing the number of fingers on nuclear triggers. Some analysts argue that, if nuclear deterrence works to keep peace among the great powers, it can do the same among other states. Thus nuclear proliferation is good. But most analysts and governments have rejected this view and endorse nuclear nonproliferation. I agree with them.

Fear of proliferation became one reason for maintaining superpower alliances and other commitments, particularly those of the Americans. Pull the United States out of the alliance with Japan, and Japan would go nuclear, it was said—and is still said today. Pull it out of NATO, and Germany would. There was something to this. When the United States was humbled in the Vietnam War, all its commitments in East Asia looked less reliable. In response, Taiwan and South Korea promptly started nuclear weapons programs. The same thing happened in Iraq and North Korea once the Soviet Union collapsed and those nations were suddenly on their own.

Thus nuclear deterrence was a tireless goad toward involvement, management, intervention, and control of the international system. In tandem, the credibility problem and the stability problem greatly reinforced the superpowers' political and ideological inclinations to carry their competition into all corners of the globe, trying to manage peace and security even as their political competition posed the greatest threat to it.

DOES DETERRENCE WORK?

In assessing deterrence, particularly nuclear deterrence, consider first why it was appealing. It was, after all, very expensive and burdensome (in many ways), and it always seemed full of risk and fear. It was often referred to as the "balance of terror" to capture the pervasive insecurity that seemed central to its character. What an odd way to keep safe—by putting everyone on the edge of a cliff. How, then, did it come to be relied upon so heavily, and how well does it work?

The Appeal of a Deterrence Strategy

The simplest answer to why they relied on it is that governments did not think they had a choice. The preferred strategy for handling regional and global security, and particularly for avoiding another world war was a great-power concert, based in the UN (see Chapter 6). The great powers would resolve or mute their differences and cooperate to make other governments do the same. But that never worked out. It was made inoperative by the Cold War. A concert did not become promising until after the Cold War ended, so something else had to be tried.

There seemed to be no possibility of nuclear disarmament either. The Cold War existed because the major states fueled their relations mainly on suspicion and mistrust—each side believing, with good reason, that the other wanted it to disappear. Neither could trust the other on disarmament matters, so some assurances, some verification, would always be necessary. Here the Soviet Union and its allies were in a serious bind. Their political systems rested on secrecy and isolation from the outside world. They sought to cope with the much stronger and healthier Western world by hiding many of their deficiencies. Serious verification would have threatened to expose defects of the Soviet bloc. Western military leaders also had reservations about intrusive verification, fearing Soviet intelligence gains. For years the West's insistence on a high level of verification, and Soviet resistance to it, doomed nuclear disarmament efforts. Even arms control (which was a long way from disarmament) made little progress until satellites in space could provide verification by penetrating the Soviet bloc from above. With disarmament impossible, deterrence involved making a virtue of a necessity.

Nuclear deterrence was also appealing because it offered a way to cope with cheap victory strategies. Fear that nuclear weapons would provide the ultimate in such strategies, especially with intercontinental-range missiles that could be delivered with a warning time of as little as twenty minutes, gave way to confidence in retaliation because missiles could be hidden or put underground. The threat of a devastating retaliation could be used to deter what was impossible to defend against. For NATO, nuclear deterrence also became the way to cope with Soviet cheap victory strategies (blitzkrieg-style) at the conventional forces level. If Soviet bloc hordes rolled over Western armies, the West could respond with nuclear weapons, nullifying the Soviet strategy.

Once they got into it, the superpowers discovered that nuclear deterrence was cheap, too. The Soviet bloc advantage was in massive armed forces—huge armies; vast numbers of tanks, planes, and artillery pieces; and immense reserves. The Soviet strategy mainly called for overwhelming the West in any war. Western governments thought that if they tried to match such forces with far more expensive Western ones, they would face bankruptcy, crippled national economic growth, or taxpayer revolts. Nuclear weapons offered a way out. Expensive to develop, they were then cheap to maintain. Soon the Soviets found that their massive forces, though cheaper than the West's, were not cheap. In the late 1950s and early 1960s they also turned to cutting those forces back in favor of nuclear weapons.

Another appeal of nuclear weapons was that they entailed no loss of sovereignty. Hence, this aspect of state security was sustained. Nuclear weapons came to seem like the ultimate guarantee of great-power status, for major states, and of national sovereignty for any other state possessing them. Remaining a great power was a strong incentive in Britain's decision to develop nuclear weapons, it was the overwhelming preoccupation of the French, it has been central in Chinese thinking right down to the present, and it was reiterated by India and Pakistan after their nuclear weapons tests in 1998.

Nuclear deterrence also fit well into the Cold War. Each side assumed the other was thirsting to attack and something had to be done to daunt it. The image of the enemy held by each side was that it was cruel, brutal, barbaric. The threat of nuclear annihilation was just what it deserved, the only thing it would understand.

But nuclear deterrence had, and still has, serious drawbacks. For instance, it was not designed beforehand on the basis of a well-developed theory or long historical experience. First nuclear deterrence emerged, then a theory appeared to help explain it and how it should be operated. The theory did not rest on a careful examination of the historical record on deterrence. This was partly because the nuclear age was widely, and incorrectly, believed to be novel; history did not apply.

The theory and practice of nuclear deterrence were controversial from the start. People objected to being so vulnerable. They did not like being the equivalent of comic strip artist Gary Larsen's bears with big targets on their chests. People thought being held hostage was immoral. After all, the hostages included kids, the elderly, art museums, churches, nurses and doctors, and even professors and students. It was as if drivers were forced to use extreme caution to prevent traffic accidents and thus had to tie their children to the bumpers of their cars.

Some objected to mutual nuclear deterrence, that is, being totally vulnerable to the enemy. Military leaders on both sides were inclined to try to create unilateral deterrence instead, by developing a cheap victory strategy or a successful preemptive attack strategy. Let the other side be deterred, not your side; let it be destroyed in the next war, not your side. Still others objected because they saw nuclear deterrence as creating a giant permanent security dilemma. Once states knew how to make nuclear weapons, they would have trouble ever giving them up for fear that someone would cheat and secretly keep some or build new ones "just in case." The critics disliked the fact that many champions of nuclear deterrence said nuclear weapons were a fact of life and that the world would have to learn to live with relying on them to keep safe.

Finally, many people objected to relying on governments, armed forces, and decision makers to never lose control, never use nuclear weapons in unauthorized ways, never go too far in a crisis, and never go crazy. This asks too much of human beings, they said. Complex systems built and run by people inevitably break down. Governments, particularly those who run them, are imperfect—burdened with misperceptions, resistant to evidence that they are wrong, inept in learning from history or past experience, and unevenly effective under stress.

Nuclear Deterrence in Practice

How accurate were those fears? How, and how well, did nuclear deterrence operate? Nuclear weapons were initially developed to be used. They were to save lives by killing the enemy. Developed during World War II they were used to bring it to an abrupt end. Then in 1946–1947 the East-West dispute emerged and Americans began worrying about possible Soviet attacks on Western Europe and about another world war. They also began to think about using nuclear weapons from the start of such a war and about using the threat of those weapons to prevent it. Then the Soviet Union tested its own nuclear device in 1949, so both countries had to start thinking about mutual deterrence. Out of this came, over the next decade, the rudiments of a theory of deterrence and the first serious deterrence strategy.

A skeletal version of the theory was presented earlier. The first strategy was referred to as **massive retaliation**. Each side built up nuclear stockpiles and delivery systems, and each promised that if it or countries it protected were attacked, it would probably respond with a huge nuclear blow to do about as much damage as it could. By 1960 the United States could have hit more than five thousand targets, but even a small nuclear power such as Great Britain could have hit one hundred or more with weapons much larger than the bomb that destroyed Hiroshima. Massive retaliation was appealing because of its low cost. It offered "more bang for the buck," it was said. Americans, Russians, and Europeans were all eager to save money for economic development. It was also appealing because the West was leery of fighting another huge conventional war and because many analysts thought no major war could be fought without each side using every weapon it had to win. So why not threaten all-out war to keep one from ever starting? East and West cut their regular forces while expanding their nuclear arsenals. The Soviet Union cut more than two million men, and NATO reduced its planned forces by over half. Each prepared to respond to a non-nuclear attack with nuclear weapons, starting on the battlefield and then escalating. The United States eventually sent to Europe some seven thousand nuclear weapons to be used by the United States and its allies (certain nuclear weapons were to be turned over to them) in the next war in Europe. NATO became addicted to nuclear weapons as a cheap way to deter.

But massive retaliation soon came under heavy fire itself. One reason was the development of deterrence theory in the late 1950s and 1960s, which put great emphasis on credibility and stability. Massive retaliation looked bad on both. Critics roughly said: "If even a small attack takes place, we expect a rapid escalation to the use of nuclear weapons. This would be unwise, however, and when the time comes our side probably will not do it. So the other side will not believe the threat." In the meantime the East and West could stumble into a crisis in which misperceptions or an accident got everyone killed. A subset of deterrence thinking called for extreme attention to stability. In a crisis there should be no benefit to attacking first, no plans to escalate, and no nuclear proliferation to put many fingers on nuclear triggers. But massive retaliation planned on nuclear escalation, thus leaders would be attracted to attacking first. And, in practice it included plans to distribute nuclear weapons to allies in a war.

The critics felt that deterrence needed less rigid strategy and forces so they endorsed what was called **flexible response**. This doctrine said that the United States and its allies should prepare to fight effectively in a war of any size, so that they would not have to escalate. As a result, attacks would be discouraged, because the West's threat of an equivalent defense would be highly credible. And if deterrence failed and a war broke out, the destruction of everything would not necessarily follow. In practice this required building larger U.S. forces trained to fight all sorts of wars (tiny wars, small wars, regular wars, large wars, or nuclear wars), hence bigger defense budgets, more ships, and so forth. NATO members and U.S. allies in the Far East were urged to get ready to defend themselves at all levels.

Flexible response had some effect but soon ran into trouble. In the United States the big problem was the Vietnam War (1962–1975). In Vietnam the United States tried to help an ally defend itself in a guerrilla war, and when that failed America escalated the fighting into a small regular war and considered escalating to an even larger conventional war. Virtually no one was happy as a result. Sizable sectors of the American public became opposed, the allies disliked the war and many other countries condemned it. As a result the public and Congress lost interest in having large forces ready to fight all sorts of wars. In the 1970s U.S. forces and defense spending shrank to their lowest levels in decades. NATO allies did not like flexible response either. In their societies little public support was found for spending considerably more on defense and putting more men into the armed forces. Allies also worried that the more they did to defend themselves, the less the United States would do to protect them. They would pay more but be no more secure as a result. They also feared that being prepared to fight a limited war could mean keeping it limited to Europe, that is, that the United States and Soviet Union might be happy to fight to the last European as long their homelands were not attacked. Europeans believed that threatening escalation to nuclear war was a better deterrent threat. Without increased allied forces, the NATO military posture never became flexible. Eventually NATO was prepared to put up a good fight only for the first few weeks and then, if it began to lose, to start using nuclear weapons and escalate to targets in the Soviet Union.

Finally, the Soviets would not go along. The Soviet government was ready to have larger armed forces (in fact, military pressures for them were immense), and it began what became a long military buildup after 1964. But it never liked the idea of another big conventional war. After all, the last one had cost the nation more than twenty-five million lives. It remained convinced that a significant war would almost certainly escalate, and it was determined to escalate first to better its chances of survival.

So by the 1970s the United States slipped into an updated version of massive retaliation, called mutual assured destruction, while Britain, China, and France retained a massive retaliation strategy, and the Russians fell somewhere in between. MAD was less a military strategy than a conception of how nuclear deterrence worked. From a MAD perspective any big conventional war could easily lead to using a few nuclear weapons, and any use of nuclear weapons was likely to lead to using many. Nuclear weapons are so dangerous that governments behave cautiously. That is how deterrence works and why nuclear deterrence threats are credible. So forget about planning for controlled wars, nuclear or conventional, and stop designing forces for that purpose.

By the late 1970s flexible response had made a bit of a comeback. Critics of MAD called it immoral because the strategy accepted the possibility of a nuclear war but wanted no preparations made to win and survive it. Such planning might save millions of lives. Critics said that MAD lacked credibility. It made governments too cautious, and eventually someone would try to exploit that like Adolf Hitler had done in the 1930s in ignoring deterrence threats.

Technology also changed in ways that undermined MAD. Missile warheads became more accurate and missiles began carrying more than one warhead. They carried **Multiple Independently Targeted Reentry Vehicles** (MIRVs). This made them better for destroying enemy missiles, even ones hidden in silos. The technology for finding missile-carrying submarines also got better, making it possible to destroy many more missiles before they could be fired. New technology made people begin to think seriously about ballistic missile defenses. All this made it seem more plausible to fight and survive a nuclear war.

The biggest shift, however, was political. Rising concerns about how poorly, it seemed, the West was doing in the Cold War was reflected in the much more aggressively competitive approach by the Reagan administration starting in 1981. Part of this approach was to expand American military capabilities; another was finding ways to fight a nuclear war successfully by destroying Soviet nuclear forces, with an updated version of flexible response as justification. But American allies once again refused to fully accept it. So did the Russians. Many domestic critics spoke out against higher military spending, new strategic weapons, and missile defenses, which put limits on how far the approach could be carried.

When the Cold War ended in 1990, what happened to nuclear deterrence? It is still around. All the major nuclear powers except China have significantly reduced their nuclear arsenals. The United States and Russia have agreed to slice their long-range nuclear weapons from more than ten thousand each to as little as seventeen hundred. British and French weapons have been cut, too. Thousands of American, British, and Russian nuclear weapons were taken off ships and stockpiled or destroyed. Only nuclear warheads on ballistic missiles on submarines remained at sea. Many strategic nuclear weapons and delivery systems were taken off high alert. The great powers finally agreed, in principle, to eventually eliminate all nuclear weapons, and a great majority of the world's nations agreed to renew the Nuclear Nonproliferation Treaty in 1995 and thus work to prevent any expansion in the number of nuclear powers.

Clearly these steps are designed to put nuclear deterrence deep into the background instead of up-front, as in the Cold War. NATO now plans to use nuclear weapons only as a last resort. Still, the nuclear powers do not expect to abandon their nuclear weapons any time soon. China is still expanding its arsenal. Two newly declared nuclear powers, India and Pakistan, are likely to keep building up, and North Korea apparently has nuclear weapons now. Several states are known to be working on nuclear weapons programs. Some states fear the huge U.S. advantage in non-nuclear warfare and hope to ward off a future American attack by threatening nuclear retaliation.

Thus nuclear deterrence is still around, it just is not nearly as important. Active movements seek to do away with nuclear weapons and nuclear deterrence as too dangerous. But some believe that only nuclear weapons can prevent wars between deeply embittered opponents. Some even support spreading nuclear weapons in places such as the Middle East or South Asia. Others say nuclear deterrence will always exist because people cannot unlearn how to make nuclear weapons. Finally, many accept nuclear weapons because they fear the return of a threat from Russia (or, in Russia, from the United States) or a new severe conflict between China and the United States, or they want nuclear weapons to cope with so-called rogue states, which get weapons of mass destruction to practice blackmail. (See the *Terms and Concepts* box, "Weapons of Mass Destruction.")

Terms and Concepts: *Weapons of Mass Destruction*

Weapons of mass destruction come in a variety of forms. Atomic, or nuclear, weapons release enormous destructive energy by processes that cause the nuclei of atoms of radioactive materials to split (fission) virtually simultaneously. A nuclear weapon sets off a huge blast as well as the release of a great amount of heat and radioactive particles. Hydrogen, or thermonuclear, weapons get their power by processes that cause atoms of hydrogen to fuse together. That fusion causes release of many times more energy than fission reactions. Fusion reactions are the source of the light and heat given off by stars. Chemical weapons use materials, usually in the form of a gas, to either disable or kill people. Many such weapons are extremely deadly. They can also be used to kill animals and crops. The use of biological weapons is basically the practice of public health in reverse. Diseases or toxins are used to either disable or kill people, and some of them—such as plague, anthrax, and botulism—are among the most virulent known. Biological weapons can be used against animals and crops as well.

ARMS CONTROL AND DISARMAMENT

Two other approaches to the problem of war need to be considered, one closely associated with deterrence and one that is the antithesis of it: arms control and disarmament. Over time nuclear and other deterrence during the Cold War went from being a national approach to security and the problem of war to something far more cooperative. This was because the deterrence practiced in the Cold War was an exercise in interdependent security. I am not safe through my own efforts alone. I am safe because you decide not to attack me. If you decide to attack and I cannot defend myself, I have to count on you not to attack to be safe. Thus in mutual deterrence my security depends in part on you and vice versa. Security is interdependent.

This perception was the starting point for Cold War arms control efforts, that is, arms control as a strategy. Deterrence can be practiced without arms control, but it has often involved arms control and Cold War deterrence was shaped by arms control thinking. Arms control is best explained by contrasting it with disarmament, which is briefly discussed later.

Arms Control

Arms control is an old idea with a long history, but it came to prominence in the twentieth century, especially during the Cold War. The general idea is that, while arms have their uses and governments clearly are not going to do away with them, everyone has to live with them. However, the harmful consequences of that fact can be lessened. The tendency of arms to provoke quarrels and war, such as in a security dilemma, can be reduced. Their cost can be lowered. Their lethality and damage in a war can be reduced. A good definition is that arms control consists of efforts, unilateral and cooperative, to limit the costs and other harmful consequences of the continued existence of arms. In the context of deterrence the effect of arms control, properly implemented, is to make deterrence more effective, more stable, more tolerable in terms of cost, and thus more useful.

For years arms control was seen as a kind of disarmament, but serious thought was given to it in its own right once it became clear that in the Cold War there was no chance of real disarmament. Soon disarmament was largely forgotten and arms control became a major focus of national and international security policies. Consideration of arms control arrangements and proposals has continued down to the present-day. Here are some illustrations.

One harmful consequence of arms is their tendency to create security dilemmas. This is not a problem among friendly states. It arises when states are unfriendly and worried about possible attacks; one state's arms can readily exacerbate suspicions and fears. During the Cold War, such concerns led to determined efforts to slow the nuclear arms race. From fears about the effects of first-strike capabilities in a crisis came strong unilateral efforts to design nuclear postures so countries were not vulnerable to attacks and to develop cooperative efforts to limit military systems that might offer a first-strike capability. That was the goal of the 1970s **Strategic Arms Limitation Talks** (or SALT) negotiations and the two SALT agreements. They limited the number of ballistic missiles the United States and Soviet Union could have, the number of warheads on each missile, and the missile defenses each could have. Fear about dangerous misperceptions in crises led to a series of hot lines (communications available for emergencies) among various states.

An extension of concern about stability was fear of nuclear proliferation and this produced the Nuclear Nonproliferation Treaty, which opened for signatures in 1968. Under the treaty states with nuclear weapons agree not to help others obtain or develop them, states without nuclear weapons agree not to try to develop them, and states with nuclear weapons agree to try to control and shrink their nuclear arsenals. The treaty has not been totally effective, but the number of nuclear powers is far lower than experts had predicted and has not been expanding fast. The treaty was renewed in 1995 and again five years later with almost all nations recommitting themselves to it. To help contain nuclear proliferation among states and to discourage growth of nuclear arsenals within states, **horizontal** and **vertical proliferation**, respectively, a determined effort has been made to ban all nuclear testing, even underground. (Success has been limited by the fact that the United States has not ratified the Comprehensive Test Ban Treaty.)

Agreements also have been reached under which states with the appropriate technologies for making weapons of mass destruction (nuclear, chemical, and biological) agree to cooperate to prevent the sale or transfer of those technologies to states without them.

Arms pose other problems. For instance, they can damage the environment. By the 1950s it was clear that testing nuclear weapons was injecting dangerous radioactive materials into the atmosphere. This led to the signing of the atmospheric test ban agreement (Partial Test Ban Treaty) in 1963 by the Americans, British, and Russians. That eliminated most testing in the atmosphere. The Chinese and French did not stop such testing until years later.

There is a long history of treating some weapons as too awful to have around, and certainly too awful to use. In the twentieth century attention has focused on chemical and biological weapons. They have been held to be inhumane and environmentally dangerous, and two international conventions outlaw the use and stockpiling of these weapons. While not universally upheld, the conventions have led to steps that will eliminate most of the weapons from military arsenals, in particular the huge stockpiles held by the United States and Russia. (However, elimination has been going slowly.) Another inhumane weapon receiving special attention recently has been the land mine, especially the antipersonnel variety. Once planted in a war mines typically stay in the ground long after the fighting has ended. They explode when civilians happen on them, killing and maiming randomly. A convention to ban antipersonnel land mines, developed largely through the work of nongovernmental humanitarian organizations, was finalized in 1997, and nations are slowly moving to sign it.

Another approach has been to limit the spread of weapons systems by putting certain geographical areas off limits. For instance, agreements have been reached to keep all of Latin America and Oceania free of nuclear weapons, to ban nuclear weapons in outer space and Antarctica, and to prohibit the installation of nuclear weapons on the ocean floor. Another kind of arms control, developed since the end of the Cold War, provides funding to impoverished countries to both eliminate dangerous weapons and buy up the materials left over from their weapons programs. The United States has arranged to help pay for the Russian government's elimination of many nuclear weapons and its chemical weapons stockpile. It helps pay for storage of Russian or other nuclear materials and warheads in more secure facilities to prevent theft. It also is buying $20 billion of surplus radioactive materials from the Russian weapons program as fuel for U.S. nuclear power plants.

Some arms control is unilateral, such as when a government designs nuclear weapons that will not go off accidentally and cannot be fired by someone (like a terrorist) without proper authorization. Much of it is cooperative, as with agreements to prevent development of some weapons, limit the multiplication of others, eliminate particularly nasty ones, and even work together in handling crises. Those who think true cooperation is unlikely in international politics argue that arms control reflects the distribution of power and that it occurs mostly when not needed, that is, when governments' interests are suitably aligned and they are not seriously at odds. When those governments again fall into serious conflict, arms control agreements will be ignored. Those more optimistic about cooperation see arms control as important in enhancing security because the process of establishing norms and rules means there is a degree of community and management in international politics, and because it limits, and provides information about, the military capabilities of states that ease their fears of each other.

Disarmament

Disarmament is different from arms control, and I have a discussion of it here only because it overlaps—in some activities—with arms control and because it is an alternative that now gets more respect. Like arms control, disarmament is an old idea. Its advocates claim that arms are, in themselves, direct causes of war and facilitators of resorting to war, that the incidence of war would be greatly reduced if arms were eliminated, and that disarmament can be carried out. It has often been put forward as a way to deal with war all by itself but can be pursued as an adjunct to other approaches discussed in this book.

The essence of disarmament is to get rid of arms, broadly defined to include military forces, and possibly going so far as to eliminate facilities for developing arms or even arrangements for drafting and training soldiers. This overlaps with arms control in various ways. Getting rid of particularly noxious weapons is certainly disarmament with respect to those weapons, but it is arms control if there is no intent to get rid of all other weapons, too. Partial disarmament results if the intent of reducing and eliminating certain weapons is to eventually eliminate other weapons, too; otherwise, it is arms control.

Proposals for disarmament are as old as international politics but were seldom taken seriously. Disarmament suffered a grave setback in the twentieth century. After World War I the winners imposed severe arms cutbacks—virtual disarmament—on the losers. They also joined in attempts to cut everyone's arms back. However, it was well known that countries were cheating. By the mid-1930s the main loser in World War I, Germany, was openly arming again; other countries were beginning to follow suit; and an international arms race was under way. World War II soon followed.

After the war the victorious allies again imposed disarmament on the losers and to this day, as a result, Japan has never become a normally armed great power. A major effort also was made to get nuclear disarmament. Under a U.S. proposal a small world government to manage all nuclear affairs would have been created, to prevent the further development of nuclear weapons by any national government. Once it was in place the United States, it said, would then destroy its nuclear weapons. The Soviet Union objected to such a glaring breach of national sovereignty and to the fact that the United States would know how to create nuclear weapons but no one else would. As a result, no disarmament occurred, the Soviet Union exploded its first nuclear device in 1949, and other countries eventually followed the same path. While disarmament talks continued on and off for the next decade or so, hope for success was never high. Western Europe and the United States substantially rearmed, and the Soviet Union never cut its forces to low levels in the first place. Instead of disarmament nuclear arsenals climbed steadily, and more nuclear powers appeared. After 1954 West Germany had an army again, within the framework of NATO, and the Soviet Union allowed East Germany to rearm. Japan never developed normal armed forces but eventually its defense budget became the third largest in the world. China, India, the two Koreas, and other countries built up large forces. Small countries such as Israel became powerful in terms of military equipment, the size of the population ready to be used for military action, and the portion of the gross domestic product devoted to military spending. In other words there was no disarmament. Interest in arms control emerged because it was so much more feasible, more realistic. Disarmament seemed like a pipe dream so arms control was pursued instead.

With the end of the Cold War, and even before it was over, the urge to reconsider disarmament returned. Perhaps the first major step was the Intermediate-Range Nuclear-Forces Treaty in 1987. This arms control treaty had important potential implications for disarmament. Under the agreement the United States and USSR (and joined by West Germany) would give up more than twenty-six hundred short- and intermediate-range ballistic and cruise missiles, based on land, that carried nuclear weapons. The missiles had a range of from five hundred to fifty-five hundred kilometers and carried nuclear weapons. The argument was that these weapons, based mostly in Europe, were too attractive as surprise or first-strike weapons there or in the Far East. After all, some could get to their targets fifteen hundred or more miles away in as little as ten minutes and strike with high accuracy. The larger implications of the treaty were threefold. First, it was a breakthrough—for the first time the superpowers were eliminating an entire weapons system. Second, the agreement required extensive verification, suggesting that similar verification would now be possible for other nuclear and conventional weapons deals. Third, the Soviet leader Mikhail S. Gorbachev shortly thereafter began saying he wanted to do away with all nuclear weapons, opening up the possibility that disarmament could spread.

With the end of the Cold War came major steps that are hard to classify. The United States and Russia have made a series of agreements to cut their strategic nuclear forces from about ten thousand to twelve thousand to about seventeen hundred to twenty-two hundred by 2012. But because many of the weapons will not be destroyed, just mothballed, the disarmament involved is half-hearted. South Africa decided to dismantle its nuclear weapons and the program that had developed them. The Chemical Weapons Convention and the Biological Weapons Convention outlawed the use of those weapons in 1993 and 1975, respectively, and the United States and Russia have begun in earnest the process of destroying their huge stockpiles. Various states established a moratorium on the production of plutonium for weapons. Almost all states signed the treaty banning all nuclear weapons tests. Campaigns emerged to do away with all nuclear weapons, efforts that involved leading ex-military officers and high officials who said their governments were badly mistaken in thinking that nuclear weapons were ever useful and necessary and could be kept on alert for decades without ever being used somewhere. Efforts to control proliferation did not die down; instead, they expanded. The United States joined with other great powers to put pressure on North Korea to abandon nuclear weapons, and after the 1991 Persian Gulf War the UN made a significant effort to force Iraq to give up all its weapons of mass destruction and dismantle its programs for developing them. And then there was the land mines treaty.

This sounds like disarmament. Given that it was accompanied by a significant drop in world military spending (the U.S. defense budget went down by one-quarter to one-third), big cuts in the nuclear weapons based in Europe, and big cuts in all European armed forces, it looks even more like disarmament. As a result disarmament has to be taken more seriously. Evidently, under certain political conditions major cuts in military forces can take place. And if **democratic peace theory** is correct—the idea that modern democracies do not make war on each other—and if democracy spreads, then less need will exist for traditional military forces designed to make large-scale war.

CONCLUSION

How well do the three strategies of deterrence, arms control, and disarmament provide security at the systemic, state, and societal levels?

Nuclear Deterrence

Evaluating nuclear deterrence has always been difficult and controversial. It has strong supporters and ardent detractors. The evidence and the debate remain inconclusive, but an attempt can be made to sort them out. At the systemic level nuclear deterrence is often given credit for preventing another world war, and some analysts feel that the world dare not try to live without it. The evidence cited is straightforward. After two world wars the international system experienced a profound political and ideological conflict among its most powerful members yet no third world war resulted. The Cold War remained a long, hard-fought stalemate. And it ended peacefully. The international system was then rearranged, which usually provokes wars, in a tranquil fashion. The great powers today live in relative harmony.

There is more evidence. The Cold War era saw the turmoil that resulted from the collapse of the European colonial empires and the end of the USSR. Dozens of new states and governments were created. Just as the decay and collapse of the Austro-Hungarian, Ottoman, and tsarist empires in Eastern Europe did much to bring about World Wars I and II, these developments offered endless opportunities for the rivalries, ambitions, and meddling of the great powers to turn into another world war. But it never happened. Instead, concern about keeping nuclear deterrence stable helped lead the superpowers to contain crises, restrain their friends and allies, limit nuclear proliferation, and prevent the escalation of small wars.

Finally, from a realist perspective, great states are so competitive, so fearful others will take advantage of them, and so driven by security dilemmas that they will fight rather than give up vital assets, lose great-power status, or be stripped of much of their territory. But the Soviet leaders accepted all of this without fighting. A realist perspective also would lead to the expectation that nuclear weapons were such a grave threat that great states must inevitably fear each other, making systemic security impossible. Yet with the end of the Cold War relations among the great powers have remained quiescent, with little fear of war among them.

Thus widespread agreement has been reached that nuclear deterrence has helped maintain systemic security. Only a few believe it was irrelevant. But is it mainly responsible? Its critics can make three arguments. First, by the end of World War II the great powers were sick of wars and would have avoided them even if nuclear weapons were not around. As in 1815, they were ready for an extended peace; nuclear deterrence was just a reinforcement. Second, with this in mind they would have been far less fearful of each other and created a safer international system, if it had not been for nuclear weapons. Those weapons helped stabilize the system but by putting the great powers and other states at constant risk of destruction. Nuclear deterrence helped control dangers and insecurity that nuclear weapons largely created.

Finally, nuclear deterrence may provide some systemic security, but deep trouble would result if it ever fails. A general nuclear war would shatter the international system. And there are too many ways a breakdown could occur. For example, the United States decided in the 1960s that deterrence stability required living with mutual vulnerability to being destroyed. Among other things this led the government to install a system under which its nuclear weapons could not be fired without the input at the launch sites of codes sent, with the order to fire, from Washington. The procedure was meant to prevent unauthorized launches. However, the U.S. armed forces felt that the only way they could carry out their mission to ensure survival of the nation was to strike as quickly as possible if a war broke out. So with nearly absolute secrecy about their planning, they designed attacks to destroy Soviet strategic forces and then arranged to launch intercontinental and possibly other missiles if controllers put in the required codes. Therefore, the weapons could have been fired with no codes being sent from Washington. Mutual deterrence was never as stable as was believed.

As for state security, no state with nuclear weapons has ever experienced an all-out war. It is unlikely this is just a coincidence. Furthermore, the states experienced no loss of sovereignty. In fact, nuclear weapons have been sought by states such as Iraq and North Korea as a guarantee of sovereignty and autonomy, much like the way Britain, China, and France developed nuclear weapons in part to be less dependent on a superpower ally.

However, nuclear weapons have proven to be extraordinarily difficult to use because of fear that doing so would bring international condemnation, more nuclear proliferation, and a weakening of barriers to deploy other nuclear powers. Nuclear weapons states have suffered attacks from and have fought with non-nuclear states. Having nuclear weapons was no guarantee of safety. Those states have even lost several wars—the United States in Vietnam, the Soviet Union in Afghanistan, and China in a short border conflict with Vietnam. They have fought at low levels among themselves at times. Nuclear weapons do not eliminate all foreign security problems. In fact, the **stability-instability paradox** contends that, when nuclear weapons provide stability, states can take advantage by attacking in non-nuclear ways and increasing the insecurity that nuclear weapons states confront. As seen in recent years, nuclear weapons offer no effective barrier to terrorist attacks. Almost all the nuclear weapons states have experienced terrorism (North Korea seems like an exception) inspired or even directed from outside their borders.

Another way nuclear weapons pose harsh threats to those who want them is the international reaction to proliferation. Both the Soviet Union and the United States considered attacking China to prevent it from developing nuclear weapons. The United States thought about doing the same with North Korea in the 1990s and did attack Iraq in 2003. Countries seeking nuclear weapons have suffered modestly (Libya, Pakistan) or gravely (Iraq, North Korea) from international sanctions. Getting its own nuclear arsenal might make a state feel less safe.

Nuclear weapons are also no antidote for internal wars. Nuclear deterrence is aimed at external threats. Governments have often hoped that obtaining these weapons would raise their prestige, make them a focus of national pride, and alleviate their domestic political difficulties (a factor of relevance in Iran, Iraq, Pakistan, and others). Often ignored is how a number of nuclear armed states have faced serious, even fatal, internal political disturbances. The Soviet Union collapsed. During the Cultural Revolution, a period of vast upheaval in China, the state nearly dissolved. While developing its nuclear weapons, France experienced a revolt, which led to the collapse of its Fourth Republic. Pakistan remains a highly precarious political system, and the fall of North Korea was widely anticipated in the 1990s. South Africa developed nuclear weapons but could not surmount the rising opposition to its apartheid system.

On societal security, any contribution to preventing large wars is of considerable value, because death and destruction are avoided. Nuclear weapons are, at least, cheap in comparison with maintaining large armies as they are less burdensome to taxpayers. Thus their real drawback is mainly hypothetical: What happens if deterrence fails and war ensues? Nuclear weapons are indiscriminate, so long lasting in some of their effects, such as radiation, that they could devastate a society. What if there is an accident or unauthorized nuclear weapons explosion? That could easily be much worse than the Soviet Chernobyl nuclear reactor meltdown in 1986. What if terrorists can use a nuclear weapon, or the radioactive material for one, in an incident? It is painful even to think of the possibilities.

Harm to societies is more than hypothetical. The sites for development and production of nuclear weapons during the Cold War have serious radioactive contamination of the ground, ground water, and installations. At times some of those sites released serious amounts of radioactive contamination, damaging the health of people nearby. Russian nuclear reactors from submarines have been dumped in the ocean. Inadequate shielding from radioactivity on Russian subs damaged the health of the crews. (Seamen from one particular base, as the joke goes, could easily be identified because they glowed in the dark.) American accidents with nuclear weapons spewed radioactive materials over wide areas. Cleaning up the aftereffects of nuclear weapons will take many billions of dollars and years to accomplish.

Nuclear deterrence can help contain, but not end, the problem of war. It is so uneven in its results, so risky, and so unavoidably anxiety-producing that the result is a warped kind of security at best. If people are safer as a result, they are far from safe, and they have to continue to worry about how safe they are. Whatever safety is provided rests on capacities to do harm that human beings probably cannot be trusted to control indefinitely. They should always be trying to do better.

Arms Control

The security that arms control affords can be evaluated in a straightforward fashion, as being primarily an adjunct of deterrence. The most significant contribution of arms control, when properly developed, is to systemic security. The arms on which states rely for deterrence are made more tolerable in the totality of their relationships. They may all have arms but the arms seem less threatening, are less expensive, and are used in ways that do less damage. In particular, arms control makes deterrence more stable by getting states to forgo some dangerous practices and to undertake some more reassuring ones.

Arms control can also make an important contribution to state security. In the form of confidence-building measures such as pulling troops back from a contested border, it can be used to relax conflicts and ease the way for negotiations. It can contain the burdens of arms racing. It can ease security dilemmas, and it can reduce the uncertainty that often builds insecurity. And it does this via states' agreement to impose limitations on themselves. It does not have to be a threat to sovereignty. No supranational authorities of any great note are associated with arms control. Most agreements are enforced by the isolation of a violator by the other parties and the threat of reprisals in the face of significant violations.

A major exception, at least for some states, is the International Atomic Energy Agency (IAEA), which upholds the provisions of the Nuclear Nonproliferation Treaty. Once states sign the treaty and claim they do not have nuclear weapons, they must accept IAEA inspections and monitoring for verification. The IAEA inspections, and many other verification efforts, are normally not meant to be invasive and confrontational. States cooperate by identifying relevant institutions and other sites to be inspected, and the IAEA announces beforehand that it is coming. The inspection is not like the police showing up with a search warrant to ransack the place. Even so, the inspections can be intrusive and, when violations are detected, an IAEA report can trigger UN Security Council action or reactions by individual states including sanctions or other serious pressure. A number of states bitterly resent this as encroachment on their sovereignty and freedom of action, especially if they fear an attack by a nuclear-armed state (such as North Korea does) or are situated near states that have nuclear or other WMD (such as Iran with its WMD-armed neighbors India, Pakistan, Russia, and, Syria). These states have the partial sympathy of China's government. It strongly opposes nuclear proliferation but thinks a state, as sovereign, is entitled to develop whatever weapons it wants. Many states accept the need to stop nuclear proliferation but resent the way the nuclear powers stress nonproliferation while continuing to maintain their own nuclear weapons. And various governments, including China, North Korea, and Russia dislike being pressured to give up lucrative sales of nuclear technology just because it might promote proliferation. China, North Korea, and Pakistan have all secretly violated the ban in the Nuclear Nonproliferation Treaty on helping others develop nuclear weapons.

The United States also now objects to some arms control agreements as threats to its freedom of action. The Clinton administration refused to sign the land mines treaty because it would have intruded on decisions to keep mines where the United States thinks they are still necessary, particularly in South Korea. Reflecting conservative views that multilateral agreements and organizations threaten U.S. sovereignty, the George W. Bush administration expressed no interest in trying to ratify the Comprehensive Test Ban Treaty and withdrew from the Anti-Ballistic Missile Treaty that bans national missile defense systems.

Arms control is also supposed to be of benefit to societal security. It is beneficial when it reduces military burdens or cuts fears of war. Arms control has always been about trying to get the destructiveness and butchery of war under control, which is another contribution to societal security. One of the earliest forms of arms control was development in the early 1600s of the "laws of war," general understandings of how civilized people should conduct that most uncivilized activity. Arms control thinking has contributed to the absence of nuclear warfare since 1945 and the emergence of earnest efforts to eliminate chemical and biological weapons. The land mines treaty may save thousands of lives and crippling incidents every year.

What can be said about its effectiveness? The record is mixed. When serious arms control thinking emerged, the ultimate objective was to convince people and governments that cooperation to control arms was possible among states in serious conflict, that they could rise above political conflicts to reach agreements in the common interest. But the modern history of arms control suggests this is not the case. Most significant agreements have emerged when there was something of a lull in conflicts or were reached among states that had few conflicts among themselves. Agreements have often not been ratified or have been ignored or violated, when the parties had serious conflicts or little domestic political agreement existed about signing the treaties. In short, international and domestic politics get in the way. When conflict is high, trust is low. A proposed agreement will be viewed with suspicion. People will charge that the other side will cheat or that if the other side wants the agreement it must be harmful to their side or that just to negotiate is displaying weakness. When conflict is high, the parties question every little thing about each other's behavior, probing for cheating or plans to renounce the agreement. They often go right to the edge of the agreement as protection against cheating or in preparation for cheating themselves, or they do everything allowed, which inevitably leads to perceptions of cheating and certainly a lack of good intent. Thus several major arms control agreements could be signed and ratified only when domestic political conditions were right. Arms control is neither an antidote to the vagaries of politics nor a way to end or evade serious conflicts.

As for specific effects, the strategic arms limitation agreements were a subject of jokes for years because they controlled weapons by setting an enormously high level on how many were allowed and because governments regularly built loopholes into the limitations or signed the agreements knowing they could get around them. The United States and Soviet Union agreed to a strict limit on strategic ballistic missiles in 1972, knowing they were soon going to put MIRVs on each missile, so their total strategic arsenals would grow by several hundred percent over the next decade. Countries have violated the nonproliferation arrangements for political reasons and commercial motives. The long-standing ban on using chemical weapons was grossly violated in the1980s Iran-Iraq war. A series of countries developed nuclear weapons in the 1980s and 1990s or had such programs under way. Attempts to impose serious limits on sales of conventional weapons have been a failure.

But there is another side. The complete absence of nuclear warfare since 1945 is a tribute to arms control thinking. The land mines treaty is a nice piece of work. Nuclear weapons are much safer from accidents and unauthorized use than they used to be. Recently, there has been a rapidly declining threshold of what is considered an acceptable level of death and destruction in a war by advanced nations. The rule in international law that only the force necessary should be used and nonmilitary effects should be held to a minimum has become more prominent. The change is attributable to a shift in attitudes and demonstrations that technology can make for much more precise weapons. Considerably more transparency exists about weapons and military forces than there used to be, partly because of agreements and because of accumulated arms control experience with developing reliable verification arrangements and technologies.

Disarmament

To date, disarmament has had limited use. Steep cuts have been made in some kinds of weapons and forces, but the reductions have leveled off. Disarmament is not relied on for systemic security, and the evidence is that it will not be for the foreseeable future. The only great power to have a low level of military might is Japan, and it is now edging toward a decision to become a normal great power in this regard. Spending on national defense indicates that few of the larger countries are counting on disarmament to boost security in the international system.

Thus in state security as well, disarmament had made only a modest contribution. In areas where the greatest progress has occurred in shrinking interstate warfare—Europe, North America, South America, and East Asia—it has come without eliminating armaments. Disarmament is evidently not considered a requirement for state security.

Disarmament has made the least progress in the area of societal security, and that has had severe effects in some places. In many countries internal warfare has been facilitated by easy access to small arms. They are available internationally—sold, resold, stolen, smuggled, and given away. The private sector in small arms alone amounts to more than a billion dollars a year (although measuring this is difficult). Modern small arms make civil wars more lethal and destructive, and civilians are usually the main victims. Little has been done to pursue disarmament with these weapons, and many experts doubt it would work if tried. When disarmament of the parties is tried as part of peace agreements it often helps, but it also often fails. (The arms are never abandoned.) Even when it helps, if the peace agreement begins to fail the parties find it easy, in many cases, to rearm.

Final Assessment

Nuclear deterrence, the foremost strategy for dealing with war's threat to international security during the Cold War, graduated from a narrow national approach into a somewhat cooperative effort at system management, involved enormous expense, and put virtually everyone potentially at risk. The approach has been important in undermining the attractions of cheap victory strategies. In conjunction with arms control it did a good deal to prevent another world war, even as the international system was mired in an exceedingly dangerous political-ideological conflict that invited despair at the chances of avoiding another great war.

At the same time this strategy was disturbing. Huge capacities for immediate destruction piled up. The stability of nuclear deterrence could not be guaranteed, even with the help of unprecedented arms control efforts. No wonder the great powers retreated from overwhelming reliance on it when they got the chance after the Cold War dissolved.

Deterrence does not require nuclear weapons. This chapter has focused on nuclear deterrence because it has been the most prominent, most elaborate, and most theoretically explored application of the strategy. However, studies of non-nuclear deterrence efforts find that the same flaws generally apply. Doubts that it can reliably prevent war are greater than with nuclear deterrence.

When the great powers reduced their reliance on deterrence, they turned to arms control measures that overlap considerably with disarmament. As such, a renewed interest arose in this approach in recent years. But the attempt to prevent the development of new nuclear powers has not been completely successful and currently there is real concern that more are on the way. While significant reductions have been made in Cold War–driven military establishments, plenty of others have stayed large or have grown. Disarmament has not displaced deterrence, and the problem of war's threat to security remains.

Disarmament requires an extreme level of cooperation among states. Arms control insisted that cooperation could be pursued in a serious conflict, and success in arms control has carried cooperation to previously unheard of lengths.

The focus here now shifts to expanded international cooperation in other ways and on other matters in dealing with warfare.

SOURCES AND OTHER USEFUL READINGS

The literature on deterrence, and on the related practice of compellence, is vast. Fairly recent works that cover much of the subject of deterrence in theory and practice include Patrick Morgan, *Deterrence Now;* Lawrence Freedman, *The Evolution of Nuclear Strategy* and *Strategic Coercion;* Robert Jervis, *The Meaning of the Nuclear Revolution;* and Keith B. Payne, *Fallacies of Cold War Deterrence and a New Direction.* Each also cites all the classic works on the subject.

On the debate over whether nuclear deterrence prevented another world war, see Morgan and Payne, listed above, who describe the arguments and list supporters of the view that it did; and John A. Vasquez, "The Deterrence Myth," and John Mueller, *Retreat from Doomsday,* who hold the opposite view.

The story of the manipulation of the launch codes on U.S. nuclear weapons is recounted in Bruce Blair, "Keeping Presidents in the Nuclear Dark" (Episode #1: The Case of the Missing "Permissive Action Links").

The literature on arms control and disarmament is equally vast. A good guide to the existing arms control agreements including their disarmament aspects is Josef Goldblat, *Arms Control.* The broad debate about arms control in recent years, with a pro–arms control perspective, is reviewed in Jeffrey A. Larsen's *Arms Control.*

CHAPTER 6

The Great-Power Concert

Strategies that governments have devised for dealing with war's threat to international security that are basically national in character or origin can be carried out by several states simultaneously as well as by one state alone. A power distribution approach calls for a national government to try to adjust the power arrangement in the international system to suit its needs, with the distribution of power then being what results from the combination of the states' individual efforts. The rivalry of the states produces the result. A cheap victory strategy is almost always adopted by a single government to meet only its needs. That government might extend its protection to others, but basically it works out a way of keeping itself safe and by its own efforts. Deterrence was constructed initially as a unilateral effort, then was extended to cover other states and via their efforts as well. But it did not involve close cooperation with the other side by plan. Only over time did deterrence, especially when arms control considerations arose, become cooperative management of a sort. Even disarmament, which would normally be undertaken in a collective effort, has sometimes been pursued by a state unilaterally.

The goal of explicitly cooperative, collectively oriented strategies is to limit or prevent costly, especially intolerably costly, wars. But the means chosen involve trying to get a number of governments to work together, including governments that would otherwise be likely to be in conflict or even at war with each other. Thus discussion of these strategies focuses not on alliances formed for winning a war or holding off an attacker but on what can be considered variants of cooperative management of the international system to maintain security.

Cooperation can be carried on in several ways, and one of the more venerable is called a **great-power concert**. No, this is not a bunch of national bands gathered together to make music. Governments coordinate foreign policies, not notes. The term *concert* refers to people concerting their efforts, that is, making their efforts go together to achieve some aim. A great-power concert is an agreement among the most important states in an international system to work together on security-related matters.

The basic idea is not strange or odd. When any group of actors must confront an uncertain environment, which is the case in the anarchical international system, and when the group's ability to get that environment under control is frustrated by conflicts among the members, one possible step involves members working together to run the system jointly. What is required for doing this?

To begin with, the great powers must have to have some strong reasons to want to behave in this way, such as wanting to avoid big wars, especially systemwide wars. Several analysts contend that the great powers are most likely to feel strongly about coordinating their actions just after a great war, when they have experienced the worst of the costs and burdens of widespread fighting. Having done each other a great deal of harm, the governments are inclined to cooperate so they can stop periodically hacking away at each other. Others believe that the same result sometimes emerges when the great powers have just passed through a dangerous crisis. For example, they were suddenly on the edge of a vast war and frightful images were conjured up of the awful things that could happen. When the crisis was surmounted, the collective sigh of relief was accompanied by fear that next time everyone would not be so lucky. The governments involved thus were amenable to working together to prevent that next time from arriving. Another reason sometimes cited is the fear found among the winners of the last great war that, if they do not continue to cooperate in peacetime, the loser(s) will eventually mount a huge war to take back what was lost. Finally, the cooperation needed to achieve victory in the last great war can have lasting effects. Having learned to cooperate in such a desperate cause the participants may find it much easier to continue to do so after the war is over, and they may entice the loser(s) into joining the group.

My view is that if the prospective harm from another great war is awful enough, then consideration will be given to a concert even if the other factors are not present. Recent developments tend to confirm this as do elements of the U.S.-Soviet relationship during the Cold War.

THE MAIN ELEMENTS OF A CONCERT

Several things define a great-power concert. All the great powers in the system usually are involved, not just some of them. All are entitled to participate and normally all of them would. One might decline to participate, and the concert could go forward without it, but that situation is rare. Normally great powers are eager to have a say about everything of importance as part of the role they see themselves playing in the world. A concert also can be said to have a significant number of the great powers participating, but this is not a popular view. For instance, at one point during the Cold War all the other great powers agreed to cooperate, to an extent, against the Union of Soviet Socialist Republics (USSR), but no one refers to this as a concert. A collection of great powers operating against another is better considered an alliance. A concert includes either the participation of all the great powers or the acquiescence to the concert's doings of a great power that does not fully participate.

In a concert, great powers agree they need to cooperatively manage the (relevant) international system—global or regional—for purposes of security.[1] They could be trying to do this to keep peace among themselves. Or they could have concluded that conflicts among other members of the system, or inside those members, are too dangerous, and too provocative and thus must be dealt with. Or they might be concerned that some conflict, if left unattended, is likely to escalate in dangerous ways, for example, into a war with nuclear weapons used or one with many states being drawn into it, or one with a high level of atrocities, refugees, and other disturbing effects.

Because all the great powers are to participate in system management, the concert will almost always act on the basis of unanimity, at least to the extent that every member acquiesces in any group decision of importance. Otherwise, a cluster of some members could gang up on another one, which would look more like traditional international politics and not much like cooperative management. If unanimity is required, then each great power has a veto. Two rules apply.

1. The members do not go forward with any decision as a group if they do not all agree.

2. No individual member goes forward on its own on a matter of great importance to the group when the group is not supportive. If members can go ahead on their own, then cooperation is being circumvented and the concert begins to collapse.

These two rules need not apply in every case. It might be, and it is to be expected, that the concert is so important to the members that it can survive their disagreement on some particular issue. For example, one member disagrees and goes off in a huff, while the others do what they agree on. But this situation cannot arise often or the concert is breaking down.

Unanimity could be a crippling requirement, preventing much action by the concert. After all, how often would all the great powers agree on everything? But it makes sense if each member is entitled to have no important decision made or action taken that it finds humiliating or damaging to its interests. Some disagreements thus would be allowed on lesser matters without bringing the concert crashing down. Members also could abstain when they could not support a matter but did not consider it vital to their concerns.

---

[1] The term *concert* usually does not refer to collective management of other things. A small group of major financial powers runs the international financial system, and a different small group is in charge of the world trade system. Neither is regularly said to be a concert, a term that is applied to security management. However, they are concerts in the way they operate and their responsibilities, and in the future they may be called concerts if a much broader conception of security continues to be employed.

A crippling condition could be created if some or all of the great powers constantly insist on getting their own way all the time and define their interests accordingly. Hence, another element in a great-power concert is that the members exercise a degree of restraint in their foreign policies. They cannot behave like they have normally in the past, each trying to get its own way as often as possible, digging in its heels to get concessions to its views, and refusing to cooperate if it does not get what it wants. And they cannot be constantly trying to make major gains at each other's expense, which has also been normal great-power behavior. Instead, the members have to accept some limits on the objectives that they pursue and the means they use. Otherwise they will not be able to cooperate for long. In particular, this means that they must

- Avoid pushing any conflicts with each other to the point of war, or even to the point of a serious breach in their relations; and

- Not go looking for opportunities to obtain a special advantage, including some gain for themselves at the others' expense.

Thus they have to try to pursue their particular objectives within the framework of the other members' interests, always keeping those in mind, too. In effect, they have to define their own national interest as requiring that they avoid stepping on the other members' toes because they want the concert to survive.

Because such behavior is rare among great powers in the history of international politics, some analysts believe that a concert is most likely to work well if the parties are homogeneous, for instance, if they are all monarchies, or are fearful of democracy, or are democracies, or are highly interrelated in some other way. Or perhaps they should all be basically status quo governments. In short, they should have enough in common that they will not be at each other's throats. This can also be a crippling requirement because great powers have often been significantly different from one another in the nature of their political systems or their foreign policy preferences. Allowances have to be made by concert members for such differences when possible.

The final element of a concert, therefore, is that each great power must largely avoid intruding into the internal affairs or spheres of influence of the others. This is problematic because concern and pressure with respect to internal affairs are considered much more acceptable than they used to be and, with rising interdependence among nations, they are increasingly hard to avoid. So it is a less absolute requirement than it once was. However, it is still necessary for members to live and let live a good deal when it comes to each other's internal affairs (in human rights abuses, for example).

In summary, a great-power concert involves limited cooperation on a voluntary basis. Hence autonomous decision making is not markedly compromised. The idea is cooperation for limited, security-related management of a regional or international system. While the great powers are supposed to take the interests of others into consideration, they likely will give primary attention in their decisions as a concert to their own interests. Limited cooperation is used to manage relations among competitive entities to keep the competition within bounds and maximize the benefits for all. Does this sound familiar? It is roughly what an **oligopoly** or a cartel involves. In an oligopoly the key firms in some industry collude to stabilize the market. They divvy much of it up amongst themselves, preventing all-out competition and thus making life easier for all the members. And no one has ever accused oligopolies of being altruistic. Consider a concert as an oligopolistic sort of arrangement, but do not call it an oligopoly because that term is usually reserved for economic management; it is a concert instead. (Occasionally, certain domestic political arrangements are referred to as oligopolies as well.)

This arrangement is enforced by the great powers acting more or less collectively. Enforcement is not against each other but against the other members of the system, making sure that they behave themselves. The great powers enforce the system against themselves only in that, if one or more of them misbehaves, the others can drop out of the concert so that it collapses. All the parties then lose the benefits of their arrangement. For the members, as for those of an oligopoly, the concert is self-enforcing. Each member has to restrain itself and keep within the limits.

This suggests that a concert is not going to be successful or will not last long unless the national interests of the great powers are roughly the same or are clearly parallel or congruent. Without this, they cannot be expected to cooperate for an extended period of time, especially on a wide variety of problems. Many analysts suggest that any concert is always temporary because the great powers are not saints. Sooner or later one will be tempted to grab too much of something for itself and ignore the interests of the others. If and when the others respond in kind, the cooperation on which the concert has rested collapses.

Finally, a concert is not associated with a particular institutional form or standard pattern. There is no cookie-cutter mold. The members might cooperate by meeting in periodic conferences, or by setting up an organization (like a board of directors), or by having constant interaction through some standard meeting place where they all have ambassadors. These days they might even cooperate through e-mail communications. However they do it, the members try to run the international system so that it is highly orderly—order is the primary objective of a concert in normal circumstances. In effect, security starts with having an orderly system. How can orderliness be determined? It is when certain kinds of behavior that the system members tend to find disturbing is repressed or sanctioned by someone so that system members behave mostly in safe, predictable ways. The concert might declare that war is unacceptable, or that the objectives of any war must be limited, or that the proliferation of some weapons is to be avoided. The unacceptable behavior would be that which violated the underlying norms. It could be domestic; for example, a declaration that steps to change governments must take place in acceptable ways. Or certain types of governments might be outlawed. Internal affairs also could be treated as beyond reach for outsiders. The only rules in play apply to each nation's foreign policy, and at home it can do what it likes. An orderly system will have various rules and norms at work, and the members' behavior will fit well together.

THE STRATEGY IN PRACTICE

A great-power concert is not simply a hypothetical community.

The Concert of Europe

The most famous example, the one from which the term *concern* originated, is the Concert of Europe. It emerged right after the Napoleonic Wars, which ended in 1815. Napoleon had run riot in Europe for two decades, making war all over the continent. By the time a suitable coalition of states figured out how to defeat him for the last time, states were ready for some serious management of the system. The Concert of Europe was the result. It was put together primarily by the leaders of the British and Austrian empires and included the empires of Russia and Prussia, and eventually the kingdom of France. The Concert and a subunit of sorts, called the Holy Alliance, involved some special cooperation by Austria, Prussia, and Russia.

The Concert rested on agreement among the members that they had a special responsibility for maintaining the peace of Europe. No one voted to hand them that responsibility, they just announced that it was theirs. After all, they were the dominant states in the system and fought most of the wars. So who else could maintain peace? As for the Holy Alliance, it concerned itself with preventing the spread of democratic revolutions, particularly in Central Europe. Such a revolution brought Napoleon to power in France, and democratic ideas made every monarchy uneasy.

The Concert tried to settle disputes over boundaries and territory, to mediate other issues, and to impose settlements when necessary. For example, the Concert helped create the nation of Belgium because it occupied a territory so strategically important that no major state in Western Europe was willing to let another major state own or control it. Belgium was created and declared by the Concert to be independent and neutral. In the end several great powers had to use force to convince Holland to go along. In addition, the Concert members agreed not to fall into quarrels over the Ottoman Empire, the "sick man of Europe." Quarrels over grabbing pieces of it would normally have produced periodic warfare. Finally, the Concert members agreed to reintegrate the defeated France into the system as a regular great power and Concert member, lest it become embittered or work to undermine the Concert. The Holy Alliance, in turn, militarily intervened to beat down democratic revolutions in several countries, earning Russia the title of "gendarme of Europe."

The members gathered in conferences whenever significant problems emerged. As Europe was going through a turbulent era (see Figure 6-1), numerous conferences were held. The Concert is usually said to have lasted until 1848 or until the 1853 Crimean War, which pitted Russia against France and Great Britain. It was just the sort of thing the Concert was supposed to prevent. A few analysts see it as having revived in a weakened form after the 1860s. Even fewer see it as having lasted until 1914, citing the resolution of several major crises by international conferences in the years prior to World War I. The fact that it collapsed and died is well known, but just when is debated. My preference is 1853.

Why did it collapse? Well, scholars do not fully agree on that either. Generating possible explanations is easy, but confirming them is tough. One line of analysis stresses memory. War is hell, but those who experienced it die out and others then

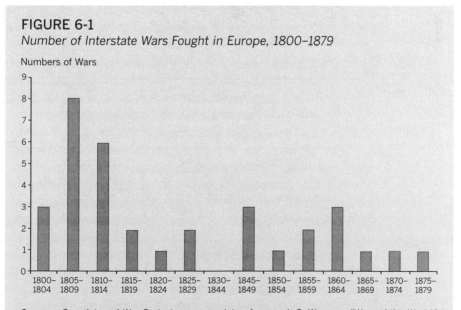

FIGURE 6-1
Number of Interstate Wars Fought in Europe, 1800–1879

Numbers of Wars

Sources: Correlates of War Project, www.correlatesofwar.org/; OnWar.com, "Wars of the World," www.onwar.com/aced/chrono/index.htm; and Wikipedia, "Napoleonic Wars," en.wikipedia.org/wiki/Napoleonic_Wars.

recall the glory or nurse the grievances. Eventually going to war becomes acceptable once more. In this view, the Concert of Europe lasted until the generation of leaders that had fought Napoleon passed on. A related explanation is that it lasted until fear of France declined, fear that the France of Napoleon would come back and wreak havoc again.

Other analysts argue that the members of the Concert gradually became less alike. Britain and France moved steadily in the direction of democracy and capitalism, while Austria-Hungary and Russia remained much more monarchical and feudal. Germany was in between, beginning as a booming capitalist system and an aristocratic political system and then slowly becoming more democratic. Also often cited is a gradual loss of consensus about the status quo. The primary examples were the efforts to create what became the modern states of Germany and Italy. The creation of Germany posed grave difficulties because the Concert members could not easily welcome a new and powerful state, and a potentially powerful Italy as well, because that would make all the others a good deal less powerful. They resisted, one way or another. The second Prussian war to unify Germany was against Austria and the third was against France; members sought to militarily offset the new Germany's power and its plans to build a colonial empire. Maintaining a consensus about propping up the Ottoman Empire also became increasingly difficult. Rising nationalist currents among the peoples in the Balkan part of the empire threatened to break it up completely, which only whetted the appetites of the neighbors to seize pieces for themselves when the end came.

The frictions and tensions over the rise of Germany and Italy and the decline of the Ottoman Empire suggest another explanation. In the highly dynamic nineteenth century in Europe, major states experienced uneven rates of development. When such a situation persists long enough, sharp alterations in the distribution of power result. Some great powers do not look so great while new ones are emerging. As a result, the influence of a Concert's members, or even its membership, is called into question. And the changing fortunes of the members can make it harder for them to cooperate and agree on how to share the burdens of management. As I said, there is no shortage of explanations. Whatever the reason, the concert broke down and then it gradually disappeared.

The Interwar Years

The idea of a concert was largely forgotten in the early part of the twentieth century. It was not revived until after World War II. Modest efforts were made to recreate a concert in the 1920s in the Locarno agreements, now forgotten, to sort out Europe's political arrangements and to avoid war. A much more serious failure in the 1930s was the attempt by the British and French to draw Germany and Italy into cooperative great-power management of the European system. The Germans, big losers in World War I, and the Italians were seeking to play a large role on the world scene at the expense, inevitably, of the power of Britain and France. The Russians, also big losers in the conflict, had dropped out as a great power and were therefore largely ignored in this scheme. The Soviet government was a pariah, living on the periphery of European affairs partly by choice and partly because of others' efforts to isolate it. (One result of a new concert would have been to reinforce that isolation.)

Facing a restive Germany and Italy and strongly fearing another great war, Britain and France began by reluctantly accepting Italy's desire to build an empire in East Africa (Ethiopia)—meaning that they resisted, but not very hard. Then they made concessions to Germany. The German border with France had been a demilitarized zone partly controlled by France since 1919. Adolf Hitler wanted it back. He also wanted to rearm Germany, ending the limitations imposed by the peace agreements. And he wanted to merge Austria with Germany. All this Britain and France eventually conceded. Then Hitler insisted that the German-populated part of Czechoslovakia also be added to Germany—a dangerous demand because Czechoslovakia was allied with France, which was allied with Britain. The solution was a summit conference of the four governments in Munich in March 1938. Hitler was allowed to do what he wanted and thus dictate the political arrangements for European international politics. The four governments announced they would cooperate to maintain peace in Europe. This is precisely how a concert would work.

But it never got started. German ambitions were much too great and the partners had little in common. The two fascist states and two democracies could get along only by holding their noses. Most important was that Hitler was willing to go to war to expand Germany's national territory even further. He felt he could win any prospective war quickly and cheaply. Thus the availability of a cheap victory strategy helped undermine the alternative approach of a concert. It took only a few months for the agreement in Munich to begin to break down. Germany gobbled up the rest of Czechoslovakia, giving some of it to other neighbors to earn influence with them, and Hitler began demanding a piece of Poland, which had belonged to Germany until 1918. The British and French would not make concessions this time, and the result was the start in 1939 of what would become World War II.

Post–World War II and Cold War Attempts at Concerts

World War II gave rise to another serious effort at a concert. The United States took the lead in designing the United Nations (UN) to help manage global security, with the following ideas in mind. First, peace after the war was going to depend, in large part, on good relations among the key Western states, the Soviet

Union, and eventually China. Next, the great powers would have to cooperate by managing the peace. They would have to restrain themselves, not interfere in each other's domestic affairs, and take action against breaches of the peace by others. This was the basis for the design of the UN Security Council. The great powers—the United States, USSR, Britain, France (at that time Britain and France still ruled a large part of the world through their empires), and China—were made permanent members, with other states rotating as the ten temporary members. Each permanent member was given a veto over decisions on any substantive issues, the idea being that the Council was to act only if the great powers all agreed. If they wanted it to work, they would have to find ways to agree. The veto each had would ensure that the Council would not interfere in a permanent member's internal affairs either. The basic elements of an institutionalized great-power concert were written into the UN Charter.

As a concert the Security Council was given extensive powers to deal with threats to peace and security. It could condemn a state's actions, order a boycott of or impose other sanctions against the offender, order UN members to send forces to deal with it, and even fight a war to maintain peace and security. Naturally, the hope was that persuasion and pressure, from the world's strongest countries, would do the trick. Hence the Council was to provide a form of deterrence. But if that did not work, then the Council members could resort to force.

Some background elements also suggested how the concert was to work. In the UN Charter and in other steps taken by the great powers there were elements of a spheres-of-influence approach. A **sphere of influence** is a geographical area a state dominates, usually because that area is on or near its borders and it is much more powerful than the others located there. The United States put in the charter a reference to regional security arrangements to permit what it soon created as the Organization of American States, for North America and South America, which were its traditional sphere of influence. The Russians soon demarcated their own sphere in Eastern Europe, while Britain and France had no intention of giving up their empires and the spheres of influence, particularly in the Middle East, that went with them. Another element at work was a shared desire to keep Germany from surging back to set off another war to recover its lost territories.

This concert never worked, virtually from the start. The political conflicts among the great powers were too great and soon grew into the Cold War, which was to last for more than four decades. They disagreed over what to do about Germany, what kinds of political systems to develop in Europe and in former Japanese colonies, how to manage Europe's affairs, the future of the colonial empires, what to do about nuclear weapons—about nearly everything. There was little great-power political cooperation in the Security Council for years. The initial lineup was the Soviet Union against the other four. China was a Soviet ally during the years when its communist government was not recognized by the United States and could not, therefore, sit on the Security Council (what is now Taiwan sat in that seat). By the time China was finally admitted in 1971, it was usually at odds with the Soviet Union. As a result, the Soviet Union often still was pitted against the other four, though China often also disagreed with the Western powers. The United States often cast vetoes as well, such as on anti–Israel votes. It did not help that the wartime cooperation between the Soviet Union and its Western allies had not gone smoothly. Even while they were allies, Soviet behavior provoked Western suspicion and irritation as did the constant Soviet suspicion about Western motives and intentions. Also important was that from Joseph Stalin's perspective as ruler of the Soviet Union, any cooperation could be dangerous. Cooperation could allow Western influences to seep in and gradually undermine his political system, and he sharply limited the cooperative interactions with outsiders he would allow. Meanwhile the British never had much confidence in a concert anyway. They believed instead in getting a suitable balance of power in Europe by drawing the United States into an alliance with Britain, France, and others to more than offset Soviet power. In the end this is what happened.

The Cold War era produced another effort to construct a concert. Henry A. Kissinger, President Richard M. Nixon's alter ego on foreign policy, had written his Ph.D. dissertation on the creation of the Concert of Europe. As U.S. involvement in the Vietnam War was winding down in the early 1970s Nixon and Kissinger, as secretary of state, launched an effort to create a concert once again. They announced that Western Europeans and Japan, now fully recovered from World War II, were ready and eager to play a larger role in managing world affairs. Nixon and Kissinger also took steps to draw China into a more normal role as a great power by radically transforming U.S.-China policy in 1971 and sought to do the same with the Soviet Union by launching a policy of détente in 1972. They claimed that an "era of negotiations" had arrived in East-West relations, with opportunities to reach major arms control agreements and settle various other conflicts. Furthermore, they said that in the nuclear age the great powers could readily appreciate the need to negotiate to avoid war. These sentiments signaled that the United States itself would be far less suspicious about negotiations than it had been earlier in the Cold War. The Nixon and Kissinger view presumed that the great powers had at least several important security interests in common and thus would be ready to restrain their rivalries and moderate their foreign policies. With intense competition being too risky, they could move to arms control deals, trying to avoid crises and practicing crisis management. Presumably, under this kind of cooperation, with every great power having a role to play and not being left out, each would be relatively satisfied with the status quo.

This was the officially presented framework for many aspects of U.S. foreign policy thereafter.

- Strategic Arms Limitation Talks (SALT) negotiations with the Soviet Union on strategic arms control;

- Agreements with the Soviet Union on trade, medical research cooperation, crisis avoidance, cooperation in space, and so on;

- Détente with China, including treating Beijing as the legitimate government of China, approving of China taking a Security Council seat, and engaging in normal relations on many matters; and

- Statements that strategic parity in nuclear weapons with the Soviet Union had arrived as a way of conceding a higher status to Moscow than before.

But it was too good to be true. Détente did not last long between the United States and the USSR, and a true concert never emerged. Why this was so is still debated (are you surprised?), but certain things stand out. Soviet leaders moved to use their new stature to rapidly expand their power and influence by such steps as increased interventions in the third world. They sought to emphasize that their power was rising while the United States, in the wake of the Vietnam War, was in decline. Soon critics were claiming that Moscow was exploiting détente, especially as its defense spending continued to rise and Soviet weapons programs did not slow down. In fact, signs indicated that the Soviet Union was seeking to erode the West's deterrence by developing a cheap victory strategy. A continuing lack of homogeneity also was evident in the great powers' political systems. For its part, the United States failed to follow through on several matters. For example, Nixon's proposed trade agreement with the Soviet Union, which Moscow wanted badly, was never implemented when Congress attached stiff conditions that the Soviet Union rejected, a reflection of the fact that détente lacked broad political support in Washington. The idea of cooperative crisis management was badly strained by the war in the Middle East in 1973. The United States charged that Moscow was using the Arab attack on Israel that started the war to seek a big gain for itself in the region, and the Soviet Union charged Washington with doing the same by arranging to end the war and pursue peace through talks run by Kissinger that left the Soviet Union out in the cold.

Just as damaging to the idea of a new concert was the continuing hostility between China and the Soviet Union. This hostility was more intense than in Soviet relations with the West. They had engaged in recent fighting along their border, were in the midst of continuing competitive military buildups as a result, and tended to regard each other as the most serious threats to their security. They would continue to struggle for dominance in East Asia for years, with the Soviet

Union trying to develop its own version of containment of China. No wonder the idea of a concert went nowhere.

The UN Security Council and Other Post–Cold War Attempts

Recently, the idea of a concert has been revived. When the Cold War ended, some suggested that, in Europe at least, a new concert was needed. Fears arose that otherwise the great powers in the European regional system would start to act independently and put an end to the North Atlantic Treaty Organization (NATO), that rivalries and tensions would increase, and that nuclear proliferation could result because Germany would want its own nuclear weapons. At the global level, the Security Council reasserted itself, becoming highly active in numerous international conflicts including intervening militarily, made possible by great-power cooperation. And a quiet cooperation was forged among the United States, Russia, China, and Japan to deal with the problem of North Korea.[2]

Nothing worked out well for the idea of a new concert in Europe. The main responsibility for security management on the continent has come to rest with a much enlarged NATO instead. Russia, which is not a member of NATO, participated in NATO interventions in Bosnia and Kosovo but only after loudly denouncing them. Only a tenuous relationship exists between the dominant Western states and a currently weak Russia—not a concert—and the Russians complain constantly about this. NATO and Russia have a regular consultative relationship. A Russian ambassador is stationed at NATO headquarters and there are monthly meetings for Russian interaction with NATO members, so a concert could easily be created. And Russia has been granted a vote along with NATO members on some matters. But Russia has never been granted a veto by NATO over European security management decisions so there is no decision by consensus. When Russia disagreed on important decisions about Bosnia and Kosovo, NATO went ahead with its plans just the same.

Things went somewhat better at first in Northeast Asia. A grave problem had been left over from the Cold War—the division since 1945 of Korea into two, usually bitterly hostile, states. The problem was of great concern to China, Japan, Russia, and the United States. South Korea was making great strides toward becoming one of the world's largest economies and a leading trading nation. North Korea, while remaining enormously militarized, began a precipitous economic decline, had a Stalinist totalitarian system, and was by its own choice one of the world's most isolated nations. By the late 1980s North Korea was trying to

---

[2] Various aspects of international economic affairs have continued to be managed by small groups of powerful states, too. These concert-like arrangements have continued to be important in the post–Cold War era.

develop nuclear weapons along with other weapons of mass destruction. Eventually it was also working on ballistic missiles, which it then sold to trouble-making states such as Iraq.

Through consultations, and some trial and error, the four great powers gradually worked out parallel policies. First, they all contributed to crippling and further isolating North Korea. The Russians and Chinese shifted somewhat toward the U.S.-Japanese position that North Korea was a troublesome, even dangerous, state. The Russians and the Chinese entered into diplomatic relations with South Korea and soon built extensive economic ties with it as well. At the same time they ended nearly all economic aid to North Korea, abandoned most trade with that country, and largely abandoned their alliances with it. Russia dropped its alliance, and while China remained willing to help defend North Korea, it indicated it would not support that government if it started or provoked another war between the two Koreas. As a result, North Korea became even further isolated and its economy went into a free-fall. Its gross domestic product shrank year after year, and a devastating famine broke out. North Korea fell into the bottom half of the world's countries in economic strength.

The United States was so concerned about North Korea's nuclear weapons program that it was inclined to continue strong economic sanctions and heavy political pressure. It withdrew its nuclear weapons from South Korea, hoping to entice North Korea into better behavior. When this did not work, it threatened to seek strong sanctions through the Security Council and even to attack North Korea's nuclear weapons program installations. By 1994 it was planning that attack. But heavy pressure from the other great powers involved helped alter its policies. Taking advice from Japan and China in particular, the United States shifted toward engagement. In that same year it negotiated an agreement under which North Korea would freeze its nuclear weapons program and open discussions with South Korea. In return the United States provided some assistance and moved slowly toward a normal relationship with North Korea, ending sanctions and promising not to attack it while anticipating normal trade and investment and regular diplomatic relations. The United States later joined the other great powers in offering large food shipments to deal with the famine. In short, it used carrots, not just sticks.

Along the way the four great powers also agreed, by implication, that unification under South Korean leadership would be acceptable but that each would respect the other's desire to have a role, even a veto, in the arrangement. And they agreed, again indirectly, that it would be bad for everyone if North Korea collapsed. That would bring heavy costs: keeping North Koreans alive, flows of refugees, and potential chaos. Great-power military intervention, which would be tricky and dangerous, also could result. These were things to be avoided if possible.

While this preliminary form of a concert has continued to work, it has been under considerable stress in recent years. North Korea and South Korea resumed talking to each other, held one summit meeting, and are trying to resolve some long-standing issues. South Korea now provides North Korea with a great deal of aid and rising foreign investment. North Korea is much less isolated, having normal diplomatic relations with many governments and more interactions with outsiders generally. It has undertaken some internal economic reforms that outsiders insist are necessary. It seems less likely to collapse, and the great powers have not had a serious clash about it in years.

Nevertheless, the North Koreans secretly started a new nuclear weapons development program within five years after suspending the old one. The George W. Bush administration was outraged and, beginning in 2002–2003, took a hard line, suspending what the United States had agreed to provide under the 1994 agreement; demanding a halt to the new program and elaborate international inspections before there could even be negotiations; and threatening to seek Security Council sanctions and perhaps even attack North Korea. The administration also insisted that any new negotiations involve the other great powers and South Korea. North Korea wanted bilateral talks only with the United States but gave in on this point. Once again, however, heavy pressure from the other great powers and South Korea led the United States to modify its position somewhat in the six-party talks and offer a few carrots. In keeping with the general rules for a concert the United States did not pursue unilateral actions that the other great powers opposed, and the great powers continued working together to get North Korea to give up its nuclear weapons ambitions. But the strain on the concert was evident as the United States wanted the others to be much tougher with North Korea and shifted toward their position grudgingly and in only limited ways, which was something Russia and particularly China and South Korea complained about strongly.

Even though the six-party talks operated fitfully, analysts proposed that they eventually be converted into a permanent management arrangement for Northeast Asian security—a great-power concert plus two. This was a natural reaction to the way the regional system had often been in a dangerous state and close to war. The concerns of the four great powers centered on the division of the Korean peninsula, the China-Taiwan dispute, a set of territorial disputes over some rocky outcrops in the sea, fears of Japan's slow movement toward becoming a normal great power, uneasiness over China's rapid rise, and the intense U.S.-North Korean dispute. Cooperative management through a concert would certainly have plenty to do. But many barriers needed to be overcome: far from homogeneous parties and several with serious frictions among them left over from World War II, the Korean War, and even Japan's occupation of Korea for decades before World War II. For many years the regional system operated under American hegemony or a bipolar distribution of power. The former is now gone and the latter is fading, so something also is needed. The obvious alternative is a new bipolar distribution, a competitive U.S.-China relationship, which many expect is inevitable and some fear and that a concert would be designed to prevent.

The most ambitious great-power concert remains the UN Security Council. Once the Cold War ended the great powers were far more ready to cooperate and the Security Council has been far more active on international security matters. Soon the Council was inundated with problems, starting with Iraq's seizure of Kuwait in 1991 and including internal wars or serious conflicts in Africa, the Balkans, Indonesia, and elsewhere. At first the concert worked well as the war to force Iraq to leave Kuwait went smoothly. Russia and China objected to the use of force but did not veto that action. Soon, however, great-power cooperation began to decline, primarily over the issue of intervening forcefully in internal conflicts. Russia and China became steadily more concerned about UN interventions the Western great powers wanted to undertake. Anticipating vetoes in the UN if forced to vote, the Western countries used NATO instead to deal with the problems in Bosnia and Kosovo.

The most serious strain on the concert developed after the September 11, 2001, terrorist attack on the United States (see the *Terms and Concepts* box, "Terrorism"). Starting in the early 1990s U.S. enthusiasm for working with and through the Security Council declined. Washington felt that the Russians and Chinese were often not helpful and the French were difficult to deal with at times. Therefore, the Security Council was inclined to drag its feet on important security issues. The United States became greatly concerned about UN administration of security efforts, particularly military interventions, and began to avoid or oppose its action. The United States came to see the Security Council as often too confining, inhibiting American freedom of action when important national interests were involved. The George W. Bush administration voiced those concerns even more strongly, and the situation came to a head over what to do about international terrorism. While the United States enjoyed considerable international support for its invasion of Afghanistan, it did not go through the UN to organize that effort. And when the United States began planning to invade Iraq it faced open opposition from China, France, Russia, and other major states. Britain was its main supporter. The administration went ahead nonetheless, organizing a "coalition of the willing" and depicting the opposition as at odds with what legitimate U.S. interests and global security required. The opposing great powers saw the United States as ignoring their views and interests, sidestepping the need for self-restraint on the part of concert members, and too ready to go around the Security Council when it felt like it. They attacked the United States for illegitimately using force by acting outside the Security Council.

Terms and Concepts: *Terrorism*

Terrorism is a deliberate strategy by an organized group for achieving defined political goals by disrupting an existing political arrangement and opening the way for something different. The disruption is sought by inflicting physical harm and psychological distress (fear, insecurity), but the ultimate aim is political. The organized group can be a government, an ethnic or religious group, a political group or movement, a guerrilla warfare force, or a small band of activists. Much terrorism arises and takes place within single states, but it is also used internationally, such as by a group across borders or by one state against another. The target may be a government or its officials, as through assassination attempts against them, or the leaders of nongovernment groups. But often the target is broader—part of or even an entire society. In both cases, particularly the latter, terrorism mainly seeks to disrupt societal security. This is meant to force a government, group, or society to withdraw its support from the existing political structure by raising insecurity markedly. Thus, terrorism is a form of coercion by inflicting harm and threatening more.

With politics involved, unanimity is impossible when trying to define who is a terrorist. Those who sympathize with the goals being sought may be reluctant to describe the actions of some groups as terrorism, instead seeing them as a legitimate form of opposition to an unjust condition. Or people may call a group's actions terrorism but feel that the proper thing to do is ameliorate the grievances from which they stem instead of suppressing the terrorists. The official position of most governments today is that this sort of coercion is unjustified under any circumstances.

Does terrorism, and fighting against it, constitute a war? The most famous definition of war is that it is a continuation or conduct of politics by other means, that is, by using force. In this sense terrorists are involved in warfare, and taking military action against them is warfare as well. However, terrorism often does not look like war because it lacks combat between organized military units. States can pursue a highly organized form of terrorism. Other terrorists may be highly organized but often they are relatively isolated groups, only partially linked if at all. And terrorists are rarely organized to operate internationally or do so only to a limited extent. International terrorism typically takes the form of efforts by domestic groups that share some broad political objective but are not centrally organized, directed, financed, or trained. They operate mainly inside the countries in which they are located.

The great concern in international politics today about terrorism, particularly international terrorism, has several roots. One is the emergence of al Qaeda, designed to have central direction, some central financing, and training centers and seeking to have broad international reach by mounting attacks in many countries. Another is that modern terrorism has sought to escalate its destructiveness and broaden its targets to include almost anyone. The harm done, on average, by specific terrorist incidents has gradually risen. The target is often random—those who happen to be in a place at the time of the incident.

A third source of the concern is suicide terrorism. For years, terrorists seemed preoccupied with delivering a message but not dying while doing so. In airplane hijackings or other hostage situations, authorities would react by giving the terrorists a platform, assuming they would then have less incentive to kill the hostages. In suicide terrorism, the death of the terrorists is part of the message; they will die to deliver harm to drive home their demands.

The final reason for today's concern is that the ideal tool for these kinds of terrorists is weapons of mass destruction (WMDs). Terrorist groups have tried to make chemical weapons, use biological agents, and purchase nuclear weapons. Plenty of WMDs are around, some are relatively simple to concoct, and a government might even sell or give them away. The United States had been worried, for example, about North Korea and Iraq obtaining such weapons. Only one terrorist group has conducted a WMD attack. A Japanese religious cult in 1995 used a form of nerve gas in a Tokyo subway, which killed twelve people. Some analysts think it is only a matter of time before a major WMD terrorist attack occurs.

The George W. Bush administration dedicated itself to a so-called war on terrorism after the September 11, 2001, attacks on the World Trade Center in New York and the Pentagon in Washington, D.C. It invaded Afghanistan to eliminate al Qaeda leaders, bases, and supporters. But in extending that war to Iraq in 2003, it toppled a government with no known connection with terrorists and one strongly opposed by al Qaeda. To fight the war on terrorism the United States built a large coalition, but many governments participated mainly to get support for suppressing their domestic opponents, whether terrorist or not. Some governments still back terrorist groups or find it politically impossible to completely subdue them, as in Pakistan. The progress being made is hard to assess. Are societies better defended against terrorism now? Are terrorists shrinking in number and options, or is terrorism spreading? Is terrorism a passing phenomenon or now a permanent weapon of the weak and frustrated? The evidence is ambiguous, and the experts disagree.

The future is unclear. The Security Council may not fully recover and could remain unable to deal with major international security matters for years to come. Political consensus among the great powers has been badly frayed, and, disturbingly, the main cleavage is between the Western democracies and Russia and China, which are far from democratic. Of greater concern is that the world's lone superpower has frequently disparaged the UN and insisted it is entitled to do whatever it deems necessary to protect its national security without regard to what the other great powers think. This is not a healthy concert.

CONCLUSION

What shall we say about the great-power concert approach to sustaining peace and security? A good place to start is to note that a concert has appealing features, just as oligopoly does in market systems. It is natural to see great-power cooperation as a way to save a large amount of grief. The great powers have a unique status conferred on them by a concert, and status is one of the major motivations in politics at any level. The great powers also gain considerably in the power and control they wield when they act collectively. When they are at odds, they feel constrained by each other and the system can seem to be nearly out of control.

Thus there is a strong natural tendency for concerts to form. There are also powerful forces at work in the opposite direction, which is why concerts have only occasionally existed. Similar factors shape the formation and decay of oligopolies. Living in a highly competitive environment and putting up with uncertainty is burdensome, risky, and costly. Cooperation can relieve these burdens somewhat. A nicely run concert may provide peace and security for everyone, as a public good, and smaller states—and their societies—can certainly benefit. In *systemic security* terms this is all to the good.

But little can stop the great powers from running the international system for their own benefit at everyone else's expense. For instance, they might devise an extreme spheres-of-influence approach: Each great power gets a geographical area it can dominate and exploit as it pleases, and the concert is about cooperating to maintain this cozy arrangement. Lest this seem fanciful, it was what Hitler proposed to Stalin in 1941 in trying to lure Moscow into joining the Axis. He indicated that Germany was building its empire across Europe, Italy was doing the same in Greece and North Africa (rather feebly), and Japan was seizing much of East and Southeast Asia. He suggested that the obvious role for the Soviet Union was to advance into parts of the Middle East and South Asia. He envisioned four giant and exploitative empires dominating world politics.

Concern about great-power exploitation is not just based on old history. In the wake of the Cold War the UN Security Council became much more active with its huge military effort, involving more than 500,000 troops, for example, against Iraq in the 1991 Persian Gulf War and a large number of peacekeeping and related activities. At one time some seventy thousand troops were involved in UN interventions around the world, apart from what had been done in the Persian Gulf. While these efforts were mounted to serve the general welfare, many states, led by China and Russia, feared that they reflected the interests and views of the Western great powers and were evidence of a Western hegemony in action. Their primary concern was that state security was being eroded because state sovereignty was being steadily undermined, and this was taking place to promote values (democracy, human rights) that these two governments do not fully share with the West. Also, Russia worried about the West interfering with the Russian effort to keep Chechnya from seceding, while China feared that the West would interfere in its problem with Taiwan. Other countries experienced or worried about direct UN, or UN-sanctioned, interventions—Iraq, Indonesia, Haiti, North Korea, Iran, and the Sudan, for example.

In another example, a current preoccupations of the great-power members of the Security Council is to prevent nuclear proliferation by leaning heavily, if necessary, on states that would like to develop nuclear weapons and other weapons of mass destruction. A standard criticism of this is that the great powers all have nuclear weapons and no desire to get rid of them, so seeking to prevent nuclear proliferation is an attempt to maintain a near monopoly on those weapons. What stings is the suggestion that their having nuclear weapons reinforces their status as the permanent members of the Security Council, able to veto any major decisions it might make. The "haves" are simply out to preserve this unusual status and the related power that comes with it.

Because being a great power in a concert carries special status and responsibility, determining who qualifies is a source of contention. There are big stakes in not being left out. Currently, Japan and Germany want to be permanent members of the UN Security Council because occupying a lesser position means their influence in the world suffers. Others periodically claim they deserve to join, too—such as Brazil, India, and Nigeria (the most populous country of Africa). Given that a Security Council member has to be ready to use force to uphold peace and security, Japan and Germany have moved in recent years to erase or evade legal and constitutional restrictions on sending their forces abroad. Because all permanent Security Council members have nuclear weapons, what if the wannabes develop their own as the price of admission? Indian commentators and leaders cited the 1998 decision to test nuclear weapons and develop a nuclear arsenal as needed so that India would no longer be underappreciated.

Another concern about concerts is that members could decide to manage international peace and security by doing as little as necessary, keeping their costs and burdens low and minimizing chances of developing serious disagreements among themselves. That would not be good for systemic security, other than in keeping great-power conflicts down. A concert does not have to be activist in character. It can cooperate in ducking many onerous responsibilities as well. This problem might arise when no one member is willing to take the lead in orchestrating the concert's response to a particular situation because no one has enough at stake or cares enough. Or it might arise when the members know they are unlikely to agree so they do not put certain problems on the concert's agenda.

While great powers have important incentives to cooperate in a concert, they may not be enough. This has been a problem in the Security Council in recent years, for example. And when the great powers disagree about one thing, members are apt to express their displeasure by making trouble for the group on another, so lack of cooperation can easily spread. This is particularly true in an institutionalized concert such as the Security Council. A concert is like a club; if a participant likes the club, likes being a member of an exclusive and powerful group, then it has a strong incentive to cooperate at least to keep the club going. But the Security Council is written into the UN Charter and will not dissolve just because the members do not get along. Instead, they can keep getting on each other's nerves and dragged into repeated clashes. Because it is a formally established group, making it work may prove more difficult.

The difficulty in sustaining cooperation means that, to some degree, a concert exists and flourishes when peace and security among the great powers are already in good shape. That is, a concert is apt to be workable and useful when little chance exists of a great-power war. But when it most needs to work—to keep the great powers out of war with each other—it begins to break down. Thus a concert is not a reassuring solution to the problem of war in international politics.

Also keep in mind what happened to the Concert of Europe in the nineteenth century. When it became clear that great-power wars could occur without being catastrophic—in the Crimean War and when Prussia defeated Austria and then France—that concert failed. What if this situation comes around again? For years there was a strong fear that nuclear deterrence would make the great powers so careful about escalation that it would "make the world safe for conventional wars." Remember the stability-instability paradox: What if a great power feels it can attack with its conventional forces with impunity because its opponent will never respond with nuclear weapons and set off nuclear war? If great-power wars come to be seen as potentially easy to limit, then the incentives to sustain a concert could decline.

Could this happen? In recent years the declining destructiveness of American conventional wars has led to the possibility that large great-power conventional wars might be fought in the future because they no longer seemed likely to be highly destructive. That could be a disturbing development in terms of systemic security.

When it comes to *state security*, a concert has considerable appeal to the members plus other governments, leaders, analysts, and citizens who care deeply about preserving state sovereignty and autonomy. For the great-power members, the only limits are the ones they set for themselves. And a concert falls far short of a being systemwide government imposed on all other states. It is unlikely to intrude on a wide variety of matters by arrogating to itself the power to decide what other states are entitled to do or not do. By the same token a concert can be less appealing to those who feel that it is the nature of international politics itself—in particular, an excessive preoccupation with national sovereignty—that is the main cause of the problem of war. From this perspective a concert is a poor substitute for something that would provide a more regular management of security in the international system.

It is, however, reassuring for state security to have a concert able to act so vigorously to protect a state from another's aggression. The most powerful recent demonstration of this was the 1991 Persian Gulf War, when the Security Council told Iraq to get out of Kuwait and then made the demand stick by mounting a military operation to drive it out. That was a powerful reaffirmation that states with a legitimate existence in the eyes of the Security Council cannot simply be seized by others.

For *societal security* preventing great-power wars is fine, but if a concert can work only when the great powers get along, then it cannot contribute a great deal to preventing a major war when they do not. That is disturbing. Having the great powers work together on other problems can reduce the likelihood that they can develop grave conflicts among themselves. They get to know each other and develop habits of cooperation. As the saying goes, however, familiarity can also breed contempt.

Another weakness is that a great-power concert may develop a habit of paying little attention to the quarrels and concerns of small states and societies in faraway places. African governments and analysts have often suggested that less attention is afforded to instances of people dying on their continent from wars compared with the kind of attention that similar cases attract from the Security Council when they happen in, for example, Europe.

However, if the Security Council or a similar institution at a regional level can be operated in a reasonably suitable fashion, then much more attention is likely to be paid to cases of aggression and cases of disastrous internal conflicts and wars, resulting in vigorous collective efforts to try to handle at least some of them. This has been true of the Security Council since 1990. It has had a greatly increased incidence of acting on serious conflicts, which has helped save a great many lives, cut down on the number of refugees, and alleviate some terrible human rights conditions. A general norm in international politics now is that states are to survive and cannot be snuffed out without the citizens' agreement. This also applies much more to their citizens than it has in the past. They are to survive, and their desire to survive deserves respect, too.

To conclude this mixed evaluation, consider the prospects for a concert approach. Concerts are more plausible now than they have been in the past, for at least two reasons. First, the world is experiencing rising interdependence among states and peoples because of a vast expansion in communications, enormous interactions of other sorts, and increasing transparency about nations' activities and capabilities, particularly about their military capabilities. These developments make it easier to create and sustain a great-power concert. The great powers typically have the range and scale of interactions, with resulting overlapping interests, that encourage developing a concert as well as the communications and transparency to contain the suspicions and misperceptions that might otherwise get in the way.

Second, great powers, at the global level at least, resemble each other politically more than they have for many generations. The democracies dominate and the nondemocracies are more open, less autocratic, than they were and are generally becoming more democratic in nature. This is not yet true in all regional international systems. A concert among predominantly or entirely democratic states may have a powerful advantage over others. If democratic peace theory holds up, then democratic great powers will find it much easier to establish and sustain a concert over the long run. This would confirm the suspicion of some analysts that one prerequisite for a concert is homogeneity in the members' political systems. But other analysts would then argue that spreading democracy would make a concert unnecessary for preventing great-power wars, so if one forms and is active it would have to be concerned with managing other things among the members themselves.

Optimism about the future of the concert approach has to be tempered, because the United States has demonstrated that the idea is not fully accepted. Significant elements in the United States do not want constraints placed on American freedom of action that working through the Security Council entails. They do not want the restrictions on sovereignty that they believe will result. They do not find the Security Council, for example, ready to deal with international security problems in a consistently rapid and proper fashion. Their view has been disturbing to many other governments.

One reason this is disturbing is that in concerts not all members are created equal when it comes to taking action. Members will vary widely in power, influence, interests, and ability to act, and these factors affect how the concert works. In the Security Council the United States has a unique level of power and potential influence, coupled with the greatest ability to act and the broadest range of interests. It is the natural leader of the Security Council. Thus its mixed feelings about the Council pose a threat to the interests of the other permanent members in being able to play a large role, and it darkens the hopes of all UN members for better system management of peace and security.

Rising interdependence, more democracy, increased communication, greater transparency, and all the other things that come with them strongly suggest that cooperative international security management in some form can now be carried much further. However, there is no certainty that it will. There seems to be no reason to object to a concert, in principle. Objections are more likely to stem from a distaste for the particular kind of international system a concert will try to create and sustain. Still, given the possible limitations, a concert seems mainly a fallback strategy, something used because other promising cooperative approaches to peace and security have not worked out. The level of community in world affairs and the prospects for community building seem to be expanding rapidly. Solutions to the problem of war that require a much higher level of community than a concert represents have more plausibility and appeal. Perhaps a concert is something to settle for only if something better cannot be arranged. What that "better" might be is the subject of the next two chapters.

SOURCES AND OTHER USEFUL READINGS

For an introduction to the idea of a concert and a brief discussion of the Concert of Europe, see Charles A. Kupchan and Clifford A. Kupchan, "Concerts, Collective Security, and the Future of Europe"; and Robert Jervis, "From Balance to Concert." As in the Kupchans' article, John Mueller proposed a concert for today's Europe in "A New Concert of Europe."

The Nixon-era effort to build a concert is recounted in Henry A. Kissinger's memoirs, *White House Years*. His version of how this effort dissolved is in the second volume of his memoirs, *Years of Upheaval*.

The North Korea problem is reviewed in Joel S. Wit, Daniel B. Poneman, and Robert L. Gallucci, *Going Critical*; Don Oberdorfer, *The Two Koreas*; and Leon V. Sigal, *Disarming Strangers*, the last of which is critical of the way the matter has been handled. Also critical but from a different perspective is Ted Galen Carpenter and Doug Bandow, *The Korean Conundrum*.

CHAPTER 7

Wilsonian Collective Security

Another approach to the problem that war poses in international security is in part, like a great-power concert, a variant of deterrence, though seldom discussed in this fashion. I prefer to call it Wilsonian Collective Security (WCS). "Wilsonian" refers to U.S. president Woodrow Wilson (1913–1921), who introduced the concept in a substantive way into international politics, although the basic idea was developed and widely advocated by others. The "collective security" is distinctive and not to be confused with other sorts of joint efforts to promote security, such as alliances, which are also often called collective security. WCS is an effort to build an unusual community in international politics, one that can operate at times like a kind of posse. It calls for a community among nations and governments higher than that of the deterrence of the Cold War and higher than a great-power concert. President Wilson had high hopes in 1919 that his proposed collective security arrangement would solve the problem of war once and for all. The rest of the century, the worst ever in terms of wars, showed how much it fell short. But it is an idea that is coming into vogue once again. What are its chances this time?

THE MAIN ELEMENTS

A WCS arrangement is a special kind of alliance among a group of governments. Normally an alliance involves governments agreeing to cooperate militarily in dealing with one or more other governments outside the alliance. An alliance can be either defensive or offensive, or a combination of both, in character. In taking military actions, the members could be defending each other against attacks or cooperating in launching attacks. By contrast, a WCS arrangement seeks to keep the peace and provide protection *among the members themselves*, that is, to protect them from each other. Wilson envisioned such an alliance of most or all of the world's governments and emphasized that they should be democratic governments. But a WCS arrangement could be created among smaller sets of states, such as those in a particular region.

In this peculiar sort of alliance the participants agree that they will not make war on each other. Because they are not going to settle their disputes by war, they are not going to threaten each other with war either. Reaching an agreement of this sort is nothing new in international politics and so, by itself, it is not significant. States have often promised that they would never go to war with each other again and have regularly broken those promises. What makes a WCS system a much more serious effort is the additional agreement among the members that if any of them breaks the peace and makes war on another member all of the other members will act against the violator(s), using force if necessary. Thus it is an alliance of all the members against any member who breaks the peace. It is a promise with teeth.

Using force against a violator is the most extreme action that could be taken. The members would normally stand ready to do other things first, such as officially condemn the violating state and its actions, break diplomatic relations, or adopt economic and other sanctions. Only when the efforts fail would the members then be committed, by prior agreement, to use force to end the fighting and restore the old situation by making the violator give up any territory it had seized. Because the violator had agreed to behave itself and then done the opposite, the alliance might even go so far as to try to do something about that government— get it ousted, impose further punishments, or keep it isolated until the offending officials had been punished.

A number of things about this simple arrangement are distinctive. First, this is not a normal alliance. However, it could have a normal alliance attached to it. Nothing prevents this. In fact, states that agree not to make war on each other and will fight to protect each other against any member who breaks that agreement would seem like good candidates for agreeing to fight together against outside threats, too. Suppose that the United States joined a North American and South American WCS group, promised to help protect Canada from other members of the group, but then sat idly by when Canada was attacked by, say, Russia. This reflects the fact that states cannot easily join a group pledging no war with each other, accepting a commitment to fight to uphold that pledge, without having developed a fairly strong sense of community among themselves. They would have to feel that they have a good deal in common, going well beyond fear of war. Such a pledge would not be made among rivals and enemies, but among states that have reason to see themselves as friends for the most part. In addition, how friendly are states likely to be if they do not help each other when they need it? Thus if they want to count on WCS to keep safe, they better not alienate their partners. For that reason, they may also join in a regular alliance, too. The feeling of community is reinforced by their interest in keeping WCS healthy and strong.

Given this higher level of community, particularly for keeping the peace, the members have to treat their security as collective in nature. Each is safe because all are protected; if any of them becomes subject to an attack, all the others are made much less safe. The members perceive that they have important interests in common, so important that each member is ready to risk its citizens' lives, its resources, and its future to help protect the others. A substantial form of community is needed to define security collectively. It is not "How can I be safe?"; it is "How can we be safe?" The result is a three musketeers arrangement: all for one and one for all.

The situation can work only if the commitment by each to defend the others is automatic. Each government has to be committed in advance to treat an attack by another member on any member as an attack on itself and to take the steps necessary to end the attack, including the use of force. When a member is attacked, the other members are ready to find themselves in a state of war. They do not get to decide whether or not to take action in this particular case. They must act if action is required.

WCS implies the creation of a decision-making arrangement. Somebody has to be authorized to decide that an attack has occurred, declare that it must be halted or else, and then call on the other members to take the appropriate action. This could be a council set up by the members, or some small committee of key members, or an emergency session of all the members. Unclear is just how such a body would operate. By unanimity? By majority rule? By some qualified majority (say two-thirds vote)? The members would have to decide when they set up the arrangement in the first place. However, once the decision is made to take action, all the members would be charged with upholding it. That is what makes the arrangement distinctive. In taking the action required, the members would also have to decide how it was to be organized and led. By the same body? By some designated leading state or states? By an appointed military commander?

Having a WCS arrangement, probably with an institution attached to guide its decision making, is not reasonable without authorizing it to take other steps to prevent a war and giving it resources to mount that effort. Thus there should be provisions for promoting negotiations, providing mediation and arbitration services, or investigating complaints and trying to sort out facts. While the heart of the agreement is the pledge to use force to uphold the peace, a WCS setup would have other resources it could apply and other steps it could take.

WCS is meant to offer a clever way around a basic problem in international politics, which is that once states have arms for security they make each other insecure (the classic security dilemma, see Chapter 1). Under the provisions of WCS states get to retain their armed forces. In fact, they have to maintain forces to fight against a member who starts, or will not stop, a war. The members also have some protection against attacks by nonmembers. They thus have a way of defending themselves against attacks the WCS arrangement does not cover. They are afforded some protection against the erosion or collapse of the WCS arrangement. A major complaint about disarmament has been that, if Nation X cheats and acquires arms, its neighbors are vulnerable. That is, the disarmament undertaken to be safe leaves them unsafe if it breaks down. Under WCS the members can have significant capabilities for self-defense but no security dilemma results.

You should recognize how the arrangement is basically to work. President Wilson proposed the first WCS setup, the League of Nations, in the wake of World War I in hopes it would end such wars. It was not only a means of rectifying the situation after a war has broken out, but of preventing wars from breaking out. And how is that to take place? The obvious answer is that military attacks are to be deterred. WCS is a deterrence-based peace and security system. It is a collective deterrence arrangement, in contrast to the deterrence mounted by an individual state or a standard alliance.

Like deterrence (see Chapter 4), WCS counts on the threat to impose unacceptable damage to keep the peace. The unacceptable damage is to come in the form of a successful defense as opposed to the deterrence by threat of retaliation that was prominent during the Cold War. The war that breaks out will, the threat goes, result in the defeat of the attacker because of the alliance that will form against it. (Perhaps WCS could rest on the threat of retaliation but none ever has.) When the League of Nations was created the prevailing thought was that, if a huge alliance confronted any attacker, no attack would take place or the attacker would be quickly defeated—probably the former.

Because the WCS is a deterrence-based method of sustaining peace, much of the analysis of deterrence applies here as well. For instance, credibility is important in WCS. The threat it poses must be credible if it has any chance of working. Are there inherent problems in making that threat credible? Furthermore, does WCS have a stability problem?

As in other modern deterrence arrangements WCS is designed to frustrate any cheap victory strategy that a member might devise to try to fight a war successfully. Country A cannot attack Country B alone, because that attack gets it into a fight with all the other members. Defeating B will not end A's war; it has to defeat the other members, too. When Wilson proposed the League of Nations, the major states had just suffered a war encouraged by cheap victory strategies so they knew the importance of trying to void them.

Another parallel with deterrence is that a WCS system has no built-in tendency to resolve a dispute. It is focused on suppressing escalation of the dispute into a war. That will likely seem inadequate in many cases. Fortunately, nothing in a WCS arrangement precludes trying to resolve disputes as well. Deterrence can be used as a backdrop to help make the pursuit of peace by other means more effective. It is useful that, unlike standard deterrence, WCS deterrence comes with international decision-making and action-taking resources that can be used for dispute resolution as well.

Wilsonian Collective Security involves a more significant, more substantial community than a great-power concert. Normally, more states are involved than just the great powers. And they carry more serious obligations. Nothing is of more concern to a state and its society than its use of force, and under WCS that would be doubly constrained. The state cannot use force against another member, but if another member does so it must be prepared to use force almost automatically. Each member also must define its security in a collective way, which is normal in human communities but not in the history of international politics.

What makes such a departure from the norm acceptable? Why would governments ever go this far? Wilson expected they would do so because of the dreadful impact of World War I. In his view the war had demonstrated that international politics as normally conducted in the past had been discredited, and governments would be so afraid of another war like it that they would subscribe to the arrangement for deterring it. States also might seriously consider WCS if the peacetime burdens of preparing for war—regular fear of attack, uncertainty about security, the costs of maintaining military forces for defense—became much too high. WCS can be a form of burden sharing that allows reduced military expenditures. The members can collectively provide the deterrence to protect any one of them more cheaply than each would spend on self-protection. And if it works, the security that each member enjoys is sharply increased. Hence the deterrence would curb the incidence of war while the cost of stamping out one that occurred would be shared.

Still, this is a considerable level of community to enter into, involving significant obligations not certain to be upheld. States do not easily trust one other, particularly on security matters. In getting states to enter into WCS, it should help considerably if the members are transparent politically and open to outside political influence. If I am to count heavily on the others, I want to know a lot about their domestic politics—the main perspectives of the political elites, the patterns of public sentiment, the depth of commitment in each member to WCS, and so on. I want to know this before joining, and I want to be kept informed of any changes because, if WCS is going to fail, I want to find out ahead of time so I can prepare an alternative way to keep safe. I also want the opportunity to play a role in the other members' domestic policy-making deliberations. I want to have ways of making my views and concerns known and to have them taken seriously. This is a much more rigorous requirement than it might appear. A famous aphorism in American politics is "all politics is local," meaning that what moves people most and moves leaders in building a domestic political base and consensus are things directly pertaining to citizens' daily lives. Political systems have a strong tendency to be driven by internal concerns and considerations even when dealing with foreign affairs. They make foreign policy from the inside out. That could worry a country in a WCS arrangement. It wants to be able to get its views across and be taken seriously even though it is from outside. Otherwise, the community could be too unresponsive to its needs and fears. When a country declares that it is about to be attacked or is being attacked, the others may not listen or care enough. Members should make some foreign policy decisions from the outside in. This is one reason WCS involves a formal alliance, a formal commitment to act more or less automatically. The hope is that parochial concerns and domestic politics will not block members from living up to their obligations.

All this suggests, much as Wilson concluded, that a collective security system is best composed of democratic states and open societies, including relatively open economies and significant levels of interdependence. Democratic states are more apt to meet these criteria than other kinds of governments. Open societies and economies would be more vulnerable to sanctions and other pressures that could be brought to bear under WCS. However, autocratic governments can make reliable partners, and democratic governments are capable of secretive behavior in foreign policy and of being misread by outsiders. Democracies are also vulnerable to outbreaks of virulent parochialism that discards existing agreements. It is hard to make war if the citizens will not stand for it or to stop one if they insist on it. And a new, highly nationalistic democracy might be intolerant of attempts by outsiders to have some influence in its political system and skeptical about advice from outside, even if through normal diplomatic channels.

Above all, this high level of community requires a substantial amount of trust among the members. They are counting on each other for defense and for getting aid under the most trying of circumstances. Relatively homogeneous political systems, transparent and amenable to foreign influence, are likely to generate the necessary level of trust. Others are apt to be much less capable of this.

CREDIBILITY AND STABILITY

As a collective deterrence arrangement WCS could, like other forms of deterrence, have either a credibility or a stability problem. In any deterrence-based system, failure is likely if the credibility of deterrence threats is low. Credibility is normally harder to achieve for extended deterrence, which is disturbing because a WCS arrangement rests entirely on extended deterrence. WCS has a credibility problem because states and societies are apt to be selfish. They care more about themselves than others, are more willing to make sacrifices for themselves than others and normally ask "What's in it for me?" when confronted with requests for help. Furthermore, there is the tendency to cheat on the provision of public goods. Public roads, for instance, are open to everyone whether or not they pay their taxes. WCS provides security for all members, but many may be able to keep safe while leaving the hard work to others, particularly the more powerful ones. Eventually, the resentment of those left holding the bag may lead to less willingness on their part to bear the burdens, which would call the entire deterrence threat into question.

An additional factor, which analysts have highlighted, is that people rarely define "attack" in the same way. They rarely agree fully as to who is attacking whom or who is responsible for an attack, and they are seldom willing to treat every attack in the same fashion. Why not? Because using force seems less like an attack when it is provoked. Suppose that rebels who want to overthrow the government of Country A are based in Country B, from which they issue lurid attacks on A's leaders, send money to support extremist elements, and arrange for guerrillas to cross into B and conduct raids. Also, suppose that B's government is sympathetic to the rebels but opposes their activities and says it has little control along the border where the rebels are making trouble. If A's army invaded B to attack the rebels, who would be the attacker? Against whom should the WCS arrangement take action? When other members are consulted, Countries C and D think badly of A's attack, but Countries E and F say it was provoked and A is entitled to stop rebel attacks because B either cannot or will not. With such a split, why would either Country A or the rebels think the security system will fulfill its threats if a war breaks out?

The example helps illustrate an additional point. Attacks on a state from inside, and its military responses to those attacks are especially difficult for an international security arrangement to handle, and this is certainly true of WCS. The problems arise not only because of reluctance to suspend sovereignty and take sides in an internal conflict, but also because knowing which side to take is often difficult.

Also calling WCS deterrence credibility into question is the reluctance members are likely to display to fight a war to avoid wars. As with nuclear deterrence, the only desirable outcome is that WCS deterrence works so well there are no challenges, no wars. When deterrence fails, for members to carry out their threat is to do something—go to war—that they created WCS to avoid. This was one of the major criticisms of WCS during the Cold War. What if a war is started by a large and powerful member, or even the most powerful member? What if it is started by a member with nuclear weapons? Or carried out by a potent band of members acting together? How willing would the others be to go to war in response, in what might be another world war?

As a variant on this problem, if states fight a manageable but costly war to uphold deterrence, and then another, getting them to fight a third would be difficult. Collective security would have worn out its appeal, and members probably would start finding excuses to evade their obligations.

The stability problem in WCS is not the classic one regarding deterrence, which is when the military systems built to keep the peace can provoke a war instead. One of the appealing features of WCS is that it is intended to guard against this. Each member knows that if it started hostilities its opponent will be joined by all the others, so it has little advantage in attacking first.

The WCS stability problem has different facets and pertains to creating reliable and effective management of security. It can emerge as an offshoot of the credibility problem, that is, doubts about the commitment of the members making certain ones willing to risk an attack. WCS can also break down in dealing with internal wars—ambiguous, intractable, and messy as they often are. Knowing this, a member might attack by promoting internal unrest in a neighboring state, a common enough pattern. It may sponsor guerrillas or other rebel groups; encourage them by aid, arms, and propaganda; and take advantage of the members' reluctance to be drawn into such conflicts.

A possible way around this dilemma is to confine a WCS arrangement to preventing only international disputes, avoiding the internal ones. But this is problematic because internal wars have a strong tendency to spill over into international affairs, and vice versa. For example, the struggle in Vietnam after 1945 over who should rule attracted outsider interest and support for the opposing sides. Eventually an interstate war broke out between the United States and North Vietnam. In 1950, once China attacked U.S. and United Nations (UN) forces in Korea during the Korean War, this led the United States to intervene again in the ongoing conflict over who should rule in China by supporting the ousted Nationalist government that had fled to Taiwan.

The internal war in Afghanistan in the 1980s brought outside support for the rebels against the government, Soviet intervention to back the government, and massive U.S., Saudi Arabia, Iranian, and Pakistani aid to the rebels. The rebels eventually forced Soviet troops to leave. However, in the ensuing civil war, outside aid to various factions came from Iran, Pakistan, the United States, Saudi Arabia, and Saudi religious leader and al Qaeda founder Osama bin Laden. After September 11, 2001, the United States sharply increased its aid to its associates in Afghanistan and sent forces to take control and set up a new government. This is how an underdeveloped, remote, isolated country ended up on the front lines of the Cold War and the war on terrorism.

No approach to managing international peace and security is sufficient if designed only for interstate fighting. Efforts always must be made to head off trouble before interstate fighting erupts, including dealing with internal struggles. In short, the stability problem mostly arises because governments have trouble looking fully reliable. If they are free to choose what to do regardless of their formal commitment, and if fighting would be costly, they can be suspected of eventually choosing not to fight. The resulting failures of collective security would prevent a fully stable peace from emerging.

Another possible source of instability is the reverse: Collective security works, which leads to a serious erosion of the military capabilities that help make it credible. With no wars in sight states let their military forces decline or find themselves unable to prevent this because of domestic pressures to spend the money on other things. Weak forces mean declining credibility. The situation would be exacerbated by the fact that the most expensive and most difficult to maintain forces are often the ones that project power at a distance, well beyond the nation's borders. Strictly defensive forces for protecting the national territory are often not expensive standing forces but largely inexpensive reserves. And because defensive forces normally do not have to be mobile, they are cheaper. Hence a long period of peace could leave the members vulnerable to a newly ruthless member willing to exploit that situation. (This could be avoided if the members maintained serious forces for dealing with threats from the outside world or for intervening militarily elsewhere in the world.)

A final possibility is that the system works so well at keeping wars under control that states, or groups within states, push conflicts to extremes. They could become falsely confident that they will not have to bear the worst of the possible consequences. A similar fear arose about nuclear deterrence during the Cold War. As a result, states would engage in conventional wars with impunity. Here conflicts might simmer indefinitely, just short of serious fighting, with little effort by the contenders at compromises to resolve them.

WILSONIAN COLLECTIVE SECURITY IN PRACTICE

We have only one clear case of WCS in the past, and a contemporary possibility that WCS will return, to discuss.

The League of Nations

The clear case is the League of Nations, set up after World War I. It got off to an awkward start and ended in abject failure, which is not a good advertisement for this approach. The League was proposed by Wilson as part of the peace settlements that officially ended the war. But he was unable to get the U.S. Senate to ratify the treaty that established the League so the United States never joined. This was not necessarily fatal because WCS is intended to work only among those who join the group. But it was unsettling because the United States was a good candidate to be leader of the League. It had just provided the critical resources that determined who won the war, its prestige was high, Wilson had proposed creating the League, and the United States was crucial to global economic recovery from the war. Who better to lead the League? Other key states were not initially members either (Germany, the Soviet Union) but joined eventually; the United States never did. Nevertheless, the League set out to prevent war.

An additional problem was the requirement under which it operated, stemming from nations' insistence that sovereignty be respected, that the League take action only unanimously. (Those being investigated for resorting to force could not vote.) The provision would bound to undermine the League's credibility if states grew wary of the burdens or disagreed about when something should be done, which they did. During the 1920s and early 1930s the League tried hard to repress war. Under its auspices there were mediation efforts, development of arms control measures, and arrangements to deal with the problem of colonies. A significant number of disputes were resolved or stopped short of war through the League's efforts. But this all began to fall apart after the onset of the Great Depression in 1929. The depression's terrible domestic effects led to retreats from international cooperation in many areas. Governments were forced to put domestic concerns first. Those effects also led to the growth of fascist groups and perspectives in many countries, and in several countries these elements eventually came to power.

However, the gravest problem the League faced was that by the mid-1930s a fundamental political cleavage had developed among its principle members. The fault line was roughly the same one that later characterized the Cold War: the leading democracies versus the leading nondemocracies (fascist and communist). The roots of the cleavage lay in World War I and its immediate aftermath. The League was generally seen by the nondemocracies in Europe and by Japan not as everyone's resource for maintaining peace and security but as part of the arrangements dictated by those who won the war. Upsetting some or all of the results of World War I was a major objective of several of these states, which they felt could require the use of force. In opposing this action, the League would be standing in the way of legitimate adjustments in the international system. At least this is how these governments rationalized their appetites to seize vast territories. So the League would have to be ignored.

Not only did the two sides disagree about many other issues, but the fascist states—Germany, Italy, and Japan—also were deeply committed to empire-building and ideologically primed for war. The Fascist perspective—that only the strongest would survive—glorified military struggle as the ultimate expression, and ultimate test, of a people and a nation. Fascist leaders were entirely unsuitable for membership in a group devoted to repressing war, something they fully understood.

Once this cleavage was clear, even leading members of the League grew pessimistic about WCS and began to fall back on other approaches. They explored the possibility of getting help by playing Italy off against Germany. This led them to avoid trying hard to stop Italy from its empire-building in Ethiopia, which Italy seized in 1935–1936. The tactic did not work. Italy became a German ally, and, as the League was uncongenial, Germany, Italy, and Japan eventually withdrew from it. In 1940 the League condemned the Soviet Union for attacking Finland, and it also withdrew. The British and French eventually decided to try to create a great-power concert to manage Europe, a less demanding form of community (see Chapter 6). When this did not work, they retreated even further to power balancing, trying to build up their forces and arrange a new alliance with the Soviet Union to offset the German-Italian axis. In the Far East the United States turned to deterrence in its efforts to offset Japan's expansion, and in this connection it inched toward an alliance with Britain in both the Pacific and the North Atlantic.

An important underlying reason for the failure of the League was that Britain, France, and their other supporters in Europe, and the United States as their potential ally, had been shocked by the slaughter of World War I and were eager to avoid anything like it again. Their citizens were visibly uneasy about rearmament, confrontations, and the idea of going to war on behalf of far-off nations. Thus the League's deterrence had a serious credibility problem, particularly in the eyes of the powerful members that started breaking the rules.

The League was also a failure in dealing with the worst internal war of that time, the Spanish Civil War of 1936–1938. The democratically elected leftist government was confronted by a rightist uprising led by elements of the Spanish armed forces with strong fascist leanings. Britain, France, and Russia came to the support of the government, though Britain and France mounted an arms embargo for a long time that hurt the government much more than the rebels. However, they would not carry this to the point of confronting Germany and Italy, which offered heavy military support to the rebels, including sending whole military units to help in the fighting. Unwilling to risk creating a general war, Britain and France let the Spanish republic go down to defeat.

To summarize, the League lacked valuable members, member unity, a strong commitment by the members to stamp out any war among themselves, and credibility. When it came time to reconsider the whole problem of avoiding war once again, after World War II, the world's leading states decided that a great-power concert was the better way to go and that is what they installed with the UN Security Council.

NATO

If this is the one example of WCS, and it did not work out, why pay so much attention to it? The answer is worthwhile because another possible example of WCS is being constructed in Europe, and it may turn out to be important. It is the only effort of its kind these days, but it involves many of the world's most powerful countries.

The arrangement that now comes close to being WCS is the current way the North Atlantic Treaty Organization (NATO) manages security in Europe. Remember that NATO started as an alliance against the Soviet Union. With the end of the Cold War, the collapse of the Warsaw Pact, and the sharp decline in military power with the disappearance of the Soviet Union, NATO became the dominant actor in European security management, so dominant that it is now a hegemonic alliance. It is not yet a WCS arrangement, but it is close. And there has been debate about whether to carry its development all the way to a full-blown WCS. It is not there yet. As a hegemonic coalition NATO applies all sorts of pressure and has imposed its will by force when necessary in its security management. But in one way or another it is a coalition that embraces the great majority of the states in the transatlantic region and Europe. Almost everyone is either a member of NATO (it now has twenty-six members), is working with NATO in a cooperative way (in joint training programs, joint exercises, joint planning for peacekeeping and related operations, participating in NATO-led operations in Bosnia and Kosovo), or is associated with NATO in agreements to cooperate (through discussions, shared programs, joint activities, and the like). Only members get to participate in making NATO decisions (Russia is a partial exception), so this is not a WCS system. But its members have many kinds of interactions and they cooperate, which reflect agreement among most European governments on the basic elements of Europe's security. This has led to something close to the kind of community WCS is supposed to embody.

To convert the existing arrangement into WCS, NATO has to expand further to include all the other relevant states as regular members. NATO does have plans to add to its membership. While this could eventually create a Europe plus North America WCS system, there are two major difficulties that must be overcome.

First, the larger NATO gets, the more unwieldy it will be in terms of making decisions and perhaps in organizing military actions as well. NATO makes decisions unanimously, and the more members it has the more difficult it will be to get them all to agree. At times it has not been easy even with the existing members. NATO prides itself on being well organized, and much better prepared to go into action when necessary than, for example, the UN. It would not like to lose this quality because of being too large with too disparate a membership.

The problem of more members is not just a mathematical one, because all large organizations normally have ways of coping. In NATO the critical way around this problem has always been that the United States has been the clear leader, providing the most important military capabilities on which the other members depended, being the key voice in making major decisions, and naming the NATO commander in chief. However, it would be wrong to conclude that the United States ran NATO and simply dictated the decisions that NATO adopted. The European members have often rejected important American ideas and initiatives and resisted being led in directions they did not want to go. In the past, effective American leadership involved heavy consultation, patient persuasion, and flexibility in adjusting to European views on many issues. Nevertheless, in getting the members to decide and to act, especially on important subjects with serious consequences, it has been useful to have one country that would normally take the lead—setting the agenda, making the initial proposals to frame the discussion, and forcing others to bring themselves to decide what they wanted to do.

It was widely expected that with the end of the Cold War this situation would change. The other members depended deeply on the United States during the Cold War as the one country that could offset the Soviet threat. So U.S. leadership in NATO was only to be expected. But the Cold War ended, the Soviet Union collapsed, and Russia ended up pulling out of Eastern Europe and being moved about a one thousand miles further away from the nearest NATO member than the old Soviet Union had been (until the recent expansion in NATO members). Russian non-nuclear military strength dissipated, and the Russian armed forces fell into a steep decline. Most observers thought that NATO would therefore become less important to the members and that the Europeans would feel less comfortable with, and less in need of, U.S. leadership. Furthermore, the United States likely would be less determined to supply it. Because European affairs would be less troublesome, and the threat there had largely disappeared, the United States would want to reduce its European burdens, politically and militarily, to concentrate on other matters.

Never underestimate the ability of the experts to misunderstand what is going on. In this case many experts were spectacularly wrong, at least in the short run. NATO did not go away and did not become less important. If anything, it became more important and was given greater responsibilities. The U.S. role did not decline, politically or militarily. And U.S. interest in Europe's security did not fade away.

What did the experts miss? Generally speaking they underestimated how concerned people would be that security in Europe be managed, that a systematic organized effort be made to keep the continent from returning to its old ways. For many years the United States has felt that international politics is too important to be left to the Europeans, but now the Europeans themselves seemed deeply afraid of international politics. When governments talked about the need to manage security, this was discounted because the assumption was that many would be unwilling to accept the necessary restraints once the great fear that the Cold War generated was no longer around to force them to do so. Many analysts suggested that Europe would lapse into one of its past patterns—power balancing or a great-power concert—or continue relying mainly on nuclear deterrence. Instead, the North Atlantic nations continued to promote what they had been relying on for decades—NATO and European integration—as the basis for European security.

NATO continued to be the foremost organization in European security affairs, and the United States continued to be its leading member. The United States was in the forefront in changing NATO from a defensive alliance into a hegemon in charge of regional security. It was the leader in the decision to expand NATO's membership. Even as NATO added new members it remained coherent, disciplined, and able to decide and act, largely because it continued to have a hierarchical structure at its core.

This is now beginning to change. The European members have decided to make NATO distinctly less hierarchical. They usually deferred to the United States during the Cold War because they depended so heavily on it. Since the end of the Cold War, they have deferred because they depended on the United States even for small operations such as the military interventions in Bosnia and Kosovo. The United States has by far the largest share of the most suitable forces. It also has the major intelligence assets. It has nearly all the capabilities to move military units and their equipment any distance in a short time. It has the smartest of the new smart weapons. It has the most portable systems for maintaining military equipment. To use force in Eastern Europe was easier for the United States than its allies. So if NATO is to be less hierarchical, Europe has to be less dependent militarily.

European members are trying to achieve this in several ways. They are seeking to create a significant military force of more than fifty thousand personnel that can intervene in situations such as Bosnia and Kosovo, complete with the transportation, communications, and intelligence elements that the United States would normally supply. It will act as a NATO force and use some NATO assets, but it will not have American military units in cases in which that is not necessary or advisable and the United States does not want to participate. In NATO-speak this means creating a "European pillar" in NATO to match the American one. It will look more like equality than hierarchy, expanding the influence of the Europeans and reducing the influence of the Americans. But in addition some Europeans, notably the French, envision this force and other European forces eventually being used without always operating through NATO, that is, without an American vote or the supervision of the American commander of NATO. The effect would be a shrinking of the American role even further. Meanwhile, the United States is sharply cutting its forces in Europe and shrinking the number and size of its military bases there, because the main security problems seem to be well outside Europe.

NATO is getting larger but the hierarchical structure that kept it from being unwieldy is going to be dismantled. Is there something to replace it, another discipline-inducing arrangement that will get decisions made? The Europeans think so. They say the answer is to put the responsibility for European management of security increasingly in the hands of the European Union (EU). They want to put even more reliance on integration. Instead of independent states that have to be pulled together to get a decision, most European members of NATO, even all of them eventually, will be drawn together on foreign policy matters as part of their overall construction of a single large political community. Eventually NATO will not need twenty-six or more governments to agree on a decision. More like three or four will do the trick—Canada, the EU, the United States, and any NATO members that do not belong to the EU.

The new arrangement is taking shape slowly and will take years to fully mature. The further development of the EU in security and foreign policy matters, and in other spheres, is politically controversial in several major societies. However, it may well work and make easy the eventual conversion of NATO into a true WCS. The situation looks promising. And the way Europe is developing, the chances of either an internal or an interstate war are low, so the WCS may be largely an arrangement on paper because there is little for it to do. That would make security management much more pleasant.

There is a second difficulty, however, pertaining to NATO's old function as a defensive alliance for protecting the members from outsiders. NATO was created and operated for years to protect its members from the Soviet Union. Currently NATO is accepting members from a long list of governments eager to join. A number of these have wanted to join so they can be protected from the Russians. But if a true WCS arrangement based on a NATO that covers all of Europe is to take form, it would require eventually incorporating the Russians in NATO. The United States talks, in broad terms, along these lines. It does not rule out NATO membership for Russia. But for some would-be members, and some existing ones, allowing Russia to join would be unthinkable. They want NATO as a traditional alliance. Perhaps they lack confidence in the progress that will be made in community-building. WCS takes a good deal of community—particularly trust—and they do not see Russia as a suitable partner in such a community yet.

The reasons they think this way are not hard to spot. Russia is a flawed democracy, and its political system has slowly been becoming more authoritarian. It has a weak and backward economic system highly dependent on selling oil and gas while being short on the institutions, laws, and practices of modern economies. The Russian government is strongly opposed to NATO's continued expansion, and Western governments are disappointed in Russia's human rights record and growing restraints on democracy. It has sought to be treated like a great power even though it is far from being one, and it has wanted what would amount to a veto in the management of European security. For many in the West the sight is familiar; an unstable Russian government and society that have inflated ambitions. That would make it a threat, not a true partner.

So the other problem with NATO expansion into WCS is Russia. Everyone agrees that Russia is a key piece of the puzzle, that securing a decent relationship between the Western nations and Russia is vital, and that Russia should be a solid participant in European security affairs. And Russians fear that if they are not involved the European security arrangements worked out by the West will be hostile to them. But nearly everyone still sees Russia as too undeveloped and improperly ambitious. Squaring that circle will take years.

CONCLUSION

WCS has obvious attractions. It could alleviate the main security dilemma, yet leave states with military capabilities as insurance. Once in place it should be cheaper than seeking security individually or in a regular alliance. Collectively the members should be able to repress wars fairly inexpensively in most cases. If it works it can alleviate much of their insecurity. With war deterred, states and their societies should be able to free up resources for other things. Also appealing is the prospect that WCS need not be complex and cumbersome. It is not a world or regional government, would not establish a whole new layer of political authority and bureaucratic management, and would not be out collecting taxes and regulating everything. And while it requires much cooperation at times, the level of community involved does not seem elaborate, which is why it is not a new level of government. In fact, WCS could be a simple functional arrangement focused on doing one thing and thus a substitute for creating a new level of government and the elaborate community that that would require. It is a way of getting results on controlling war without states and societies having to undertake the difficult task of learning to live closely together. The members just have to agree that they want no more wars, will fight any member who starts one, and will cooperate sufficiently to do that. Sounds simple enough. If they want more extended efforts to reduce or manage conflicts they can set up the necessary organizational resources.

Security at the Three Levels

WCS can attend to security at all three levels. WCS can provide significant security management, which could produce a high level of *systemic security*. Unless the only members are poor and weak, a WSC arrangement will have the resources to deter many wars, internal or interstate, if the threats have credibility. And it can be durable if the members keep in mind that they must always be prepared to go fight somewhere else, when necessary, to keep themselves safe. The payoff could be the end of warfare in a WCS-dominated international system.

It could also be acceptable in promoting *state security*. The members retain their autonomy except in having to fight to maintain peace and in agreeing to stop making war for any other reason. And in return for this modestly circumscribed autonomy, states get relief from the insecurity of traditional international politics and some of the costs of dealing with it—more security from attack at less expense. In particular, a state gets help when it is attacked, that is, when it needs help the most. Perhaps the members would act to provide help in resolving internal wars, which can be a difficult burden.

By curbing most or all wars among the members, and possibly helping on internal conflicts, WCS can be of great benefit in terms of *societal security*. Death and destruction from warfare would be markedly reduced, as would the costs on citizens of sustaining military forces. Any war undertaken by a WCS coalition likely would be less harmful to citizens of the country or countries involved than wars among states. The coalition would try to avoid unnecessary destruction, atrocities, looting, and so on. because it was fighting only to end a war, not to gain something (territory, wealth, power) for itself and not out of hatred for the other side.

But Wilsonian Collective Security is not without drawbacks. One of its complications is credibility. It can be hard to get people to die for their country; it is harder to get them to die for an ally; it is harder still to get them to die for a member of a club. The more powerful the violator that has to be defeated, the greater the reluctance to undertake the task. Imagine finding governments to sign up to try to defeat the United States because it started a war against Iraq. WCS deterrence has a credibility problem and, as in the League of Nations, it could gradually lose the ability to prevent wars. This is a particular concern at the systemic level. How can people and governments be convinced to regularly care enough about others beyond their borders to be willing to fight for them? Europeans may know enough about, and feel close enough to, each other to do this, but would they always risk their lives for people in Africa or South America? The solution is to create a strong sense of community with others, which is more likely to exist regionally than globally and is in short supply now in most regions. Thus, WCS may not be feasible in many places.

This leads to another point. If WCS is most feasible when member states and their citizens feel close to and comfortable with each other, then WCS is not much of a substitute for having an elaborate community after all. Which raises another question: If a group of states has achieved such a high level of community, how likely are the members to attack each other? If attacks are unlikely, why would the members need WCS? Would it be of benefit? The existence of that solid community would do the real work of preventing wars. This question may apply to the Europeans in the relatively near future if the level of community among them continues to rise, which seems plausible.

However, trouble may arise in building a suitable community, where wars do not occur, among states with a long history of fighting, so WCS could be an important interim step in that direction. And even in well-established national communities, and in those not well established, sometimes something goes terribly wrong and people start killing—in riots, terrorist attacks, atrocities, war. This is certainly possible in seemingly decent communities of states. So WCS as an insurance policy might be wise.

At the state level, Wilsonian Collective Security may not be attractive to a government, and its people, if it sees the status quo as unfair and harmful, because WCS is designed to prevent it from fighting to change this situation. There are always governments that feel the system is unfair or that the neighbors are taking advantage of them or that they suffer from some past mistreatment. Governments and their citizens get frustrated if they see no peaceful way to get what they want. Adolf Hitler expressed and played on these feelings in his country when evading or attacking the role of the League of Nations in the 1930s. He insisted Germany was entitled to use force if necessary to get back the territory it lost and save Germans from mistreatment by the Czechs or the Poles. In addition, many states may oppose losing even a modest amount of autonomy. Many Americans, including a U.S. president, have asserted that the nation must not be required to ask permission to do whatever it thinks is vital for national security. States and their citizens may also feel that WSC costs are too high. The larger and longer the first war to end a war, the less likely members will want to fight another.

Concern about being free to fight when one sees fit is particularly likely to arise for a state in connection with an internal war. Once such a conflict erupts, the government is apt to resent outside interference with its efforts to defend itself and crush the opposition. This is particularly so if the opposition is trying to secede from the country or oust the government. The opponents may feel the same. They want the right to fight to destroy what they perceive as an unjust government or break away from the country in which they are mistreated.

With all these drawbacks it is hard to imagine that WCS will be highly effective in dealing with interstate and internal wars in many places outside of Europe any time soon. As a solution it will fall short of saving societies and individuals from the costs that wars impose. A high level of cooperation among states to prevent wars among themselves may be attainable only if they also agree not to interfere in each other's internal affairs. Thus in seeking to work with Russia on improving security, the Americans and Europeans have somewhat soft-pedaled their criticism of the Russian government's war against the Chechens.

Having a fairly strong community among states is important if real progress is to be made. This suggests that WCS is best thought of as an interim solution on the way to something better. It takes a certain level of community to get it started but much more community will be needed to resolve the problem of war, and the best WCS can do is help that community-building along. This is not a bad way, in fact, to describe what is going on in Europe now. A large group of nations is inching toward creating WCS. But for the long run they have put their money on two higher levels of community, which are the topics of Chapters 8 and 9.

Consider once more the question of costs and burdens, which will recur in later chapters. Remember how WCS is supposed to deter—or fight to repress—a war. Imagine yourself handling the problem of preventing wars. If there are highly contentious parties and you do not want a war, you would probably spend much time and energy promoting negotiations between them, mediating the dispute or providing financial inducements for them to agree. Perhaps you would have to insert peacekeeping forces between the parties to minimize frictions that keep everyone on edge. Maybe you would have to develop common projects for the parties to handle some of their complaints or get them used to cooperating—maybe joint development of a waterway or building roads to promote trade. Maybe the parties will trade off disputed territories to settle their conflict if you pay the costs of resettling people who have to move.

What does that sound like? It sounds like government—having numerous international agencies to do these things, with bureaucracies and substantial budgets. In other words, WCS is not necessarily cheap because it is likely to expand over time into other activities. In Europe, where states have been moving from a hegemonic security arrangement toward true WCS, the costs and complications have already been substantial. Once trouble began in the Balkans, governments trying to stop it have found themselves

- Accepting many refugees—legal and illegal;

- Paying significant economic costs to uphold embargoes;

- Paying significant costs to blockade and bomb;

- Paying large costs to occupy Bosnia and Kosovo militarily;

- Paying large costs to promote rebuilding and development—for constructing new governments, reestablishing the police, rebuilding schools, setting up health care and transportation, and so on; and

- Making commitments for large long-term aid and trade to foster development of the Balkan region.

Final Assessment

Wilsonian Collective Security is a good alternative to keep in mind. With the end of the Cold War the most serious wars or war-threatening conflicts are normally regional, or bilateral, or even internal (not global). Hence they are of intense concern to only a limited number of states. WCS might be an attractive response in various places, where a limited group of states tries to keep safe from each other given that it is from each other that they face their most serious threats. This could be particularly the case if WCS emerges and seems successful in Europe, providing a powerful and attractive model. "After all," people elsewhere will say, "with their awful history, if the Europeans can do it maybe we can, too."

In any cluster of states there are significantly larger ones—the great powers— and they are the biggest potential headache for WCS. If one misbehaves it could take a serious war to get it to stop, and in some cases it might be impossible to stop. Imagine the other governments in South Asia trying to stop India from conducting a war. This suggests that behind every successful WCS system lurks a great-power concert that is important for it to work. The most powerful countries had better agree to get along and not start wars if their agreement with the other members to repress anyone who starts a war is to have teeth. Thus significant overlap could exist between a concert and WCS in practice, particularly when WCS is just getting started, even though the WCS arrangement had added on to the concert a broader membership and shared decision making.

WCS takes a strong helping of community to work, seemingly more than first appears, and apparently that does much of the serious work of preventing war, particularly for the major states. Thus even higher levels of community than WCS involves may be more potent still. The next chapter looks at one sort of community that is particularly appealing.

SOURCES AND OTHER USEFUL READINGS

Among the many discussions of the theory and practice of collective security is Inis Claude, *Swords into Plowshares,* which is justifiably famous for its analysis. The subject is revisited in *Collective Security beyond the Cold War,* edited by George W. Downs; and Thomas G. Weiss and Laurse S. Hayes Holgate, "Opportunities and Obstacles for Collective Security after the Cold War." A fine examination of Wilson's approach is Thomas J. Knock, *To End All Wars.* A good critique of collective security is Lynn H. Miller, "The Ideal and Reality of Collective Security."

CHAPTER 8

Complex Multilateralism and Integration

Progress on the problem of war can require a high level of community within nation states and in relations among them (see Chapter 7). Operating Wilsonian Collective Security in an effective way takes a well-developed community of states if warfare is to be deterred or suppressed. Alas, that much community is hard to find in international politics, which is not a good sign. Another solution requires a significant community and is even more ambitious. However, in at least one part of the world, the necessary level of community has been found.

The general idea is simple enough: War is the opposite of community. In a true community people feel that they share important things—a common home, a joint culture, similar values, and a common fate. Because of this, they feel that they should look out for each other, more so than they would look out for others and especially when some outsiders pose dangers and threats. When people feel that way about each other they normally expect to settle or contain their differences well short of having to kill each other. Deliberately hurting the members would mean that the community, particularly the sense of being a community on which it rests, has broken down. This means going well beyond the level of community represented by Wilsonian Collective Security, which is just a community among states. The kind of community discussed in this chapter reaches into the societies that states govern and directly involves elites and ordinary people.

Such a level of community is both hard to develop and hard to maintain. Many analysts believe that international politics, the realm of anarchy, is devoid of community. They are not surprised, therefore, that war has been such a stubbornly persistent feature of relations among states. But the communities those states represent are also often fragile or on the verge of collapse, leading to severe conflict, violence, and even war within them. Community has been fleeting in places such as the Balkans, Afghanistan, the Congo, Northern Ireland, Sri Lanka, and the Sudan. According to political scientist Ted Robert Gurr, nearly one hundred minority peoples were involved in violent conflicts within their countries between 1945 and 1990, resulting in almost fifty episodes of genocide and mass political murder, between ten million and twenty million total deaths, and well over twenty million refugees as of 1995. Each number has gone up steeply since then. He indicates that about one-sixth of the world's population, more than one billion people, consists of politically active peoples struggling for independence, autonomy within their country, or basic human rights.

In the last five or six decades much effort has been made to try to construct strong, effective international or transnational communities on the expectation that in a healthy community there will be no warfare and little other severe violence and conflict. A strong community of states would largely eliminate interstate fighting. The community would have to go beyond a simple alliance, however. Alliances are common in international politics, but studies have found that alliance partners, trying to protect themselves from attacks by third parties, are prone to getting into wars with each other. The strong community of states could also help suppress warfare inside states, in at least two ways. One is deterrence. The international community could assert that internal wars are unacceptable and that the community will act to suppress them wherever they break out. The community would supplement this by providing assistance in settling major problems and ending the conflicts from which such wars grew. The other is community pressure against any state that deliberately mistreats its citizens. Such mistreatment often fosters or reinforces serious domestic conflicts and helps turn them into outright civil wars.

Even better, however, would be an international community that dealt with the problem of war not by upholding or enforcing peace but by eliminating conditions, foreign and domestic, that breed war. For instance, states could cooperate to settle serious problems that might otherwise provoke serious fighting sooner or later. They could work together to eliminate border disputes, deal with common problems in areas such as health or agriculture, promote general economic development, or do joint research on other problems. The expectations would be that developing habits of cooperation that produced widespread benefits and common achievements would promote expectations of more. People would grow more prosperous or healthier or better educated together.

What should such communities of states look like? How can they be created? This chapter considers two different, though related, forms of community building. States cooperate all the time, in trade, catching criminals, fighting epidemics, promoting tourism, and permitting study abroad. They build **intergovernmental organizations** (IGOs), and many private **nongovernmental organizations** (NGOs) also carry on this work. But cooperation is not community. Cooperation needs to be carried to a special level.

COMPLEX MULTILATERALISM

The first variant is **complex multilateralism**. Ordinary multilateralism involves a temporary alliance, or an arrangement to coordinate flows of things such as mail or tourists or kumquats. It is a cooperative association of more than two states for some purpose. It emerged in a significant way in the nineteenth century and then blossomed in the twentieth century. Complex multilateralism is newer, appeared in the twentieth century, and took hold after World War II. It combines a high degree of intimacy and interaction among states with continuation of substantial national autonomy. That is, governments accept important restraints on their behavior without being swallowed up by a superior ruling center. In search of controlling war, this approach reduces state security to a significant degree to boost societal and systemic security.

Much of its development can be traced to a particular government. It is largely a product of U.S. political experience combined with a strong American dislike for ordinary international politics. In fact, complex multilateralism became the vehicle by which the United States accepted its shift from a somewhat detached (isolationist) stance to a highly active involvement in international politics, a transition about which the country still debates today. In turn, complex multilateralism would not have amounted to much if the United States had not become the world's most powerful country during and following the Cold War. American power forced other countries to give advanced multilateralism serious attention. That is why many analysts over the years have wondered if advanced multilateralism could flourish without the United States. What if Americans abandoned it for a more self-centered foreign policy or a new isolationism? Others have contended that the existence of the Cold War was crucial. Otherwise, would complex multilateralism have broken down? The best answer to each question is maybe. But right now it is being used so seriously in Europe and being explored enough in a preliminary way in other places that it must be considered an important approach to the problem of war.

Complex multilateralism emerged mainly from American disgust with normal international politics and its warfare, a disgust as old as the republic. However, the United States was not powerful enough to do something about it until well into the twentieth century. Americans insisted that, for the most part, nations can live harmoniously, particularly if they have the right sorts of governments. That is, international politics is not inherently war-ridden. The assertion that the problem of war could be solved within international politics fit well with a strong desire to resolve the problem without sacrificing American sovereignty. Another ingredient has always been American dismay over how other countries were ready to leave the major costs, complications, and casualties of running international politics to the United States. Disgust, desire, and dismay produced an American willingness to push cooperation with certain states to a high level, in arrangements that limited American freedom of action but kept the nation from being overly exploited.

Its first manifestation was President Woodrow Wilson's desire to build a new international relations on the basis of the League of Nations. This faltered when membership in the League was rejected by the U.S. Senate and when the League collapsed in the face of the rise of fascism (the opposite of a cooperative approach to international politics) in the 1930s. The United States returned to complex multilateralism after World War II. The first component was extensive cooperation among selected nations for keeping themselves safe. The United States finally agreed to join alliances but insisted they involve much higher levels of cooperation than typical alliances. The members were to develop and act on shared security perspectives and relations and not just on some temporary security interests. The alliances were not to be temporary but to represent substantial, semipermanent security cooperation.

Furthermore, all the allies had to contribute (and not leave everything to the United States). The alliances were run by endless consultation, debate, discussion, and consensus-seeking and involved some shared effort. Finally the cooperation and shared effort was unusually broad and deep. The alliances became real communities not just temporary associations of convenience (of which the United States had several as well during the Cold War). In practice, to take the example of the North Atlantic Treaty Organization (NATO), the alliance of the United States, Canada, and Western Europeans called for

- Some members keeping military forces on other members' soil for decades—an unprecedented scale of cooperation;

- An elaborate integrated command headquarters to coordinate cooperation in peacetime and to run the alliance as a military force if war occurred;

- Integrated logistics, shared intelligence, integrated communications, some shared weapons, and a broadly shared strategy for security;

- Constant efforts by members to contain disagreements and maintain consensus; and

- Contacts, conversations, debates, and discussions—lectures, briefings, joint schools for officers, summit meetings, phone calls, and other communications among officials.

The U.S. alliances with Japan and South Korea developed along the same lines. The United States had the greatest influence (as the largest military power) but never just dictated. The allies periodically said and did things the United States opposed, and often the United States adjusted its policies to take allied views into account.

Going beyond the alliances, the United States insisted on considerable economic associations among nations, too. Major international organizations, such as the World Bank and the International Monetary Fund, provided some governance of the international economic system and oversaw development of extensive economic interdependence among the participating countries. Huge flows of goods, money, technology, culture, tourists, and students were involved. Each member came to have a big stake in the others' economic health. Many of these states also accepted high levels of cultural interdependence, in academic life, science, entertainment, music, consumer goods, fashion, and cuisine.

The United States and most of its close associates came to strongly prefer that they all have similar (democratic) political systems. Undemocratic allies were tolerated but never with comfort. Spain could not join NATO for years because it was not democratic. Frictions arose between the nondemocratic members (Greece at times, Portugal, Turkey) and the democratic ones. The United States worked hard at promoting democracy in Japan, South Korea, and Taiwan and eventually promoted it in the Philippines.

In short, complex multilateralism grew up as detailed, intimate interactions and cooperation, on many levels, facilitated by important international organizations, multilateral corporations, and eventually some international unions and private interest groups. Five general principles emerged.

1. Common security—keeping safe together, not separately—is required.

2. Rules for cooperation apply to all the participants equally.

3. Human rights and democracy are important.

4. Consultation and consensus building are vital.

5. Diffuse reciprocity is practiced.

Only the fifth principle might be unclear. One way to make a deal or reach other joint decisions is for each member to ask "What's in it for me?" and insisting on a big payoff to agree. In a real community, people regularly agree to go along with deals or decisions that carry few immediate benefits for themselves because they expect to get good results later. I make concessions now because I expect that on other matters in the future other members will do the same and also because, if we all go on cooperating, I will be much better off in general. That is **diffuse reciprocity**. In trade, for example, the United States has supported Western European integration even though it somewhat limited American sales to Europe, figuring (correctly) that a strong, prosperous Western Europe would be of great benefit to the United States in the long run. A general acceptance of diffuse reciprocity makes multilateral arrangements work much better. Participants can be less concerned about free-riding, and every decision is less of a hassle. Diffuse reciprocity is a kind of trust, allowing more cooperation than otherwise would develop.

COMPLEX MULTILATERALISM IN PRACTICE

Complex multilateralism is supposed to result in states that get along so well they cannot imagine, and thus do not worry about, going to war with each other. When they have disagreements, war is never how they settle them. The technical term for this situation is a **pluralistic security community**. The "pluralistic" part is the presence of separate, independent states and societies; "security" refers to how safe they feel among themselves; and they get that way via a "community" of cooperative interactions.

NATO

Complex multilateralism has been most highly developed among the rich countries of the world, especially in the regional international system of the North Atlantic and Europe, which was the heart of what was the West during the Cold War. It was a Cold War phenomenon initially. That it happened in the West was partly because it is typically the richest, most developed nations that have the greatest level and variety of interactions with each other. In the West, NATO has been the most integrated peacetime alliance of sovereign states in history. Western nations (plus other countries such as Japan) have for years operated a highly interdependent global-scale economic system with open national economies dealing with each other on the basis of shared principles. Running these and other multilateral arrangements—with recurring stresses and strains, grumbling, and the like—often has been painful, but over time the application of complex multilateralism has steadily increased. The governments involved figure that they must be doing something right.

What is remarkable is that these governments had historically been exceedingly sensitive about their sovereignty. Their societies displayed powerful nationalist feelings. They had been making war on each other for centuries, culminating in two vast world wars in the first half of the twentieth century. They had good reasons to hate each other and had often done so. Their shift to profound cooperation was hardly a good probability.

In fact they took up cooperating in such a big way partly out of desperation. They feared that if they did not they would end up killing each other in bigger and better ways in the future. Ultimately, they cooperated to deal with the problem of war *among themselves*. The general feeling was that these governments had for too long been preoccupied with narrow nationalist concerns and had been living with old hatreds and grievances, nourishing grudges and quarrels about historical events and even the smallest slices of territory. This pattern of behavior was clearly holding back the development and prosperity of the entire North Atlantic region.

While it was easier to cooperate because these countries faced a serious threat from the Soviet bloc, they also cooperated to stop being at each other's throats.

The Warsaw Pact

During the Cold War, the communist governments in Eastern Europe tried to develop complex multilateralism also to compete with the West, but it was a flop. Led by the Soviet Union, these countries tried to construct a highly interdependent economic system, establish an integrated military alliance, and greatly expand cultural and other ties. They proclaimed that this socialist community of nations, and only a socialist community, could overcome the problem of war by living together in unprecedented levels of peace and harmony despite only recently having been at war with each other and having long been deeply suspicious of each other.

However, the Soviet Union proved overbearing, too insistent on making the key decisions itself, even though over time the other members did become less repressed and either became more influential in community decisions or opted to go their own way. In the 1950s and 1960s Moscow used military interventions, as well as threats to intervene, to keep or put governments they liked in power. This happened in East Germany, Hungary, and Poland and was hardly the epitome of cooperation to preserve the peace. A larger problem was that the governments in the Soviet bloc were undemocratic and unpopular at home. By the 1980s the main point of their political cooperation was to prop each other up.

Finally, though their level of cooperation was much higher than normal in international politics, they were not nearly as successful domestically, as a result of that cooperation, as Western governments. They achieved too little economic growth (eventually they had almost none), the living standards of their people were low, they offered poor health care, their institutions were infused with corruption, and their cultural life was drab. Life in these societies was dull, gray, and hard. Cooperation did not promote enough progress, and elites all over the Soviet bloc eventually wanted to break out of it in hopes that things might get better.

In the end, that is what they did. As the 1980s ended, cracks appeared in bloc solidarity. Once it became clear that they would not prop each other up any longer, they began to dissolve, one by one. Their replacements did away with communist-style multilateralism and most, including the former Soviet republics in Europe, began trying to join the multilateral arrangements of the West. Western complex multilateralism had clearly triumphed in a direct competition. That blend of national autonomy and international cooperation was immensely appealing. It seemed to offer a more decent way to conduct international politics without war or the threat of war.

Both the North Atlantic states and the Soviet bloc states created communities. But only the former developed into a pluralistic security community in which all the nations felt safe with each other. Many of the members disliked and feared the military power of the Soviet Union, and with good reason. They experienced a Soviet, or Soviet-led, invasion; they feared Soviet domination; and they knew that the political systems they had and did not like were ultimately in power because the Soviet government insisted on it. In short, the members were not safe among themselves.

The West developed a broad community, not just a bunch of IGOs and NGOs. To join its community, a country had to begin to make elaborate political (democracy), economic (capitalism), cultural (Western), and interdependence (trade, investment, and people flows) adjustments. Since the end of the Cold War, Eastern Europeans have found that hard to do, but most have seriously undertaken it.

ASEAN

Complex multilateralism has not readily spread around the world because it is hard to do. The best effort to develop it elsewhere was eventually mounted, oddly enough, in Southeast Asia. A group of nations—Indonesia, Malaysia, Singapore, Thailand, and others—emerged in the first decades after World War II either from colonial rule or wartime occupation and soon fell into the standard pattern in international politics. Little cooperation existed among them. Instead, they quarreled, and sometimes fought, over territory. Ethnic conflicts erupted and internal political strife emerged in several of these nations in which the neighbors eagerly meddled. Various governments built up their arms and went looking for friends or allies among the great powers of the world, especially the United States, the Soviet Union, Great Britain, and China, which were eager to do their own meddling in the internal affairs of these countries and ready to play one faction or one country against the others. The situation was all deplorably familiar.

Just as in other parts of the world where similar things happened, political elites and governments in Southeast Asia became alarmed. By the 1960s the Vietnam War was pushing the Cold War ever more deeply into Southeast Asia. The war was so vicious and destruction was so rampant that the prospect of more of the same was scary. To their credit, these governments decided to do something. In the late 1960s the largest of them, Indonesia, began to promote regional cooperation. Others liked the idea, and the result was the Association of Southeast Asian Nations (ASEAN). The members began holding regular high-level meetings to resolve some of their conflicts, expand economic links, and work out common positions on important matters so they could present a united front and not be played against one another. They devised several principles and practices as the basis for their relations.

- Moderation in foreign policy—curbing grand and imperial ambitions.

- No threats or use of force in dealings with each other.

- Promotion of economic cooperation and increased economic links.

- Serious efforts to reach a consensus on ASEAN positions.

- Openness and candidness in discussions—more transparency.

- No meddling in each other's internal affairs.

ASEAN members made good progress in putting these principles into effect. They ended meddling in each other's affairs, eased their territorial and other conflicts, and expanded trade and cross-border investing. Over time they moved into joint action to resist superpower influence and cooperated to offset the power of Vietnam after it had defeated the United States. That cooperation eventually included action, jointly with the United Nations (UN) and various great powers, to bring an end to the war inside Cambodia that killed upward of two million people. Eventually ASEAN's membership was expanded (Brunei, Cambodia, Laos, Myanmar, the Philippines, and Vietnam now belong, too) to cover almost all the states in the area. They take a common position in the dispute that many of the members have with China over who owns the South China Sea, insisting that the principle of peaceful settlement of disputes applies. Their broad desire is to stand together against possible domination by any great power, particularly China but also Japan and the United States. ASEAN is also committed to becoming a free trade area (such as that created by the North American Free Trade Agreement, or NAFTA), which will require some painful and ambitious adjustments. ASEAN organizes the annual Asian Regional Forum, during which members meet for high-level conversations on East Asian security with U.S., Chinese, Japanese, Russian, and European Union (EU) representatives. The goal is to get the great powers to talk frankly about major issues and to allow the ASEAN members to make their views known and have some influence.

Thus these nations have been trying to avoid war and make themselves more secure by building a community, going well beyond simple agreements for limited cooperation. However, their activities fall short of complex multilateralism. Their community is not that well developed yet. They do not have a comprehensive alliance and are still some years away from even a free trade area, much less the kind of economic interdependence of the West. The principle of noninterference in internal affairs means that they do not have highly similar domestic systems either. ASEAN is now under strain because Indonesia has gone through serious domestic political problems in recent years.

Eastern Europe Today

An intense effort to expand complex multilateralism for purposes of preventing wars and building security is taking place in Eastern Europe. As noted earlier, when the Cold War ended in 1991 members of the old Soviet bloc in Europe, as well as Estonia, Latvia, and Lithuania and other former Soviet republics, were eager to get themselves accepted in the West's complex multilateralism arrangements. They were determined to join the West. (This is not surprising. Several states that had been neutral during the Cold War—Austria, Finland, Sweden, and Switzerland—were thinking about doing the same thing.) And the key Western countries considered this a good idea.

The first step was to get nearly everyone in Europe, plus the United States and Canada, to reaffirm their endorsement of the West's basic principles and Western concepts of the proper behavior that nations in a safer Europe would display. In agreements signed in 1990-1991 those principles and concepts were laid out. States would

- Be democracies and respect human rights at home.

- Have capitalist economies open to foreign trade and investment, with a high level of economic interaction so that everyone could be prosperous.

- Respect existing borders; changes could be made by mutual consent of the parties.

- Not use force or the threat of force in their relations with each other.

- Avoid excessive use of force in big domestic quarrels.

- Implement major cuts in military forces and weapons; military forces were to be designed and deployed mainly for defense and definitely not for a cheap victory attack.

- Accept the idea of common security, which is that you can be safe only collectively and trying to achieve safety for yourself alone is ultimately destructive.

These broad principles became the basis for a new IGO, the Organization for Security and Cooperation in Europe (OSCE), which monitors the treatment of human rights by Europe's governments, tries to make elections democratic, and works to ease conflicts and discourage the use of force. Other new institutions were developed as well, such as the East European Development Bank to promote economic development. And it became possible for East European nations to join the Western institutions if they met the requirement.

What has all this looked like in practice? Principles are easy to announce; the devil is in the details. Thus far something like 100,000 or more pieces of military equipment have been eliminated across Europe; Soviet forces were withdrawn from Germany and Eastern Europe; U.S. forces in Europe were cut by two-thirds; British, French, and Russian nuclear weapons were reduced; and most of the American nuclear weapons that had been stored in Europe were removed. Germany has been unified in arrangements under which it accepted the permanent loss of the territories taken from it at the end of World War II. Concerted efforts have been made to strongly discourage attempts by separatists to change national borders by succession, unless the succession is done in collusion with the national government, as happened in Czechoslovakia and the former Soviet Union.

Eventually NATO began to enlarge by adding Poland, Hungary, and the Czech Republic, which is controversial because it can be seen as building a threat toward Russia. But it is better understood as extending Western complex multilateralism eastward. The European Union added Sweden, Finland, and Austria as members. Border controls were cut back, permitting greater flows of people and goods. Censorship has been greatly reduced in Eastern Europe.

Thus the broad solution to the problem of war in Europe has become, in large part, to reproduce for all of Europe what the United States and the Western Europeans developed for themselves during the Cold War. Complex multilateralism needs careful evaluation, but a review is first necessary of what Europeans have been doing on their own, without the United States.

INTEGRATION

The most powerful, and the most extreme, approach to the problem of war in Europe is the use of **integration** to gradually do away with international politics. Advanced multilateralism creates high levels of interaction and builds an elaborate community among a set of states that remain separate and sovereign. No agreement is made in advance or along the way, no master plan is drawn up, requiring that states begin to merge. Integration also seeks to generate high levels of interaction to erect an elaborate community. But the underlying plan is to develop that community to the point where, for many important parts of society, the distinctive and separate identity of the members begins to dissolve. Parts of their societies gradually become less like separate nations and more like a single state. Champions of integration typically urge that this gradually be extended to more and more parts of society, eventually turning the independent states into something more like the fifty states of the United States, no longer separately governed but components of a single large country.

In view of the huge preoccupation with national autonomy in the history of international politics, this is clearly an extreme step. Total integration tries to end war among its participants by ending international politics itself. Because this book is about dealing with the security problem of war within international politics, integration is only of interest, in its early stages, when governments are clearly separate and independent even as they get together for certain purposes.

Because it is a drastic step, integration is difficult to pull off. While it has been tried, in some form, in various places, only in Europe has it taken hold. Its difficulty to implement makes it hard to count on as a great way to resolve the problem of war. But the concept deserves attention because it is important now in the most war-torn area in the history of international politics.

Integration starts out like advanced multilateralism in that it builds a community by promoting beneficial interactions among the participating nations and expands their cooperative activities. The difference is that, in at least a few activities, those nations develop not just cooperation but also a higher authority to supply rules, make decisions, and serve to manage. For example, suppose that states have common problems with crime. Criminals in one nation hide in another, make money illegally in one and stash it in another, or operate from one state to prey on people in another (selling phony investments or illegally shipping them guns). The states decide to cooperate. Their police agencies share information; the governments agree to extradite criminals to each other; and an international organization is set up to facilitate cooperation. Such action constitutes normal international politics. But the states could decide instead on complex multilateralism: letting police in one country work on investigations with the local police in another country, conducting joint operations against major crime (drugs, terrorism), developing common principles and changing their laws so as to reflect them, and moving to use the same sorts of legal and police procedures. Some of this is happening today but not much. If states decide to create a common police force, set up a single court system (or common rules, laws, and principles for any of their courts to apply), and establish standard punishments for specific crimes, and particularly if they create one legislature and one prosecuting agency to apply the law in all of the nations simultaneously, that would be integration.

How does integration deal with the problem of war? First, it can be used to build a strong, highly satisfying community among separate states on selected matters, such as crime, environmental problems, and economic growth. As a result the members presumably develop good feelings about each other, and about cooperating, and (as with complex multilateralism) they end up with something like a pluralistic security community. Thus they become safe from war among themselves because through integration they find war less plausible. The more integrated they become, the more complicated it would be to fight each other. They would have to disentangle themselves to do so.

Second, integration can deal with war by eventually replacing the separate states with a single new state. International politics is eliminated by these states among themselves so that war will disappear along with it. Why go this far? Because the members do not trust themselves to sustain their pluralistic security community indefinitely. They fear that without carrying integration further they will someday, somehow fall back into quarreling, competition, and conflict. They feel they will be safer inside a single community with a unified political system.

Thus integration is a big deal, a massive and daring step. In fact, it is so massive that a concern about war is not enough to carry it off. Some other important payoffs are needed, such as prospects for much higher living standards and much improved chances that the people involved will live under democracy, to get enough support to carry it through. It is not guaranteed to work either. The states involved could get partway integrated and then come to blows about something. They could build a single nation, and then it could fall apart in a civil war. This is one reason that only a single example exists—the European Union. Some states pursue integration in some specific sector but not for security reasons. Canada, Mexico, and the United States are slowly moving toward creating a single huge economy and maybe someday they will get there. But it would not be a step taken to keep the peace. These three countries have had a pluralistic security community for decades, and it seems likely to continue. Thus this is not a pertinent example.

THE EUROPEAN UNION

The initial pressure for integration in Western Europe came from people determined to avoid any more wars. World War II was enough, and they thought building at least some integration would help. The United States agreed, and gave the idea a boost by announcing that it would help pay for Europe's recovery from the war if European governments designed their recovery programs to work together and thus greatly improved their economic cooperation.

The first target was coal and steel. West Germany, France, Italy, Belgium, Holland, and Luxembourg agreed to set up an agency to manage their coal, steel, and steel-related industries (iron ore, ore shipping, and so forth). The European Coal and Steel Community began to make binding decisions on the production and sale of coal, iron, and steel, particularly to get individual governments out of protecting these industries from competition and thus promote greater efficiency and better growth. But the main reason for targeting coal and steel was that in the major wars of Europe over the preceding one hundred years the main bulwark of national military power was iron and steel production. The iron and steel industries produced the weapons, the ships, and many other components of military might. If these countries entangled their coal and steel industries, going to war would be just that much harder. Doing so would require disentangling them first.

The second target was the military sector. These same countries set out to create an integrated army. At the time, it looked like it would be difficult to cope with a possible invasion from the Soviet bloc, because not be enough military power would be available. Hence the United States was pressing to let West Germans arm as well, but the thought of Germans being rearmed scared many Europeans half to death. The idea behind an integrated army was that the Germans could carry guns again but only by being absorbed in a larger military entity called the European Defense Community (EDC). An alliance would protect against the Soviets. An integrated army would protect these Western Europeans from themselves. It turned out to be too big a step, too radical. A suitable treaty to create the army was signed, but in the end, France, whose government had pushed hard for it, refused to ratify it and the whole scheme collapsed.

Integration did not. Instead, it developed in three other directions. The first was to enlarge the integrated sectors. The same six countries set up another agency—Euratom—to oversee their nuclear energy development, using the same justification as with the European Coal and Steel Community: getting some supranational control over a sensitive area in terms of security. Then in 1957 these nations set up the European Economic Community, the common market. Their intent was to steadily move toward eliminating economic barriers among themselves so that goods, labor, and capital could flow freely. One important goal was rapid economic progress, but another was to make these countries ever more closely associated so that the possibility of war among them, particularly between France and Germany, would steadily fade away. One direction integration took, therefore, was to shift into other sectors of life.

The second direction it took was horizontal expansion—the addition of new members to the community. In 1972 Britain, Ireland, and Denmark joined. By 1986 Greece, Portugal, and Spain had been added. Since then Sweden, Finland, and Austria have joined, and in 1993 the name of the community was changed to the European Union. In 2004 EU membership took a turn to the east, adding Cyprus, the Czech Republic, Estonia, Hungary, Latvia, Lithuania, Malta, Poland, Slovakia, and Slovenia. As of 2005, the European Union was expecting Bulgaria and Romania to join and was in membership negotiations with Turkey and Croatia. Expanded membership is believed to be crucial for knitting all of Europe into a peaceful region.

The third direction, and the most important, is the deepening of integration so that the members are slowly shifting toward ending international politics among themselves. Their economic integration has become steadily more elaborate. The EU has acquired more power to direct economic policy, regulate economic activity, and negotiate with the outside world on trade and other economic issues. In the 1990s the big step was to create a single monetary system for most of the EU members, replacing the franc, the lira, the mark, and other national currencies with the euro and putting the newly created European Central Bank in charge of adjusting the money supply to control inflation and promote economic growth instead of relying on the central banks of the member countries. This was a huge commitment. Participating states had to give up one of the most important, and most symbolic, elements of their independence. Naturally that took a long time to agree to and then to implement. Not everyone, Britain in particular, was ready to agree by 2002, when the new currency appeared. Beyond economic matters, over the last two decades the European Court of Justice has also expanded its power as the authoritative interpreter of the European integration treaties. National courts have agreed that those treaties normally overrule conflicting laws and regulations, as well as conflicting practices, of national and local governments or elements in society.

What matters here is why this broadening, horizontal expansion and deepening have taken place in the years since the end of the Cold War. One reason was to keep up economically with the competition by creating a single economy on a scale with the other huge economies that exist or will soon exist: the United States (and NAFTA), China, India, maybe a revived Russian bloc, and perhaps a group in the Pacific led by Japan. But if this was the only reason, why spread integration to other areas, too, such as in human rights matters or environmental concerns, which is what has also happened? The other major objective was, and is, security. For about 150 years Germany was the most powerful country in Europe. When Germany was reunited in 1990, the question was: "What if it went back to its old ways?" Just the thought of this scared everyone, even the Germans. The response was to embed the new Germany into an even larger and deeper EU, to use integration to reduce even further the possibility that Germany, or any other European government, could go back to promoting itself at its neighbors' expense—by grabbing territory, for example, or turning weaker states into semicolonies or economic vassals, or by other forceful steps.

Shortly after the start of the twenty-first century EU members came up with yet another big project. The most politically sensitive area in which to try for integration has been foreign and national security policy (remember the failure of EDC in the 1950s). The ultimate expression of independence for a nation has long been that it controls its dealings with other nations and it controls the means by which it guards against them. It has a foreign policy and an independent military capability. That is the hardest thing to tamper with in integration, the hardest emotionally and politically. The EU has long handled some important aspects of foreign policy, such as economic negotiations, and for years the member states of the EU have coordinated their foreign policies on various issues to produce a single position if they could. But these were modest steps.

Now the EU is going further. In the 1990s during the crises over Bosnia and Kosovo, European governments were embarrassed. They had difficulty agreeing on what to do, so the decisions took too long to make and implement or the decisions were what they could agree to, not what was effective. When it came to taking effective action, particularly military action, the United States took the lead in making the decisions. The best equipped, best staffed, and most experienced resource for military action was NATO in which the United States, not the European nations, played the dominant role. It did so because the Americans had the most mobile forces, and ones most suitably trained and equipped for being sent far away for a fight. They also had the best resources for moving and supplying military forces far away from home, the most suitable intelligence resources, and the best communications. Sending military forces long distance meant, for most European governments, a few hundred miles. The United States found it easier to send sizable military forces to the Balkans than the Europeans, even though the Balkans were in their own backyard. This state of affairs was somewhat annoying to the Americans, and the United States grew reluctant to keep on fighting small battles on behalf of Europeans who could certainly do the job if they wanted to.

Out of this came a European decision to set up an intervention force in the EU. European governments have moved to make forces always available, and suitably equipped, to intervene with up to sixty thousand troops in a place such as Kosovo for up to a year. That meant creating a permanent command structure, staff, planning unit, and intelligence resources. This is not an integrated army; instead, it is a closely coordinated collection of national forces like NATO's. But it puts European integration institutions, the EU, into the business of foreign and security policy and, just as has happened in other areas, the level of integration will almost certainly expand.

This all came about because of the problem of war. In this case it was the problem of small wars inside a decaying state (Yugoslavia). Europeans have decided that to have a peaceful continent they need not only rules of good behavior but also some way to deal with those who ignore the rules. They could have left dealing with this to the most powerful states, having them act as a great-power concert. Instead, the Europeans decided to pursue a collective response to the problem by further extending integration. After all, if the major states carried out the interventions that were involved on their own, maybe they would cooperate and maybe not. Maybe they would end up competing with each other over these interventions, which is what they did for centuries. Integration is seen as better. Europeans do not trust themselves to live together peacefully forever within international politics.

But what about Europe's pluralistic security community? Clearly it is highly developed. Integration could hardly have gone far if the members were still concerned about fighting each other in future wars. Their pluralistic security community is flourishing. Nevertheless, their faith in it has never been complete; they do not totally trust themselves. All around them are reminders of their violent past, of the millions killed, the nations upended, and the destruction suffered on a vast scale. Beyond the economic benefits it provides, the European Union remains their best bet for security.

CONCLUSION

Complex multilateralism and integration overlap a good deal but are basically different solutions to the problem of war.

Complex Multilateralism

Complex multilateralism as a way to resolve the problem of war looks appealing, and it has a highly successful track record in one part (historically the most violent part) of the world over the past fifty years. But can it be used elsewhere? Thus far the evidence is not reassuring, and who needs a solution to the problem of war that is useful in only one place?

To see if it might be used elsewhere, analysts have tried to figure out what makes complex multilateralism tick, what makes it feasible and workable. Here are some of their conclusions. One is that a considerable degree of homogeneity helps. The participating governments and societies should be significantly alike. Much emphasis has come to be placed on democracy in this connection. Democracies virtually never go to war with each other, even though they fight with nondemocracies. In fact, they do almost nothing to prepare for possible wars among themselves. In short, they seem to find it easy to maintain a pluralistic security community among themselves.

We are not entirely sure why. Democracy is common in countries that are highly developed economically, so maybe a high level of development is the key and not democracy. Or maybe it is the combination of a high level of development and democracy. Another possibility is that many democracies have been allies for decades, battling fascism and then communism, so perhaps they have been peaceful among themselves because they had such powerful enemies in common. Or it may be simply that the major democracies are homogeneous specifically in terms of their current interests and policies. They get along because, at least for now, they agree about many important matters. As Russia and China contend, the great Western democracies seem to agree that they ought to dominate the international system and run the world, putting their preferences—such as globalization or human rights—ahead of those of other kinds of governments.

Yet another possibility is that democracies get along because of their transparency. Democracies are easy to monitor politically and in policy making because they do so much of their decision making in a highly public way. That can make it much easier for a group of governments to trust each other, which is good for developing a pluralistic security community. Still another explanation, and the most popular one, is that democracies are used to settling political conflicts at home by compromise because they respect their citizens' right to disagree, and they carry over this mindset into their dealings with each other.

One relevant element is that democratic governments are open to political penetration from outside. That is, a democratic government permits foreigners to press their views inside its country and try to influence its decisions. It will accept the flow of information from outsiders that challenges its policies. Such interchanges among democracies, which are carried on at many levels, keep their policies from getting too far apart and allow their governments to take each other's views seriously.

Whatever the explanation, it is now the broad view of Western governments that what makes for peace in the world is more homogeneity via proliferating democratic political systems. For instance, governments that want to join NATO, the EU, and other Western organizations are typically told to be or become more democratic. But if a strong need exists for this political homogeneity as a prerequisite for spreading complex multilateralism to promote peace, it poses a serious limit on what can be done to stop war. In many parts of the world democracy is scarce, and it looks like this will not change for many years to come.

Maybe the homogeneity needed is not political but economic. Several versions are available of this general argument: What promotes peace is that governments are eager to cooperate, such as in complex multilateralism, and what usually makes them amenable to cooperation is their realization that rapid national economic development (getting rich) depends on vigorously participating in the international economy. But a government cannot fully join the world economy if it is bullying, blustering, warlike, aggressive, and self-centered. Instead, it has to deemphasize conflicts, pursue a moderate foreign policy, and open up all sorts of interactions with others. The rapid national development that results makes citizens less restive and allows the country to keep up with nations that might otherwise become too powerful and turn into threats. Having an open economy, while facing little chance of war, is the best way to attract foreign investment, get new technology, expand trade, and attract help from other countries or IGOs such as the World Bank if a state should fall into an economic crisis. Serious internal conflicts and troubles, war or the threat of war at home or abroad, disrupts the economy. Foreign investors are not interested in countries experiencing such things, and IGOs are less helpful. In addition, a country in deep trouble at home or facing serious threats abroad is often reluctant to be dependent on outsiders and is more inclined to have authoritarian rule to hold the nation together. This may lead to neglecting domestic economic and other reforms, as too many resources are tied up in fighting, arming, repressing dissidents, or suppressing terrorists.

The argument concludes that the solution to the problem of war, at least for a time and perhaps indefinitely, is to have political elements come to power, at roughly the same time, in countries with serious conflicts that are determined to promote rapid national development by opening up their economic systems and jumping vigorously into the world economy and that want to undertake domestic reforms for this purpose as well. They moderate their nations' foreign policies, ease conflicts, and reduce tensions. This explanation would indicate why complex multilateralism, so successful in the North Atlantic area and Europe, has gone nowhere in a place such as the Middle East where war and violence have flourished. Almost all the major governments there, and several minor ones, have been unwilling to follow this course of action, either out of political and ideological concerns or because huge oil revenues permitted national development by following other policies.

This is an attractive explanation because opening up economic systems, while often difficult, is normally easier than democratizing political systems. Creating more of the necessary economic-system homogeneity is easier and faster, bringing more peaceful international relations even though many governments remained undemocratic. But in instances in the past, especially in the period from 1890 to 1914 in Europe, rapid national economic development stimulated in part by rising trade and flows of foreign investment led a group of nations into war. Rapid development, plus the domestic strains that both development and a more open economy produce (fears about foreigners taking "our jobs," complaints about foreign investors "taking over" and "exploiting us"), and the appeal of nationalistic slogans to people upset by the many social changes that were taking place contributed to the coming of World War I. Widespread concern exists that the same thing might happen again in East Asia, where national economic development has been proceeding at a furious pace. What is now a peaceful region might fall into a grim cycle of violence.

Yet another explanation for complex multilateralism is that it flourishes only when it has a powerful patron—a hegemon. Hence this is typically called the hegemonic stability thesis. Complex multilateralism flourishes because a dominant state, or dominant set of states, insists on it. The dominant state or coalition can do much to promote cooperation among states by making life difficult for those who are uncooperative or cheat on their agreements, giving subsidies or providing some other relief for those countries that face high costs from cooperative agreements, promoting the resolution of conflicts, or helping IGOs work more effectively. This argument can easily be applied. Complex multilateralism in the West during the Cold War succeeded because of the enormous power of the United States that was behind it. It is spreading now in Eastern Europe because a dominant coalition of Western states is pushing it. Thus complex multilateralism is less important for squelching the problem of war than the existence of a hegemon. Get the wrong sort of hegemon (Nazi Germany) and peace will not result; get into a period when the hegemon is becoming steadily weaker and complex multilateralism will die out, along with the contribution it makes to keeping international politics peaceful.

Complex multilateralism can be self-sustaining—and maybe it is. Some analysts expected it to unravel once the Cold War ended. They said the United States would be less interested in the burdens of making it work, Europeans would be more resentful of the dominance of the United States, and Europeans would be less dependent on U.S. protection, so U.S. leverage for making multilateralism work would decline. Maybe this will happen but it has not yet.

Efforts to explain the incidence and success of complex multilateralism have not resulted in a consensus. One of its attractive features is that, unlike deterrence or power balancing, it promotes conflict resolution and the easing of tensions. States are never eager to cede some of their power, so it is good that complex multilateralism develops slowly, not abruptly, giving states and peoples time to adjust. Enhancing cooperation can take place with regard for the concerns of leaders and nations about autonomy. *Systemic security* is enhanced, because conflicts are eased, without unduly disturbing state security. A pluralistic security community is very attractive because it means peace with sovereignty. In addition, if governments are suitably inclined, complex multilateralism can go a long way toward eliminating the security dilemma. States continue to have military power, but that, in itself, does not make them afraid of each other. The key is an appreciation by everyone of the interdependence of security, of the foolishness of everyone trying to be safe alone no matter how their actions affect others. This can be a hard sell politically, psychologically, and in many cultures. But moving toward it seems much better than treating security as a zero-sum game, in which a state is safe only if it is so strong that everyone else is fearful.

The benefits to *societal security* can be substantial as well. Eliminating wars and shrinking fears of it can reinforce the payoffs from rising economic, cultural, and other interactions that advanced multilateralism promotes. That allows it to be carried further. In addition, knowledge that these effects are likely can be a powerful incentive. In Eastern Europe the prospect of joining the Western communities, and then membership in them, has stimulated many of these nations to move toward democracy, introduce economic reform, promote social change, and set aside ethnic or religious quarrels. As a result, improvement in the lives of people in these societies promises to be substantial in the future.

Yet problems and defects are apparent with the complex multilateralism approach to peace. Critics think it works only because the participating states already get along well. That is, it is not why they get along, it is the result of their ability to get along. That would mean it is not a solution to the problem of war. This may be true. It is suspicious that complex multilateralism has flourished mainly among Western countries that have much in common and not much to disagree about. Evidence suggests that complex multilateralism is more important, more useful, than this, but further studies and more experience with it are needed to be sure.

Also disturbing is that, even it if works, it may not work well in much of the world. That is a disturbing possibility because in various ways complex multilateralism is now the world's foremost approach to the problem of war and the one given great attention by most of the world's most powerful countries. In pushing globalization and pressing for democratization, Western countries are also trying to lay the basis for spreading complex multilateralism, anticipating that it will make the world much more peaceful. A considerable amount is riding on it, so the desire for it to work is great. However, if what is needed to make it work will not be available in many parts of the world, at least not soon, then someone has to come up with something else.

Consider, for example, complex multilateralism and the global great powers today. Multilateral management of the problem of war is supposed to take place largely in and through the UN Security Council, with the great powers and others moving beyond running a simple great-power concert. But China is not a democratic political system, and Russia is only marginally one. Both are only partly market-oriented economies. Sure enough, the main dividing line on the Security Council is between those two states and the Western democracies. If this situation continues and hardens, the lack of consensus will keep the Security Council from acting to deal forcefully with either conflicts among the great powers or conflicts of other sorts between or inside other countries.

Integration

What about integration as an alternative solution? When integration is in its initial phase, it is much like complex multilateralism. Rising interactions, spreading cooperation, and greater interdependence lead to or strengthen a pluralistic security community. The benefit to *state security* when it comes to avoiding wars is gratifying. *Societal security* is enhanced in the same fashion as it is with complex multilateralism. However, many of the concerns about how applicable complex multilateralism is applied to integration also. For instance, how far can integration get if the participating states and societies are not alike? The European Union is not interested in adding nondemocracies, or socialist economic systems, or dirt-poor countries. It is leery of adding a non-Western culture (Turkey), and some people think that the non-Western elements of Russia will always keep it from being admitted. In much of the rest of the world countries that constitute a region are often far more heterogeneous than those in Europe. Also countries elsewhere are not so afraid of war that they will readily embrace such a drastic solution as integration to avoid it. If integration is the way to go to achieve peace but many countries cannot or will not embrace it, then it is not a promising solution.

Integration is also harsh on state security eventually. States get to be safer from military attacks but slowly lose the essence of being states. Their sovereignty is ceded in the name of systemic and societal security, plus their own safety. That is a big price to pay, and not just for states. Many people cherish national autonomy and would feel less safe, less complete, and less comfortable in their identities as peoples without their independent states. Integration pushed too fast can easily promote societal insecurity.

This problem has cropped up repeatedly in Europe, which is a major reason that integration has developed slowly, taking more than fifty years. In Britain, for instance, there have been persistent doubts about carrying integration too far, doubts that other nations share. In referendums Norwegians have repeatedly refused to join the EU. The Swiss are far from certain that they want to join. Public support across Europe for developing a single currency was consistently tepid. Though barriers among the participating states have been taken down, citizens of the various nations still maintain their differences and speak their separate languages. They do not move in great numbers either. French workers do not flood into Germany when the French economy is slow and Germany is booming. As a result, available jobs have often been filled by immigrants from outside Europe, who are not received with open arms. This has helped spawn political movements that stress nationalism, national independence, and—naturally enough—resistance to further integration.

Clearly integration is not a universal solution to the problem of war either. The great powers will not be integrating. No support is found in much of the world for pursuing integration with neighbors, who are despised or hated or feared. Weak states and small societies sometimes feel the need for integration to be safe, but they often also react in just the opposite way—fearing that they will be swallowed up by a large new community in which much larger peoples will be dominant.

Final Assessment

Thus far this book has been discussing approaches to deal with the problem of war that involve adjusting the international system and relations among governments in the context of that system. Now it turns to techniques and practices that focus more directly on war itself and on the political conflict that gives rise to it. These approaches can be applied within various arrangements of the international system. They are more practical than strategic in nature, designed to cope with conflicts and war no matter what the broad systemic arrangements are.

SOURCES AND OTHER USEFUL READINGS

The statistics on ethnic conflicts are from Ted Robert Gurr, "Minorities, Nationalists, and Ethnopolitical Conflicts." Also useful is his book on the same subject, *Minorities at Risk*. The broad conception of complex multilateralism used in this chapter is derived from John G. Ruggie, *Multilateralism Matters*. A good account of how the United States stressed multilateralism during the Cold War in relations with Europe is John G. Ikenberry, *After Victory*. A shorter review of the use of multilateralism in the Atlantic community is Patrick M. Morgan, "Multilateralism and Security: Prospects in Europe," in *Multilateralism Matters*, edited by John Gerard Ruggie.

The concept of a pluralistic security community is discussed and applied in *Security Communities*, edited by Emanuel Adler and Michael Barnett. The concept goes back to Karl Deutsch, Sidney A. Burrell, and Robert A. Kann, *Political Community and the North Atlantic Area*. On the theory of integration, see Dimitris N. Chryssochoou, *Theorizing European Integration*. To review the development of the European Union, see David P. Lewis, *The Road to Europe*; and Desmond Dinan, *Ever Closer Union*.

The enlargement of NATO and the EU is discussed in Robert Ruchhaus, *Explaining NATO Enlargement*; and Wade Jacoby, *The Enlargement of the European Union and NATO*.

CHAPTER 9

Negotiation and Mediation

In general terms, **peacemaking** is the effort to resolve a serious conflict, one in which peace could easily break down, or already has, into killing and other mayhem. Various possible outcomes would constitute a success. One side could quit, give in, or surrender to the other, with the help of some conflict resolution efforts. This is possible but, in serious conflicts, unlikely. Or the parties could reach an agreement and settle all the issues between them. Again, possible, but not likely. Otherwise, the parties might ease the situation by relaxing the conflict either temporarily or indefinitely, such as by adopting a truce or a more elaborate deal. This happens fairly often. Finally, antagonists sometimes just set a conflict aside. They agree to disagree about contentious issues and shift their attention to other matters. Usually this occurs only when other problems have arisen for the parties involved, problems that are more important or more pressing. In each of these instances peace is either preserved or restored, at least for a time, and in that sense the conflict ends.

How can such outcomes be achieved? Some of the tools developed in international politics are

Negotiation—a process used for all sorts of purposes but the concern here is with reaching a mutual agreement to ease or resolve serious conflicts.

Mediation—an effort by one or more outside parties to help those involved in a serious conflict to negotiate their way out of it.

Arbitration—the use of an outside party, by agreement in advance, to settle the conflict, thereby avoiding negotiations among the antagonists.

Adjudication—the use of an outside judicial party, a judge or court, to try to settle the issue; the parties might agree in advance to accept the decision as final or to treat it instead as informational and advisory.

This chapter is concerned with negotiation and mediation because they are far more commonly used for serious conflicts in international politics. Arbitration and adjudication are commonly used in domestic conflicts but have had little impact in international conflicts and normally have little impact on serious domestic disputes as well, ones on the verge of or already caught up in internal warfare. In serious international conflicts, states are rarely willing to let an outsider decide. The more important the issue, the more they care about how it comes out and the less they feel they can leave determining the outcome to others. In serious domestic conflicts, the same is basically true for all the parties involved.

NEGOTIATION

Negotiation is a familiar way of tackling conflict, with a long history. It is, basically, an exchange of ideas by the parties to a dispute as to how it should be settled. Those ideas are typically exchanged directly. The parties talk with each other. Sometimes the exchange is indirect; the parties make public pronouncements aimed at each other (for example, when the protagonists "negotiate in the newspapers") or have another kind of channel through which messages get passed. In negotiation by force, the parties inflict harm as a way to send messages and bargain about possible outcomes to the conflict. In the exchange of ideas during negotiation, the point is to reach agreement—to settle, ignore, abandon, or temporarily halt it. (As every couple knows, conflicts are often ended without being settled.)

According to Louis Kriesberg, renowned for his analysis of conflict situations, a conflict emerges when two or more parties have incompatible goals about something important and realize that this situation will either deny them other things they want or make achieving them much harder or more costly. Disliking this situation gives them a grievance and moves them to do something about it—to persuade, to bargain, to threaten, or to fight. Negotiation can be used to strike a deal that prevents escalation of the conflict to more intense levels or to fighting. The persuasion involved can be instructional, emotional, or compulsive. Compulsive persuasion includes when negotiation is used to convey or accompany threats designed to force an agreement—like *The Godfather*'s "I'll make him an offer he can't refuse." Once the use of force begins, negotiation can be tried to prevent the fighting from growing, then to halt it, and finally to deal with the conflict. Similarly, if the fighting has escalated to outright war, negotiation can be used to suspend it or to end it and settle the conflict. Thus negotiation is an option at any stage of a conflict, and often negotiation and continued disagreement, even violence, go hand in hand through many phases of the dispute.

There is debate about when negotiation is most appropriate. On the one hand, it may seem best to have negotiation early to get a settlement before the conflict deepens, positions harden, opposition to negotiating grows, and the costs mount. On the other hand, it sometimes seems best to put off negotiations until the conflict gets serious and each side figures out what is really at stake, how determined the opponent is, and what the possible consequences are of reaching no deal (Will fighting start? If so, with what result?). Each side must also assess its political situation (Do its supporters want a deal?). Like labor-management talks, a deal often emerges only when pressure mounts, a crisis builds, and a resort to coercion (a strike, a lockout) is imminent.

Once fighting starts it would be nice if negotiations would bring it to an end, preventing more bloodshed and destruction that, if not stopped, will likely breed more bitterness and make the conflict harder to solve. Otherwise, the fighting could escalate, feeding on itself like a bad fire. But there is that alternative view: Negotiation will not work until either one side is clearly winning or both sides are clearly not winning. Negotiations, those critics say, mostly end fighting when both sides feel further fighting will not change the outcome and will just add to the costs they suffer.

Negotiation as a Process

A vast literature exists on negotiations—historical accounts and memoirs, assessments of negotiation styles, descriptions of the psychology of negotiation, and so on. After all, negotiations are common, and the stakes are often important so failure is costly. Courses and programs to train negotiators are available. Nevertheless, major disagreements are voiced not only about when to negotiate but also about how to negotiate, and even about how to think about negotiation. There are also signs that negotiation has limited value. In many cases it fails or negotiated settlements soon collapse. Either it is an unreliable solution to the problem of war or its proper use is hard to define.

One of the more influential approaches to negotiation is linked to specialist on international negotiation Roger Fisher and his associates at Harvard University. In this approach, negotiation is seen as technique. Negotiations often fail because they are badly conducted. Certain ways of negotiating maximize the chances of success in almost any conflict situation. Fortunately, the essential elements of good negotiating are not hard to grasp and can be readily taught. Fisher and associates have produced numerous how-to books, offered courses, and held seminars, workshops, and the like throughout the world.

Assume that negotiation is important and how it is conducted makes a difference. This sounds obvious, but there is an alternative view. What if international conflicts are decided by the distribution of power? Then negotiations are often just window dressing. Or maybe the key is whether the parties are politically ready to agree. When the Israeli-Palestinian peace process collapsed in 2000–2001, analysts said it was the result of bad negotiating, but maybe it was because powerful elements on both sides opposed the negotiations and there was no consensus in either camp on what to settle for on the big issues such as the future of Jerusalem. Maybe negotiations and ways of negotiating matters only in certain cases.

The response of the Fisher school is that in many disputes good ideas are put forth concerning how to settle them and the main components of a workable deal are understood, so maybe the problem is poor planning, poor negotiating strategies or poor techniques on things such as communicating with the other side. How should these things be done? If you are a party in a significant conflict, the first step is to think through the conflict carefully in terms of your interests (what you need, what you have at stake) and then in terms of the other side's view (its assumptions, goals, view of you, and what it needs and has at stake). It is also important to appreciate the other's side's priorities, plus its feelings and emotional or political commitments, as they emerge from its underlying perceptions and values. In a negotiation you want the other side to make the decision you prefer. Unless you grasp how it sees the situation you cannot figure out how to make that decision appealing—how to describe the issue, how to frame it, and what concessions or incentives to offer.

To formulate your negotiating stance you need a good sense of who will make the decision for the other side and what that person or group is like. You design your messages accordingly. And it is not what you say that matters, it is what the other side hears. What is reasonable to you may sound unacceptable, even impossible, to those across the negotiating table. Or your message may be clear to you but not to others, conveying elements that you did not mean to impart or asking for things you did not mean to request.

In this undertaking a decent working relationship with the negotiators on the other side helps. People are not automatons; social relations matter. And you cannot expect the other side to share your values, agree with your assessments, typically make the first move or offer the initial concession, and always be pleasant. So you need to be patient, communicate carefully, be reliable in what you convey as your view and position, use persuasion instead of threats or withdrawal, and listen carefully.

It is also necessary to review the conflict, the issues, and the parties' positions in detail. Sometimes the official position that each side takes does not accurately reflect its interests or clearly grasp the essential disagreement. Often more compatibility exists between the two sides' positions than it seems. This is because an official negotiating position can reflect many different things: a temporary political or bureaucratic compromise back home, the need to project a tough image there, the desire to ask for more than one expects to get so that later shifts can be called big concessions that the other side should match, and so on.

For the Fisher school the ideal is to convert the negotiation from a competitive exercise in trying to get the most out of the other side into a process the parties see as "a joint search for a principled solution." This calls for an accommodative attitude. That is, the real enemy is the problem and the opponent can be an ally in solving it. Together the negotiators work out the principles an agreement should embody, take everyone's real interests and concerns into account, and jointly tackle the obstacles that exist to resolving the problem posed because of the parties' clashing positions. One side does not get a successful conclusion by just announcing its position, pounding the table, rejecting the other side's stance, staking out the maximum in demands, and hanging tough on every possible concession. Instead, it tries to figure out what is blocking agreement and, using reasoned persuasion and flexibility, encourage the other side to join in creative thinking about how to overcome it.

Therefore inclinations to negotiate by threats and force must be curbed. Threatening others usually makes it harder for them to agree. They resent the threat, resist giving in to it, and fear that to do so will only invite more demands with more threats backing them up. They may even seize on your threat as an opportunity to show how tough, how determined, they are. And if you carry it out, maybe because you do not want to look as though you were bluffing, you add to their grievances and possibly reduce their readiness to compromise, especially if they had psychologically prepped themselves for that harm so the cost does not seem so bad. Outsiders will criticize you for using pain instead of talk, especially if you are the much stronger party (you look like a bully).

Ultimately, what matters is whether the **best alternative to a negotiated agreement** (BATNA) is better, for either party, than a prospective agreement. If the BATNA is better for both, why negotiate at all? If the BATNA is better for the other side than what you are offering, you better improve your bargaining leverage—reducing the other side's BATNA and boosting your own—by softening your offer or upping the costs to the opposition of not getting a deal. Other useful techniques for getting out of an impasse are

- Reframing what you are asking for by shifting your position;

- Asking the other side to agree to do something eventually, instead of right away;

- Dividing the issue into pieces and taking up some of them at a time;

- Arranging to deliver your part of the proposed bargain sooner so the benefits for the other side will be more apparent;

- Setting a date when your offer will expire; and

- Starting to prepare to carry out your offer, so it looks more credible that you will come through with it when a deal is reached.

In explaining how negotiations often go sour, Fisher proponents are wary of how governments work. Inside an agency consensus is prized so innovative thinking is scarce, and an agency will be preoccupied with its own interests and perspectives so it will not listen well to the other side's concerns. To gain a consensus position for an agency or for the government as a whole takes trade-offs and compromises; agreement is typically reached at the lowest common denominator. The result is a negotiating approach highly attentive to what the various parts of the government want but not to the other side's needs and concerns. And it can be rigid. To change the official position means undoing the compromises in the government on which it was built, leaving that position not particularly imaginative. So governments talk past each other. Their internal negotiating dialogue can overwhelm the negotiating process with the other side.

Negotiation as Politics

Two significant approaches, and variations on them, emphasize the *political* dimension of negotiations as opposed to being concerned with technique. The first includes what Fisher and colleagues describe as hard bargaining and others sometimes consider a **rational decision approach**. It starts by seeing conflicts as the result of real differences in goals. That is, people want incompatible things. Negotiations, at least in international affairs, are often seen as tests of each side's power and determination, and the parties more or less rationally calculate what they can get given the relative power distribution between them. A negotiation is a political trial of strength and will, an effort by each side to politically defeat the other. Sometimes the matter at hand is less important in itself than as an opportunity to display the other side as politically, morally, or ideologically weaker and thus having to make concessions. As a result almost anything can be worth arguing about. During the Cold War the Soviet Union wanted East Germany to be accepted as a legitimate government, so for any East-West talks it kept trying to get East Germany invited as a separate state. When Western governments refused, the response was often a protest and a delay in the proceedings. Hard bargaining can lead to a fight over the agenda—a negotiation about negotiating. The hard bargainer wants the items he prefers on the agenda and listed his way (not as "discuss X" but as "discuss the other side's misbehavior with regard to X"). He wants to determine what will be discussed first. He hopes to stipulate where the talks take place. The process is an effort at political one-upmanship from the start. This can extend to using the negotiations as a platform to publicize the hard bargainer's position and grievances while making the other side look bad. The negotiations are used as a pulpit more than as an opportunity to reach a deal.

In a particularly extreme version, once the talks begin you, the hard bargainer, do not make suggestions, you make demands. Or you offer no proposals, to convey the impression that the other side is in the wrong and should therefore come up with a proposal on how to fix things. When you adopt a position, you stick to it rigidly. You challenge the other side's motives, its decency, its legitimacy, and its intentions. Lack of progress is always the result of the other side's inadequate response to your fair position. If the other side makes a concession, it is only being realistic, and it is about time. You accept it and press for more. You wait to the last minute (the talks are about to collapse) to make a concession yourself to keep things going. Otherwise, you woodenly repeat your position, over and over. The goal is to disorient and frustrate the other side and exploit its desire for an agreement. Meanwhile, you wait for the other side to start rethinking its position and be conciliatory, making concessions to get the talks moving. Until then he rebuffs friendly overtures. The working relationship is not likely to be pleasant, just formally correct.

Western governments ran into this negotiating pattern on numerous occasions with many communist governments and gradually came to see it as a deliberate style, a consciously crafted approach. Those governments often wanted to reach agreements, were willing to bargain seriously, and could make concessions, but much patience and persistence were required to craft agreements. There are various explanations for this combative approach. One is that these states were ideologically predisposed to treat each Western government as an enemy seeking their destruction. Negotiation was a ploy the West used, so extreme care was needed to get what they could and not give anything away. Another is that communist governments had an inferiority complex. Being the weaker side and having suspect legitimacy, they felt they should look as tough and suspicious as possible to make the most of their limited assets.

North Korea continues to illustrate this hard bargaining pattern today. It has long bristled with nasty responses. It condemns actions of others that it dislikes and regularly threatens military action or a withdrawal from agreements or a halt to negotiations. It often operates as if the outside world is so hostile that it will only get what it needs by forcing others to give in. It is combative, assertive, insulting, demanding, and highly repetitive—the opposite of the Fisher approach. When it gets a tough response it regularly charges that it has been insulted, mistreated, or not taken seriously, and it suspends or cancels negotiations—it goes off in a huff.

Has this tactic worked? Assessments vary. For years critics charged that the West (the Americans, the French, the West Germans, and so on) was outmaneuvered, snookered by the Russians, the Chinese, and the East Germans. Western countries went too far in seeking détente, gave up too much in arms negotiations, and the like. These were calls to adopt either a hard bargaining approach or something closer to it. After all, that approach was, supposedly, working for the other side. North Korea, once again, remains as an example today. For years it insisted on isolation, being as self-reliant as possible, and it negotiated with little interest in getting along with others. But eventually, in the 1990s, the United States and

North Korea conducted a series of talks on North Korea's nuclear weapons program, on its development of missiles and its missile sales, on U.S. aid, and on the U.S. recovery of bodies from the Korean War (1950–1953). Critics said that North Korea's hard bargaining was successful.

According to these critics, North Korean leaders decided some years ago that isolation was not sustainable. The country needed more respect, more trade, more aid especially in food, and some foreign investment. But it had little to offer (it was too poor) except for things it did not want to give, such as domestic political and economic reform. So instead North Koreans threatened, demanded, and were obnoxious. They started developing nuclear weapons and selling some of that technology, and they built and sold ballistic missiles especially to states much of the world finds unappealing. When the United States and others complained, North Korea denounced the criticism; when economic sanctions were threatened, North Korea called it an act of war and threatened to attack South Korea and U.S. forces there. The United States' drive to end North Korea's nuclear weapons program eventually led to a crisis, the opening of negotiations, and a deal in 1994 under which North Korea froze its nuclear weapons program in exchange for a variety of concessions by the United States. But this was not the end of the conflict. Soon North Korea was in terrible shape, especially from a severe famine, and had to accept a great deal of foreign aid. Nonetheless, it continued its hard bargaining. It limited access to a significant portion of the country for the aid givers. Therefore donors could not fully check on whether aid was properly used. It refused to adopt reforms so the aid could be reduced, and it resisted making other concessions. The world could either bow to North Korea's demands or deliberately let thousands, maybe millions, of North Koreans starve to death.

When the outsiders clearly were not going to ignore or abet starvation, talks were finally mounted on things North Korea badly wanted. At that point North Korea was businesslike, the negotiations went fairly smoothly, and the hard bargaining dropped away, strongly suggesting that it has always been a negotiating ploy or strategy.

To the critics North Korea successfully bullied and blackmailed others. It became the leading recipient of American aid in Asia; received huge amounts of aid from South Korea, Japan, Europe, and elsewhere; and ended up getting normal diplomatic relations with much of the world. The cost? It gave up its nuclear weapons program but refused to reveal whether it has any nuclear weapons. It subsequently started another nuclear weapons program, setting off (in 2002) another crisis with the United States and more negotiations—and more hard bargaining on its part. It did not become less authoritarian, was slow to pursue economic reforms, and remained the most militarized state in the world—still poised to attack South Korea. While it eventually made a huge concession by agreeing to

hold a summit conference with South Korea, it was slow to develop major cooperation with South Korea. What it had done, say the critics, was to extort enough
aid to allow the regime to survive.

The George W. Bush administration was full of such critics. In 2002 the administration tried to develop a hard bargaining approach of its own, demanding that
North Korea admit it had violated the 1994 agreement and give up its new nuclear
weapons program, plus any nuclear weapons it had from the earlier one, before
real negotiations could even begin. Predictably, critics at home and abroad said
this was more coercion than negotiation. The United States could even be just
going through the motions to make North Korea look bad so it could attack. But
when the United States adopted a more flexible position, other critics, also predictably, charged that North Korea was getting away with extortion again.

Is hard bargaining just a ploy or is it rooted in certain cultures? On the one
hand, at times the North Koreans were all business and accommodating, which
was true earlier of other communist governments. On the other hand, a recent
study of the Russians finds that they see negotiations as a struggle, with victory as
the goal. The key is power. Compromise may be necessary but mostly it stems
from weakness. It is shameful, not the epitome of success. Tactics include
stonewalling; laying out extreme positions from which to move only in exchange
for major concessions; seeking agreement in principle, which is then exploited to
justify the Russian position; and generally practicing a high level of secrecy. In
short, the study concludes, much that had been thought of as Soviet bargaining
was more typically Russian behavior.

Is hard bargaining the way to go, in general or at least for dealing with the
world's North Koreas? Often opponents of North Korea advocate hard bargaining
in return; confront North Korea with serious demands, insistent criticism, and
threats, and if it does not come around, refuse to negotiate at all. That is tempting. The West, especially the United States, often took that route in the Cold War.
However, the classic hard bargainers during and since the Cold War—the Soviet
bloc nations, North Korea, Iraq—had short-term successes but were often long-
term failures. Their negotiating tactics alienated others and limited their opportunities for beneficial international cooperation. That lack of cooperative interaction had a good deal to do with their overall failures.

Another approach to negotiation that stresses politics, called the **two-level
game approach**, was developed by political scientist Robert Putnam. When leaders seek an agreement with another country, they enter into a bargaining game
with the other side. There are various ways to play the game, but the goal is an
acceptable political deal. So if State A wants a military base on B's soil and B wants
to get paid for this, A and B have to agree on a price. Suppose A will pay from $50
million to $70 million annually, and B would take as little as $65 million but

wants $90 million. That range of possible deals on each side is its win-set. The negotiations are about determining the price—between $65 million and $70 million—which is where the two win-sets overlap and deals within that overlap would be acceptable to both sides.

But an agreement almost always has to be approved by someone back home. That is, it must be ratified. Who is the someone? It might be the public. Governments that agreed to join the European Union have usually asked for public approval in a referendum. Sometimes it is the cabinet, because the cabinet represents a majority of the parliament. If the agreement involves the United States and is a treaty, the U.S. Senate must approve it by a two-thirds vote. Other U.S. agreements often require implementing legislation passed by a majority in both houses of Congress. In communist countries the top leaders of the party had to approve. In other words, normally somebody has to okay the agreement. If so, says Putnam, those negotiating the deal have to play in a second bargaining game. They must negotiate with the ratifiers at home and, once again, the key is the range of acceptable deals. If State B is ready to agree to accept $70 million but its legislature must approve and insists on at least $80 million, the deal is in trouble.

Thus negotiation is at least a two-level process in international politics, which sometimes can be used to advantage in the international game. You insist that I pay at least $75 million, and I say that I would be happy to but Congress will never approve more than $60 million. Each side has good reason to try to alter the other side's win-sets in its favor, which may require trying to influence the other's internal negotiating game. For instance, you contact members of Congress to say that a deal at $70 million will lead to good business opportunities for Americans in your country. Each side should try to figure out what the other side can get agreement on back home. I say I will not pay more than $60 million, you find out that Congress will approve $70 million, so you hold out and hope Congress will pressure me to offer more. Those negotiating on a controversial matter clearly should be thinking about ratification on both sides and, in crafting the agreement, how to convince the ratifiers to approve it. Thus you and I cannot agree on $75 million because Congress will object, but both agree to see if Congress might go for a deal of $60 million in the first year and $2 million more each year after that. Furthermore, cooperation helps to get deals ratified. We both sign for $60 million the first year and $2 million more each year after that, then I tell people in your country that you were tough and got the best deal available and you do the same in mine.

Notice that this approach to understanding negotiations ignores many things in other approaches. What matters is whether the two sides' win-sets overlap or can be adjusted so they overlap; whether a possible agreement fits the win-sets of the ratifiers on each side; how well each side understands the real limits on what can be agreed to; and how well each negotiates to get the best deal it can within the limited range of possible agreements. For instance, many analysts believe that Chinese and North Korean leaders have trouble grasping how powerful Congress can be when they negotiate with the United States. What does not matter much is negotiating style, other than within the two-level game. For instance, having good timing is important only if the win-sets can easily shift or be shifted. If they do not overlap now and will not six months from now, timing on when you make your best offer is irrelevant. The best negotiating skill might be in manipulating the opponent's domestic political situation to shift his win-set. The Fisher sort of recommendations would not be useless, just not important to the outcome in many cases.

The Putnam approach is great for understanding why negotiations on difficult conflicts can be so lengthy and often unsuccessful. During the Strategic Arms Limitation Talks (SALT) that U.S. and Soviet officials conducted in the 1970s, American officials often spent more time and energy negotiating inside the government or with Congress or important interest groups on what the negotiating position should be than they did on talking with the Soviets. Noting this, President George Bush took a sharply different approach as the Cold War was ending. Instead of official negotiations with the Soviet (later Russian) government on how, and by how much, to cut nuclear arsenals, he began, after some prior consultation with Moscow, to announce unilateral American cuts in weapons. Then the Soviet leader would announce parallel cuts. Sometimes the Soviets would take the first step and the United States would match it. Each leader had to not outrun what domestic elements would support, but each leader gave those elements little room to react—no formal talks, no treaties, no elaborate details about a possible deal to chew over. Significant cuts in arsenals were agreed to quickly and mostly implemented during the 1990s. President George W. Bush tried to revive this strategy on arms control (and some other matters), in part to get around the onerous complications of negotiating with all the interested parties. His administration much preferred to unilaterally announce the steps the United States was going to take and let others decide whether they wanted to cooperate. As an example, this was the way the Anti-Ballistic Missile Treaty was cancelled.

Understandable though this practice may be, it is often an uncomfortable way to proceed. It is most appropriate when the leader wants to get something done that relevant foreign leaders and domestic actors basically support. When he acts, they react appropriately, with approval. But when they do not agree, this practice looks arbitrary—a leader doing what he wants regardless of the views of others who believe they are entitled to help shape the decisions. It is the rare leader or government that can display a unilateralist disdain for negotiations and agreements for long without provoking nasty reactions.

The other problem is that agreements, carefully negotiated, normally bind future decision makers in the governments that sign, which makes international politics more stable and predictable. That is valuable and a costly thing to lose. One of the driving motivations behind the flood of international agreements negotiated each year is the desire to control uncertainty in the future, no matter how imperfectly. Sure enough, the Central Intelligence Agency (CIA) has suggested that the strategic arms cuts President George W. Bush arranged in a simple, one-page agreement with the Russian government cannot be fully verified. The negotiation and the agreement avoided all real discussion of verification.

Negotiation and Culture

Another analysis of negotiation illuminates important aspects of it in international politics. The approach is associated primarily with political scientist Raymond Cohen, who accepts that negotiation expertise and technique are important and that an overlap in the parties' goals and interests is crucial. However, he finds that ways of negotiating are heavily influenced by **culture**. People from different cultures often negotiate differently, opening up endless possibilities for miscommunication, misperception, and misunderstanding. Language differences contain traps. Translation cannot entirely capture the nuances of one language in another, and sometimes one language conveys clearly something that another language cannot. An example is the term "deterrence" in English, which comes out meaning something more politically oppressive in its nearest equivalents in Russian and Chinese.

Then there are major cultural differences as to what is fitting or proper behavior, that is, what is suitably polite in social situations, conversation, and negotiations (see the *Cases and Context* box, "Cultural Aspects of Negotiations"). Cultures put a different emphasis on the relative importance of the individual or the group and thus on respecting and preserving face and honor vis-à-vis other individuals and groups. Some cultures allow for cutting to the heart of a problem and directly dealing with it. Others call for an approach that is carefully respectful of personal, social, and cultural needs and considerations, so the sensitive difficulties at the bottom of an issue are much better approached indirectly. Negotiation via confrontation and direct debate is appropriate in some cultures and considered insensitive in others. Cultures vary in their sense of time and history. Americans are often irritated when others cite events from hundreds of years ago to explain and justify a conflict and their stance on it. To Americans history can be irrelevant or overcome and what matters is defining, then dealing with, problems here and now. In some cultures time is important, not to be wasted. Hence a serious conflict should be confronted and dealt with, resolved so as to get on to other things. In other cultures, time is less important. Cultures also vary in terms of how they regard lying—in some it is fine, in others awful—and in their attitudes toward taking risks.

Some cultures treat the world as readily manipulable: Problems can be solved or fixed and relationships can be adjusted or changed. But to others the world seems not easily changed; the world's complexities and difficulties must be accommodated. In cultures in which rank and face are important, interactions (including negotiations) should seek to avoid even slight suggestions that a participant

Cases and Context: Cultural Aspects of Negotiations

Cultural elements can shape views on negotiations. For example, despite their many positive interactions, particularly in economic relations, China and Japan have an uneasy, strained political relationship based largely on each seeing the other as a rising threat. Both could benefit from a more relaxed relationship that allows productive negotiations on political and security matters, because neither would benefit from a full-blown rivalry. However, a major barrier exists to starting such negotiations. China insists that Japan has insufficiently apologized for its crimes against China before and during World War II, and this failure to accept responsibility indicates it is still dangerous. In particular, China objects to visits by top Japanese officials, particularly the prime minister, to the Yasukuni cemetery and shrine to Japanese war dead, where some Japanese leaders convicted of war crimes were reburied in 1978 as a protest over their convictions and where an attached museum presents Japan's view of the war. Because Japan has often apologized to China for its past actions, the Chinese complaint is that it has not been sufficiently abject. This reflects in part the Chinese sense of morality—a great wrong requires total remorse. It also stems from the Chinese view that, as a great nation, society, and culture, China's experience of being invaded and abused by Western nations and Japan in the nineteenth and twentieth centuries was not just a string of defeats, it was a national humiliation. A core element of Chinese culture is that China is, and must be appreciated as, a great society. Only a complete apology is suitable, and achieving it is part of the restoration of China's dignity, of China finally returning to its proper position as a great nation in the eyes of the world.

From the Japanese perspective, the essence of a good relationship is mutual respect, which must rest on never treating others in a way that is degrading or disregards feelings. This is a central element in Japanese culture. In negotiations, the Japanese typically avoid directly saying no and rejecting the other side's view outright or making peremptory demands. Candor is set aside so as not to appear insensitive, disrespectful, or belittling toward the other side's feelings. China's demands for an apology are therefore inappropriate, as they are lacking in proper respect. This crude insensitivity to Japanese feelings is insufferable, and catering to it would be humiliating, particularly for such a unique and important society. Furthermore, it suggests that China will be a threat to Japan in the future. Resisting Chinese demands is especially necessary now, because standing up for Japan's stature and dignity is required to complete its recovery as a nation and a great power, restoring the respect lost with its defeat in World War II and never fully regained because of Japan's deferential and low profile foreign policy thereafter.

Americans readily sympathize with Chinese resentment about past Japanese crimes. However, they have difficulty understanding why that should cripple better relations and effective negotiations now between the two most important nations in East Asia, particularly when so much is at stake. After all, World War II ended a long time ago. They can understand why Japan resents China harping on this matter but tend to suggest that Japanese leaders should continue apologizing and stop visiting the cemetery so that Sino-Japanese relations can move on to the important issues and problems of today. Because these steps have not been taken, Americans are given to suspecting that each side must have more pragmatic reasons for their behavior, as that makes more sense. Perhaps important domestic political advantages or constraints make the two governments behave this way. Or maybe each government, operating with a realist picture of international politics, believes that the two will inevitably be rivals, and are already rivals in fact. Therefore this dispute is just a symbolic expression of their emerging competition over more substantive matters.

Each view reflects important elements of a national culture, which leads to three different conceptions of how the Sino-Japanese relationship should be understood and how that bears on the chances for negotiations on important issues.

lacks stature, is incorrect, or is not to be trusted. Therefore, someone from such a culture insists being treated with respect, even in small things, from the opponent. When members of different cultures interact, endless possibilities exist for each side to irritate the other, intentionally or not.

One implication is that negotiation can hardly be taught from a manual like teaching someone to fix cars. Any negotiation, but particularly an international one, is an elaborate social process, varying from one set of participants to another. Cultures vary on how important it is to not look weak or incompetent. Years ago India desperately needed American aid, but in the negotiations it was important to India that the United States offer the aid first and let India deign to accept it—to avoid India having to openly ask for it—and that the United States then defer to India on many details as to how the aid was to be delivered and distributed. Cultures also diverge as to the art of the negotiation process. Americans like to be all business: Get right to the issues, lay out their position, hear from the other side to see where the differences lie, then debate and haggle over an agreement that settles matters. In this process, compromise is appropriate and welcome. But negotiators from other cultures often prefer to move slowly. The initial stage should be used to get a clear sense of the broad context and develop a relationship between the parties. Direct confrontation, tough debate, and argument should be avoided.

Only through discussions of general principles and broad concerns should the issues emerge, in an indirect way. Open disagreement strongly expressed is painful, disruptive, even threatening. Compromise is not particularly good, because it is considered a sign of weakness—something to hide, not to be proud of. Thus much of a final agreement may have to be put in vague terms to conceal the compromises involved, or skirt key issues, or prevent an ignominious failure of the negotiations and loss of face. This leaves important issues to be dealt with later and, if possible, in a lower-profile way.

Numerous examples can be cited of how cultural clashes distort negotiations, and Cohen groups them into two models. A **low-context culture** is familiar to Americans and other Westerners—straight talk preferred, positions stated clearly, getting right down to business is good. The point is to get results (reach a deal) and sharp debate is fine while compromise is valuable. But in a **high-context culture** communication should be indirect, nuanced, often nonverbal. To protect people's sensibilities, retaining face is important in negotiation meetings and direct debate. Haggling is therefore unacceptable. It is crude and indelicate because direct confrontations are bad. And for a party to lose an argument outright would be embarrassing.

Within the two broad negotiating styles are variations. Negotiation thus is more than a matter of the right techniques. This approach is not compatible, therefore, with the Fisher concept of negotiation. Critics, however, temper the Cohen view. Perhaps the impact of culture is limited or, at least, not overwhelming. If so, it is not a big worry. Maybe the major differences are captured by the two models and a negotiator just needs to understand which one he is dealing with. That would make negotiation fairly easy to teach. Or maybe in a globalizing era the world is becoming more like the West on negotiations. Maybe all diplomatic negotiators, who work closely together, are often away from their home cultures, speak the same languages, and have similar educational backgrounds, are becoming more like each other and socialized into an **international diplomatic culture**.

Still, some negotiators do not fit the mold (like the North Koreans). Many negotiators are not trained diplomats, only politicians or bureaucrats sent off to deal on behalf of their governments. In addition, the biggest negotiating problems arise inside countries in internal conflicts. Those negotiators are military officers, politicians, guerrilla leaders, heads of NGOs, or religious leaders. No common diplomatic culture applies. Even though the parties are from the same country, they are often vastly different culturally. And even when they share a culture and speak the same language, they often fail to resolve their differences and continue fighting instead. Maybe culture differences are not the key, at least with some domestic conflicts and wars.

MEDIATION

With so many difficulties involved in getting negotiations started, conducted, and successfully concluded, negotiators often need help. **Mediation** helps. It is an effort by an outsider to aid the parties in a conflict in establishing and conducting negotiations to deal with it. Mediation can be used for all sorts of conflicts, especially ones that are persistent and seem all but impossible for the parties to settle themselves. The concern here is its use in conflicts in which fighting is possible or has already taken place. In fact, for the purposes of this book, mediation is more important than negotiation. When outside governments, international organizations, or others intervene to deal with the problem of war, their first recourse is usually to encourage the disputants to deal with the conflict themselves, starting with negotiations. They try to get the parties interested in talking, help to start the talks, or assist the parties through the talks to reach an agreement. Sometimes they even help the parties live up to that agreement.

Mediation Activities

Parties to a conflict sometimes negotiate at a distance, without formal talks. They issue public statements or take various actions—even by using force against each other. In a severe case, however, they are often not negotiating at all. Even if meetings take place the parties may simply be going through the motions. Thus the mediator's initial task may be to suggest that they give negotiations a try, take negotiations seriously, and offer to assist in getting them started. The mediator might do this in a low-key fashion, even behind the scenes, but sometimes mediators go public and complain loudly to apply pressure. At times mediators offer incentives to stimulate talks. Often it helps if the mediator takes the initiative to propose an agenda, arranges a place where the parties can meet, suggests a time, and so on.

Once the parties agree to talk the mediator can then be of assistance in many ways: providing a meeting place, chairing the meeting, providing security for the negotiators if the parties are nervous about this, and keeping a record of what is said and agreed to (to resolve later disputes). Sometimes the mediator turns into a phone line. Just because the opponents arrive at a meeting does not mean they are ready to actually talk with each other. President Jimmy Carter often carried messages between the Egyptian president and the Israeli prime minister while the two were meeting, with his help, in 1978 at Camp David. The mediator may inject proposals on various matters into the discussions or design possible agreements, especially on a sensitive issue or when the talks are deadlocked. Going further than this, mediators sometimes put considerable pressure on the parties or orchestrate pressure from others to make a deal. The other side of that coin is to offer incentives. Examples include offering to provide or help pay for verification of any agreement reached, to help enforce any agreement, or to supply side payments ("Sign the agreement and we will give you some other things you want").

When agreement is reached, the mediator may still have more to do. As the two-level game approach indicates, ratification of the agreement could be a problem. Sometimes the mediator tries to help the situation along by campaigning for the deal and helping defend it against critics. The implementation of an agreement commonly runs into problems and controversy. Here the mediator can help by, for example, collecting arms that are supposed to be turned in, monitoring military pullbacks, or holding meetings to resolve disputes. A powerful mediator might threaten to directly intervene to punish any violations of the agreement. More often, the mediator calls attention to violations and coordinates pressures on the violator to stop.

Mediation Performers

Mediators come in all shapes and sizes. The United Nations (UN), usually through the secretary general and his representatives, offers to mediate in many conflicts, frequently under instructions from the Security Council. Individual governments do a great deal of mediating. Powerful governments are common mediators, particularly when they are in the neighborhood or have other reasons to be deeply concerned about a conflict. They can more readily twist arms or grease palms to help create deals. But smaller mediators, including ones far from the conflict and with no stake in it, can also be effective. Being far away, they can easily look suitably neutral, honest, and nonintrusive. For example, Canada has been involved in various mediation activities, Algeria helped mediate an end to the U.S. hostage crisis with Iran, and Norway has a special fund to promote mediation and peacekeeping efforts. Private organizations also pursue mediation in international politics. The International Committee of the Red Cross has mediated often in Africa, as has the Catholic Community of Sant'Egidio based in Rome, Italy. IGOs have sometimes worked side by side with governments in mediation activities, for example, in Burundi and Tajikistan.

A popular approach these days is the use of **Track II diplomacy** efforts organized by outsiders who are usually nongovernmental agencies or groups. People from each side who are not officials or official representatives are brought together by a third party for discussions meant to help settle a conflict. The technique often is employed when the conflict is severe. Sometimes the discussions involve officials who appear in a personal, not their governmental, capacity. This has been true of discussions for years on disagreements between China and several nations in Southeast Asia about sovereignty over the South China Sea. More often the group will not have officials participating but people who are just outside the government or, for a nongovernment entity such as a guerrilla movement, just outside its ruling group—a former high official or a close friend or relative of a guerrilla leader. The idea is that they have access to the leaders of the parties in the dispute, know what the issues are, and understand what the views are of their side, but, not being leaders, they can talk more freely, raise and consider a wider range of ideas and options, and debate options in a more flexible way. Then they can talk to their leaders about the possibilities that emerge. This is often a good way to probe issues in depth and to try out possible proposals. It is a more productive way for opponents to communicate while not talking directly with each other. Sometimes the people involved are not semiofficials but instead are distinguished experts (scientists, intellectuals, business leaders). Their status lends weight to the discussions, which can make Track II a way to deeply explore the issues and float trial balloons on how to resolve them.

Another variant is discussions among ordinary people who serve as examples, politically, ethnically, or in some other way, of the contending sides—Jews meet Palestinians or Catholic mothers meet with Protestant mothers in Northern Ireland. The hope is that, in confronting the issues, these people broaden mutual understanding and tolerance, which then will spread. The theory is that a conflict often reflects powerful emotional and other needs and attitudes, and part of resolving it is to deal with those factors. Or meetings might initially ignore the issues and try to get the participants working on some common problems—rebuilding schools, starting a clinic, improving distribution of food aid—so that they build habits of cooperation, a certain amount of mutual respect, and an appreciation of their shared interests.

Still another approach is the use of distinguished individuals as mediators. They might be acting in an official capacity on behalf of a government or IGO or they might be acting on their own. Jimmy Carter is a good example. As the U.S.-North Korea dispute got nastier in 1994 and the United States planned direct military attacks on North Korea's nuclear weapons facilities, the former president suddenly dusted off an old invitation he had received to visit North Korea. The White House was surprised and the State Department uneasy, but he was given a message to carry. Carter went beyond message-carrying to work out a compromise, which he then announced in South Korea (on his way home), once again to the surprise of the White House. The two sides agreed to open negotiations on halting North Korea's nuclear weapons program in exchange for the United States supplying aid and beginning to move toward normal ties with North Korea. Another example is George J. Mitchell, former U.S. Senate majority leader. He served as a mediator in Northern Ireland, a thankless task, for a number of years and then headed an international team to develop the framework for trying to end Israeli-Palestinian violence in 2001 and get negotiations started again. In both cases he acted at the behest of the U.S. government. Long and complicated mediation was undertaken on the Bosnia situation by Robert Owen (former British foreign minister) and Cyrus Vance (former U.S. secretary of state) in 1992–1993, with Owen being the representative of the EU and Vance named by the secretary general of the UN.

Swedish professor Peter Wallensteen, well known for studies on resolving conflicts peacefully, once was invited to mediate in a conflict between guerrillas and the government on an island in Southeast Asia. After talking with the military commander, he was dropped off in the jungle to meet with the guerrillas.

Mediators play many roles. As one summary puts it, these roles include "instigator, communicator, persuader, organizer, precipitator, legitimizer, convener, moderator, manager, funder, teacher, and idea formulator." Put another way, mediators have various kinds of power: as rewarders, coercers, experts, sources of information, embodiments of legitimacy, and actors the parties may need good relations with. Some are clearly outsiders—standing apart, being detached. Others work as insiders, such as Americans mediating in the Middle East who care greatly about the dispute and are attached to one or both parties. Sometimes mediators facilitate steps by the parties, but at other times they have to maneuver and manipulate to force the negotiations along. Examples of the latter include Henry A. Kissinger and his associates who, after the October 1973 Yom Kippur War in the Middle East, ran every facet of the ensuing negotiations and dominated the crafting of the eventual agreements. Richard C. Holbrooke and his team did the same in developing the settlement to end the fighting in Bosnia in 1994. The United States hauled the leaders of the various parties to an isolated air base near Dayton, Ohio, and pressured them into accepting an agreement the Americans had largely designed.

There are not only many kinds of mediators, but also, increasingly, multiple mediators dealing with a single conflict. Sometimes they operate simultaneously, both governmental and nongovernmental entities. In other cases they operate sequentially. One mediator operates earlier in a conflict, another at a later phase of it. The process can be complicated and confusing, and sometimes it gives rise to a problem of too many cooks, but conflicts themselves can be complex, with multiple layers and, over time, involving many different circumstances and participating leaders. So intervention by multiple mediators may be inevitable and valuable.

Also complicated is what constitutes success. Mediation may be undertaken to end the fighting, but is that success? To a mediator it could be, at least temporarily, but if the underlying conflict remains, then the success may be too short-lived. Who is to be the judge? The parties to the conflict or the outsiders determined to get it under control? The mediator may be, or represent, an outsider more interested in getting the conflict under control, leaving an end to it for another day.

And is stopping the fighting or easing the conflict acceptable if the solution is clearly unjust? The fighting stops, but if an awful government is left in place or all those who committed atrocities are pardoned, is that success? These questions often arise and there are no easy answers.

GENERAL FEATURES AND PRINCIPLES

Certain generalizations apply to negotiations and mediation. One is that democracies negotiate all the time but only occasionally use mediation to deal with each other, probably because they so seldom push their disagreements to the edge of war. Whatever mediation there is is informal, not an organized effort. Next, while negotiation and mediation can be productive at any point in a conflict, experts feel they are most likely to be successful either relatively early in a severe conflict or relatively late. "Early" means before the conflict is well under way. Grievances are still modest, and the emotional-political intensity is limited. There has been much interest in **preventive diplomacy**, in which outsiders try to intervene before conflicts boil over. "Late" means after the parties have become tired of the conflict—weary of it never ending, its costs, its frustrations. So "early" usually means before fighting starts or gets far, while it still shocks each side and before grievances escalate as lives are lost. And "late" generally means when the two sides are tired of fighting, killing, and dying. They reach a point that political scientist I. William Zartman describes as a **hurtful stalemate**, perhaps the best-known term in studies of negotiation. In a hurtful stalemate each party has demonstrated that it cannot be defeated, will not collapse, and will not quit, and that it will continue hurting its opponent. Thus the conflict is painful and seems ready to continue indefinitely. If each side is feeling the strain or fears that, while it will not be defeated, it might lose ground if fighting continues, the situation can be exploited by a mediator.

The idea that it can take a hurtful stalemate to get progress in ending a conflict is disturbing, which leads some people to resist it. After all, it means the conflict has to get worse to get better—more strife, more fighting, more death and destruction, especially if the stalemate is a long time coming. But it is intuitively appealing, too. Strikes and lockouts, for example, often end only when the costs have piled up. Some analysts like to stress that ripeness is somewhat malleable. It is subjective, and an astute outside party may promote a sense of it. Another possibility is that the outside party is the one that finds continuation of the conflict intolerable, the one for whom the stalemate is most hurting. This is one way to explain the settlement in Bosnia. The parties were willing to continue fighting, but the Western Europeans and Americans demanded that they stop because the conflict had become intolerable to them.

The notion of a hurtful stalemate also helps explain how outsiders' efforts can often fail. While the conflict is still early, outsiders may be unwilling to make an all-out effort to intervene; the situation is not urgent enough. When the conflict gets serious, the outsiders want to do something—stop the fighting, halt the flow of refugees, stop the atrocities. But, when they try, little is achieved because a hurtful stalemate has not yet emerged.

Next, some types of conflicts are tougher to handle. When the core issue is security (the Israel-Palestine case), when sovereignty is at risk (the Tamil Tigers versus the government in Ceylon), or when national territory is the issue (the China-Taiwan dispute), then the participants see the stakes as very high (see the *Cases and Context* box, "The China-Taiwan Conflict"). Commitment on each side is strong, making compromise difficult. Also tough are internal disputes of other sorts that have become protracted social conflicts, conflicts with self-sustaining hostility and violence. Thus some conflicts are, or at least are widely perceived to

Cases and Context: The China-Taiwan Conflict

When the Chinese Communists won the civil war in 1949, the defeated Nationalists fled to Taiwan, a large island a little more than one hundred miles from the mainland. The new government in Beijing laid plans to invade Taiwan, but the United States moved to protect it when the Korean War broke out in 1950 and eventually signed an alliance with the Nationalist government. It supported the Nationalists' claim to be the true government of China, and the "two Chinas" remained bitterly hostile. Not until 1971 did President Richard M. Nixon agree that the Communist government was legitimate and that Taiwan was a part of China. However, U.S. leaders insisted that unification take place peacefully, threatening to intervene if China sought unification forcibly. Direct negotiations to end the conflict have never taken place, though in 1991 the Taiwan government dropped its claim that it was the legitimate government of China. Since then Taiwan has never declared that it should be independent but has never accepted unification either, saying that unification might be possible at a future time.

This conflict might seem an ideal candidate for resolution by negotiation. The people on both sides are Chinese. Since the 1980s, billions of dollars in investments have flowed from Taiwan to the mainland and hundreds of thousands of Taiwanese have moved there, often to oversee those investments. Trade has expanded enormously. Millions of Taiwanese visit China, and Taiwan is about to allow a major increase in the small number of tourists from China it has permitted. Yet Taiwan continues to spend billions on national defense to be safe from China, while China is alert to the slightest sign of Taiwan moving toward independence, threatens to use force not only to prevent independence but also to compel unification if necessary, and is steadily increasing and positioning its forces to carry out that threat. Nevertheless, negotiations could be seen as a plausible solution.

With the huge, rapidly growing, and highly valuable interchanges between the two sides, which are ethnically, culturally, and linguistically the same, why would Taiwan want independence? Even if it does, declaring independence would not change much. The U.S. government says it will not recognize that independence, which means few others would either. An independent Taiwan could hardly be a threat to China, and it is bound to be intimately involved with China in many ways. Why would China have to react with force?

Then why have there been no negotiations? Some limited forms of negotiation have taken place. Influential people have met occasionally to exchange views, and each country has an officially private organization for conducting interactions with the other side. The two governments also negotiate through the media via official statements and leaders' speeches, as well as by their military steps. They have also had secret contacts periodically. However, direct open talks have not taken place. Beijing insists that a settlement can easily be reached, that it will provide Taiwan with generous benefits to get one, but only if Taiwan agrees, before the negotiations, that it is a province of China. Taiwan insists on being negotiated with as an independent state. China wants no negotiations that, by taking place, legitimize Taiwan as independent; Taiwan wants negotiations that, by taking place, confirm its independence.

What about mediation? The plausible mediator would be the United States, but China rejects the idea. China sees America's past interference, in supporting the Nationalists during the civil war and then on Taiwan, as the source of the problem. The future of Taiwan is an internal Chinese affair that Chinese must settle. In addition, the United States says it will neither mediate nor pressure Taiwan to negotiate.

This case illustrates a number of points: the onerous difficulties in fully resolving civil wars, the way internal conflicts can attract outside involvement, the use of indirect forms of negotiations including Track II efforts to try to bridge gaps, and how holding negotiations can appear to one party as symbolically and politically too beneficial to the other. It also displays some of the limitations of negotiations, and mediation, for tackling intractable conflicts, because the Taiwan issue is more than an interesting case study. The United States says it will not permit unification by force, a more credible threat now that Taiwan is a vigorous democracy and China is not. The one time in recent years that China threatened forcefully, firing test missiles into the sea near Taiwan in 1996, two U.S. carrier task forces were deployed in response. China says it will not permit Taiwan independence and will fight American military interference. As a result, each government's armed forces are planning for a possible war, developing and redeploying their forces accordingly. No negotiations have taken place about this aspect of the issue either, because neither side seems willing to budge.

Many experts see the Taiwan issue as the most likely source of a future great power war and therefore as the world's most dangerous ongoing conflict. The continued absence of direct negotiations (between China and Taiwan and between China and the United States) makes many governments in East Asia uneasy.

be, intractable. As such they discourage mediation efforts so few or none are undertaken.

It is commonplace to think that a mediator must be impartial, but analysis and experience have shown this is not so. What is required is that the mediator seem fair enough, which can be achieved even when the mediator is known to favor one party. One reason mediators cannot always be impartial is that on some issues they inherently favor one point of view. If you are fighting to secede, an outside government is unlikely to agree (unless you want to join its territory), because governments do not want ideas of secession to spread. If you are using terrorism, many outsiders will disapprove in principle. While you are fighting, the UN will insist that you stop. It will not endorse fighting because its central purpose is to resolve disputes peacefully.

A mediator who is not impartial can be acceptable at times because he will bend over backward to be fair and thus preserve his influence, especially if he fears that the side he favors will be seriously harmed if the fighting is not stopped. Such a mediator may also have unusual credibility and influence with the side he favors. This was the argument Kissinger used after the October 1973 war. To get parts of their land back, the Arabs would have to make a deal with Israel. and only the United States, as Israel's strongest supporter, could get Israel to make the necessary concessions. By that logic, Arabs should accept the United States as the intermediary. This view has influenced some Arabs ever since. If the mediator favors the weaker side in a conflict, that government or other actor may say to itself, "Being weaker makes negotiations a risk for us but our friendly mediator will help us get the best deal possible and will help us if the deal falls through or the other side reneges."

Thus it often helps to have a powerful, influential mediator, a mediator with muscle, that favors one side but is unhappy enough about the conflict to try to get it resolved. By trying to be fair but determined to end the conflict, he makes suggestions on the compromises needed that may be much more politically and emotionally acceptable to each party than if they came from the parties themselves.

CONCLUSION

Are negotiation and mediation valid and useful tools for enhancing security by resolving the problem of war? It is difficult to put too much confidence in them. What is discouraging from the start is that war and negotiation have coexisted for too long. On wars among the great powers, negotiation has a mixed record. Sometimes it has been an adjunct or extension of those wars, instead of a substitute and remedy. Nazi Germany used negotiations to demand that others give it what it wanted. If that did not work, it used war instead. As a negotiator it was often more like a bully.

The Track Record

Negotiations have sometimes done much to prevent or end great-power wars. In ending the several decades of the Napoleonic Wars, a lengthy set of negotiations arranged settlements, adjusted borders, established several governments, and laid down some rules for the future. Analysts have often praised the results, concluding that because the negotiators knew what they were doing almost no great-power wars were fought for the next one hundred years. It was not only the settlements but also the development of habits of negotiation. International conferences were used for years to tackle sensitive issues and crises, and a great-power concert imposed settlements on weaker states, intervened in troubled states, and generated compromises among the great powers themselves. Not until 1914 and World War I did this ready resort to negotiation fully collapse. Analysts such as Hans Morgenthau and Henry Kissinger later argued that the terrible history of war and Cold War in the twentieth century was mainly the result of devaluing negotiations and negotiators. Fierce nationalist, religious, and ideological zealots, popularity-driven politicians, and stodgy bureaucracies took over instead.

It is widely accepted that the negotiations to settle World War I were a failure. A sickly League of Nations was born. The patient survived for two decades but was all but dead in the 1930s. The settlements left various great powers frustrated and resentful toward the international system built on them. When those states got the chance they tore the whole system down, setting off World War II. Arrangements for the international economic system were also inadequate and collapsed in the Great Depression of the 1930s. World War I destroyed the old empires in Eastern Europe, but agreements based on the principle that oppressed peoples were entitled to their own states had woeful consequences. Bad governments, weak states, and ethnic conflicts emerged, and the aftereffects still rumble in Eastern Europe today. Outside Europe the post–World War I settlements ignored that principle and produced—or did not preclude—equally bad consequences: heightened resentment against the colonial empires, Japan's eventual effort in World War II to throw those empires out of Asia, and endless conflicts, fighting, and destruction for years after those empires broke up.

Negotiations after World War II, in 1945–1950, seemed equally disastrous. Members of the winning side started quarreling almost immediately, so efforts at a grand settlement ended in a competitive truce. Major issues were left unresolved and became topics of bickering for years. Europe was divided; the two halves had little to do with each other until the late 1980s. With no agreement on what to do about Germany, the two sides divided it and eventually they did the same to Korea, China, and Vietnam. Each case then posed a severe threat to regional and global security for years. Governments could not agree to eliminate nuclear weapons either, so each great power, and a few others, developed nuclear arsenals. Negotiations helped only in getting the arsenals stabilized and only after two of them grew to fantastic levels, with tens of thousands of nuclear weapons each. With no agreement on an international economic system the great powers built two—each barely interacting with the other and each competing for third-world countries to join. This East-West competition went on everywhere for almost fifty years, fostering competing factions in dozens of countries, the excessive arming of friends or clients, extended propaganda battles, military interventions against the other side, and secret maneuvers to back friends and undermine opponents.

This did not seem much like peace. Negotiations often seemed futile and the UN Security Council was regularly deadlocked. Only limited agreements were ever reached, and negotiations never directly settled the major issues left by World War II or produced during the Cold War. Fortunately the eventual result was not as disastrous as the failure in 1918–1919. The dominant states decided to agree to disagree and live with that. They competed sharply but without another great war. The conflict was unpleasant, unsafe, and certainly not cheap. Governments learned to put up with the fact that real peace was not at hand.

Because it was expected to go on indefinitely, when the Cold War ended it was a shock. As it abruptly died, its major issues were peacefully resolved. The dominant view in most places was that communism should be abandoned, so it was; that the Soviet empire was an anachronism, so it disappeared; that what the West was building was better, so formerly communist countries in Europe set about becoming democratic and capitalist. Those who disagreed, such as Yugoslavia, Belarus, and Russia, were on the defensive. Thus the peaceful end of the Cold War was not a triumph of negotiations. It was the collapse of one side—of its energy, legitimacy, and self-confidence. Until then, the Cold War had been a conflict so fundamental that it was beyond the capacity of negotiations to resolve.

A good illustration of the limited impact of Cold War-era negotiations was the 1954 Geneva Convention on Vietnam and its aftermath. Vietnamese nationalists under communist leadership moved to toss the French out of their empire in Indochina in 1945, first through negotiations and then by guerrilla war. Eventually France was losing the war and ready to leave, but the Cold War made this a complicated matter. A communist Indochina was not acceptable to all the great powers, so the Geneva meeting was held to negotiate a settlement. It was agreed that France would leave and a new state, North Vietnam—run by communists and backed by the communist world—was created, something the United States strongly disliked. The rest of Indochina was divided into three noncommunist states—South Vietnam, Laos, Cambodia—backed by the West, particularly the United States, something North Vietnam strongly opposed. Soon every other aspect of the agreements broke down. Plans to unify Vietnam were blocked by the United States. Plans for a peace collapsed so North Vietnam turned again to guerrilla war, communists versus noncommunists, which started in Laos, spread to South Vietnam, and seeped into Cambodia. By the 1960s the United States had joined the fighting, greatly intensifying the war and conducting immense bombing and shelling on all of Vietnam and part of the rest of Indochina. The fighting ended in a negotiated settlement in 1975, but that soon collapsed into more fighting in South Vietnam and Cambodia. The results were millions of Indochinese killed, millions more injured and maimed, and hundreds of thousands fleeing to other countries. The entire region has not fully recovered to this day.

In the end, negotiations between France and communist guerrillas failed, the Geneva Conference failed, and the settlement ending the Vietnam War mostly failed to create a peaceful Indochina. The most gruesome loss of life in Cambodia came after that settlement. Various other negotiations to end the war sooner also failed. Was it cultural differences? Maybe. Bad negotiating techniques? At times, but not always. Two-level games problems? Sure. But basically, actual or proposed compromises were seldom acceptable to the parties, so either they were not adopted or did not hold up if they were.

Of course, there are examples of successes, even successes in serious conflicts among the great powers. In great-power crises from 1890 to 1912 negotiations repeatedly staved off war so successfully that some observers thought they could do so indefinitely and were surprised when they failed in 1914. In the Cuban Missile Crisis in 1962 the United States and Soviet Union were on the brink of war and negotiated their way out of it, after scaring themselves so badly that they never got into a confrontation like that again. One study describes how great powers peacefully end bad conflicts. First, the conflict has become severe, and each side has concluded it will have serious problems if the conflict continues. Second, each sees no sign the other side will quit. Third, each side starts by taking little steps to improve relations. When it comes to negotiations they start with less important, less difficult issues. This establishes a record of success and eases hostile feelings and perceptions. Finally, on the most sensitive issues they resort to secret contacts and talks, particularly among the top leaders who are powerful enough to make controversial compromises. If some disagreements cannot be settled, they agree to put off these matters by using ambiguous, face-saving language. They highlight the agreement they have reached, not the remaining disagreement.

Negotiations are hardly useless but not always effective. Mediation essentially has the same record.

The Three Levels of Security

Negotiation and mediation are widely pursued to enhance societal security, especially in the present day when almost all wars are internal—civil wars, guerrilla wars, competing terrorisms. Often these wars go on for years. The parties are stalemated in continued fighting or the fighting stops only to bubble up again. The big losers are the societies and the citizens caught in the middle. Each side disrupts and terrorizes. Citizens become gruesome examples used to try to get others to join or to scare the other side. In Algeria's civil war, a particularly grim case, forces from both sides long crept into villages or seized busloads of people on highways and killed everyone, including children, by slitting their throats. An awful practice in many African conflicts has been to enlist children as soldiers, mostly boys but some girls, too. Civilians are often forced to inform on the enemy, contribute food and money, and carry supplies, which makes them targets for the other side or turns them into refugees eventually.

Unfortunately, negotiations and mediation regularly fail in these conflicts. The parties often use talks or mediation efforts, truces, ceasefires, and even agreements mainly for propaganda or as breathing spaces to rest and regroup before fighting again. Many internal conflicts have been eased or resolved through negotiation and mediation, but they are not always a reliable recourse in terms of societal security. This is so clearly the case that there is now a significant set of studies on why negotiated settlements often fail.

The impact on state security in uneven as well. Negotiations between states can heighten state legitimacy and autonomy by confirming that it is states that decide, that they are in charge. This can be reinforced when mediation from outside emphasizes that the parties to the conflict must resolve it themselves; it is in their hands. In such cases negotiation and mediation are not serious threats to state security in themselves, and when they work to produce a peace the states are made safer.

But external mediation is sometimes much more intrusive and manipulative, taking important aspects of an interstate conflict out of the hands of the states involved. That is what the Security Council is supposed to do—to insist that the parties avoid fighting or stop fighting. The less powerful the parties, and the more awful or politically obnoxious their conflict, the more they may face real interference from outside. However, the vigorous use of sanctions or incentives by mediators is rarely the key to getting a successful, long-lasting deal. Usually the parties must take the important steps on their own. Outside help is not guaranteed to be available either. When Iran and Iraq fell into war in 1981, the general response of the major powers and the UN was to keep hands off. Negotiations were tried only after a massive slaughter.

The larger problem in terms of state security is that negotiations and mediation often do not work. This applies to interstate conflicts, including conflicts among the great powers. And it also applies to internal wars that afflict states. As a result of the lack of success, conflicts pose serious security threats, often remain unsettled, or are only temporarily contained. Fighting continues or soon returns as the issues are neither resolved nor shelved. States are therefore threatened with harmful outcomes. A state may lose an important conflict, or it may win but at such great cost that it is gravely weakened, or it may be gradually exhausted by the strain of the conflict. Iraq lost the Persian Gulf War, putting its state at serious risk thereafter from heavy sanctions, military pressures, secessionist elements, and political unrest. Tsarist Russia lost the support of the armed forces and citizens for its incompetence in administering its involvement in World War I and subsequently collapsed. The Chinese government was at war from 1927 until 1949. Despite its original popularity and some powerful outside help, the fighting gradually sapped its resources, its public support, and its political cohesion. The government retreated to Taiwan to survive only as a fragment of its former self.

Why is it so hard to negotiate or mediate away a severe conflict or war? According to Putnam, if the win-sets of the parties do not overlap and cannot be changed, getting anything other than a cosmetic agreement is unlikely. Some observers assume that severe conflict means there has been a failure to communicate. But many conflicts arise because the parties intensely want incompatible things. As a result, talking things over does not help much. Particularly difficult are deep internal cleavages over ethnic, religious, or political differences, especially when group identities are at stake. First, the parties feel that what is at risk is enormous—survival itself. If the rebels win, the state will be destroyed; if the state wins, the rebels will be wiped out. If Protestants (or Serbs, Tutsis, or Russians) win it means the destruction of the Catholics (or the Croats, Hutus, or Chechens) and vice versa. These conflicts reflect deep-seated feelings of insecurity and strong perceptions of being threatened, and the conflicts then reinforce such attitudes. The fears are intensified by being collectively held. People feed on each other's insecurities.

Second, parties to internal conflicts often do not recognize each other as legitimate. The rebels are just bandits or criminals; the state is just a corrupt, brutal, and unrepresentative entity. Negotiating with such a despicable opponent is disgusting, even degrading. "They don't deserve to be in the same room with us," one side might say. Thus it is politically unacceptable to negotiate anything other than the other side's surrender. The point is to destroy it or to escape from it, not talk to it. These are highly conflictual attitudes, to say the least. Even if individual leaders want to negotiate, and mediators create an opportunity for that, their compatriots may reject the idea.

Negotiations and mediation are therefore suspect out of concern about the legitimacy they would grant the opponent. Governments feel that just to hold talks with a group in revolt grants that group status as a recognized political entity. Having a mediator set the talks up is even worse because an outsider is treating the rebels as an equal of the government. Such a group is often eager for talks precisely for that reason. However, it may also be reluctant instead. Because it condemns the government as illegitimate, why negotiate with it? An outside mediator will insist on getting the fighting stopped to have talks, but that leaves the government still running the country, which is the image its opponents want to undermine.

Such conflicts then escalate. Everything is potential fuel. Even little steps by the hated other side look like big threats, provoking anger and outrage. Conflicts become part of the parties' self-identities, and one's identity is not something to be negotiated away. Each side nurtures its grievances, introduces them to its children at an early age, develops and cherishes its martyrs, and thus passes the cause from one generation to the next. Adding intensity is the tendency to demonize the other side and "angelicize" one's own. The other side's awful behavior is seen as inherent in its nature or character, while you are just reacting to the terrible things done to you and to a conflict forced on you. The other side commits atrocities, while you inflict only justifiable retribution.

Psychologists know that perceptions such as these carry strong resistance to any conflicting or self-critical information. You ignore suggestions that you are provocative, threatening, and unjust. Meanwhile, any decent or conciliatory behavior by the opponent is a trick or has been forced on him by your staunch opposition. There is a terrific fear that your side will lose cohesion or look weak, which is something the enemy will exploit. Empathizing with the enemy becomes a form of betrayal, and contact with the enemy should be minimal and primarily hostile.

When interstate conflicts become this deep-seated and vicious, the same barriers to successful negotiation and mediation apply. The Cold War displayed all of the things just described. Each side fervently declared that the future of civilization, of the world, was at stake. Each saw the enemy as constantly poised to attack and wipe out its foe if it could find the right opportunity. Each considered the other side basically illegitimate. Each piled up grievances that were carefully calculated, so even small matters could provoke confrontation. The Cold War became an integral part of each side's identity. Because the other side was inherently evil, negotiations were useful only when some temporary problem might be eased. For ending the conflict they were futile and pressing hard for them only made your side look weak. Proposals to negotiate were often treated with suspicion or alarm.

Mediators rarely make a serious difference through substantive contributions to the negotiations. They do not normally design the breakthroughs that produce agreements, uncover clever ways of refashioning each side's concept of its interests so they are not so far apart, and so on. Even mediator expertise on the conflict itself is not important. The main contribution of mediators, in this view, is procedural, facilitating talks among the players who in the end have to sign and live with an agreement.

As a broad conclusion, conflicts most likely to result in wars nowadays, or the conflicts underlying contemporary wars, are frequently the kinds of conflicts least amenable to negotiation and mediation. The Cold War resisted negotiation for decades. Now myriads of internal conflicts also resist negotiated solutions. As a consequence, states are often insecure.

Most analysts would say that systemic security has greatly improved but do not credit negotiation and mediation. No conflict among the great powers today is as intense as the Cold War. When the great powers disagree, they are in regular contact and periodically use negotiations, which is a part of applying policies of engagement instead of trying to isolate each other. But the conflicts among them that exist have not steadily yielded to negotiations.

Meanwhile, internal conflicts also continue to damage systemic peace and security. Fear exists that sooner or later the great powers will begin lining up on opposite sides of some internal conflicts again, leading them toward competitive intervention and confrontation. Fortunately this has not happened yet. The Western states clashed with China and Russia over how to handle the conflicts in Bosnia and Kosovo but not about whether the situations were bad and needed to be fixed. However, U.S. exploitation of the internal conflict in Afghanistan to oust the Taliban was of more concern to various governments. Even more worrisome is that internal conflicts could threaten the stability of important governments because when major states collapse or are gravely weakened, the global international system or regional systems can be seriously strained.

Internal conflicts are now more disruptive to the international system as well because, to reiterate a point made in Chapter 1, the concept of security has been shifting. There is more concern at the systemic level about serious, large-scale, violations of human rights and about terrorism. There is a more widespread reaction against humanitarian disasters, including those driven by civil wars.

A systemwide capacity for inducing negotiations, including by mediation, adds to systemic security. It is good that in the past decade it has been reinvigorated. Such a capability has existed in all international systems, and it is probably more substantial around the world today than it has ever been. There is plenty for it to do—plenty of encouragement for negotiations to prevent or end wars and many kinds of available mediators. What is disturbing is their uneven effectiveness.

SOURCES AND OTHER USEFUL READINGS

Louis Kriesberg's analysis of conflict is *Constructive Conflicts*. He reviews various forms of conflict resolution, including mediation. The negotiation-as-technique approach to negotiation is explained by Roger Fisher, Andrea S. Schneider, Elizabeth Borgwardt, and Brian Ganson in *Coping with International Conflict*. See also Roger Fisher, William Ury, and Bruce Patton, *Getting to Yes*. Some other valuable works on negotiation are I. William Zartman, *The 50% Solution* and *The Negotiation Process*; P. Terrence Hopmann, "Bargaining and Problem Solving"; and Brigid Starkey, Mark A. Boyer, and Jonathan Wilkenfeld, *Negotiating in a Complex World*. Raymond Cohen's approach is presented and explored in such works as his *Negotiating across Cultures* and "Language and Conflict Resolution." For other discussions of the cultural element in negotiation and mediation, see the pertinent parts of Luc Reychler and Thania Paffenholz, *Peace-Building*. An example of the memoir literature on negotiation is Joel S. Wit, Daniel B. Poneman, and Robert L. Gallucci, *Going Critical*, on negotiating with North Korea.

Mediation is also a popular topic in the scholarly literature. Some examples are *Herding Cats*, edited by Chester A. Crocker, Fen Osler Hampson, and Pamela Aall, and *Resolving International Conflicts*, edited by Jacob Bercovitch. For a broad review largely devoted to mediation, see Lilach Gilady and Bruce Russett, "Peacemaking and Conflict Resolution." Numerous first-hand accounts of mediation have been published, including Richard C. Holbrooke, *To End a War*; and Henry A. Kissinger, *Years of Upheaval*.

The concept of a hurtful stalemate as making a conflict suitable for negotiation or mediation or both is discussed in I. William Zartman, *Ripe for Resolution*. For a critique of this concept, see Landon E. Hancock, "To Act or Wait." On difficult conflicts for any mediator, see *Taming Intractable Conflicts*, edited by Crocker, Hampson, and Aall.

A number of studies consider the concern that many negotiated settlements do not take hold or eventually break down leading to more violent conflict. A good example is *Ending Civil Wars: the Implementation of Peace Agreements*, edited by Stephan John Stedman, Donald Rothchild, and Elizabeth M. Cousens. Others include Fen Osler Hampson, *Nurturing Peace*; Barbara F. Walter, "The Critical Barrier to Civil War Settlement"; and *Civil Wars, Insecurity, and Intervention*, edited by Barbara F. Walter and Jack Snyder.

CHAPTER 10

Peacekeeping

Negotiation and mediation are well and good but they are not foolproof. What can be done when they do not work? In truth, they often do not work, with conflicts getting more severe and large-scale violence occurring as a result. When the violence is grievous enough and destructive enough, it is called a war, civil or international. What is to be done then? How else might a conflict be brought under control? Apart from negotiation and mediation, what can be done to keep a war from breaking out or, if a war is already taking place, what can be done to try to stop it?

In modern times, one of the more creative solutions to the security problems that war causes is peacekeeping. Along with peace enforcement, peace imposition, and peacebuilding (see Chapters 11 and 12), it can be undertaken when war seems about to occur or already has. The general idea behind peacekeeping is that when the parties to a conflict are close to war or already in one they may have a strong desire to stop short of or end the fighting. But fighting is a messy activity and can be hard to control. The parties might need outside help to get the fighting under control. Peacekeeping is one kind of outside help.

Peacekeeping is a particular kind of external intervention into either a violent conflict between governments or a conflict inside a state. Interventions of this sort have occurred occasionally throughout the history of international politics, particularly interventions by great powers in regard to their neighbors or others in their spheres of influence. Today, peacekeeping is typically used to refer to a particular kind of intervention that is taken, actually or supposedly, for the general welfare of the people caught up in the conflict, the region, or the global system.

If the parties in a conflict need help because their fighting is too messy to control, how, exactly, is fighting "messy?" It does not mean scrambling a society and its economy, spreading devastation, and turning people into refugees. Instead, a messy conflict can be hard to control, including hard to stop. It may have poorly defined boundaries, mixed kinds of violence, odd collections of fighting forces, uneven command systems over the forces involved, and the like. For example, suppose each side in a conflict says it would like to stop fighting. One side sends out a patrol to see what the other side is up to—not to make trouble, but to see whether it is planning to attack instead of ending the fighting. When the patrol is spotted by sentries, they shoot. The patrol fires back in self-defense. The other side increases its fire so the patrol's compatriots lay down an artillery barrage to help it get back to their lines, and the other side replies with its own barrage. In the end, just trying to check on what the other side is doing triggers a firefight, all unplanned. That is messy.

Or, for example, a truce is declared but each side is afraid the war might start again so it continues to rigorously train its forces and keep them on high alert. Each side is afraid it might soon be attacked, so it tries to look tough and ready to fight so as to send the other side a message—"Don't even think about it." If an incident occurs—a sniper kills someone, for example—each side may blow the incident out of proportion. Finally, suppose a civil war is being fought between two ethnic groups. A truce is declared, and it works. But some adherents of one side (not its soldiers) are so angry that they attack people on the other side—committing an assassination, starting a riot, burning a village, or carrying out any number of violent acts. Some of the other side's citizens respond in kind, and soon the local military forces on each side join in. There goes the truce. Why the anger and the resort to force in these examples? Fighting is emotional; it can build tension. It creates grievances, scores each side wants to settle, and the desire for revenge. Given such emotions and situations fraught with tension and suspicion, violence can easily flare up and then escalate.

So maybe outside assistance is needed that goes beyond mediation. Peacekeeping is the insertion of outside military forces that are intended to use nonmilitary means to help the parties behave peacefully. These are true military forces. They have a chain of command, wear uniforms, carry at least some weapons, but they are not there to use force. Instead, they are meant to get between the two sides, to dampen down any incidents that occur, and to diffuse nasty situations. As will be seen, this can turn out to be more like a good intention and peacekeeping may involve a limited use of force, but that is not what is intended in creating the operation.

Peacekeeping was primarily developed by the United Nations (UN), or for the UN by some of its members, relatively early in the Cold War. At that time there were plenty of conflicts around and often the UN could do little to settle them because the Security Council was too divided to take decisive action and mediation efforts by the secretary general had their limits. But once the UN had been drawn into a few peacekeeping efforts, Secretary General Dag Hammarskjöld led the way in declaring this to be an important UN function. Specialists on peacekeeping trace UN operations back to 1956 and the war that year in the Middle East. Israel handily defeated the Arab forces, and a UN Emergency Force was stationed between Israel and Egypt in the Sinai desert as part of the truce that followed. This action came to be widely seen as a valuable step, and the UN forces stayed there for eleven years, setting a model for future UN peacekeeping. It has been developing ever since.

WHO DOES PEACEKEEPING?

The UN Security Council has mounted numerous peacekeeping operations (see Table 10-1 for a list of UN operations in 2005–2006). It has even had one operating continuously on Cyprus since 1964! In that year a long-standing conflict between Greek and Turkish residents of the island culminated in an invasion by military forces from Turkey. They seized roughly 40 percent of Cyprus and turned the area into a haven for the Turkish Cypriotes, while the Greek Cypriotes congregated on the rest of the island. A line was drawn through the island and its capital city, Nicosia, by the UN mediator and has been patrolled by UN peacekeepers ever since. The line keeps the two sides apart, replacing war and internal violence with peace.

In 1991–1992 a serious conflict broke out in Yugoslavia when the individual states, or republics, which made up the country, began to declare their independence from the dominant Serbs, the nationality of those who controlled the central government. This set off a civil war inside several republics. Serbs in those areas were about to become minorities if the republics gained independence, and they would probably be persecuted minorities at that. They set out to seize areas that could be theirs and that might eventually be combined into a larger Serbia, a country just for the Serbs. Other nationalities also reached for guns to carve out territories for themselves and perhaps to drive other nationalities out of those territories. Into this vicious struggle the European Union inserted thousands of peacekeepers. Troops from all over Western Europe were sent to help the parties stop fighting and committing atrocities. The operation was authorized by the UN Security Council but the heart of it was an effort mounted by European states.

In 1994 the United States decided to tackle the situation in Haiti. Its ruling elite, often topped by a military junta, has a long history of brutally mistreating and exploiting the citizens, leaving Haiti the poorest country in the Americas and usually filled with violence. With Security Council approval but operating mainly on its own initiative, the United States sent troops to restore order and to try to install a somewhat democratic, civilian-run, political system. They were there for five years, then supplemented by UN peacekeeping forces. So this was peacekeeping by a single state, at least initially.

In 1992 a civil war broke out in the newly independent state of Georgia, which had been a republic in the Soviet Union. The Georgians had been eager for independence, but once they achieved it, several minority groups in Georgia were no longer subject to Russian rule, which they felt had been bearable, but to Georgian rule, which in their view was intolerable. Soon there was serious fighting in Abkhazia, a portion of the country, between Abkhazians who wanted to avoid Georgian rule and the regular Georgian army that was trying to hold the country

TABLE 10-1
UN Peace Support Operations, 2005–2006

Mission name	2005–2006 budget (millions of dollars)	Troop level	Start date
Minor operations			
UN Truce Supervision Organization— Middle East	29	150	1948
UN Military Observer Group in India and Pakistan	8	42	1949
UN Peacekeeping Force in Cyprus	47	180	1964
UN Disengagement Observer Force— Golan Heights	44	1,047	1974
UN Interim Force in Lebanon	99	1,994	1978
UN Mission for the Referendum in Western Sahara	48	28	1991
UN Observer Mission in Georgia	36	a	1993
UN Observer Mission in Kosovo	253	a	1999
Major operations			
UN Mission in Sierra Leone	113	944	1999
UN Organization Mission in the Democratic Republic of Congo	403	15,051	1999
UN Mission in Ethiopia and Eritrea	186	3,132	2000
UN Mission in Liberia	761	14,656	2003
UN Mission in Cote d'Ivoire (Ivory Coast)	387	6,701	2004
UN Stabilization Mission in Haiti	495	7,265	2004
UN Operation in Burundi	308	5,336	2004
UN Mission in Sudan	316	3,683	2005

Notes: At the end of 2005 the United Nations (UN) had approximately seventy thousand military personnel and police personnel serving in its peace support operations, with another fifteen civilians involved. The budget for these operations was $3.5 billion for 2005–2006. The major operations are coping with serious situations. Sierra Leone is coming out of a civil war but has only an interim central administration because of continuing political strife. The eastern part of the Congo has been torn by invasion and internal warfare for years, fighting that now involves a large number of tribes, guerrilla organizations, refugees from neighboring countries, and marauders. Ethiopia and Eritrea were edging toward another border conflict in 2005. The last one, in 1998–2000, killed approximately eighty thousand. UN forces ended a long period of civil war in Liberia and in 2005 oversaw a presidential election; the country was at the bottom of the UN development index. The Ivory Coast has been in constant danger of having a peace arrangement break down, after a civil war that started in 2002 divided the country roughly in half. Haiti remains a source of despair, making little progress toward stability from years of mismanagement and civil unrest. In Burundi the situation has stabilized so that some of the 400,000 refugees from the 1993 civil war can go home. The western Sudan has had a vicious civil warfare for years, producing many civilian casualties and refugees.

a. No troops, only military observers and civilians.

Source: United Nations Department of Peacekeeping Operations, www.un.org/depts/dpko/dpko/bnote.htm (accessed December 2005).

together. Outside efforts to end the fighting eventually led to the insertion of Russian peacekeeping forces. This was done at the instigation of the Russian government and was not authorized by the UN.

Thus, peacekeeping can be a UN operation or a UN-authorized effort left to a specific state or states, or action by a state or states acting outside the UN. It can be carried out by, or under the auspices of, regional organizations such as the Organization of American States or the Organization of African Unity.

CLASSIC PRINCIPLES OF PEACEKEEPING

Troops could be sent into a country or a war zone between countries to do all sorts of things: seize the territory involved, impose an outside party's rule, grab the area's assets, or pursue some other self-serving purpose. States, acting alone or together, have often done these things; they can certainly be greedy enough. When they mount an intervention, keeping the peace might be the least of their objectives. Therefore, the first principle of an honest peacekeeping effort is that it is carried out on behalf of the general welfare. That is, for the benefit of the parties suffering from fear of a conflict or the fighting, the neighbors that could be affected by refugees or a spread of the fighting, and the entire human community in keeping with poet John Donne's admonition: "Ask not for whom the bell tolls, it tolls for thee."

The second principle is that, within the limits of looking out for the general welfare, a peacekeeping operation is impartial. The point is not to intervene on one side against the other. Sounds simple enough, but it is not. For one thing, often one party is seen as doing more harm to the general welfare than the other(s). Hardly anyone from outside Haiti took the side of the ruling elite, for example. Thus an intervention may be technically impartial but have a distinct orientation toward one side. In addition, a peacekeeping intervention is likely to affect the parties unevenly. It is impartial about ending the conflict but the effects of doing so are not. In Cyprus the peacekeepers have frozen in place a peace under which, as they see it, the Greek Cypriots have lost almost half their island.

The third principle, therefore, is very important: Peacekeeping is undertaken because the parties want to stop fighting and want the peacekeepers there. Peacekeeping units are invited by all the parties to the conflict. Presumably this means that the parties are willing to put up with some or all of the adverse effects peacekeeping may impose on them. Peacekeeping may not be totally impartial in spirit or effect, but that is tolerated because it is welcomed by the parties anyway. Some analysts, reflecting on the Bosnian case, have suggested that being welcomed by the parties may not be enough, though. They feel it is important that the local population actively supports the peacekeepers and wants them there, because otherwise they may not cooperate with the peacekeeping mission and that will make it harder to get anything accomplished.

With these three principles in mind and the desire that peacekeeping forces, above all, not make things worse, the fourth principle is that peacekeeping forces are to be lightly armed. The idea is that they can defend themselves against a small attack and will use force only under those circumstances, which will presumably be rare because they have been invited to come. In a proper peacekeeping operation a minimal amount of force is used. Because the military forces involved are not to be employed in a standard military way, the fifth principle that emerged was that peacekeeping is best left to specially trained forces. After all, regular forces get orders to do something then go out and do it by, if necessary, threatening or using force. They are trained with that in mind. As a result, their first instinct when encountering resistance is to impose their will. In peacekeeping that is not desirable, so regularly trained forces might not help the situation or even make it worse.

These principles were worked out over time. They emerged from peacekeeping in practice. In important ways they also fit the circumstances provided by the Cold War. Saying that peacekeeping was for the general welfare helped limit the pressure from either the United States or Soviet Union to have peacekeeping that served only its particular purposes. One early peacekeeping effort—the ONUC (Operation des Nations Unies au Congo, Operation of the United Nations in Congo) in 1960–1964—went badly and reinforced this point. When the Congo suddenly became independent in 1959–1960 it was a mess. There were just a handful of college graduates in the country, no working political system, no unity (some sections of the country began to secede), and the economy collapsed. UN peacekeeping forces were sent to try to provide some order and eventually found themselves taking sides among the political elements competing to run the country; soon they were being used to try to hold it together. The president of the Congo was kidnapped and killed, something the United States was not unhappy to see, and a pro-Western government was installed. The Soviet Union therefore objected strenuously to the lack of UN neutrality, stopped paying its share of the cost of the operation, and thereby threw UN finances into deep trouble for years. The United States was concerned that so much initiative was being displayed by the secretary general. The combination of U.S. wariness and Soviet displeasure meant that the consensus necessary for the Security Council to take action via peacekeeping vanished for years, and even when it returned it remained tenuous until the end of the Cold War.

Impartial operations using specially trained, lightly armed forces were ones for which the UN's smaller or less powerful members were ideally suited. Many of these states were strongly committed to neutrality, such as Sweden, or nonalignment, such as India. Many had forces with no history of fighting real wars abroad, such as Latin American countries. Others—Canada, for one—did not seriously train for real wars. So they could, and did, embrace peacekeeping as their specialty, moving to train some of their forces for this purpose. They saw themselves as making a distinctive, important contribution to peace and security—a contribution the great powers could not readily make under the circumstances.

EXPERIENCE WITH PEACEKEEPING GROWS

Peacekeeping was not widespread during the Cold War era but experience with it slowly accumulated. Peacekeeping forces could be found performing various functions.

- **Observing and verifying peace arrangements**—Includes going beyond observation, and reporting on what had been observed, to helping mediate disputes that arose, doing additional fact-finding, encouraging cooling-off periods between the parties, and the like.

- **Serving as a buffer**—Usually is done by positioning peacekeepers between the parties to cut down on confrontations and incidents. It is also done politically, with the peacekeepers representing outsiders' commitment to getting the two sides to keep the peace.

- **Offering humanitarian assistance**—Could be used directly by having peacekeepers help people out of dangerous situations, distribute assistance, discourage reprisals after incidents, and get basic services (garbage, electricity, and so on) going again. Humanitarian aid could also be offered indirectly. For instance, peacekeepers could protect shipments from theft or being siphoned off through bribery, corruption, or blackmail of aid workers. They could also protect aid workers as they went about their duties and provide good information about emerging threats, places to be avoided, and groups not to trust.

- **Helping generate law and order**—Also could be done directly or indirectly. Peacekeeping forces sometimes acted like the local police: directing traffic, discouraging disturbances, and halting looting. Or they could be employed to help train and equip the local police and military forces to provide order and security for the citizens.

All these activities and more are still a part of peacekeeping operations. Peacekeepers can be found pursuing them every day in many parts of the world. Ideally, peacekeeping would be entrusted to a well-financed, carefully staffed international organization or organizations (the UN or others), which either had their own peacekeeping forces—trained as such—or could quickly draw on specially trained and equipped military units from various states. This organization would have become experienced over time in setting up a command, installing the necessary communications systems, and creating the logistics arrangements needed. The peacekeeping forces would have a common language or languages plus a common understanding of peacekeeping and all the tasks involved, knowledge the forces had built up over years of peacekeeping service together. The forces would go into peacekeeping for a lengthy period if necessary, years or even longer, developing a deep understanding of the local situation, the local people and their culture(s), and all the other things necessary to operate effectively. Alas, nothing like this has ever emerged.

Instead, no specific international organization has been designated as responsible for peacekeeping. Normally each new operation must be put together from scratch. The UN, or the North Atlantic Treaty Organization (NATO), or some other organization or government asks for help and has to take what is offered. While a number of countries have specific military units earmarked for peacekeeping and related activities, often with specialized training and equipment, most states do not. So the force put together is often a hodgepodge. The units are unevenly trained and led, with limited common communications systems, with language differences among the forces, and so on. And the budget is limited and uncertain. The UN has relatively small administrative capacities (members must supply most of the money, logistics, communications, and other capabilities) and many other organizations are even worse off in this regard. Countries typically send their own military units for only a limited time, say six months or a year, so the units are constantly turning over. When one country's commitment to the peacekeeping effort is up, units come from different countries—a Pakistani unit departs and one from Uganda replaces it. Countries rotate units of their forces regularly—the United States usually does so every six months—for any number of reasons, but one result is that most of the soldiers never get comfortable with the situation, the local culture, and the population. Not surprisingly, peacekeeping efforts have an uneven record.

Nevertheless, the practice of peacekeeping received an enormous boost with the end of the Cold War. Few of the older efforts at peacekeeping that were still operating were brought to a conclusion and a host of new ones were developed, often in a great rush. As Yugoslavia broke up, the situation in the Balkans became unstable and received great attention. The Soviet Union disintegrated into fifteen different states, some of which were soon chaotic and needed peacekeeping help. The Security Council suddenly, and briefly, had a high level of consensus that various trouble spots needed to be dampened down. There was a burst of enthusiasm and a surge of UN and other peacekeeping. However, nearly everyone now agrees that this was too much too soon. And it became clear that amidst all this activity the very nature of peacekeeping was shifting.

The major turning point was probably the peacekeeping operation in Bosnia. With the end of the Cold War the unstable coalition of peoples that had made up Yugoslavia began to dissolve. Various peoples—Croats, Slovenes, and others— began thinking about becoming independent. In the fighting that resulted, forces drawn from these ethnic groups used brutal tactics to seize territory and drive out (actually clean out) other ethnic groups. This came to be called **ethnic cleansing**— driving all the unwanted people out of an area, people typically unwanted on racial or ethnic grounds.

The United States was outraged, the UN members were deeply disturbed, and Europeans were horrified at the appearance of something akin to the policies the Nazis had practiced toward the Jews, Gypsies, and various Slavs. The Europeans sought, under UN auspices, to take the lead in dealing with the conflict in Bosnia by sending peacekeeping forces. The trouble with this plan was that the fighting had not stopped and in many cases the parties did not want to stop. Peacekeepers were being plopped down in dangerous and unstable situations, violating many of the basic principles of peacekeeping. Everyone outside Yugoslavia wanted the fighting and atrocities to stop, and they did not want to wait for the parties to be ready to do so because it seemed likely that they would not stop and their terrible behavior would continue. Hence the general good that outsiders were promoting was not necessarily what the locals wanted. That left the peacekeepers sitting in the middle of ongoing battles and less than impartial. They were unsympathetic to those who wanted to continue fighting.

Things went downhill from there. As the fighting and atrocities continued, the peacekeeping forces were frequently threatened or ignored and were sometimes attacked. They often knew of impending atrocities but had no mandate to try to prevent them. The forces were only lightly armed in any case. But not doing any- thing about atrocities occurring right before their eyes brought strong criticism from people on the scene, from governments not involved in the peacekeeping, and from the United States, especially Congress. Efforts by peacekeeping forces to use even modest force to contain the worst excesses were also handicapped by the command system. Officers on the scene would have to seek approval from their commanders, who in turn had to gain approval from the UN official charged with overseeing the operation. He had to clear everything with the secretary general who had to seek support from the Security Council. In addition, the whole point of the UN is to try to prevent the use of force by others so it is almost always wary of using force itself. Thus when the peacekeeping forces wanted to apply even lim- ited military pressure it was uphill work to get approval.

Pressure mounted, especially from the United States, for the use of NATO members' planes to bomb the local forces that were the worst offenders. European governments resisted, fearing that those forces might take reprisals against the peacekeepers. Eventually the United States won the struggle and bombing was used, but as was feared the Bosnian Serbs replied by seizing dozens of peacekeepers as hostages. That made their governments unhappy at the idea of using even more force, unless some changes were made in the peacekeeping operation. Ultimately the solution to getting the fighting to stop was to

- Turn the operations over to NATO, because it was expected that considerable force might have to be used and NATO would have far better command arrangements than the UN.

- Pull the peacekeepers back into consolidated positions and then add much more heavily armed forces to augment them, so they could no longer be attacked or seized as hostages.

- Bomb the Bosnian Serbs heavily and assist, or do nothing to hamper, offensives by Croats and Bosnians to force negotiations on ending the war.

- Have the United States use extreme arm-twisting at the negotiation held in Dayton, Ohio, to get all the parties to agree to stop fighting and welcome a NATO peacekeeping force.

- Send a heavily armed force of more than fifty thousand troops from NATO and associates of NATO in Europe, Russia, and several other countries to do the peacekeeping. They were to deter attacks on themselves, deter violations of the peace agreement, and respond with serious firepower if the deterrence did not work.

That got the fighting and atrocities halted so that efforts to build a long-term peace could get under way (see Chapter 12).

The Bosnian case differed from traditional peacekeeping. In the end, outsiders forced the parties to stop fighting and accept peacekeeping. The parties did not invite the intervention; the outsiders took action without being invited. The forces involved were not lightly armed, and they were not specially trained for peacekeeping. They were regular military units. The force used in the bombing, and then the threat of force posed by these units, was not minimal in scale in terms of its potential destructiveness. The intervention was also far from impartial. Those in charge were particularly tough on the Bosnian Serbs for having been the worst offenders on ethnic cleansing, for committing the worst atrocities, and for having persisted in the fighting for the longest time.

Since then, in another operation, in Sierra Leone, peacekeepers were sent into an ongoing conflict, were killed and held hostage, and were supplemented by much stronger forces. In a case in East Timor, as it seceded from Indonesia, fear of similar events unfolding led to sending regular, heavily armed units to do the peacekeeping. In addition, several more traditional peacekeeping operations have been run since the end of the Cold War.

Mainly as a result of the experience in Bosnia, another important change took place in peacekeeping (see the *Terms and Concepts* box, "Human Rights"). This was the rise of what has been termed the **humanitarian impulse** as a motivation for peacekeeping. It refers to a growing interest in getting organized international interference in internal situations in which grievous harm is being done in terms of human welfare and human rights as a deliberate part, or an offshoot, of a violent conflict. Since the situation in Bosnia, humanitarian interventions have become a feature, and a highly contested one, of international politics. No one objects to the humanitarian impulse. What is under debate is whether it should be allowed to override sovereignty, particularly as an extension of Western countries' foreign policy pursuits.

GENERAL RULES FOR TODAY

The classic principles of peacekeeping do not fully apply today. While some operations are conducted in keeping with those principles, analysts and practitioners, in observing the many operations that sprang up in the 1990s, have reached broad agreement on a number of amendments or additions to them when circumstances require. Forces specifically trained for peacekeeping are not necessary—maybe useful but not necessary. Regular military forces can do the job. However, they need

- A clear mandate—some initial conception of what they are there to do;

- Unity of command;

- Significant autonomy for the commanders to carry out their job; and

- Clear rules of engagement, such as how far the peacekeepers can go to defend themselves, prevent atrocities, and maintain order.

And the rules of engagement, apparently, can now include using a good deal of force when circumstances call for it. The military forces sent in thus have to prepare to be flexible, be ready to adapt to the rapid changes in circumstances that can occur. The mandate and rules of engagement cannot be set in stone. Regular forces have to be carefully primed to be friendly and patient in hostile situations, instead of just imposing superior force. But they must be prepared to use force when necessary.

More widely accepted, though not universally, is that peacekeeping need not be entirely neutral in character. As with mediation, the important thing is that

Terms and Concepts: *Human Rights*

Human rights has emerged as a leading issue area in international politics in recent decades, with profound effects on peacekeeping and peacebuilding. There has been steady expansion in the scale of human rights activities; the number and variety of rights involved; the interest in and attention paid to human rights; and the potential costs for governments, corporations, international organizations, and others of neglecting them.

The rights involved are well known. They include standard democratic rights (freedom of speech and the rights to vote, assemble, have a fair trial, not be tortured, and so on), nondiscrimination rights (no discrimination based on race, ethnicity, religion, sex, or political beliefs), and rights of well being (to health care, a decent environment, adequate nourishment, and the like). Such rights have been endorsed in international conventions and conferences as well as in many national constitutions. Relevant for this book is that wars can emerge from struggles over these rights, and wars often seriously damage them. Thus many contemporary interventions to stop or prevent wars, including humanitarian interventions, and most cases before international war crimes tribunals are driven in part by human rights considerations.

Promoting human rights expanded after World War II, boosted by trials of German and Japanese leaders and their underlings for violating rights deemed so universal that their actions were depicted as crimes against humanity. Human rights efforts were then reinforced by the United Nations (UN) commitment to them during the Cold War, when the West called itself "the free world." In the Helsinki Accords of 1975, an agreement to promote détente in Europe, the West insisted among other things on progress on human rights in communist countries. However, this goal was neither deeply nor consistently pursued, and President Jimmy Carter's call for making human rights central to U.S. foreign policy was not taken seriously by other countries. It was therefore a surprise when numerous groups in Eastern Europe cited the accords to raise human rights complaints that put pressure on communist governments, and even more surprising when the Soviet Union's Mikhail S. Gorbachev displayed interest in making progress on human rights.

After the Cold War an explosion of interest in human rights took place, which continues today. The most powerful force behind this has been that human rights progress makes for peace. The broadened appeal of the idea, such as in democratic peace theory, has shifted the politics of Western and other societies. Until late in the twentieth century, groups promoting peace, including human rights advocates, operated on the fringes of political systems and collectively had little leverage in international politics. Human rights considerations typically gave way to state or systemic security concerns and economic issues. With an emphasis on personal autonomy and people's freedom from being unfairly restrained, human rights are fundamentally about societal security.

The collapse of the Cold War was a turning point. The immediate reaction of Western societies was to try to bury that conflict by promoting human rights improvements in Eastern European societies. The troubles in the Balkans, particularly over Bosnia, helped reinforce the sense that this was urgently needed if Europe was to remain peaceful. Spreading democracy, economic progress, and other human rights improvements in the former communist states had strong appeal across the political spectrum in Western countries. Thus the concerns of peace activists and human rights proponents now had much more impact in mainstream politics. Western governments created huge programs for fostering human rights to promote peace in Europe, programs that drew on and helped stimulate the rapidly expanding private sector activity along the same lines. It was virtually inevitable that the West would then apply the same thinking beyond Europe. As a result, resources for peacekeeping and peacebuilding efforts today are being mobilized by proliferating networks of private groups or are granted by intergovernmental organizations, the European Union, and national governments to such groups to support their activities. Nearly every contemporary peace operation has a human rights component.

This change is not always well understood. Many non–Western governments (China is a good example) treat human rights campaigns and pressures that originate in the West as a form of political warfare, as threats to their rule mounted by political enemies at home and abroad. They think of these activities as a tactic that Western governments turn on and off to suit their foreign policy needs. They insist that progress on human rights can be delayed to avoid disrupting national stability priorities or unduly disturbing national political and cultural traditions. In fact, these activities enjoy a much broader political base than before and have deeper roots in the basic values of Western societies. Western governments are less able to manipulate these activities because they enjoy such broad support politically. Human rights elements are well organized internationally, thanks to resources such as the Internet, and can bring substantial pressure to bear. Linking human rights to peace has had a profound effect.

Dilemmas for policy makers will grow. For example, the U.S. government, particularly Congress, and human rights groups have moved to put ever more pressure on North Korea over its poor record on human rights. The South Korean government has resisted this effort, raising few such complaints with North Korea and refusing to vote with Western countries on this matter at the UN, because it wants to avoid antagonizing North Korea so interactions and good will between the two Koreas can continue to grow. As a result, pressure is rising on the South Korean government from human rights groups charging that it should be ashamed for not standing up for fellow Koreans to the north.

the peacekeeping looks like an effort to be fair, evenhanded, and focused on helping to end the fighting. A peacekeeping force is likely to find some combatants far less eager to stop fighting than others, especially if they feel the fighting has left them at a serious disadvantage that they would like to eliminate or if they saw the fighting as having been going their way when it was halted. Thus the intervention affects the parties unevenly; it is not impartial in its effects. Unless the peacekeepers are seen as being fair in getting the fighting to stop, they could come into direct conflict with those not very eager to quit.

Next, it is now clear that peacekeeping needs substantial political support to be successful, not just from the parties to the conflict but from the outside. A Security Council operation would be best served if a strong consensus on the Council backed it; a NATO plan would be enhanced if the individual members are in fairly strong agreement about the operation. States that send forces should have strong support for having done so back home, particularly if there could be casualties. And it is particularly important that the states next door to the conflict are supportive. Otherwise they can easily stir up trouble by supporting one of the parties in violating the agreement, sabotaging sanctions, encouraging continued violence, providing a refuge for troublemakers, and the like.

There is also more acceptance of the need for effective intelligence operations to support peacekeeping. Intelligence in peacekeeping is a sensitive subject. Parties that invite peacekeepers in do not want the peacekeepers to then be engaged in spying on them. However, peacekeeping operations need information about potential trouble ahead, any changes taking place in the attitudes of the parties and the population, outbreaks of fighting that occur, and related concerns. If peacekeeping forces are attacked and need to decide how to respond, their intelligence needs rise sharply. This intelligence is not easy to get. The information normally available has often been of a distant, technical nature such as satellite photography or secret listening to communications. It takes time to build up reliable local sources to provide insider information, and this is often highly specialized work.

In this media-driven age, a major peacekeeping operation needs a well-organized effort to handle the media. The initial operation in Bosnia was burned by weaknesses of this sort, which made those running later operations wary about making the same mistakes. Efforts must be made to clarify the mandate and explain what is being done and why, dispel unfounded rumors, and provide the background information to put the whole operation in context. Otherwise support in other countries can be eroded or it could decline in some of the nations participating in the operation. In Bosnia the peacekeepers ended up taking steps to shut down some of the most rabid, sensationalist media associated with the parties to the conflict while developing their own media output.

Finally, it is now likely that a significant peacekeeping effort will be expected to intervene to prevent, slow, or halt a human rights catastrophe if that seems feasible. Great impetus for this kind of action came out of the developments in 1994 in Rwanda. The government, dominated by members of the Hutu tribe and with the help of Hutu extremists, set out to do something about the problem, as they saw it, of having to live with the members of the minority from the Tutsi tribe.

They used a simple and direct solution: Kill as many Tutsis as fast as possible. The UN had an aid mission in Rwanda, including a force of some 21,500 peacekeepers. The French also had some troops in Rwanda. France, Great Britain, the United States, and others rapidly evacuated their citizens. The French soldiers took in many fleeing Tutsis to protect them, only to be pulled out eventually, with the other peacekeepers, leaving the remaining Tutsis to their fate. Numerous governments decided they had no important interests at stake and saw no reason to care much about what happened in faraway Rwanda. The United States was particularly determined not to get involved, so much so that officials were told not to say anything about genocide in their reporting or policy proposals. UN bureaucrats were similarly instructed.

Four years later President Bill Clinton formally apologized (after a fashion) to the people of Rwanda for U.S. inaction. It was much too late, of course. During that murderous frenzy in 1994, perhaps 800,000 people were killed by guns, knives, and machetes—a giant *Friday the 13th* horror film come true. Even a modest effort by the peacekeepers would have saved thousands of lives. They would have had to fight or be ready to fight—maybe even fight hard occasionally—and accept a few casualties. Sometimes peacekeeping is not enough. But a frenzy can often be stopped if a pause is imposed, if even modest resistance appears.

While intervening to prevent a human rights catastrophe is now more expected, doing so is not firmly established as an operating principle. It is, however, the general direction in which events have been pushing international organizations and their members. To human beings' credit, in a media-driven age it is becoming ever harder to know that a great crime is taking place and look the other way.

CONCLUSION

After the surge in UN-led or -authorized peacekeeping in the early and mid-1990s as well as some big failures (early on in Bosnia, in Somalia), the feeling was a widespread that the UN had gone too far. Various governments sought to cut back significantly on peacekeeping under the UN or otherwise. But this did not work. In the current decade UN peacekeeping efforts have risen to their earlier levels in terms of the number of cases, the troops involved, and the costs being incurred.

Assessment

Nations often have serious reservations about getting involved in peacekeeping. Usually they have to bear some or all of the expenses involved in sending their forces, and governments rarely have loads of money to spare for helping other societies, other than in efforts such as disaster relief. It is odd that this should be so. A tidal wave or giant earthquake can stimulate huge foreign assistance, while an equally deadly international or civil war does not arouse the same sentiments. On top of that, all relief efforts, and particularly ones for internal conflicts, normally result in far less aid being delivered than is officially pledged. Talk is cheap, and governments talk a good game on the aid they will provide.

Governments are also sensitive to the fact that in peacekeeping some risk always exists of casualties, especially if the nation sends ground forces. Those casualties can be hard to explain back home because they relate only indirectly to national defense. If the forces involved are regular military units designed for fighting, their commanders dislike diverting them from their regular positions, training, and duties to learn things not relevant to their primary mission. Peacekeeping always produces wear and tear on expensive military equipment. There may be morale problems. After all, peacekeeping troops are far from home, usually in a strange place, maybe pursuing a fuzzy objective. Governments and their military officers frequently are uncomfortable with the command arrangements. Taking orders from foreigners is never easy. Governments in peacekeeping sometimes are participating because they disagree with the operation. They want to have influence on how it is conducted, and they seek a way of monitoring what is being done so they can support the interests of one of the parties. (Such was the case with Russia's participation in the NATO intervention in Bosnia.) With this as the main motivation their participation may well be a bit odd. Some governments may disagree completely with a particular operation, refusing to take part or offer any support or even trying to inhibit the operation. Their opposition may affect participation by other governments.

As a result of all this, when trouble arises somewhere, there is often no rush to act, a point made repeatedly in this book. Peacekeeping is likely to be undertaken later than it should be. This has important implications for a frequently discussed variation on peacekeeping usually referred to as **preventive diplomacy**. The idea, developed by analysts such as international relations consultant Michael S. Lund, is that when international organizations or their key members see serious trouble brewing in a conflict they should be prepared to intervene—forcefully if necessary—before things go too far and great violence takes place. That sounds good; it is a logical extension of the idea of peacekeeping. However, everyone who has considered the matter admits that a good workable strategy, and the capability for carrying it out, is lacking. Governments are often too busy with other things to act on a problem early enough, and politics always hampers decision and action. In particular, the best time to intervene to keep a conflict from deteriorating into serious violence is not the best time politically for deciding to take action. The best time to act is before things go too far. But usually it is only when things go too far for too long—much death and destruction, fleeing refugees, atrocities, and media reports that stir revulsion—that the parties are ready to stop and a public clamor arises in places such as the United States, Europe, Japan, and Russia that something has to be done.

Governments' reluctance to act also means that once a peacekeeping operation is organized and then gets under way, many officials will want to get in on the act. Governments want a say in the strategy; they want to try to micromanage how (and how not) to use their specific forces; they want to help decide what risky steps, if any, to take; they want to monitor the command structure; and so on. It is easy to see how peacekeeping can get overly complicated and cumbersome. Governments and politicians then complain loudly that the whole operation was inefficient, badly administered, and torn by conflicting views.

About the only thing that offsets this is that conflicts are usually obnoxious to at least some governments, while others join peacekeeping efforts as a way to play a role in managing the world and have a say about what is done. But otherwise, as happened in the late 1990s, governments are all too ready to announce that the UN (or NATO or the United States) is involved in too many peacekeeping efforts. Imagine a fire department or its city supervisor deciding it was involved in too many fires and would answer just half the calls.

Naturally this cuts the success rate of peacekeeping. It has had a mixed record for other reasons, too. Often peacekeeping helps stop the fighting, especially now when peacekeepers may be armed and dangerous. However, its record as a way to promote conflict resolution is discouraging. When political scientist Paul F. Diehl looked closely at ten cases some years ago he found almost no real success at ending the conflicts. Just getting the fighting stopped was not enough. When it stops, one or both parties often feel less pressure to reach an agreement, especially if it will take painful political decisions and concessions. In this way peacekeeping can make a peace settlement less likely. This is not good.

The Three Levels

In revisiting the three levels of analysis, there are other things to note. At the societal level peacekeeping is likely to have a beneficial effect. The fighting stops and may be suspended indefinitely, as happened on Cyprus. Normal life can resume and in this sense things get much better. There is a decent atmosphere for peacebuilding by outsiders, too (see Chapter 12). The reestablishment of a peaceful society is often the foremost initial objective of peacekeeping.

But a true peace is not created if the underlying conflict has not dissipated and is not being tackled. Peacekeeping can help, of course, but often the fighting is just in remission and later flares up. In many cases, if the conflict has not been settled, people may be unable to go back to their homes and are unable to live as they used to. For example, UN peacekeeping on Cyprus locked a division of the island into place, cutting many thousands off from their homes indefinitely. Traveling in

Cyprus today, you can see across a valley perhaps a cluster of abandoned homes that were once a village, an eerie reminder that peacekeeping is not peace. Hence peacekeeping is only a start at dealing with the problem of war at the societal level and sometimes is just a large bandage to stop the bleeding.

There is another, and uglier, side to peacekeeping. In several countries peace-keeping forces are volunteered mainly to make money. The UN, NATO, or others will pay the troops much better than their governments do. This kind of partici-pation in peacekeeping will not produce a consistently effective result. Moreover, the troops sent are often poorly led, ill-trained, and unenthusiastic. They may look around for opportunities to sell drugs, steal, or rape. An attractive option is organ-izing prostitution rings or smuggling ventures. This has been a problem in both the Bosnian and the eastern Congo peacekeeping operations. When the UN is running the operation it has no power to punish the participating military per-sonnel. All it can do is send them home and ask that government to take action, and the results are predictable.

At the state level, peacekeeping has important attractions. It is action taken to cope with conflict but it is not intended to trample on sovereignty. Peacekeepers are supposed to be invited in and to operate only as long as the combatants want them to, so each government involved in the conflict is not being overridden. And because peacekeeping is carried on with the forces made available by individual countries, those governments control much of what is done. That is, responsibil-ity is not in the hands of an international organization operating over their heads. When peacekeeping works to resolve conflicts, normally it is because the parties themselves reach a settlement. The solution is not imposed by outsiders. States get out of a serious situation in this way without losing any autonomy.

Peacekeeping can also be valuable in forestalling the collapse of a state or a secession from it. With peacekeeping forces in place a government gets a breather—a chance to enhance its popularity, reestablish its legitimacy, and get its economy functioning. Negotiations also could end the conflict. If a government acts to make improvements and exploits the negotiations, it can greatly improve its chances of survival, either by ending the fighting for an indefinite period or doing much better at fighting in the next round.

However, for a sovereign state to accept the arrival of peacekeepers, on its ter-ritory or along its borders, is embarrassing. It is a highly visible sign that a state needs help—that it cannot defeat the opponent at least for the time being, may have to settle for the situation as it is even if this means losing territory or hav-ing less control over it, or may have to accept the continued existence and power of a rebel group. This is hard to take and may be politically perilous over time if resentment of the settlement builds up and political opponents of the govern-ment exploit the situation. Peacekeeping may also be accompanied by outside pressure on the state to mend its ways by ending corruption, arbitrary rule, and human rights violations. The trouble for many states is that moving in that direction can get its leaders tossed out of office, probably arrested, and perhaps even shot.

Another point should not be neglected. Governments, especially powerful ones, may not undertake peacekeeping missions out of the goodness of their hearts. (This may have crossed your mind.) Intervening in another country to keep the peace can be a way to bring it under one's control, to get rid of a troublesome government, or to open up economic opportunities. During the destructive civil war in Lebanon on and off from 1975 to 1990 there were several foreign interventions—by Israel, UN peacekeepers, the United States and other Western peacekeepers, and Syria. Eventually the Syrian government ended the fighting by bringing Lebanese politics, government, and foreign relations under its control, a situation that lasted until 2005. Syrian control was in keeping with that government's long contention that Lebanon should be a part of Syria. Thus its peacekeeping operation was not disinterested in character. In the same way, Russian peacekeeping in areas that used to be part of the former Soviet Union has been widely viewed as an imperial effort to construct a sphere of influence. The United States often intervened in the Caribbean, Central America, and Mexico from the turn of the century to the early 1930s. Such interventions are threatening to the autonomy of the targeted states.

At the systemic level peacekeeping operations that are successful can be a great relief. Wars between states and some wars within states often put great strain on an international system. The small wars in southeastern Europe as the Ottoman Empire decayed and the Austro-Hungarian empire declined, in the late nineteenth and early twentieth centuries, repeatedly had this effect and eventually played a major role in the outbreak of World War I. Some feared that something similar was occurring in the 1990s, before peacekeeping operations sharply altered the situation. Peacekeeping can play an important role in easing strains of this sort, but it is likely to be applied later than is desirable, after considerable strain has already been caused. In addition, peacekeeping operations have repeatedly been hard on the UN—damaging its finances, the political consensus among its most important members, and the political support in various governments for its administrators. It is not helpful to have a management capability for the problem of war that can be damaged if used.

Also of concern is how peacekeeping has recently come to encompass something much more forceful. If it has a weak record on conflict resolution, and it often takes a real threat of force, or force itself, to get a conflict under control, this suggests that peacekeeping as a solution to the problem of war has only limited value as it works well only in selected circumstances.

SOURCES AND OTHER USEFUL READINGS

Paul F. Diehl's *International Peacekeeping* and "Forks in the Road" are central works in the study of peacekeeping. The development of peacekeeping over time from the traditional approach to the more muscular version is recounted in *The Evolution of UN Peacekeeping*, edited by William J. Durch; Donald C. F. Daniel and Bradd C. Hayes, *Beyond Traditional Peacekeeping*; and Adam Roberts, "The Use of Force," which looks at military intervention deeper than peacekeeping as well. The complaints about peacekeeping and its shortcomings are discussed in Dennis C. Jett, *Why Peacekeeping Fails*; and Wolfgang Biermann and Martin Vadset, *UN Peacekeeping in Trouble*. An interesting brief article on peacekeeping today for the general reader is James Traub, "Peacekeeping."

For peacekeeping and even more extensive interventions much depends on the UN and its agencies. Discussions of this can be found in Jim Whitman, *Peacekeeping and the UN Agencies*; and Richard Caplan, "A New Trusteeship?" An overall look at the UN Security Council that assesses its potential is *The UN Security Council*, edited by David M. Malone.

The early development of the Cyprus peacekeeping effort can be traced in Farid Mirbagheri, *Cyprus and International Peacekeeping*. The NATO efforts in the Balkans that turned into peacekeeping are recounted in Dana H. Allen, "NATO's Balkan Interventions."

The negative reaction to the broadening of the criteria for peacekeeping and deeper interventions, in China as an example, is reviewed in Bates Gill and James Reilly, "Sovereignty, Intervention, and Peacekeeping."

Perhaps the best discussion of why governments are so slow to act when confronted with a serious internal conflict is James E. Goodby, "Conflict in Europe." A case in point is the Bosnia situation. To understand the reluctance to act on it in the U.S. government, see Ivo H. Daalder, *Getting to Dayton*; and David Halberstam, *War in a Time of Peace*. And a nice explanation as to why American commanders find that peacekeeping duties are not good for regular military forces is William Langewiesche, "Peace Is Hell."

Finally, this chapter, like others, includes several indications that internal wars can be destructive and violent in their consequences. A powerful analysis of how long-lasting those effects can be is Hazen Ghobarah, Paul Huth, and Bruce Russett, "Civil Wars Kill and Maim People."

CHAPTER 11

Peace Enforcement and Peace Imposition

Peacekeeping started out as a simple military activity. Peacekeepers would arrive lightly armed because the parties to a conflict had invited them to come. They were just there to assist. If being lightly armed showed that they posed no threat and intended no harm, how could keeping the peace mean shooting people? Responsibility for ending the fighting remained clearly with the parties. Peacekeeping would help but it was up to those directly involved in the conflict to ensure that the fighting stopped and remained stopped.

This fit in well with the idea that states are sovereign. The United Nations (UN) Charter said there were to be no wars among states and the Security Council was empowered to take steps, including military measures, to enforce this. But states are sovereign and an organization composed of states was naturally not eager to trifle with sovereignty. So members felt it would be far better if the parties in a conflict worked things out for themselves, with help from peacekeepers if necessary.

However, experience with peacekeeping moved it toward being more forceful in character. What was proper and acceptable peacekeeping behavior changed. In some operations strong pressure (sanctions, threats) was placed on the parties to stop fighting, eventually including having peacekeepers arrive in a fairly heavily armed condition. It was also no longer always assumed that peacekeepers would be safe when they came, especially when inserted into conflict situations when the parties had not yet stopped fighting and perhaps did not particularly want them there. In these cases they had to be decently armed, in part to protect themselves and also at times to deter the parties from further fighting. The peacekeepers could threaten the parties via their presence and their military strength.

The real turning point was the North Atlantic Treaty Organization (NATO) intervention in Bosnia. An attempt at classic peacekeeping had failed in that sad place. The parties did not stop fighting, ignored UN peacekeeping forces, and took some peacekeepers hostage. So when NATO replaced the UN it did so with heavily armed troops that, fortunately, never had to do any fighting. NATO was determined that its personnel not end up as hostages. They were sent in part to continue the military arm-twisting NATO had used, particularly on the Bosnian Serbs, to get the parties into a peace agreement. On the whole, even though there was no fighting that operation was not much like normal peacekeeping. It is treated as peacekeeping in Chapter 10 only because the NATO forces never had to defend themselves or use force to stop the parties from fighting. The peace agreement held. But a gray area clearly exists between muscular peacekeeping and a military insistence on peace, which is the subject of this chapter. The Bosnia case was a bridge between the two.

MAIN ELEMENTS OF PEACE ENFORCEMENT AND PEACE IMPOSITION

This chapter is about two overlapping phenomena. Each involves outsiders saying, in effect: "We're here to promote peace. And if you don't stop fighting we'll kill you if we have to." Together they represent a major escalation in the remedies available within international politics for the problem of war. Perhaps the most profound aspect of a successful political community is the effective order and security that it provides, by nullifying violent threats to order and security from conflicts among the members and by protecting the community from outside threats. While much can be done for this purpose, when all else fails order and security have to be upheld by force. Communities use force not only to repress and punish outbreaks of violence or attacks from outside but also, they hope, to deter such outbreaks and attacks from occurring. A fairly well developed political community is needed to do this properly so that, on the one hand, force is seldom needed for this purpose domestically and, on the other, force and the fear of foreign threats are not used to terrify and oppress the citizens.

With this in mind the international political environment is often cited as an example of a poor, even nonexistent, political community because war among its members is insufficiently deterred, repressed, and punished. Strategic political arrangements that analysts and statesmen hoped would get the problem of war under control—such as nuclear deterrence, hegemony, a great-power concert, collective security—would bring the proper amount of force to bear when necessary without, in theory, unduly trampling on other things that nations highly value. As noted, these arrangements have their limits. However, interstate wars are now relatively rare even though there are more states than ever. Perhaps good progress has been made in developing at least a minimal level of political community in international politics.

However, interstate wars have not disappeared, and although wars inside states have declined in number in recent years, and possibly in total fatalities, they are still common. Among the more tactical, practical actions that international strategic arrangements can use are steps that only a serious level of political community can readily undertake because they involve force to suppress violence when all else fails. This is an ambitious enterprise for international politics, a leap into relatively unknown territory.

In one of these approaches, **peace enforcement** (PE), outsiders use threats and fighting if necessary to get the parties to agree to stop fighting and then to stop.

The parties have agreed to quit but cannot manage to do so, and peace enforcement is used to make them toe the line. The NATO Bosnia operation started out as peace enforcement and then, fortunately, slipped back into peacekeeping. For a domestic U.S. analogy, PE is like calling out the National Guard to halt a riot or other violent demonstration when appeals by the community leaders and leaders of the demonstrators to stop are having little effect, then keeping the guard around for a while to make sure the violence does not flare up again.

In **peace imposition** (PI), by contrast, outsiders are ready to use force and may do so to defeat at least one (or more) of the parties because it will not stop fighting or give up what it wrongly seized by fighting. In short, war is made if necessary to stamp out a war. A domestic U.S. analogy is when the authorities go beyond calling out the National Guard to declare martial law that puts the armed forces in control of an entire area. It is a bit strong to cite defeat of a party as the prime justification for PI. Sometimes that is the goal. In other cases the goal is to frustrate a party's political and military objectives in the conflict. That could be done by defeating it outright but also by just militarily preventing it from achieving a victory. PI can use force to stop a war or to undo the results of a war already finished because efforts to stop it got started too late. After all, if a war ends because one side has defeated the other and nothing is done about that, then the triumph of the victor is allowed to stand and he gains the spoils, which does nothing to reduce the problem of war and exacerbates it instead.

Who, Where, and Why?

Various examples exist of pure peace enforcement. However, once a peace enforcement operation gets started it may turn into peacekeeping, as happened in Bosnia, or deteriorate into an effort at peace imposition. The latter is what happened in Somalia, culminating in the incident chronicled in the movie (and novel) *Black Hawk Down,* and it also took place in Sierra Leone in recent years where the British were doing most of the peace imposition. The best modern example of using force to undo the results of a war is the 1991 Persian Gulf War against Iraq. The ONUC (Operation des Nations Unies au Congo, Operation of the United Nations in Congo), discussed in Chapter 10, also took on aspects of a peace imposition operation.

PE and PI can be carried on by a hegemonic state, by a set of states in a power-balancing system, by a concert of great powers, by both ordinary and advanced multilateral institutions, and by a collective security system. As for who might specifically act, many are eligible: the UN Security Council, other groups of states, and individual governments. However, it can be difficult to know how to treat specific military interventions by individual governments. What this book cares about is PE and PI undertaken for the general good, because the international community considers war harmful to everyone and thus unacceptable. Sometimes an individual state intervenes militarily for this reason, too. It might be disgusted with a war and its effects.

However, when a state intervenes it is often because fighting inside another country, or between countries, is not turning out the way it prefers. The wrong side is winning, or the right side is not winning because there is a stalemate. The United States militarily intervened strongly in South Vietnam in 1965 in hopes of ending the war there, saying that it sought to discourage communist expansionism and aggression and to show small states that they were safe. That is, it was acting to promote the general welfare. But it was actually trying to keep the communists from winning the civil war there after having prevented them from winning via an election. That was its foremost foreign policy objective. It was not against the war in South Vietnam per se; it was against North Vietnam winning it. The United States would not have intervened to halt a successful war by South Vietnam against North Vietnam. Some analysts argue that many conflicts would end, in that there would be no more fighting, if outsiders let the battling parties alone and let one side win decisively. Their view is that outside interventions to promote peace are misguided. In contrast, individual states often militarily intervene because they fear the wrong party will win decisively, not because they dislike the fighting itself. In intervening to prevent a defeat of their side, they are not trying to solve the problem of war. By using force to achieve their political objectives, they are part of the problem of war.

The easy way to classify interventions properly might be to say that a true case of PE and PI for purposes of this book exists when intervention was authorized by a regional or global organization—such as the UN Security Council—acting on behalf of the general welfare. Alas, this will not always work. When, for instance, the Security Council acts, is it because the general UN membership supports doing so? What if action is taken only when it suits the Security Council members' political objectives and fits their national interests, regardless of the general welfare? What if a particular coalition dominates the organization? Others then claim that the Security Council acts not in the common good but in the West's interest. This view is particularly likely to spread if the organization is dominated by a specific state, such as the United States. When the George W. Bush administration sought Security Council approval in 2002-2003 for its plan to invade Iraq and oust Saddam Hussein—for the general welfare, it said—many members felt that Security Council approval would reflect overwhelming American influence and not the general welfare. Sometimes what a government wants for its own purposes fits nicely with the general good and sometimes governments want the general good, so when a government mounts a military intervention this need not automatically offend the international community. But the opposite conclusion as to what is taking place is usually plausible.

Peace enforcement and peace imposition operations range from a potent threat to intervene forcefully if fighting starts (that is, deterrence) or is not halted (compellence) to direct military action such as bombing or an invasion to fighting an extensive war. That last possibility has disturbing elements that must be considered here because it is, in effect, waging war against people because they are waging war. That stimulates moral qualms not unlike those about a state that executes, that is, murders, murderers.

Legitimacy

Peace enforcement and peace imposition by outsiders depart from traditional international politics, a subject raised in connection with Wilsonian Collective Security. In traditional international politics, war is a standard, acceptable tool of statecraft. Iraq and Kuwait have a serious dispute, which cramps Iraq's ambitions. No agreement can be reached, so Iraq settles the dispute by attacking Kuwait. War is the ultimate way of settling international disputes. However, when PE and PI are used on behalf of the general welfare to stop a war this is because the international community, or some part of it, considers war no longer normal and acceptable. Aggressive warfare to settle disputes is out of fashion. In the case of Iraq and Kuwait, the Security Council condemned Iraq, authorized a war that threw it out of Kuwait, and punished it with further restrictions and sanctions.

This may not be the only reason the Security Council acted. After all, the United States organized the Security Council response and led the war on Iraq partly because it did not want a dictatorial, anti-Western, expansionist Iraq dominating the Persian Gulf and thus controlling world oil exports. The United States and others had economic, strategic, political, and other objectives in mind, not just the principle that aggression is intolerable. However, the war enjoyed wide support among UN members because one banner under which it was fought was the principle that aggression is intolerable and when it occurs the Security Council must do something.

But who decides these things? What makes it proper to change the basic rules of international politics in this fashion—aggression used to be common, but now it is illegitimate? Using force is serious business and if it is to be allowed only for certain purposes, this limits governments in an important way. How is it legitimate to ban a tool that was once common?

One way that banning force for aggressive purposes has been legitimized is saying so in the UN Charter, with enforcement to be provided by the Security Council. Because virtually all governments belong to the UN, and thus have subscribed to the charter, every government has officially agreed that aggressive war is unacceptable. The charter says the Security Council is to mobilize the members to do something about a war or other threats to peace and security, so when the

Security Council authorizes a military action that makes it legitimate. Thus what generates the legitimacy is a compact by the members, an established process for deciding when force is being improperly used, and a process for authorizing action. An agreement by an established institution lays down some rules and an established process is used for upholding them—agreement, institution, rules, process.

Deviating from this invites strong criticism. The Bush administration, for example, experienced this in going to war against Iraq in 2003, when it led a coalition on its own without the approval of the Security Council. Because Iraq was not at war and was not committing aggression, it was difficult to mobilize governments to go to war against it. And they were uncomfortable in supporting a war even if they did not have to join in fighting it. Most wanted the Security Council to be asked to authorize any war against Iraq because otherwise it would look like the United States was aggressively using war, not Iraq. By insisting it would attack Iraq on its own if it had to, the Bush administration was violating the basic agreement—in the charter—that war is not acceptable unless authorized. By then attacking without Security Council authorization the United States avoided the agreement, the institution, the rules, and the process that had been set up for deciding on military action. It was ready to put U.S. policy and objectives ahead of those things. The United States insisted its cause was just, that it acted in the general interest to forestall aggressive action by Iraq in the future, and that Iraq deserved to be attacked for ignoring past Security Council decisions critical of its behavior. All this may have been true, as various analysts claimed. But it did not eliminate the fundamental problem of legitimacy for the administration's actions. Anyone can claim his or her cause is just; in fact, everyone always does. Legitimacy ultimately derives from a prior agreement, institution, rules, and process.

The NATO countries, led by the United States, were in far better shape to use force against the Bosnian Serbs and then against Serbia on the issue of Kosovo even though they, too, went around the Security Council by avoiding referral of their proposed action to it for approval. The NATO countries had officially designated their alliance as Europe's security manager. This would have been an aggressive claim if they had not then developed elaborate links between themselves and most of the other countries in Europe—links that had to do specifically with helping to prevent wars, resolve conflicts peacefully, and intervene if necessary to uphold the peace. This rather strongly suggested that the nonmembers of NATO in Europe were on its side in dealing with problems of war, and many were in fact supportive. Finally, the NATO countries had rules for deciding on when they would collectively use force and the proper process was used. When they did use force, in each case the members were criticized for not going through the Security Council, that is, for acting illegitimately. While the criticism was technically correct, it did not have much impact politically. NATO countries had acted on the basis of a broad agreement among the great majority of the European and North Atlantic nations, through an established institution, following established rules, and through a standard decision-making process. When they used force it was clear that most European governments approved and would help; that is, it was a collective decision made in accordance with the relevant procedures. So the action was largely accepted as legitimate.

In traditional international politics power matters most and legitimacy often follows power. States often do what they want and what they can and then declare the results legitimate. Shifting from doing things this way requires, at the start, reducing the dominance of power in favor of legitimacy. If that can be made to work, when states do something violently it can sometimes be declared illegitimate by representatives of the international community and because of this it becomes more difficult, even impossible, to carry out.

The other way that PE and PI depart from traditional international politics has to do with reacting to internal wars. When PE and PI are used to halt an internal conflict this often directly challenged sovereignty, or national autonomy. Sovereignty means a state is entitled to be free from outside interference in its internal affairs, particularly on its internal political affairs. Classically, how a sovereign government treats its citizens is its own business. In addition, sovereignty means people inside are free from outside interference. If they want to tear down their government, shoot the officials, and build another, that is their business. Of course, sovereignty has always been an ideal and not uniformly upheld. States have interfered in each other's internal affairs, and often that interference has been aimed at the citizens, not the state. However, sovereignty is a powerful ideal. It is the core of autonomy, and autonomy is a compelling value in politics at any level. Thus governments are normally reluctant to be involved in or approve of international PE and PI efforts for conflicts inside a state. Such operations usually have to be justified in a special way—made to appear legitimate, despite sovereignty—to have widespread support. In each case the question is, Why doesn't sovereignty apply?

As with efforts to deal with interstate wars, discussion can start with the UN Charter, but extracting legitimacy for interventions from the charter is not as easy as it is for wars between states. Here is how that legitimacy is usually sought and achieved. The charter empowers the Security Council to act when it detects "a threat to international peace and security," and the Security Council is left to decide when such a threat exists. So if the Security Council decides that something inside a country is a threat to peace and security in the world outside, this is said to justify intervening militarily to stop it. Because UN members are governments one obvious reason for this justification would be that what was happening was a threat or serious burden to other governments. The Security Council might decide that fighting inside a country was likely to provoke or tempt others to seize its territory or help their ethnic compatriots caught up in the fighting and fear that a wider war would result. Or it could emphasize humanitarian considerations with regard to the refugees and other suffering civilians, or decide that refugees from the fighting were too big a burden on other governments. It can cite the International Convention on Genocide as justification for taking action, when applicable.

Raising humanitarian considerations means embracing the notion that an international community exists. The idea has become more attractive, partly because of rising interdependence and the globalization of communications and partly because of the huge number of organizations that now exist devoted to promoting universal values—groups normally referred to as elements of **international civil society**. As a result states and individuals sometimes feel deeply affected by what happens in other countries, including wars. Why? One answer is that human beings care about the human condition. A human community exists even if many people do not see it and governments often do not want to see it. People care about the community and everyone in it. When hurricanes, earthquakes, or epidemics occur, they rally, send help, and intervene. Why not when a disastrous war occurs?

Thus for internal wars the legitimacy of forceful intervention rests on a jumble of elements. The fighting may be threatening sovereignty. Because states like sovereignty they may support intervention to prevent that from happening—it might be infectious. What if a state has broken down, with society dissolved into civil war and chaos? Then intervention is not contravening sovereignty because there is, at that time, no state to be sovereign. Others suggest that sovereignty is ultimately lodged with citizens, not the state. If intervention protects citizens from a terrible state or halts fighting to reestablish order and security, sovereignty is reaffirmed, not violated, because the citizens once again enjoy a decent, safe community. A widely voiced argument is that sovereignty is not absolute. If terrible enough things happen inside a state, that is justification enough to intervene. If damage to outsiders is great enough that, too, justifies ignoring sovereignty and intervening.

Arguments like these are never clear-cut as to when an internal war threatens peace and security, so the best conclusion is probably that an internal situation justifies forcible intervention when the most relevant international community says so. The relevant community might be the neighbors; it might be a regional organization for security management such as NATO; it might be the UN Security Council. Thus, in international politics we have been feeling our way in recent decades toward acceptable justifications for forceful interventions into states and their societies. Progress is slow because consensus is missing. Sovereignty is too attractive to abandon, but wars can have atrocious consequences. So the international reactions to violent internal conflicts are uneven—sometimes something is done, by force if necessary, and sometimes little or nothing is done. International community action sometimes is justified by one argument, sometimes another. At times reactions are swift, at other times slow or tentative or nonexistent. A constant backdrop is that governments and citizens feel that killing people to save them from war should be done only when absolutely necessary. Otherwise, why risk getting shot, getting drawn deeply into the conflict, and straining the national budget?

This makes PE and PI an odd resource. Justifying forceful interventions, and vigorous ones, is easiest in blatant cases of interstate aggression, as when Iraq invaded Kuwait. Unfortunately this is statistically the least common kind of war today. When aggression is less clear-cut, international reaction may be muted. Beginning in 1998 and running on for years the eastern part of the Democratic Republic of the Congo was an arena for fighting by units from seven or eight countries, some by invading and others in defense of the Congo. Some analysts described it as Africa's version of a world war. Yet the only serious justification offered for possible UN intervention was the humanitarian effects, not the aggression. You do not remember the UN's War to Stop the War in Central Africa because it never happened. The outside world made only a feeble attempt to develop a peacekeeping force. No serious consideration was given to real PE or PI to end the fighting.

In summary, states, and many people, are increasingly inclined to regard military intervention as proper for stopping highly unacceptable behavior—outright attacks on others, death and destruction inside a country, and genocide. Sovereignty is not protection against intervention in such cases. But not everyone agrees that, or agrees on when, things are bad enough to justify military action. So states do not want to try to develop explicit definitions of such conditions, that is, clear indicators as to when force is called for. That would lead to endless discussion with no consensus. Even if they could agree, they might want to ignore the rules and do nothing the next time a clear case arose. Instead, states and their citizens want to choose which situations to respond to, when they want to, and avoid universal rules and indicators.

PEACE ENFORCEMENT AND PEACE IMPOSITION IN PRACTICE

The first serious effort at UN peace imposition occurred in 1950–1953 with the Korean War. This was no modest affair; several million people were killed. Much like Germany, Korea was occupied at the end of World War II by Soviet and

American forces and then divided when the Cold War made it impossible to reach agreement on the government Korea should have. When North Korea invaded South Korea to reunite the country, the United States persuaded the Security Council to intervene militarily against the invaders. Early military success led to a UN effort to occupy North Korea and unify the two Koreas, a step blocked by China's military intervention to support North Korea, which made the war larger and more costly. So what started as peace imposition by defeating North Korea turned into a long war with China. A truce in 1953 ended the fighting along a line not far from the earlier one between the two countries, but the result was not particularly satisfactory. The demilitarized zone between the two Koreas has remained an area of continuing tension ever since and for years was one of the most heavily militarized zones—huge forces on high alert—in the world. Not much peace and security resulted from that PI effort.

For years thereafter, the Cold War made similar actions almost impossible. The members of the Security Council would not reach agreement. The closest was the Congo intervention in 1960–1964. When the Congo became independent it was in such poor shape that UN peacekeeping forces were sent to help get the new government on its feet. A rebellion against that government broke out and UN peacekeepers were eventually used to defeat it, going beyond peacekeeping into something closer to peace imposition. This was a long way from what had happened in Korea. Even so, it was so controversial that nothing like it was attempted again for more than thirty years. The UN was badly divided and nearly bankrupted by the intervention.

But as soon as the Cold War ended the Security Council plunged back into the business of PE and PI, this time against Iraq in the Persian Gulf War. As in Korea this was for reversing an act that was perceived as aggression. With the United States once again in the lead, a large military force was put together to throw Iraq out of Kuwait. Much like in the Korean War, some thought was given to carrying the invasion of Iraq all the way to Baghdad to oust the government responsible for seizing Kuwait, but President George Bush decided not to go that far, hoping Saddam Hussein's government would collapse instead. When it did not disappear, used brutal repression against internal opponents, and resisted UN inspections, there was no desire to restart the war, so sanctions were imposed and limited applications of force were used to cripple the government's ability to fully control the country, force it to accept inspections, and compel it to give up the weapons of mass destruction it possessed. That situation lasted until the U.S. and British attack on Iraq in 2003.

After the Gulf War there were several additional cases of PE and PI: in Bosnia and Haiti, where PE soon turned into peacekeeping; Somalia, where PE and PI collapsed in failure and the forces were withdrawn; Kosovo; Sierra Leone; Sri Lanka, by India; and the Ivory Coast, by France. A muscular peacekeeping operation was launched in East Timor in 1999, headed by the Australians, that was ready to use force to suppress violence there if necessary but did not have to.

The members of NATO became steadily more concerned about the situation in the province of Kosovo in what was left of Yugoslavia after the fighting in Bosnia. The population of Kosovo was about 90 percent Albanian, and the Yugoslav government had steadily reduced its autonomy and increased repression of its population, fearing that the province would try to secede. When a movement to secede emerged and began using force—terrorism and guerrilla warfare—against the Serb government and its forces, the government reacted in kind and began a campaign to terrorize people into fleeing the province, much like the ethnic cleansing during the war in Bosnia. NATO warned that it would not permit this. The Serbian campaign was too violent, was too much like genocide, was creating waves of refugees, and was too much like Bosnia where NATO had already intervened. Not getting the desired cooperation, NATO launched an extended bombing campaign of Yugoslavia and its forces in Kosovo, and it eventually began moving toward the use of army units as well. This went on during March-June 1999 and forced the Yugoslav government to suspend its actions in Kosovo and remove its forces, which were replaced by NATO forces for peacekeeping and, if necessary, more PE and PI.

The Kosovo case is interesting in several ways. It was not the UN but NATO that acted. NATO members knew the Security Council would not approve a war (Russia and China were opposed), felt they had no choice but to use force, and argued that, because the Security Council had repeatedly condemned what Yugoslavia was doing, an attack on it would be in keeping with the clear intent of the Council. Furthermore, NATO members insisted they did not want Kosovo to secede from Yugoslavia; the intervention was not to undermine the sovereignty of the government but to get Yugoslavia to run a multiethnic state in a fair and democratic way. NATO forces went to Kosovo to do PE and PI if necessary by opposing the political objective of the Kosovo rebels. NATO also insisted that it wanted Kosovo to be safe for the 10 percent or so of the population that was Serbian. Here is the evidence of the reluctance of the relevant international community to undermine sovereignty and to set a precedent of supporting an independence movement against a government.

How did this turn out? The peace imposition worked in ending the fighting and repression in Kosovo, allowing hundreds of thousands of refugees to return. But the Serbian population in Kosovo knew it would not be safe after the fighting ended and largely moved to Yugoslavia proper. The Albanian population was almost completely opposed to remaining a part of Yugoslavia, and NATO made no attempt to turn it over to Yugoslavia to become a province again. Instead, the outsiders were left running the province or getting Kosovar governmental units established to do so. So the PI achieved its initial objectives but not the subsidiary ones.

Action in Kosovo was the last major peace imposition undertaken after the end of the Cold War involving large and powerful forces and notable killing and destruction. Because many wars are still being fought around the world, almost all intrastate or civil wars, the limited use of PE and PI indicates that this is not a popular or standard way of dealing with the problem of war. It is the ultimate forcible recourse now not only because it involves such potentially large forces but also in the sense that it is seldom applied and appears to be a last resort.

EXPLAINING THE USE OF PEACE ENFORCEMENT AND PEACE IMPOSITION

After the Cold War, peacekeeping operations surged and peacekeeping drifted toward more forcible intervention (see Chapter 10). Most of the instances of PE and PI were an extension of that surge. Interest even was expressed in military intervention to prevent serious wars from developing; that it, preventive PE and PI were used for humanitarian purposes. This is a forceful version of **preventive diplomacy**. If the international community is willing to intervene by force regularly to stop wars, why not intervene to prevent the wars from breaking out or building up in the first place? This idea probably emerged mainly because of the results in Rwanda stemming from the international community's unwillingness to act when the slaughter began and its reluctance to do anything after the massacre was well under way. With no outside intervention the consequences were much like the slaughter in Cambodia when the Khmer Rouge tried remaking the entire society by killing those who they thought would not fit into the new one. The big difference was that, in Rwanda, the slaughter took only a few weeks.

Militarized preventive diplomacy has not developed as a regular tool, however. And by the end of the twentieth century eagerness for interventions to deal with the problem of war had diminished. As with peacekeeping, a surge of interest and activity in the 1990s in PE and PI was followed by a much diminished level of effort. An attractive explanation of the surge is that after the end of the Cold War the media found other conflicts to focus on that were seemingly small and remote but were collectively killing and destroying on a large scale. This is sometimes referred to as the **CNN effect**, in which suffering presented in a graphic way leads to rising pressure on governments to do something.

The most direct explanation for the eventual drop in PE and PI activities is Somalia, where a peacekeeping operation developed into much more and went terribly wrong. When the corrupt and repressive government of Somalia collapsed in

1991 after lengthy civil warfare, there was no government, just a set of warring clans. In the chaos and fighting, thousands of innocents were soon dying, not just from the conflict but also from starvation, disease, and other maladies of a society in collapse. International aid efforts were overwhelmed, while the warring clans were stealing up to half the aid and endangering the people providing humanitarian assistance. At the insistence of the United States, in one of President George Bush's last official foreign policy actions, the UN agreed to send forces to help—with American forces as the most prominent participants. These were to be peacekeepers, who were put there to protect supplies and aid workers. The intervention was opposed by African states because there was no Somalian government to invite it. Sovereignty was being ignored, and they feared a precedent was being set. Because food was the key thing to control in their fight to dominate the country, the clans were not about to stop seizing the aid, so the peacekeepers' mission soon was changed. They were to go after the thieves and break up the clan armies to provide enough order and security for humanitarian efforts to save lives. This meant combat operations and the fighting soon led to the deaths of twenty-four Pakistan soldiers and eighteen Americans. Many commentators cite the CNN effect at work here, because Somalis dragged the bodies of two Americans around the streets in well-televised jubilation. Evidence showed that this did not destroy American public support for the Somalia intervention. However, the armed forces had a deep aversion to such involvements, Congress was bound to be leery, and the public might have soured on the intervention after more fighting. In any case, the Clinton administration had seen enough. The United States announced it would pull its forces out and the other participants did the same. The UN has never again run a peace enforcement or peace imposition operation itself. The United States has done no more of these kinds of operations.

Were there larger factors at work? No one can say for sure. There are several possibilities, including some discussed earlier. As for why the UN revived PE and PI, there is the rising interdependence of states and societies globally and especially in some regional international systems. Trouble in Yugoslavia quickly scattered refugees all over Europe. They cost governments a considerable amount of money, strained social services, sometimes increased the crime rate, and attracted ethnic opposition. One justification for the U.S.-led war in Afghanistan was that the civil war there in the 1980s had eventually produced such grave conditions that radical fundamentalists (the Taliban) were able to seize power and then assist, even nurture, international terrorist groups such as al Qaeda. That is, civil war in a place most Americans could not find on a map eventually had something to do with destruction of the World Trade Center on September 11, 2001. Economic interdependence is evident in the way wars in the Middle East drive up the price of oil, creating serious economic strains.

The trouble with this explanation is that interdependence does not look that critical. While military interventions surged after the Cold War, peace and security in the world actually looked less related to interdependence than before. During the Cold War virtually unknown places such as Angola seemed vitally important to the superpowers and others, if only for symbolic reasons, so their internal struggles attracted outside intervention. In Angola, for example, intervention of one sort or another came from the Soviet Union, the United States, China, Cuba, and South Africa. Since the Cold War major states are more inclined to treat small-state wars or internal conflicts as worth little time and attention. Rwanda was the most glaring example. While refugees are a problem, it is hardly new. The world has had major refugee burdens from wars for nearly a century. If concern about refugees can drive interventions it must be because the sensitivity to their plight is greater. The same is true with economic interdependence, which also features nothing new. In some ways the major economies in the world were more interdependent in the late nineteenth century than they are now. Most states do not like depending on others for oil but seem unwilling to fight about it.

A better explanation is probably that the end of the Cold War elevated the West to greater preeminence in world politics than before, which led to more emphasis in the international system on Western humanitarian values. Western countries dominate the Security Council, other international organizations, the international economic system, the world's military capabilities, and most of the world's information flows. The surge in military intervention for peace and security after the Cold War was stimulated by the West's interests and concerns, and then it faded primarily because the West lost a good deal of interest. The West now seems unlikely to regularly expand the use of PE and PI. For one thing, Western countries consistently disagree on when and to what extent to use military intervention for the general welfare, that is, on when war should be used to do something about war. In particular they do not agree on how much they should risk and pay to control war. They display a strong reluctance to intervene in internal wars if significant costs—casualties, long-term commitments, big aid programs—would be incurred. Thus the rise of the West has certainly moved forceful interventions to control wars higher up on the world's agenda, but it does not seem to consistently dictate interventions.

So what determines which conflicts draw intervention? A favorite explanation (the CNN effect again) is the media. They are newly globalized and driven by the need for dramatic pictures and stories, hence offering hypercoverage of fighting, genocide, famine, and destruction. Supposedly the media have made it much harder to ignore war-driven catastrophes, much harder to dismiss them as irrelevant or far away, and much easier to say "let's do something." Remember how the Clinton administration issued instructions to officials to avoid talking about

Rwanda, even inside the government, with language referring to it as a case of genocide because if the media got hold of that loaded word the pressure to intervene, something the administration was determined to avoid, would grow. Thus if the media hype the consequences of a particular war the world or some part of it will be moved to react strongly; when they do not, nothing much happens.

But how powerful are the media on this? If the media ignore a war, outsiders likely will do little about it. But sometimes the media play up a war and still nothing is done. After all, news of violence and destruction is so relentless that it tends to routinize violence and distance people from it psychologically. Like sex in advertising, over time it loses some of its power to grab their attention. And coverage of so much violent conflict can make it seem unavoidable, not something that could be stopped or eliminated. It can also make violent conflict look irrational and its perpetrators beyond help—all the more reason to stay out. Such situations seem like ones that should be avoided unless they have a direct effect on a society. In short, familiarity with the worst people do to each other often breeds pessimism about trying to stop it. This may even occur when "other people's wars" do directly affect a country. The media seize on any violence against their country's soldiers and citizens, as happened in the United States with the Somalia intervention. This can easily produce disgust and a deep desire to get out and stay out of such situations. Since the Somalia incident the United States has not joined any humanitarian interventions expected to use force, and it used force in Kosovo only in ways that guaranteed practically no U.S. casualties. Only when the administration said the United States was directly threatened, in Afghanistan and then Iraq in 2003, has its forces been used, not to stop others from fighting but to defeat those who attacked or seemed ready to attack the nation.

Thus sometimes the media have a significant effect and sometimes not. Media help direct public and governmental attention, and they often reflect it. If people or officials do not care about a situation, it often does not get much coverage. If early coverage generates no interest, media attention shifts elsewhere. So the CNN effect exists but has an uneven impact.

The most interesting possible explanation for greater attention to wars and more attempts to mount international interventions to stop the fighting is a growing revulsion toward war itself, making it slowly but steadily less acceptable as a tool of statecraft or governance and treated instead as a last resort. This revulsion stems from disgust with its destructiveness, loss of life, and other costs, especially because war is often ineffective. The price is paid but without the intended results or the results end up costing far too much. That means war is becoming increasingly unacceptable unless properly authorized, which harkens back to the justification for using force to prevent wars, a rationale that is slowly being applied even to internal wars. When war is not properly authorized and justified it lacks legitimacy, can be condemned, and therefore is worth suppressing—at least sometimes.

If this is so it is a profound and notable development. It is a turning point. A marked decline has taken place in interstate wars, and maybe revulsion is the main reason. But the revulsion toward war has not fully extended to internal fighting. Violent domestic conflicts have diminished but not disappeared. Since World War II they have killed many millions of people, mostly civilians. People still feel driven to violence in dealing with others in their own societies, so the most potent revulsion thus far—in its impact on internal wars—is that felt by outsiders. And if this is a real turning point it is in slow motion. The so-called international community simply does not treat all wars as so awful that something must be done about them.

Probably a combination of all these factors, and others, is responsible for increased use of PE and PI. Their collective effect is not overwhelming. The international community and individual governments are rarely eager to militarily intervene. Much fighting is largely ignored. Hands are wrung, dismay expressed, pious resolutions passed, but no outright intervention is undertaken or even proposed. So direct intervention to halt warfare takes place intermittently.

Partly this is because a widespread sense exists that all violent conflicts are not the same and not all should be suppressed. In managing forests, not all forest fires should be put out. In the same way some conflicts seem like legitimate revolts against oppression. Another reason forcible interventions do not occur is that one party to a war is exceptionally strong and opposes intervention, which raises the prospective costs considerably. Two of the world's most unfortunate conflicts that display both of these elements are the Israeli-Palestinian war that has been grinding on for years and the war between the Russians and the Chechens. Many people sympathize with the Palestinians for violently resisting suppression by Israel and with the Chechens for resisting Russian rule in their homeland, while others regard both Palestinians and Chechens as brutal terrorists. In regard to both conflicts there has been no interest in forceful intervention against the weaker party's violent struggle, and none contemplated against the Russians and Israelis either because of their military strength.

Inevitably available resources are inadequate for interventions as well. There is never enough to deal with many of the conflicts that exist. So the UN, the United States, and others decide not to attempt to do too much. Another concern is that an intervention that turns out to be long and costly may leave participants with little to show for it. Interventions have often done some good, but many interventions have not. Another concern is that dangerous precedents will be set via military interventions. The fear is setting a precedent for action in the future: People will insist that because action was taken to end a war in Country A, the same must be done for Countries B and C and other cases that arise. Or the precedent could be that sovereignty ignored in one case means it can be ignored in deciding whether to intervene in the future. Another fear is setting a precedent that justifies inaction: Because intervention turned out so badly in one case, doing so again must be avoided elsewhere. Obviously, if an intervention creates more cost and frustration than success, less support will be found for further interventions.

Because states are good at thinking of reasons for not doing anything about a war somewhere else—no national consensus on intervening, uneasiness about chances for success, dismay over the probable costs, uncertainty about what other governments will do—often the real reason PE or PI is mounted is because a particular state or group of states, hopefully acceptable to the international community, is ready to do most of the work and pay most of the cost. Frequently that key state has been the United States. It is not just that U.S. opposition to an intervention is likely to kill it. The United States is so powerful that its involvement means the risks of failure are sharply reduced and the United States can be counted on to bear much of the cost, making it easier for other governments to decide to join. U.S. power includes not only its combat forces but also its intelligence, logistics, and communications assets, which an intervention will need and few other governments (sometimes none) can supply. Thus interventions to impose peace are often carried out by a so-called coalition of the willing, that is, by a few, not the many. Even then, interventions rarely come soon enough. A military intervention, as with peacekeeping, typically comes after much death and destruction have been inflicted.

PROTRACTED INSECURITY AND PARTITIONS

Once a PE or PI intervention occurs, what happens? For internal wars, getting the fighting to stop initially is often not too difficult. If the outside forces are large and determined, and the parties to the conflict get little outside help, the parties often quit fighting for the time being. After all, they have a powerful new incentive. Neither wants to be the one that refused to quit and thus lead the angry outsiders to gang up on it. For big interstate wars the largest PE or PI interventions—in Korea and against Iraq in the Persian Gulf War—have had mediocre outcomes. In each case the aggressor was ousted from territory it had seized only after large-scale fighting, while its government remained in power, and expensive and difficult efforts were required to keep it contained. So there was peace but not true security. The threat of another war remained real.

In internal conflicts intervention stops the fighting, which is good. But the outcome is often much the same. There is no fighting, but real peace is absent because another war seems possible. Ethnic conflicts are particularly prone to this outcome. They are not necessarily difficult to stop. People are often willing to quit fighting, temporarily, and seize on the intervention as a good excuse. But conflicts are difficult to resolve, particularly ones that are deeply rooted and that people have lived with for a long time. Conflicts like that get woven into the collective identities of the parties. Like family heirlooms, they are passed down from one generation to the next and become part of the self-identities of individuals. If you are a Northern Irish Catholic, part of the concept of yourself may include hating Protestants. As a Palestinian a cornerstone of your identity is probably opposition to Israel. In such conflicts what makes you who you are is, in part, hatred for some other, emphasizing the differences between you and the other. That does not disappear when fighting stops.

If the conflict is not deeply rooted, a military intervention can sometimes do more than stop the fighting. Studies indicate that if the prior state and society were reasonably satisfactory for the citizens, particularly if they were democratic, then an intervention may produce a durable peace. Here the inability of outsiders to intervene early hurts. The more intense the fighting and the longer it lasts, the more the parties may move toward incorporating the conflict into their identities, leaving little room for them to associate peacefully with each other again in the future. This is possibly what happened in Yugoslavia. While there had been serious past conflicts among Bosnian Muslims, Croats, and Serbs, during the Cold War these peoples lived together peacefully in Bosnia. A good deal of intermarriage went on among them, considerable political and economic cooperation took place, and ties of friendship were forged. Once fighting started and built up, outsiders did little to stop it until horrendous levels of destruction, refugees, and ethnic cleansing had been reached. Once NATO intervention ended the fighting, efforts to rebuild Bosnia as a multiethnic community have foundered on the new identities that the war helped build and deeply instill. The three communities remain separate physically, politically, and psychologically (see Chapter 12).

Thus one outcome of internal wars with no decisive winner because of stalemate or outside intervention may be partition. The parties get to the point where they cannot live in a single community, even when fighting stops. As with peacekeeping, outside intervention may reinforce this by halting the fighting and freezing the division of the country it has produced into what each party sees as "ours" and "theirs." In Kosovo, NATO intervened to prevent Serbs from driving out the 90 percent of the population that was Albanian. But when the fighting ended, the area remained overwhelmingly Albanian and fiercely hostile to Serbs, many of whom quickly left. Yugoslavia has been partitioned; a country with that name no longer exists. The territory in which it formerly was situated now contains five separate states: Croatia, Bosnia and Herzegovina, the former Yugoslav republic of

Macedonia, Slovenia, and Serbia and Montenegro (containing the area of Kosovo, which will likely secede eventually).

Partition is a solution both obvious and troubling. Because it is an obvious recourse, I should explain why it can be a bad idea. Internal wars can be vicious and deep-rooted, so partition often seems the best, even the only, solution—like divorce for a broken marriage. It can appeal to outsiders who want the conflict to disappear so they will not be bothered with it again. Many places were partitioned in the twentieth century—Ireland, India, Pakistan, Korea, Vietnam, Germany, and China. Sometimes this happened after considerable fighting, such as Yugoslavia in the 1990s or Pakistan in 1971. Sometimes it was carried out in time to prevent fighting, such as in the Soviet Union and Czechoslovakia after the Cold War. Several of these partitions have an uncertain future. The country could unite once more or stay partitioned (for example, Cyprus, China, or Korea).

Unfortunately, partition often does not work well. Typically, one side thinks it was robbed of much of its territory and schemes to get that part back. Ending the partition may become the focal point of its foreign policy, as was the case with West Germany about East Germany or is true of China now about Taiwan. Unification has dominated the foreign policies of the two Koreas for more than fifty years. In such cases the conflict is not settled by partition, just deferred. Every analysis of the most dangerous trouble spots in the world today puts the China-Taiwan issue high on the list, right up there with the two Koreas and the division of Kashmir between India and Pakistan.

Another problem with partition is that people in the affected areas often refuse to move to their side of the territorial division. They stay where their homes are and their ancestors lived. Life seems better there than they envision it would be if they moved. They insist they are in their country already. Many Catholics remained in Northern Ireland, and many Muslims did not leave India and move to Pakistan in 1947. Those who refuse to leave are apt to become disaffected minorities. Given that they live among people who want them to leave, they usually face discrimination. This is not new, but because of the partition they are a much smaller group than before, a smaller minority and therefore more insecure. Meanwhile, they have friends and supporters abroad, who have resources from running their own government. So these minorities can become security risks for the states where they reside or at least get treated like security risks and threatened by members of the majority who would like to drive them out.

Partition can easily lead to border disputes, not only because people define their areas as ones where they live, not where the new dividing line happens to run, or because they feel that their areas include all the places where many people just like them live, but also because people may define a place as theirs for historical reasons long after they left it. This happened to Jews about Palestine, and then to both Jews and Palestinians after Palestine was partitioned. Many Palestinians dream of getting their land back, which is now the state of Israel, while many Israelis dream of adding Arab parts of Palestine to modern Israel because Jews controlled those areas thousands of years ago. These sorts of conflicts attract outsiders. Some care because they sympathize with one side, for instance on ethnic or religious grounds. Others care because they have strategic or other interests at stake. India seized on Pakistan's civil war in 1971 to help get Pakistan divided to greatly weaken the military threat Pakistan had posed to India.

Another problem is typified by the Abkhazians when Georgia split from the former Soviet Union. A minority living uneasily with another and larger minority inside a large state will feel much more threatened if the large state is partitioned. It is still a minority but the other minority may now be running the new state created by the partition. Serbs were a minority in the Croatian part of Yugoslavia, but Croats were a clear minority in Yugoslavia and did not control the government. However, in an independent Croatia these Serbs feared for their future under a Croatian government and they posed a potentially serious security problem for Croatians because their complaints might stimulate Serbian intervention or they might want to secede from Croatia and join Serbia. That provided much fuel for a war, and one of the most significant of the conflicts in Yugoslavia as it disintegrated was between the Croats and the Serbs in Croatia once it declared its independence.

Many Russians stayed in the new states formed out of the former republics of the Soviet Union, and since then have claimed, with some justification, to be mistreated minorities. After all, the republics typically chose independence because they felt discriminated against in the Soviet Union and because they were tired of Russians dominating their affairs. Now these republics often treat their Russian citizens poorly. Several regard them as potential threats. After all, they can appeal to Russia for support and it might militarily intervene on their behalf. It does not help that Russia, naturally enough, vigorously protests mistreatment of these Russians.

Conditions created by partition can hamper the development of democracy. Jews remain deeply divided in Israel over whether Arabs living there should be normal or second-class citizens, something Latvians also debate about Russians living in Latvia. Democracy looks less appealing if the minority could position itself to exploit political divisions among the majority and become the power broker that decides elections or forms cabinets. In the United States after the Civil War, fear of blacks in the South not only as a majority but also as a politically active minority led southern states to curb democracy for almost one hundred years. The states denied blacks voting rights and other forms of political participation and operated one-party systems with no black participation in shaping and running state and local governments. This was the closest the South could come to the partition of the United States it sought in the Civil War. When partition has occurred the same distaste for democracy may be strong in a new state.

Partition might be attractive for ending a war if it can be clear and complete; everyone is civilized when it occurs; or it seems a good possibility, as was the case in Canada and Czechoslovakia. But if people have been killing each other, a good bet is that partition will be a bloody mess and, as with India and Pakistan over Kashmir, pose constant risks of war thereafter. Even an initially peaceful partition is likely to be deeply opposed eventually by some of the people involved, as in Germany, Korea, and Vietnam during the Cold War. In each case, the people involved resented the division of the nation and were eager to change it.

The final strike against partition is that most governments hate the precedent it sets. They fear the idea will spread. NATO intervened to protect Kosovars from Serbia but not to separate Kosovo from Serbia. African states have a rule against supporting secessions on that continent because every country is vulnerable to them. China does not support secession because that would weaken its effort to prevent Taiwan from remaining separate from China and encourage the Tibetans or others in China to continue seeking independence.

If partition is unattractive, another option is granting a degree of autonomy to those who have tried, or might otherwise try, to secede. Alas, this is also difficult to bring off. Sometimes it works. Puerto Rico and the United States have such an arrangement. Puerto Rico is part of the United States, but, as a commonwealth, it has considerable autonomy. However, a long military struggle over the island never took place between Americans and Puerto Ricans, unlike other cases around the world. Autonomy is most likely to work when the area in question has a distinct population, as with Puerto Rico. Where it does not have a distinct population, the people who dominate the area are seen as threatening by the minorities who live there. The local Serbs in Kosovo feared oppression by Albanians if Kosovo became ever more autonomous, which led President Slobodan Milosevic to cancel Kosovo autonomy, a politically explosive step that led to war and NATO's intervention.

One difficulty with creating an autonomous or semiautonomous area is that it can be accompanied with what amounts to second-class status for the people there, particularly in the national government's budget, universities, roads, welfare programs, and the like. This happened to Native Americans on reservations in the United States. The result could be further pressures for independence. Offering a restive area autonomy is often taken by the people involved as the first step toward independence anyway. Even if this is not the case initially, the second-class treatment that comes with it can incite separatist sentiments. A final problem for many governments is that they rule over a number of minorities, and creating one autonomous area brings endless pressures to create others.

CONCLUSION

Peace enforcement and peace imposition can be evaluated from the three different levels of analysis.

Systemic Security

At the system level, major benefits can be derived from PE and PI. Often a major conflict, and occasionally even a minor one, between states or within them can seriously threaten order and security in part or all of the international system. The concept of sovereignty was initially developed among states to contain the spreading of internal religious wars in Europe from one state to another in the seventeenth century. An interstate or internal war along ethnic or religious lines can spread to neighbors who are similar to the parties involved or can incite similar fighting elsewhere by its example. The fighting in the eastern Congo in recent years started in Rwanda, spread to the Congo, then drew in several different tribes there, and eventually came to involve forces from a number of other states. Internal or interstate warfare in a strategically sensitive region can disrupt international politics in general, something that has been true for decades in the Middle East. In an ever more interdependent world, sovereignty does not contain this enough. Now, sometimes sovereignty is ignored and interventions take place in such internal wars (still based on religion, ethnicity, tribal affiliations, and the like) before they spread.

Another important consideration is that for an international system, global or regional, to seem orderly and safe it has to periodically display a significant capacity to respond seriously to outbreaks of warfare, including internal warfare in particular as it has become more important in an increasingly interdependent world. States and their citizens have to be shown, repeatedly, that an international community (regional or global) exists, that it can act, and that its actions can be powerful and effective. Without this even governments and peoples not threatened at the moment can feel insecure. They imagine threats and envision a nonexistent or insufficient international response, or they seize on a disastrous war elsewhere as evidence of what could happen to them. And if their part of the world seems disorderly, why make serious commitments to international communities? Why take risks and bear costs on behalf of those communities? Because international communities are often still fragile, their solidity can easily be undermined by such thinking. A periodic demonstration that a community, particularly its powerful members, will respond forcefully if necessary to a war is important for international order.

At present the world is in a relatively favorable situation with regard to interstate wars in the global international system; they rarely occur. However, this is not the result of PE and PI. The powerful states now seem disinclined to fight each other. The only serious risk of a great-power war currently is between the United States and China over Taiwan. In recent decades the great powers have also not been eager to fight with other states, as has been evident for the great powers in Europe, plus Russia, Japan, and China. The only exception is the U.S. and British war on Iraq. However, this great-power restraint does not stem from the threat of PE and PI from other states. China might provoke a military response from the United States if it attacked Taiwan but probably would not face military opposition from the others. In general, peace enforcement and peace imposition cannot be applied against a great power. The potential costs are too great. Thus one weakness of PE and PI is that they cannot curb wars among great powers. The states have to do this themselves, by behaving themselves.

Powerful states are sometimes willing to use military intervention to stop interstate wars among less powerful states, as was the case in the U.S.-organized Persian Gulf War against Iraq in 1991. Maybe the threat of a similar international reaction has helped prevent other wars since then. But whether the Gulf War example could be easily replicated is unclear. It was not repeated in Central Africa in the late 1990s when a regional war broke out and the major powers were unwilling to intervene. Whether military intervention can be repeated more clearly and effectively elsewhere remains uncertain. Hopefully, not many occasions will arise to find out.

What about military preemption as the way to deal with war in the international system? This was one justification offered for the war against Iraq that the United States and some of its friends undertook in 2003. In principle, preemption is good. It would prevent much destruction and loss of life. The problem is to do this in time and in a sufficiently collective way. An additional problem is that it would reflect an expansion in the available justifications for interventions, and states are uneasy about that. An excellent example is the response to the U.S. campaign for an international attack on Iraq in 2003. The international community was strenuously divided over whether the war was needed at that time or could be delayed. Was war necessary to prevent a war later, or could Iraq be contained sufficiently to accomplish the same task without fighting? Pressure for delay came from countries that did not want a war, but Iraq's evident weakness after years of sanctions made it doubtful that a war was needed even to governments not opposed to the war in principle.

By forcing the issue the United States greatly exacerbated this uneasiness. It suggested that preventing nuclear proliferation, possibly even to terrorists, was enough to justify the use of force by the international community. In other words, just the possibility of nuclear proliferation justifies using force. The wars to be dealt with are imagined future wars and the other threat to be dealt with is from imagined future terrorist incidents. Presumably the same logic could be applied to deal with threats from the proliferation of other weapons of mass destruction or from other developments. If states have trouble endorsing military interventions for real wars, usually waiting until those interventions look unavoidable, they will not approve of interventions for possible wars. It is one thing to intervene militarily to stop a war. It is another to intervene militarily to prevent a future war. While the latter provides more military security more effectively, the former is politically more feasible and tolerable. The trade-off is between acting when it is cheaper and easier versus acting when it is more feasible.

Another problem with the war in Iraq was that when states such as the United States insist on retaining their nuclear weapons while heading campaigns for using force to prevent others from having them, this is seen by many governments as seeking to maintain a discriminatory situation. The world is on record as predominantly opposed to nuclear proliferation. But it has yet to decide that preventing nuclear proliferation is worth a few wars, especially if that would not lead to the complete elimination of nuclear weapons.

It is but a short step from such concerns to the conclusion that all this trouble is the result of a mistaken retreat from treating sovereignty as sacrosanct, however laudable the goals in that retreat may have been. If many states take this view it will be harder to get internationally approved PE and PI operations in the future. The U.S. government may have poisoned that well for years to come. Unless a collective decision process is devised for using force to keep the peace, the most powerful states may feel free to make war whenever they want and claim it is for the general welfare. Many governments saw no reason for the United States to promote another war on Iraq in 2003. They feared that U.S. goals had little to do with terrorism and mostly to do with strengthening Western control over the Middle East and its oil.

State Security

Moving to the state level, having states use force to preserve peace is inherently dangerous without general agreement on how to decide to do so and thus on how to sort out aggressive ventures from legitimate ones. That is why the UN Security Council was created—to provide a decision-making vehicle and some rules for identifying an inappropriate use of force and using force to do something about it. A similar structure can be set up regionally, too, with collective decision vehicles like NATO with suitable rules. But decision procedures and rules must be explicit, and the most powerful states have to abide by them.

This is something the George W. Bush administration ignored. Even before the September 11 attack, the administration was inclined toward making security and other foreign policy decisions by itself. After the attack the administration was even more determined to do this for dealing with terrorism and the threat of weapons of mass destruction proliferation. It argued, in effect, that making a good decision and dealing resolutely with terrorism and proliferation problems was much more important than how it was made. That is, it was fine to decide and act unilaterally as long as the results were good. Other than when immediate action is needed, this is short-sighted. In no decently organized system are members entitled to decide individually to use force or even to uphold peace and security because the use of force is such a potential threat to peace and security that the decision must be constrained by an acceptable process for making it. The United States did much to establish this as a general principle in building multilateral institutions during the Cold War and many felt it should not have been abandoned for the war in Iraq.

Thus that war resulted from a lack of collective decision making in the view of other governments. Their concern was then exacerbated by American denigration of the institutions and processes normally used when no endorsement of the American position was forthcoming from those institutions. What seemed clear was that the United States put its immediate national interest ahead of any contrary position that others, even close friends, might take. In fact, this was one of the themes in President Bush's reelection campaign. It was natural to fear that the United States would do this in the future and that others would then do the same.

Peace enforcement and peace imposition have other effects at the state level. The effects on sovereignty are mixed. A peace imposition operation such as the Persian Gulf War bolsters state autonomy by rejecting outright aggression, but many states are uneasy about PE and PI for internal wars or humanitarian disasters, fearing that they erode sovereignty too much. Thus far, at least, states and international organizations have been reluctant to discard sovereignty wholesale. Thus there are many more wars than interventions to stop them. However, enough forceful interventions have taken place to make the point that a tough reaction by the international community is at least a possibility. That may help contain some internal wars while offering a suitable precedent for almost any step that might be considered appropriate. The range of military steps that can be taken has been expanded considerably.

Societal Security

At the societal level, PE and PI are no panacea. A military response is mostly a last resort, made possible by suffering instead of incited by the possibility of suffering.

So societies and individuals suffer considerably from wars. This is unlikely to change any time soon. Power and management in the international system are too decentralized to respond rapidly and effectively, and too many states and societies like it that way. Doing something about war does not seem urgent enough to them. War is awful when you are involved, but not so awful as to make big sacrifices very often for halting it when it is happening to someone else. However, it is comforting that it has become harder for the world to ignore wars, to dismiss many of them as not everyone's concern. There is now more inclination to do something, including taking drastic steps such as PE and PI, than ever before. That is small comfort to the hundreds of thousands killed every year in internal wars around the globe, but it holds out the hope that this number will continue shrinking.

Putting an end to a war does not end the suffering it causes. Much time and effort are needed to recover. The world is now interested in this, and more international assistance is available for those trying to recover than ever before. What is important for this book is that much of the assistance is available because of the spreading belief that wars happen at least partly because of deplorable conditions and doing something about war requires taking steps to eliminate those conditions. That has given rise to energetic efforts at peacebuilding around the world today, which is the subject of the next chapter.

SOURCES AND OTHER USEFUL READINGS

The well-known argument that interventions for peace often do more harm than good by preventing a decisive settlement via war is raised by Edward N. Luttwak in "Give War a Chance" and "The Curse of Inconclusive Intervention." On sovereignty as an ideal that is often violated see Stephen D. Krasner, *Sovereignty*; and for a general review of sovereignty in theory and practice, see Thomas J. Biersteker, "State, Sovereignty, and Territory." The notion that sovereignty can be ascribed to citizens and not, or not just, the state is raised in Boutros Boutros-Ghali, "Empowering the United Nations," and his *An Agenda for Peace*.

The idea of a preventive intervention, including a forceful intervention, to stop wars before they go very far—saving everyone from more serious wars and the burdens of halting them—has occurred to a number of analysts. To trace their thinking, see Michael S. Lund, *Preventing Violent Conflicts*; Donald C. F. Daniel and Bradd C. Hayes, *Coercive Inducement and the Containment of International Crises*; and Kevin M. Cahill, *Preventive Diplomacy*. The one good example in recent years of a preventive military intervention is recounted in Abiodun Williams, *Preventing War*. The difficulty of pulling this off in other cases is explored early on in John Stremlau,

People in Peril. There has also been some exploration of the possibility of using incentives, instead of deterrence or force, to control wars and other violent conflicts. See *The Price of Peace,* edited by David Cortright; and his summary chapter in that book, "Incentive Strategies for Preventing Conflict."

William Stueck's *The Korean War* provides a good recounting of that conflict. On the use of force in the Bosnia and Kosovo cases, see Peter Jakobsen, *Western Use of Coercive Diplomacy after the Cold War,* or David Halberstam, *War in a Time of Peace.* On the difficulty of getting a successful multiethnic community in Bosnia, see the Elizabeth M. Cousens and Charles K. Cater study *Toward Peace in Bosnia.* The finding that parties to a conflict that have had prior experience with democracy are more likely to arrive at a lasting peace settlement is in Caroline Hartzell, Matthew Hoddie, and Donald Rothchild, "Stabilizing the Peace after Civil War." The best discussion of the difficulty in using partition to end conflict is Chaim D. Kaufmann, "When All Else Fails."

CHAPTER 12

Peacebuilding

The most elaborate recourse yet devised in international politics for addressing the security problem that war creates is **peacebuilding**. In this survey, it is the most ambitious, most complex, and most difficult. Not necessarily the most costly, peacebuilding is nevertheless not cheap. It is meant to be the most effective for the long run but no one would say it is quick and easy or will even make the problem disappear. Peacebuilders do not expect to be out of work any time soon.

The central idea behind peacebuilding is that, while conflict is normal, violent conflict within and between societies arises from and is sustained by unfortunate attitudes and defective social arrangements, that those attitudes and arrangements can be corrected, and that enough is now known about how to do so. Thus peacebuilding aims to get at the roots of war in seeking to create inherently peaceful communities. That is quite a claim. Whatever else may be said of them, peacebuilders do not lack ambition.

Technically, peacebuilding can be undertaken within any of the security strategies discussed in the first half of this book. In a power distribution system, peacebuilding might be pursued by a hegemonic state. It can make a nice adjunct to deterrence and arms control. A concert could authorize and promote peacebuilding, as could a collective security system, and it has been closely associated with advanced multilateralism. It can also be undertaken in dealing with any stage of a conflict through the practices explored in the second half of the book. In theory it can prevent a conflict from becoming violent, by ending it before it gets that far. It can make negotiation and mediation work better, and it is a valuable adjunct to peacekeeping and peace enforcement and peace imposition. But it is not used in all these ways often. It is too complicated and costly, requires too much effort and commitment, and asks too much of those who fight and those trying to get them to stop. Instead peacebuilding is usually more like a last resort and is mainly used after a war. Normally peacebuilding is turned to because the war was so awful that the parties must never fight again. War drags the parties and outsiders into making the necessary commitment to peacebuilding.

THE MAIN ELEMENTS OF PEACEBUILDING

War is a serious problem both between and within societies, and peacebuilding can be applied to both. It is now mainly a response to internal wars, not interstate ones, and that is the context in which it will mostly be discussed in this chapter. First, though, consider peacebuilding for international wars. In fact, it has already been discussed. Complex multilateralism involves pluralistic security communities, which are clusters of states and societies that create elaborate relationships among themselves in which using force is never considered so the members do not worry about being attacked by each other (see Chapter 8). These societies live near each other and have a long history together, including warfare, and they have significant military forces. (If states that are far apart and have limited interactions, and show little capacity or inclination to fight each other, that is not a major achievement.) A pluralistic security community is a tremendous achievement when the members interact extensively, could easily attack each other and do great harm, and did fight in the past. Building a pluralistic security community involves peacebuilding, using many of the same steps found in peacebuilding within countries that have suffered disastrous wars.

Luc Reychler, an analyst and a practitioner in peacebuilding, has a useful set of qualifications for what constitutes the practice. Peacebuilding is

> all efforts required on the way to the creation of a sustainable peace zone: imagining a peaceful future, conducting an overall needs assessment, developing a coherent peace plan, and designing an effective implementation of the plan.

Notice that peacebuilding does not just happen; it is designed to happen. The people involved have an idea of what peace would look like, develop a plan—in broad terms—for getting there, and make efforts to implement it. The goal is a peace zone, where people feel safe with each other.

How is this done? Effective pluralistic security communities (PSCs, see Chapter 8) are characterized by

- The existence of a hegemon, to push others into getting things started;

- A cluster of complex multilateralist institutions that carry cooperation much further than normal in international politics;

- The development of huge interactions so that the members are in contact for common purposes on many different matters; and

- The development of common values (democracy, human rights, capitalism, free trade, common security) and rules (equal treatment under the rules, consensus to be vigorously pursued, no use or threat of force).

Using complex multilateralism to build a PSC has been done either among states and societies that are largely alike or after hard work to make them much more alike. In the history of complex multilateralism in the North Atlantic community and the rest of Europe, the focus has been on making those societies more alike: in democracy, on human rights, in having free market economies, and in achieving a high level of economic development.

Peacebuilding on the international level is difficult and has been successfully employed among only a limited number of countries. Fortunately, it has been effective among many of the most powerful countries in the world. Unfortunately, much of the world seems unsuited to it, so it has not been seriously tried in most places.

As for peacebuilding within countries, these efforts reflect much the same conception of both the problem and the solution. The goal is, once again, a peace zone—to turn a country torn by war into a peaceful place for its citizens. As in international politics, the solution is to build, or rebuild, an effective community where one has been lacking. Either the community collapsed, which brought on a severe civil war, or a civil war gradually developed that tore the community apart. Building an effective community after a war is a major undertaking, pursued in unpromising circumstances and surroundings. The initiative and then the pressure to follow through on it comes largely from powerful outsiders, which act like a hegemon and carry out most of the initial steps. Of particular interest here is what can be done in international politics by the outsiders through peacebuilding about the problem of internal wars.

Efforts at this kind of peacebuilding have become common recently, but it is worthwhile to look at its historical development. The first major instances of modern peacebuilding developed after World War II in Germany and Japan. The military occupiers—the United States, France, and Great Britain in West Germany; the United States in Japan; the Soviet Union in East Germany, to an extent—set out to foster changes in Germany and Japan so they would no longer be militaristic, aggressive, and expansionist. They tried to tear down elements of the old order that, arguably, had brought those governments to launch World War II and start building new political, economic, and social systems. In West Germany and Japan, that led to developing new constitutions, democracy, more market-oriented economic systems, and social systems that allowed greater opportunities for ordinary citizens. For the United States this meant making these countries more like itself. In East Germany the Soviet Union sought to install a system that reflected its own authoritarian, communist party-dominated, socialist elements. It was not that the outsiders were to do all this themselves. They were to get the ball rolling and then the Germans and Japanese were to take it from there. They would do most of the work after a good push in the right direction.

These efforts were successful in West Germany and Japan. Historians report that the Germans and Japanese were clearly more responsible for the outcome than the occupiers; they did indeed do most of the work. But the occupiers certainly helped. As a result West Germany and Japan were slow to develop new armed forces and those forces were then constrained. Oriented strictly toward national defense, they were too small even for that, and they relied heavily on the former occupying powers as allies for protection. Each became a strong and stable democracy. Each built a powerful modern economy, and both are now among the world's most prosperous societies. They created more open and flexible societies. Each became so devoted to peace by nonmilitary means that they did not accept responsibilities even for peacekeeping until almost fifty years later. In 2003 public opinion in both countries was strongly against the war in Iraq, and neither country sent forces to participate in the fighting.

It is harder to conclude that peacebuilding worked in East Germany. It was never a fully viable country and state, and the Soviet forces based there during the Cold War were so large that, in a sense, the postwar occupation never ended. While none of the communist countries in Eastern Europe went to war with each other, Soviet troops battled rioters in East Germany (1953) and insurgents in Hungary (1956) and, along with other East European forces, invaded Czechoslovakia (1968). Maybe peacebuilding Soviet-style did work and that was why East Germany collapsed in 1989 and united with West Germany with no fighting. But, it seems much more likely that those developments were the result of disgust with Soviet-style rule and attraction to what West Germany had achieved.

As of 2005, the United States, with some help from others, was engaged in a huge peacebuilding effort in Iraq. The most unusual aspect of this project was that it was initiated in the midst of an insurgency, a perilous enterprise. Perhaps the situation in Iraq will play out like postwar Germany and Japan, but Iraq seems unlikely to fare as well. At the same time, the United States has been leading a peacebuilding effort in Afghanistan. Internal resistance there was somewhat less violent but that was partly because the central government was too weak to challenge the regional warlords and their well-armed forces, which run much of the country. For that reason, it is hard to be optimistic about the long-term outcome in Afghanistan either.

Another element that shaped modern peacebuilding is the history of the North Atlantic community and European integration. Western countries pursued peaceful relations among themselves after World War II, and their success has led to applying the same recipe recently in relations between eastern and western Europe, which called for

- Advancing multilateralism in international arrangements;

- Promoting huge domestic changes;

- Developing European integration beyond a peace zone among European governments into a peaceful European community; and

- Spreading democracy, free market economies, better human rights practices, and more open societies.

The pluralistic security community, a peace zone, first developed in the West is to spread across the rest of the continent.

Another taproot of modern peacebuilding is a Western belief that a long-standing violent conflict gradually creates its own perverse social system (or systems) and thus tends to become self-sustaining. The conflict continues because it feeds on itself. For instance, as fighting builds hatred and grievances those feelings gradually are communicated to children and become part of their identity. Opposing cultures emerge, not just different cultures but also ones in which part of the group identity is hatred for and grievances against the other side. Practices emerge—in schools, in how history is written, in the media, and in social relationships—dictating that to be a proper member of the community is to share this hatred. Prolonged fighting builds military subcultures in which violence is accepted, honored, or becomes the only way of life many men and some women have known. Whole institutions—internal security forces, governments, warlords who dominate regions, large military forces of the government—are rooted in violence. The conflicting parties fall into profound security dilemmas, with each side believing that it can never trust the other, must therefore arm and fight, and must mistrust any conciliatory steps or offer. The other side's arming and fighting becomes evidence that it can be regarded only as hostile. Peacebuilding therefore requires breaking up these social and cultural elements, replacing them with new ones that do not reinforce conflict and violence.

Still another reason peacebuilding has emerged is the growing emphasis by some governments, international organizations, nongovernmental organizations (NGOs), and others on broader conceptions of human rights and security. This book gives some attention to the notion of societal security, which can simply mean that citizens are physically safe—from attack, from crime. But it is now widely argued that security ultimately means, as well, a good opportunity to have a decent life. That is, a chance to earn a good living; freedom from discrimination based on ethnicity or sex or religion; access to education, health care, and a fit place to live; and a reasonable opportunity to help run one's community and society. Around the world people are often denied or stripped of these things by force and violence or by systems kept in place by violence. In turn, they frequently turn to violence—against the state, each other, and outsiders—because of their bitterness over life in such conditions. The resulting killing often makes everything worse. This, arguably, is one cause of much of the world's warfare, and one of its greatest consequences, so it is something that peacebuilding should try to correct.

Finally, peacebuilding is partly driven by the shift away from wars among states to wars within states—civil conflicts. Many internal wars are highly brutal and destructive, particularly when they drag on for years or decades. They inflict profound cultural and psychological scars as former neighbors, friends, or even family members turn on each other. Over time they often completely disrupt and exhaust their societies politically, economically, and socially. Even when one side wins, the conflict can simmer and do damage for years thereafter. Often one side wins only temporarily; the conflict eventually breaks out again and again.

Take an example from an earlier time of what peacebuilding now is trying to tackle in various countries. In the nineteenth-century United States, settling of the West was violent. Wars were fought with Indian tribes and violence was rampant in many Western towns where the murder rates were high. Much of this was because the West was settled by men who had been through the Civil War, seen and committed mayhem, been part of guerrilla raids, lost friends and relatives, were used to carrying guns, and made a living with them. Jesse James, perhaps the most famous postwar outlaw, saw himself as carrying on the guerrilla warfare against the North that he and his brother had begun during the war. Often the gunfights celebrated in Western movies were between northerners and southerners, still holding grudges from the war. In the South bitterness gradually eclipsed efforts to reconstruct the country. The result was that eventually the U.S. Constitution was unofficially suspended there. A one-party system controlled political life so that blacks could not participate effectively. It was a system in which lack of competition stimulated corruption. Blacks in large numbers were denied the right to vote, subjected to segregation, denied equal access to education and decent jobs, and barred from service on juries. Trial by jury for blacks was sometimes superseded by lynchings. Treatment of prisoners under state and local governments deeply violated civil liberties. In Washington, D.C., the power of longtime-serving southerners (elected with almost no opposition) in Congress kept the federal government from doing anything about the situation for generations. And in the North, attitudes toward blacks also hardened, in part because of their flight from the South. The mistreatment of blacks, which the Civil War in part was fought to end, grew into accepted practice including discrimination in jobs, housing, schools, and other public services. One result was the emergence of a criminal subculture (black gangs, drug culture, gang warfare) and dysfunctional black families. The Civil War did not end the conflict in 1865. Its effects haunt the country still, damage the security of Americans, and play a large (often hidden) role in politics that is harmful to the nation.

WHO DOES WHAT?

Luc Reychler, drawing on many studies and available experience, lists specific components of a sustainable peace zone inside a country. First, there should be a consolidated democracy with elections, power decentralized and shared, the rule of law, and respect for human rights. Consolidated means well established, not just in place until the next coup. Second, there should be an effective, legitimate, and restorative justice system. Hence governments, police, prisons, and other justice agencies uphold the law and live within it—ending terror, torture, legal favoritism, bureaucratic disdain for laws, and other lawlessness. Restorative means a system that deals with past crimes and atrocities, plus other deep injustices, in ways that help build a cohesive society again. Third, a social free market system should be developed. A market system can stimulate economic recovery and growth but often leads to uneven living standards, so steps must be taken to help the poor. Fourth, sound education, information, and communication systems must be established because they are vital for creating, maintaining, and strengthening a community. Fifth is reintegration. A bad civil war turns many people into refugees and expatriates or drives them into isolated areas to either hide and fight or hide from fighting. People often drop out of sight—going underground, staying out of politics, or abandoning sensitive jobs. They all need to come back into society, into normal life, and be reconciled within the society so that they can trust each other to work and live together and take up the peaceful management of conflicts. Finally, both objective and subjective security must be created. People, groups, and leaders need to be safe—crime drops, assassination and terrorism stop. But they also need to feel safe by having confidence that security will continue. Often this requires leaders who put forward an effective, appealing vision of a peaceful future—someone such as the Rev. Dr. Martin Luther King Jr.

Not everyone would list all of these elements, and disagreements exist about which components are the most important. But in this view peacebuilding has major political, military, economic, and social-psychological dimensions. Outsiders can do only so much to build a peace zone; much of the heavy lifting must come from the people themselves.

The Political Dimension

Peacebuilders from outside typically enter a country in which the state has been either too strong or too weak. Either it has survived and been effective by being too authoritarian, using force and repression too much, or it is about to collapse (if it has not already) because of war, the loss of legitimacy in the eyes of the people, and general exhaustion. The political system is in disarray in the aftermath of a war. No way exists to select leaders, make decisions, and carry them out. The peacebuilders want to transform or recreate the state and the political system. They want a political system that the outside world can tolerate and is an effective arena for resolving political and other conflicts—a substitute for fighting to pick leaders, make decisions, and get things done. Here is what they get into as a result.

The state may need a new constitution. Usually peacebuilders do not write it, as the United States did for Japan after World War II. They work to get a commission formed to do the job but then offer advice, as has been the case in post-Saddam

Iraq. They usually want democracy established, and they start taking steps to develop some of the prerequisites. They help to reorganize or newly establish political parties and assist people in setting up interest groups and establishing media to distribute political information. The eventual goal is elections, and peacebuilders may design and help conduct them. Peacebuilders supply experts to get the state up and running and to give advice and assistance to departments on how to conduct the various functions of a government. Peacebuilders often help to rehire, recruit, and train civil servants to staff the government. A major objective is to reestablish a government not only that works but also that people have confidence will work—deliver the mail, pick up the garbage, control traffic, and police the streets. The country is apt to have gone a long time without getting much of those kinds of things from its government, and people are apt to have little confidence in government to manage important elements of their lives.

Who does this? Peacebuilding is run by the United Nations (UN) or other international organizations, by a coalition of governments, or sometimes by one government. They may send their own experts or hire others. There are thousands of nongovernmental organizations eager and able to participate vigorously in peacebuilding. They bring in and distribute aid, provide advice and services, administer programs, and offer training. Each year NGOs spend billions of dollars of their own and collect billions more under contracts with intergovernmental organizations (IGOs) such as the UN, governments, or the countries being helped. Many provide medical assistance, some promote agricultural improvements, some help with education, and many work to develop elements of democracy. At times NGOs are so important they temporarily run parts of the government. They can do these things for all sorts of countries, but they gear up for peacekeeping efforts. They are a remarkable addition in recent decades to the world's resources.

IGOs and NGOs constitute a huge pressure group in support of peacebuilding, which is a major political role for them. When a peacebuilding mission is being put together they insist that their particular concerns (civil rights, women's rights, environmental problems, health) be given priority. They call attention to the problems that will be encountered and press governments to allocate enough money to handle them. They also monitor peacekeeping and peacebuilding operations, calling attention to weaknesses, difficulties, or failures. They may provide an early warning system, in which they draw on their people in the field and their contacts to spot and highlight emerging political difficulties in a country in which peacebuilding is being attempted. They spot administrative defects or corruption. They cry out about an impending famine or deadly epidemic. They lobby continuously for better, and better funded, peacebuilding efforts.

Often it is necessary for peacebuilders to run the country for some period. In effect, the country is put into a kind of trusteeship because it is politically bankrupt. In Kosovo, the North Atlantic Treaty Organization (NATO) has created and run an interim administration for years. In Bosnia, continuing political infighting among the Bosnian Serbs, Croats, and Muslims slowed the development of a decent state so badly that the Office of the High Representative of the NATO countries and others gradually assumed more power to run the country. It enacted laws, set up a currency, devised a national flag, designed and issued car license plates, and dismissed elected officials who were obstructing the peacebuilding process by blocking efforts to return refugees or promoting continued ethnic tensions. It also shut down media that continued to foster ethnic hatred. In Iraq, the United States led the Coalition Provisional Authority that governed the country after Saddam Hussein until the Iraqi interim government assumed control.

Also vital is to get a funding base for the fledgling government. Initially, the money comes from outsiders. When Cambodia and Mozambique were entering into their peacebuilding phases over half the two governments' budgets came from foreign aid. Frequently that outside aid remains vital to the nation for years. Aid or foreign investment is often used to develop or redevelop some of the nation's key resources damaged in the fighting so that money from oil, diamonds, copper, bananas, or coffee can flow into the government coffers.

All this sounds good, but peacebuilding faces serious problems and difficulties. The international system is not set up well politically to do peacebuilding. The UN has experience with it in various agencies, but it is decentralized and undercoordinated. The agencies that, for example, provide food, aid refugees, and help children have their own budgets and operate largely beyond the direction of the secretary general. They were also not designed with peacebuilding in mind and have had to adapt on the run to taking on such responsibilities. All of the agencies, and the UN itself, operate on small budgets. Many governments feel too poor to make a serious financial contribution to the UN and specialized agencies, and the rich countries are unwilling to contribute much. The United States, the largest contributor, says the UN is grossly inefficient and too often reflects the views of countries with the wrong sorts of governments and values. Both sympathy for supporting it and U.S. aid available under UN administration are low in Washington. Finally, coordinating peacebuilding efforts can be difficult. Bureaucratic rivalries exist among sections of the UN and the specialized agencies. The secretary general struggles to keep them working together but many of them do not want his coordination. The same is true for NGOs. They have their own interests and perspectives, funding sources, and personnel, and they resist coordination even among themselves much less with the UN or other IGOs. In short, peacebuilding faces complex political difficulties among the people doing it, not just with those for whom it is to be done.

Political peacebuilding starts with outsiders who come in to run things, but imagine how difficult that is. They arrive in Country A to help but most of them do not know its language(s), people, culture, or history. Because it is not their country they often do not stay long. Just as with peacekeeping forces, the programs and projects in peacebuilding are often staffed on a rotating basis; people stay a while and are replaced. Next, governments promise money for peacebuilding—for their own personnel and programs, for the UN and other agencies, for the government of Country A—but they usually do not deliver anything like the amounts they promised. Or they deliver it slowly. Peacebuilding operations are run on the proverbial shoestring.

Politics further complicates the peacebuilding effort. The outsiders want their money spent for activities, and in ways, that local officials often dislike. (Western-style rights for women is often a good example.) Local leaders in Country A may want to restrict the help to only certain people—"Give aid to us in Country A, forget those in Country B." They wish to benefit their supporters and penalize those they dislike. Or they see aid as an opportunity for theft. Or they want to use aid to build up their political machines or to employ their cousins, uncles, and the rest of their extended families. Sometimes their last priority is using aid to help the country as a whole. But governments that send aid may have a similar approach. They want their money to go for a showy project that looks good back home, even though it may be useless in Country A. Much of their aid may be spent back home to buy things to be sent to A, even if it would do much more good and more efficiently spent locally, because buying at home is politically more attractive. They want to staff the aid program with friends, relatives, or political supporters or give contracts to friendly groups and firms back home whether they can do a good job or not. They bring ideological and cultural views that clash with local preferences. The United States will not fund abortions or abortion training abroad, for example.

The outsiders' concerns usually are at odds with the insiders' politics. A government is more than officials who govern. It is the result of elaborate struggles and compromises among politically important forces. These forces, particularly their leaders, want numerous things. A government will not work unless the political forces are reasonably supportive, that is, unless they get some or all of what they want regardless of whether it is legal or fair or just or efficient. For instance, some local leaders often resist any agreement to stop fighting unless they get an amnesty for things done during the war. This poses a dilemma: Is it more important to get the fighting stopped or be able to pursue justice after it stops? In the same way, important political forces in the country will resist a serious pursuit of justice for wartime crimes by the new government. They will want to control at least part of the government for themselves, their relatives, and their members and supporters, even if those people are poorly qualified for holding office. Some will want to be able to steal. Thus the politics of building a working government will clash with what outsiders want done on democracy, human rights, the economy, and other matters. Working this out is complicated and people on all sides are likely to be dissatisfied with how it goes.

Serious political problems arise in connection with people who fought the war. For instance, many of those who know the most about running the country were associated with the government so they may be hated or at least mistrusted by those who were against the government during the war. Yet their knowledge, skills, contacts, and supporters might be useful. Sending them into exile, to jail, or isolating them could be wasteful. It may also be dangerous. They may start organizing to undermine the new government. But allowing them to remain active politically poses big problems, too. Can the government look new to the citizens if people from the old days have important positions? Will people who were deeply involved in a repressive or corrupt government adhere to norms of democracy?

As for the other side in the war, those who led the conflict against the government usually have few of the skills and inclinations needed for governing. They know about fighting, but not much about constructing compromises, public administration, or economic policy making. They may have been involved in terrorism and other criminal acts. Yet trying to exile them, or send them to trial, may be politically counterproductive by stirring up opposition and undermining the peace agreement.

Another difficulty is that each side is likely to have agreed to stop fighting because it hopes to win instead through peacetime political activities—winning elections when they are held, holding the biggest share of the positions in the new government, and using those political advantages to advance its cause. Thus each regards losing influence over the government as potentially disastrous, because then the other side will use the government against it. Thus the conflict that drove the war continues and may poison peacetime politics. The result can be an eventual resumption of the fighting.

A huge concern in peacebuilding is that democracy is complex. It takes many kinds of behavior that are learned only over time and with practice, including ways of operating a government and attitudes about dealing with a government and a political system. Among these are respect for authority and the law, willingness to accept losing on a political issue and to win with restraint, the ability to discuss and disagree peacefully, and acceptance of compromise. Skills are required to get groups work together and to build a political party or an interest group to press for decisions and actions. Such skills include developing and circulating information, holding meetings, developing leaders, and shaping a political agenda. The buzz of activity involving many people in making a democracy and its political system work is referred to as a civil society. It develops slowly and elements of it cannot be easily taught. In fact, even established democracies have flaws in their civil societies—discrimination against some groups, readiness of groups to go outside the law to manipulate the government or use it to manipulate the law, pressures to repress views or criticisms (and their advocates) that are uncomfortable, and the use of force (assassination, terrorism, riots, repression) when democracy brings unacceptable results. In the wake of a war, especially if the country had little prior experience with democracy, the whole society can be an obstacle to political peacebuilding in some ways.

What can peacebuilders do about all this? Space allows only a few examples. While the peacebuilders are in control of the country they can arrest people guilty of terrible crimes, promote new leaders to replace ones likely to provoke the conflict again, and round up competent people from former governments and put them to work. They can help design political institutions that limit the power of leaders and require them to cooperate to exercise power. Neutral experts can be brought in to shape election systems, teach people to organize politically, and suggest ways to ensure that power is shared. Outsiders can help set up initial government structures, particularly at the local level, that give people experience in running things in a democracy. Governments or international organizations can threaten to cancel aid unless the society makes progress toward democracy and cut off those groups that do not move in the right direction. Peacebuilders can circulate books, articles, films, and TV programs that describe democracy, criticize racism, and promote concern for human rights.

However, debate continues about whether democracy should come first or be a lower priority. Democracy might be crucial for getting people to see that there are ways of dealing with conflicts that are better than fighting. But a raucous, deadlocked democracy might lead to despair about what it will ever lead to and thus promote a renewal of the fighting. This is one of the recurring dilemmas in peacebuilding.

The Security Dimension

A vital function of government is to provide security, so to establish a government security must be a top priority. After all, the outsiders intervened because security had disappeared, and an environment was created in which one or both sides terrorized and abused people. The new government has to provide security just to get peacebuilding started, but without security a new government is hard to establish.

One thing needed is the **rule of law**—creating or reinvigorating a legal system. In authoritarian systems the law is ignored or is deliberately designed to exploit and terrorize citizens. In a civil war, the law largely disappears. Guns settle disputes and keep whatever order there is. Bringing back the law is difficult. Often those who ran the old legal system were incompetent, corrupt, and guilty of grave crimes. Under those circumstances, the upstanding legal professionals may have moved on to safer pursuits. The former have to be ousted and the latter convinced to come back, and many new people need to be trained, including prosecutors, defense lawyers, and judges. The prison system will also need reform; the prisons typically are in terrible shape.

But rule of law usually cannot return until security has been established and citizens feel safe enough to go out on the streets, to shop, and to go to work. Safe streets and roads are needed to get economic activity flourishing, schools open, and public services up and running. So getting the police working is vital. But often the police were part of the problem in the old government—corrupt, tyrannical, brutal. Or they may have disappeared because they were targets in the war, because no one was listening to them, or because there was no law to enforce. So police officers have to be recruited or rehired and the bad ones weeded out. Normally, they need retraining, to learn how to protect people and not exploit them, respect human rights, to implement new procedures (on arrests, interrogations, investigations) in keeping with the rule of law, and to build good relations with communities, all the things people in settled societies expect. It is also often necessary to integrate the police. Because of the war officers were drawn mainly from particular parts of society. Citizens may not feel safe if they do not see their sorts of people serving on the force.

All this takes time. So the outsiders must temporarily provide security, sometimes for quite a while. They have to operate a kind of martial law and use soldiers partly as police to prevent rioting and looting, direct traffic, arrest criminals, and so on. Rarely do soldiers like this work. Sometimes they handle it well and sometimes not. They are happy to turn it over to others. Reorganizing and training the police is often done by a UN Civilian Police mission or a program set up by a particular country. These missions recruit foreign police officers to teach, train, monitor progress, and, in some cases, be adjunct administrators to run the police. This is a difficult task, not one for which those involved were originally trained. The foreign police officers have to leave behind their families, departments, and responsibilities for a lengthy period to tackle frustrating and risky situations. Grumbling is heard because no country has a surplus of good police officers to spare, which is one reason that retired police are often used in these missions. They have to adjust to a different legal system that is often in disarray, different cultural traditions on justice and authority, different security situations, and strange languages. They also must make do without much money for their programs. Furthermore, there will be conflicting conceptions of reform, as when affirmative action considerations clash with an emphasis on professionalism.

These difficulties are minor compared with dealing with the armed forces. After a war, security requires demobilization and military reform. Many young men who have lived with violence, used it to get what they want, and often know little else must now have something else to do, some other way to live. Military units and guerrilla forces must be disarmed and disbanded. Otherwise those who fought the war will be easy recruits for crime or new guerrilla fighting or just banditry. But most have no job skills, often no real education, and little experience with living in a regular society. With the economy a mess, there are few jobs. Demobilization is also sensitive because the forces that many people depended on for their safety and survival will gradually disappear. That means they are gambling that the peace process will work. Naturally, people would rather hedge their bets and keep their forces around until it is clear that the other side will behave. Some leaders may want to keep forces around so that later they can attack and defeat the other side. They never intend to keep the peace.

Demobilization is particularly sensitive to those who have been in charge of the forces. Often this control of forces is their source of power. It may provide them with a criminal livelihood. They use their forces to seize valuables, blackmail people into paying for protection, or collect money for feeding twice the number of men in their units and then pocket the extra funds. Through their units they may maintain the intensity of the feelings that drove the war and is the basis of their power. Thus demobilization will strip them of resources, stature, and power. In many cases, therefore, resistance arises to demobilization as people try to hang onto their guns. Often a faction goes underground instead and mounts attacks to disrupt the peace process and keep the war going.

One tactic to avoid this problem is to merge people from the armed forces with people who were fighting against them into a new armed force for the nation. In this way these fighters have a livelihood, a new career. This, however, is difficult. The people involved were killing each other for years. They come from different tribes, castes, social classes, and parts of the country. Some were trained to be soldiers, others to be guerrillas, still others to be terrorists. Now they are all supposed to work together effectively. That is not likely.

Another approach is to reform the armed forces so that they do not have to be demobilized. The country needs the military. It may have been the bulwark of the old government, even running it because of repeated military coups and rule by military juntas or strongmen. Their opponents may be no better. They may have been operating like a violent gang, in units that alternate between guerrilla activity and outright crime or in movements that practiced terror, such as the Tamil Tigers in Sri Lanka. Needed is a military force that is professional, not inclined to interfere in politics, attentive to human rights concerns, disciplined, and honest.

In the meantime, the outside forces may have to run things for a long time as part of peacebuilding. In nasty cases they face resistance and have to fight to settle down the country. The outsiders start to retrain the army's officer corps, get new recruits, and teach people from the old forces for service in the new ones. This assignment rarely helps foreign officers with their careers back home and, as with the police, they have to cope with unfamiliar problems, cultures, and languages. Political difficulties exist in weeding out those associated with the brutality and corruption of the old government or the terrorism, blackmail, and other crimes of the opposition, because of the various political concerns mentioned above. The new forces have to be paid and equipped but the foreign intervention, not surprisingly, is always short of funds. Perhaps the biggest problem is that in many countries the military forces never existed to defend the country from foreigners. They were deeply involved in domestic politics instead. Asking them to stay out of politics now is contrary to their past experience and the society's.

Security involves more than police and military reform. Internal wars often result from security dilemmas. One of the key themes in studies of ethnic conflicts, for example, is the security dilemma that arises for ethnic groups when a state is dissolving and groups are tempted to gather weapons just in case they will have to defend themselves. In Bosnia today there are Bosnians, Croats, and Serbs. The Bosnians may feel that the government is fair and will protect them, but what about next year? What if their side loses the next election? Or the government collapses? It would help if everyone in the country disarmed so that the Bosnians feel their neighbors cannot attack them. But, if everyone fears attack, every group also fears that another group will cheat (hide some weapons) or could easily get weapons shipped in by outside friends. As a result, everyone is tempted to cheat at least a little. It would help if there was a strong state, able to protect everyone, provide order, and maintain stability. But each group fears that if another group controls the state it might use the state to wipe out rival groups, so all the groups are reluctant to see a strong state created. For instance, it would be good if the courts, the police, and the military were nonpolitical so groups cannot abuse them for their own purposes, but how is that to be guaranteed? You can see why groups often would rather be able to defend themselves if peacebuilding breaks down. For instance, if the Bosnians all live together instead of being scattered in villages among the other groups, then they would not be vulnerable to attack. But if they all live in one place, and the other groups cluster together, too, how is an integrated society to be recreated? And won't this encourage the Bosnians to insist on their own state, on an area where they are all clustered together? (See the discussion of partition in Chapter 11.) And if that does not happen, won't the groups living together and protected by their own forces continue to generate security dilemmas?

This is where the forces of outsiders, called on to supply security, can perhaps play an important psychological role. They can guarantee to protect various groups, and if that promise has enough credibility, then the pressures on groups to develop or maintain their own forces—thus making each other nervous—would be much reduced. Unfortunately, the intervention forces will not be around forever, and governments get unhappy about the burdens of keeping troops on a peacebuilding (or peace enforcement, peace imposition, or even peacekeeping) mission indefinitely.

This suggests trying another approach: building a state and political system with mutual restraint of the parties built in. The government can be designed with various power-sharing arrangements. If there are two main factions, each faction gets a portion of the cabinet seats or they always split the ones in charge of security. If, for example, the Sheep Party gets the police, the Goat Party runs the defense ministry; if the Sheep Party runs the local militia, the Goat Party heads the ministry of justice. It can be arranged that a government formed by one side must always get the other side's agreement for a constitutional amendment or any major new policy. In other words, each side has a veto. These kinds of arrangements can work, but they can also easily degenerate into political paralysis, then frustration, then a coup to get rid of the ineffective government, and ultimately to civil war again. That was what happened years ago on Cyprus, resulting in the current division of the island into Greek and Turkish Cypriote sections.

Plenty of other security issues are available to tackle. To take just one particularly nasty problem, the war may have left mines strewn about the country. Unless they are dealt with, innocent people continue to be killed or maimed. But demining takes money and there is never enough. Outside help is needed but it is expensive. So it is handled badly. Signs are put up to identify minefields but some fields are forgotten and not labeled, or the signs fall down, or illiterate people cannot read them, or desperate people need to get into those areas and thus take the risk, or their animals wander into the fields and people are killed trying to get them back. One of the saddest sights in many countries today is many people missing an arm or a leg.

A real concern in peacebuilding is security for the peacebuilders. In a desperately poor country full of guns it is dangerous to have anything of value, and peacebuilders have medicines, food, cell phones, trucks, watches, and boots. Any aid distribution point can be a target for raids. Women in the aid organizations can be targets of sexual violence. Or gangs can extract protection money; they will not steal or pursue other criminal activities if they get paid off. This leads to all sorts of problems. Starving people cannot be helped if the food is hijacked, so peacebuilding military forces will be asked to provide protection. But that disperses them all over the place, providing less protection elsewhere. As a result, the military insists that aid workers not go anywhere until they can be protected. Meanwhile, the aid workers insist that they have to go so people will not starve or die from disease. Many aid agencies or IGOs are uneasy, in principle, about accepting protection. They fear that a military escort interferes with fully reaching out to the people and winning their trust. The International Red Cross normally refuses military protection, for example. But officers are not happy if aid workers are getting hurt because this suggests military people are not doing their jobs.

Unfortunately, serious problems sometimes arise with the peacebuilding military forces, too. In the Balkans, for example, certain peacebuilding units set up criminal activities such as running drugs, smuggling, and the like (see Chapter 10). In the eastern Congo (see the *Cases and Context* box, "The Violence in the Congo") forces sent to do peacekeeping and protect aid workers also turned to rape, extortion, developing prostitution rings, and other crimes. These are difficult situations to handle. The peacekeeping forces come from different countries, and the UN or other command authorities usually have no jurisdiction over them for such behavior. The governments that sent the forces are responsible. But often those governments are not much interested, especially if their forces commonly behave the same way back home. The offending troops can be sent home but that may spell the end of the peacebuilding effort.

There is a larger problem. Many aid suppliers are private NGOs. They are unlike military organizations—decentralized in their decision making, flexible, loosely organized in the field, and inclined to adapt to situations instead of doing elaborate advance planning. These two cultures clash. Aid people insist in going to dangerous places because that is where they are most needed; military people want to keep aid workers out of dangerous places until the danger can be neutralized. Aid workers see the military as too uptight and conservative. Military people respond that the aid workers are irresponsible and, by getting in trouble, may get soldiers killed in rescue efforts that could have been avoided. In addition, NGOs (and IGOs) have their own agendas, funding bases, missions. Furthermore, they often are not closely coordinated. In fact, they resist being coordinated if it hampers doing what they want to do. Thus they overlap, compete, and exceed the boundaries of any plans the peacebuilding authorities have drawn up. To military people this can be a real headache. But it can also be beneficial because these scattered outsiders can generate much needed intelligence about what is going on in the country, and spot trouble before it gets out of hand.

The literature on peacebuilding reports that aid organizations and military units have made progress on improving their relations, learning first that they need each other and then how to get along. Military units are accepting the need to be more flexible on providing security and even to help out in aid distribution. Aid

Cases and Context: *The Violence in the Congo*

Sustained violence in the Congo, known for years as Zaire, is rooted in the sudden, unexpected creation of that forlorn country in 1959 when Belgium, its colonial ruler, abruptly pulled out. The country was unprepared for independence and quickly fell into disarray under its new president, Patrice Lumumba. Twenty thousand United Nations (UN)-authorized peacekeeping troops were sent to maintain order but were drawn into fighting to hold the country together by suppressing secessionists. Approximately 250 peacekeeping troops were killed in that mission. Eventually, Lumumba was assassinated and the Congo then was ruled by Joseph Mobutu. He probably holds the world record for looting a poor country. After his ouster by Laurent Kabila in 1998, via a short civil war, the country was still basically unprepared to govern itself. Kabila had been sponsored by the Rwandan government. The spring 1994 slaughter in Rwanda of Tutsi tribesmen (and moderate Hutus) by radical elements of the Hutu tribe had incited a Tutsi invasion from outside to take over Rwanda. Many radical Hutus then fled across the border to the Congo and continued to attack or harass Rwanda. Kabila was supposed to help the Rwandans end this problem but his government could not control the Hutus, and he appears to have also wanted to stop taking orders from his Tutsi backers. So the eastern Congo turned into a no-man's land, as Rwanda continued supporting local tribes against the Hutus and, in 1998, with the support of Uganda, invaded the Congo and seized a good deal of it. The government survived with assistance from forces sent by Angola, Zimbabwe, and Namibia, and this fighting among six nations is sometimes referred to as central Africa's World War I.

Several peace agreements have been arranged through mediation by African governments. One in 1999 was negated by Kabila. Another in 2002 was unsuccessful because the government could not control the eastern Congo. Rwanda continued supporting violent opposition both to the government and the Hutus there. A 2003 agreement called for power sharing and the merger of the rival forces, plus elections to produce a viable Congo government. However, rival tribal militias continue marauding, drawing on mineral wealth (such as diamonds) in the eastern Congo and subsidies from outsiders. These militias often feature child soldiers. At least six of the militias are composed of people from Uganda, Rwanda, and Burundi. The rebels were forced to flee to the lawless eastern Congo.

Estimates of total casualties, mostly civilians, start at three million from direct fatalities and victims of malnutrition, disease, and other ills related to the fighting. The world's governments were reluctant to get involved in that lawless and violent region. However, small numbers of UN peacekeepers were eventually sent, inadequate in number and purpose because the region needed not peacekeeping but peace imposition. By 2003 the UN had several thousand troops there, but they were in danger of being mauled like the peacekeepers in Bosnia a decade earlier. The UN sought emergency help in June 2003 and the European Union, under French leadership, sent eighteen hundred heavily armed troops as an interim emergency force to the Bunia area where fighting was particularly bad. This eased pressure on the peacekeepers for a while but they were often attacked in late 2003 and 2004 and their forces had to be increased to eleven thousand by late 2004 and fifteen thousand or more in 2005.

organizations are working harder at accepting coordination and understanding the military forces' concerns. Everyone is learning about peacebuilding on the job.

The Economic Sphere

One reason peace agreements are often signed in internal wars is because the economy of the country is a shambles and everyone is desperate. Unless something is done about this the prospects for long-term security are bad, as are the prospects for political stability. Thus certain economic objectives must be at the heart of a peacebuilding effort.

- Getting the economy to recover—getting farms working again, markets and stores open, goods produced, banks operating, and reestablishing a currency.

- Getting the economy to grow and develop—just returning to how things were will mean too little money to ease grievances and repair the country.

- Getting economic results usefully distributed—putting payoffs from economic recovery and growth into the most useful hands.

A central task is to get major infrastructure restored. During the war the bridges may have been downed, communications destroyed, roads bombed or left unrepaired, airports damaged, power plants and power lines disrupted, or irrigation systems abandoned. Other infrastructure items that may be needed include a working legal system, a financial system, a solid currency, banks and other credit systems, a tax system, and a decent education system. If these systems do not work the economy will not function well. Here outsiders are normally crucial. They supply the funding, provide the equipment needed to demine roads, rebuild dams and power plants, and bring in other necessary things—power lines, cement, textbooks, and trucks. The financial system may start by using an international money, such as the dollar, until the local currency can be established as usable again. Outsiders often run the economic agencies initially or serve as advisers and make many of the key decisions.

In doing all this the outsiders usually emphasize reforms and institutions that reflect capitalist concepts and practices. Government economic operations are discouraged. The country is told it should emphasize private economic activity, including steps to attract foreign investment to stimulate the economy. A major outside contribution is economic assistance—aid for economic recovery, development, humanitarian assistance, security improvements, and education. This comes from governments directly, from UN agencies' regular funds and special donations by governments, from other IGOs such as the World Bank, and from NGOs. Much of the aid is in the form of money, but there will be tools, equipment, food, medicines and drugs, and experts as well. Some of it is technology transfers or foreign investment. Often the country can be helped by special trade concessions so it can export products to earn money.

Getting economic benefits usefully distributed is something that outsiders can help with but eventually is a job for local authorities. Benefits should be distributed so they mute conflicts, not promote them. If one side in the war gets most of the benefits a resumption of fighting could occur eventually. It is good if economic benefits are distributed in a way that promotes reconciliation, particularly by emphasizing and exploiting the various groups' interdependence and by seeking cooperation so that all benefit. Outsiders can play a role, by insisting that aid be distributed with this broad objective in mind and rebuilding or designing newly developed infrastructure accordingly.

As with political and security aspects of peacebuilding, the difficulties are extensive. For example, broad economic reforms and changes often produce serious problems for many individuals, groups, businesses, and regions. It makes sense to end wasteful government activities (especially those rife with corruption) except to the people who are then made unemployed, or to improve tax collections except to those who have to pay. Ending subsidies for farmers can make agriculture more efficient, which is good, but can put many people out of work, which is not so good. Economic reforms also produce political problems. If a change will adversely affect groups with leaders who are important for the new government's stability, then it is not likely to be adopted. If the reforms mean ending subsidies or rationing for food, fuel, and other necessities, then prices will rise along with unemployment, which is not good for any government politically.

Broad reforms, including the introduction or expansion of capitalist elements, always produce uneven benefits and costs. Some parts of the society get few of the benefits or pay much of the cost. In developed countries the government can help ease the pain. In poor countries, just coming out of a war, that is impossible. Reychler's notion was that peacebuilding should put a social free market system in place. Economic reformers argue that in the long run the road to prosperity is an efficient economy. But that is not true for many people in the short run, which, as economist John Maynard Keynes pointed out, is where people live. (He said, "In the long run we are all dead.")

Remember also that economic power is political power. The distribution of economic benefits does much to shape who has the most political influence in the future. Fighting over pieces of the economic pie is therefore also a struggle over who gets a political dessert. Instilling economic reforms can have long-term political consequences that peacebuilders hope will be beneficial, but there is no guarantee.

Foreign aid can easily be a can of worms. Aid pouring in may substitute for local economic resources. With an abundance of food aid everyone gets enough to eat, but the price of food in the markets will drop and farmers' incomes therefore drop, too. Thus they have less to invest in improving their production. In some countries, governments exploit farmers by requiring that they sell their products to the government at set low prices and then these governments sell it for much more and keeping the difference. So, the food aid may cost the government a good deal of revenue. Foreign aid also will flow into sectors that outsiders think are important, for instance, to develop mining for exports that will bring in foreign exchange the country badly needs. But if the mining pollutes lakes and streams, killing the fish that people rely on for food, those people are likely to pour into the cities, establish shantytowns, and add to political unrest.

Aid is seldom politically neutral. It is often used by the local government and its leaders for their own political purposes. Leaders insist that the foreign aid has come because of their effective negotiations with the outsiders. They take as much of the credit as possible. Agencies or groups want to be in charge of distributing aid so they can steal some, make sure their relatives and political supporters get most of it, or use it to build coalitions with other leaders and groups to enhance their power. Aid given directly to those in need, as outsiders often insist on doing, may be used by the recipients to build up their power against the government, something the government will not appreciate and perhaps lead it to stop cooperating with the donors.

Constant struggles take place over priorities in economic recovery and development. Which should come first, economic recovery or political stability? A good case can be made that each is vital for the other, so they should go together. Alas, decisions must often be made that benefit one at the expense of the other, so which is more important then? And who should decide? The same is true in promoting human rights. Economic recovery may include boosting industries that rest on child labor. Which is more important, human rights or getting money to desperately poor families? To run the economy some high-level decision makers must be installed. Should they be democratically selected and removed, or treated as specialists to run the economy and insulated from political pressures? Without insulation for them, needed economic steps may be politically impossible; with insulation for them, the tough decisions can be made but confidence in the government and public support for its policies or for democracy itself may erode. These are hard choices.

PEACEBUILDING IN PRACTICE

Here are a few recent examples of peacebuilding. (For details about conflict and peace in the Sudan, see the *Cases and Context* box, "Sudan and Its Darfur Region.")

Cases and Context: Sudan and Its Darfur Region

Sudan is a large country with an Arab Muslim north and a black African Christian and Animist south. Sudan is a country with a long history of conflict, as in many parts of Africa, derived from past Arab exploitation of blacks. Objecting to domination and mistreatment by the government run by Sudanese Arabs, the Sudanese People's Liberation Army (SPLA) fought an on-and-off civil war for some twenty-one years, well known as a vicious struggle with atrocities and civilian harm that never attracted sustained outside relief efforts. There is a belief, but no great confidence, that the fighting has now been ended, via peace negotiations and a treaty in 2003–2005 that the United States helped sponsor.

The Sudan has discovered significant oil deposits in the north and wants to exploit them. Under the agreement the south gets half the oil revenues for its recovery and development and the SPLA is to stop attacking the oil installations. After a new constitution is created 30 percent of the national assembly seats will be reserved for representatives from the south, which is also to get a significant portion of government jobs and substantial autonomy. In an unusual step, the Sudan is to have three armies: one in the north, one in the south, plus twenty thousand northerners and southerners merged into a joint army. The south is to have its own regional government, including newly established laws, courts, police, and other institutions. All this will require massive foreign aid, almost all of it from the European Union and the United States. After six years a referendum is to be held in the south on whether to become independent.

The south has other problems, too. With a population of about 7.5 million it must prepare for the return of up to four million who fled elsewhere because of the fighting. Life expectancy there is forty-two years, and it has one of the lowest rates of primary school completion in the world. Average income is less than $1 a day.

However, as the conflict was ending, ten years of tensions in the western desert of Sudan erupted into still more fighting. In the Darfur region black (Muslim) tribesmen had suffered attacks by Arab tribes and in early 2003, with an eye on the north-south negotiations, black guerrillas began military operations in response. The government retaliated by arming some Arab tribes to create militias, the most lethal of which are referred to as the Janjaweed. Darfur is one of the most isolated and desolate regions in the world, so the fighting attracted little attention at first. In addition, governments played down the situation so as to not disrupt the north-south talks. Gradually word seeped out, partly from those engaged in aid operations, that the Janjaweed and some Sudanese forces were systematically driving blacks out of villages in sweeping campaigns to destroy homes, rape women, kill many people, and damage oases.

The outside world was slow to react. The African Union (AU) eventually sent a small police force, then peacekeeping units (totaling fewer than two thousand troops) that could do little. In part this was because the AU was reluctant to override Sudan's sovereignty. Sudan objected to outside interference and insisted no serious conflict was occurring. Pressure built as aid agencies reported the atrocities, African governments offered to send more troops, and the United States took up the matter and began urging a strong response by the United Nations (UN) Security Council. What might have galvanized a stronger response was a UN declaration that Darfur was a case of genocide, but no agreement was reached on this. The United States officially labeled it genocide in the fall of 2004 but the European Union and the African Union did not agree and nongovernmental organizations such as Amnesty International and Human Rights Watch said it was unclear. What everyone did agree on was that over a million, probably more than two million, people had been displaced (many into neighboring Chad), and that at least 50,000 and perhaps 300,000 were dead. Hundreds of thousands more were at risk from disease and malnutrition.

The United States pressed for sanctions on Sudan, particularly on its oil industry, but France, China, Russia, and Pakistan, among others, did not agree. China, for instance, has signed agreements with Sudan to buy oil, while the others are anticipating lucrative trade deals. However, by the spring of 2005 the number of AU troops was approaching three thousand and there were plans for twelve thousand by the spring of 2006. This has allowed more aid personnel and aid programs to operate. Nevertheless, the UN secretary general reported in late 2005 that the situation was deteriorating again. The heaviest part of the peacebuilding, including an extensive aid program, is yet to come.

Cambodia

In Cambodia, for a while known as Kampuchea, the Khmer Rouge revolutionaries took over in 1975. They moved, in a totalitarian fashion, to control and remake the society. This included driving many people out of the cities into the countryside (the Khmer Rouge envisioned a rural utopia), imposing a new economic and social system by force, and killing hundreds of thousands of people—perhaps as many as two million—who opposed the regime or did not fit into its plans. One Khmer Rouge target was the Vietnamese minority, many of whom were badly treated or fled into Vietnam. This helped the Vietnamese government, which wanted to control Cambodia, decide in 1979 to invade to drive the Khmer Rouge out and install its preferred government. The Khmer Rouge were largely defeated but hung on in the jungles at the western edge of the country, with support from Thailand and China because those governments disliked Vietnam's control of the country. So fighting continued, adding to the devastation of Cambodia.

Eventually, under great pressure from all the great powers, the parties agreed to end the conflict in 1991. In the presence of UN peacekeeping forces, the UN took over running the country while arranging for elections. The Khmer Rouge objected to having to be disarmed, so the peacekeeping forces and others continued fighting it while a government was elected and a huge peacebuilding effort continued as well. The country, its government, and its society had to be rebuilt, which required major international subsidies. Progress was made in settling down the country, ending the Khmer Rouge as a fighting force (by 1998), getting the economy working, and keeping the coalition political system—a precarious balance between antagonistic factions—afloat. However, the man the Vietnamese had installed years before as president eventually mounted a successful coup, dispersed the coalition government and any semblance of democracy, and took over. As of 2005, he was still in charge, and Cambodia has remained stable and peaceful but very poor.

El Salvador

El Salvador, one of the world's poorest and most densely populated countries, experienced a devastating twelve-year civil war that flattened the economy and, through numerous atrocities, terrorized the population and killed more than seventy thousand. The United States played a large role by supporting the government with money and weapons against the leftist guerrillas that were seeking a more equitable society. A negotiated settlement was finally arranged in 1991–1992, under the auspices of five neighboring countries, that ended the fighting and the terrorism. The UN then organized one of its most notable peacekeeping and peacebuilding efforts. Peacekeeping forces went to unprecedented lengths in rebuilding the police and the legal system while demobilizing the combatants. Peacebuilding also concentrated on getting the economy running, including giving some of the combatants land and setting up a democratic system that provided for elections in 1994.

One notable feature was development of a commission to seek national reconciliation by investigating the killings and other atrocities during the war. The idea was to truthfully record what had happened and identify those who were responsible, not to punish but to help people face up to what had been done and come together to keep it from happening again. This innovative step has been imitated in peacebuilding efforts elsewhere. The political system is still operating and fighting has not broken out again. But the economy has never fully recovered and development to ease the plight of the ever growing population has not taken off. So poverty and underdevelopment, plus the sharp social divisions reinforced by a high concentration of land ownership in few hands, which were the main causes of the civil war, have not been erased.

Bosnia

The struggle in 1991–1995 among Croats, Serbs, and Bosnian Muslims to control the newly independent country of Bosnia (after its secession from Yugoslavia) destroyed most of it, collapsed the economy, produced 1.2 million refugees and perhaps 1 million displaced persons inside the country, killed about 250,000, and wounded or traumatized many more. A U.S.-led imposition of a peace agreement followed by a NATO peace enforcement operation ended the war. A peacebuilding operation involving NATO, the European Union (EU) and other European states, the UN, and the United States is still in charge of the country. It has tried to install a democracy that involves an elaborate sharing of power, rebuild the economy, get refugees and displaced persons returned, and create a multiethnic nation. The greatest success came in ending the fighting. Some of the displaced have been able to return, the economy is at least working again, several elections have been held, and progress has been made on legal reforms and rebuilding the police. Forces from the European Union members have replaced some NATO units.

Despite these moderate successes, the economy is still weak, violent protests have kept some refugees and displaced persons from returning, and in elections the most hostile nationalist and separatist elements regularly win. Because their parties represent largely ethnically homogeneous parts of the country, dislike each other intensely, and propagate ethnic conflict they cannot together form an effective government. As a result, there is none. The international community representatives govern the country. Many observers believe that if they and the peacekeeping forces left, the country would fall apart and fighting would resume.

However, more than a million refugees have returned, and a Bosnian army is slowly being formed. In 2005 the U.S. government drafted a constitution for a new parliamentary democracy with a cabinet system and began seeking approval from the three large ethnic groups. The hope was that these groups were finally ready to cooperate in creating a viable political system.

Iraq

The war on Iraq that commenced in 2003 was not a peace enforcement or peace imposition action but a straightforward attack, mainly conducted by the United States. The United States then initiated a major peacebuilding effort run initially by the occupying (mostly U.S. and British) forces but eventually involving some elements from the rest of NATO, the EU, and others. The situation in Iraq combined the aftereffects of an interstate war and the ongoing effects of a large internal war, so it was particularly important to do the peacebuilding effectively. That, however, has not been achieved. The goal was a government far less threatening to its neighbors militarily and able to pull together Kurds, Shiite Muslims, and Sunni Muslims into a stable and peaceful country with democracy and a fully recovered (oil-rich) economy. Hence the peacebuilding is more like the peacebuilding efforts developed in Germany and Japan in 1945, but it also reflects other contemporary efforts in terms of what it is trying to achieve. The United States had not succeeded in fully securing even the capital from the insurgents, yet it was trying to get a democracy established, an economy rebuilt, and a stable cohesive society knitted together. Unfortunately, it has also been typical in terms of the problems and difficulties encountered: political factions unable to cooperate, slow progress in rebuilding the economy from the interstate war and postwar looting, and considerable difficulty in getting democracy started. Two features of this case are of special interest. First, the United States was reluctant to turn over peacebuilding to the UN, regarding it as inept and too reflective of those governments who opposed the war. In response, other governments avoided major participation in peacebuilding under U.S. auspices. At issue was a major disagreement over who should be in charge of an international peacebuilding effort. Second, Iraq is the first country in decades getting a major international peacebuilding effort that has a strong national economic base and plenty of potential national income from oil. One reason for arguments over who would run peacebuilding was fear that the United States would keep the bulk of the contracts for itself. Peacebuilding is normally hampered by a shortage of funds. If it does not work well in a country as rich as Iraq, support for it will be diminished around the world.

However, the George W. Bush administration was slow to take over and dismantled the remnants of the Iraqi police, armed forces, and government before there was anything to put in their place and before alternative jobs were created for these men. As a result, order and security rapidly deteriorated. The occupying forces never caught up with this situation, so security was not well provided, particularly for Iraqis serving in the interim government and its forces. Resistance to the occupation sprang up in the chaos that ensued and turned into an outright insurgency, which soon focused on interference with the peacebuilding—attacking the occupation forces, sabotaging economic recovery projects, undermining security in many parts of the country, assassinating Iraqis trying to rebuild the political system, sowing interethnic and interreligious conflict, blowing up aid projects and headquarters, and trying to prevent elections. As a result the economy did not strongly recover in the first years of the occupation and the insurgency regularly damaged Iraq's oil industry and oil exports. With widespread violence and insecurity, peacebuilding made slow progress even though elections were eventually held in 2005 that allowed the formation of an interim government to develop a constitution. The elections in December 2005 to establish a government will probably not be a breakthrough. Insurgents were reportedly forcing people in smaller communities to segregate themselves residentially into Sunni and Shiite groups for greater security, and neither the newly formed Iraqi army nor the fledgling police were close to being capable of suppressing the violence. Iraq is a good case study in how not to do peacebuilding, even if the mistakes are eventually overcome and things turn out well in the end.

CONCLUSION

Peacebuilding is the most ambitious effort yet that actors in international politics have devised to solve the security problems that war creates. In comparison with the other solutions considered in this book, it involves

- The greatest changes to be made in the parties to violent conflicts;

- The deepest penetration of nations by outsiders—the greatest erosion of sovereignty;

- The deepest penetration of societies as well;

- The most expansive conception of peace; and

- The largest, most lengthy commitment by outsiders to a process meant to create a sustainable peace.

Systemic Security

With respect to the systemic level, during the Cold War, Western nations carved out a zone of peace among themselves, which constituted a huge achievement. It shows no signs of disappearing. Today Western nations are busy trying to expand that zone of peace. They are working hardest in the rest of Europe, trying to bring the formerly communist part into that zone. So far it seems to be working but it has taken strenuous efforts in the former Yugoslavia. The nations are also working, more indirectly, by trying to spread democracy and capitalism to other parts of the world in keeping with the concept of the democratic peace and the belief that rising economic interdependence does much to prevent war among nations. Whether this is working is not yet clear. Not many international wars are being fought these days. But democracy has certainly not spread everywhere, capitalism is not universal, and economic interdependence is uneven. Maybe the Western nations are on the right track and the low level of international warfare is the result, but maybe it is the result of other things instead. It is too soon to tell.

As with peacekeeping, peace enforcement, and peace imposition, the West is also leading international efforts to deal with internal wars via peacebuilding inside societies. This involves declaring internal wars to be threats to international peace as violating international values and, in extreme cases, intervening massively to try to reorder a nation and its society internally. Thus far progress has been poor. There are still plenty of harsh internal conflicts, some that have had drastic effects on their regions. A few have provoked terrorism activities that are a serious threat at the systemic level. The world does not look orderly some days. But at least the international community is trying hard, at times; is no longer always constrained by a narrow conception of what is allowed by sovereignty; and has had some partial success in peacebuilding.

However, the peacebuilding effort in general has many limitations—in funding, in the unwillingness of governments to use it in many places, in the disorganization that often characterizes the whole effort, and in the scope of activities that the UN or, in Iraq and Afghanistan, the United States can take on. It reflects not only how far international management of peace and security has come but also how far it has not come.

In addition a serious complaint about the entire enterprise has been lodged at the systemic level. The West is mostly in charge of peacebuilding through Western governments, the international organizations they dominate, and the major NGOs, which are Western in origin, financial support, and orientation. The complaint is that modern peacebuilding reflects Western values and practices and is therefore a thinly disguised version of Western imperialism. The West is telling others what to do and how to behave, how to live and make a living, and how to govern themselves. The West does this in other ways, too—injecting capitalist practices into other societies and insisting their economies reflect Western ways; intervening against governments it dislikes and propping up governments it favors; promoting Western culture through consumer goods, movies, and other entertainment; proselytizing Christianity; educating foreign students; running military training missions; conducting arms sales; and asserting political and economic pressures on other societies to accept Western practices on medicine, women, marriage, sex, eating habits, and the environment. Now it is able to do this and more, openly and directly, through peacebuilding, all in the name of peace. The model on which peacebuilding rests and toward which it is pushing others is a Western conception of society and government. Many object, seeing this as Western arrogance, insensitivity, and exploitation. The most ferocious opposition comes from Islamic fundamentalists but others, including some Western critics, also see peacebuilding as too often one-sided and unacceptable because it strips people of what makes them who they are—their cultures, their ways of life, the groups they identify with, their social universe.

The complaint is significant because it attacks the basic design of modern peacebuilding. It reflects either a rejection of the idea that those in the West know what is best for the nations of the world if they are to live peacefully with each other or a belief that adopting the model is too disruptive of other values and ways of life to be worthwhile even for peace. Furthermore, it questions the motives of peacekeeping, which is seen as extending Western domination of the international system.

On the charge of Western imperialism, one possible response is that no other obvious model exists. The alternative ways peoples might learn to live in peace, put forward in many places, have proven to be defective in today's world. People cannot live in extended families, kinship groups, tribes, and the like any more. They need to live in, and as, nations. What many internal wars are about is the shaping of those nations—which peoples are to constitute nations and have states, who is to control the creation and shaping of them, and who shall govern them and for what purposes. But the ultimate answers are not entirely open to debate because people want nations in part to gain many of the things Western nations have. States that do not figure out how to get those things for their peoples eventually face rejection and extinction. As for international security, states of all sorts could theoretically coexist peacefully, thus solving the security problem. But no other large set of powerful states has ever coexisted peacefully, and eliminated internal warfare as well, to the extent the Western nations have in the last fifty or so years, particularly the Western democracies. The West seemingly offers the ultimate solution to the problem of war, among nations and societies and within them, which is that all nations and societies become prosperous, developed, and democratic. It is the ultimate solution because nothing else has consistently worked.

Whether this is the best answer to the charge that the West is promoting its way of life in an imperial fashion is often irrelevant because people want their society to be theirs, regardless of whether it is ideal in terms of some set of standards and values. They are likely to resist many changes simply because they are changes, and because they fear becoming more like somebody else and less like themselves.

State Security

Regarding the state level of analysis, peacebuilding poses a grave threat to some states and national sovereignty. Partly it is the states' own fault. The main targets of peacebuilding are failed states. These states are close to collapse or have collapsed because they cannot run their countries decently. They face serious internal opposition and even civil war, have little political legitimacy, operate poor economic systems, reek of corruption, stay in power (if they do) largely through repression, and have populations that are starving, poor, and unhealthy. Peacebuilding suggests that sovereignty is not absolute or permanent. A state can be dismissed by the international community for crimes and incompetence and the society can then end up a ward of the world. Thus some governments fear that they might someday be subjected to a humanitarian intervention and subsequent peacebuilding that strips away their autonomy. Others, such as China, are afraid of the precedent set by ignoring sovereignty.

However, the point of peacebuilding is to rebuild a state and its society. It rests on the idea that the proper community for people is a nation-state. It emphasizes that a nation-state should properly care for all the ethnic and religious groups within it so that existing nation-states need not be endlessly fragmenting.

Peacebuilding is, in a way, a powerful reassertion of the importance of sovereignty, of statehood.

Societal Security

At the societal level, the picture is also unclear. Peacebuilding is a last resort, undertaken when conditions in a state are terrible. Thus the immediate effect is to substantially improve societal security—fighting stops, law and order is restored, schools open, the police are retrained, and government services revive. Life gets better, much less brutal. It is marvelous that the international community will plunge into such a complex and expensive effort to fix things in some of the poorest, most underdeveloped, and most damaged places.

However, such an effort is no good if a permanent change is not made. A major complaint about peacebuilding is that it is just a rerun of a great failure in the past and thus will likely fail spectacularly again. These critics are referring to the huge effort by Western countries during the 1950s-1970s to promote nation-building and development in the third world. They feared that, if these countries did not develop into stable nations with a good rate of development, they would be unstable, fall prey to the influence of communist countries and movements, and be undemocratic and anti–Western. So they poured money, expertise, arms, and technology into the development of these new nations. They failed. Not everywhere, but often. (The competitive communist efforts also failed.) The critics say peacebuilders now are making the same mistakes.

Their central mistake, according to critics, is trying to do for a society what only the society itself can do. Some things can be easily learned from outsiders: building the trappings of a modern state, using some modern weapons, and constructing buildings and roads. But democracy, a national commitment to the nation, modern economic behavior, the use of advanced technology, and the like cannot be so readily learned. Elements can be borrowed but not their essence. A few people can learn much of what is required but many cannot learn enough. So governments have emerged that are not managers of national resources but kleptocracies, using power only for the enrichment of themselves and their friends, families, and supporters. In too many places people have remained loyal primarily to those groups, not the so-called nations in which they live. Economies have developed a modern veneer but remained basically undeveloped. Ways of life have taken on surface aspects of change but remain much as they were in the past.

Hence giving societies a crash course via peacebuilding will not work. The governments that emerge will not remain democratic and adhere to international human rights standards. Their economies will not achieve sustainable growth and meet people's needs. The armed forces, the police, and other security forces will again become threats to citizens' security as repressive rule returns.

The most sophisticated version of this criticism is that national development is—as it was in the West—driven initially by **state-making**. Someone has to consolidate power and construct a state, force the disparate elements in the country to conform, and extract resources to build the state and then the nation. This is harsh because the entire society must be transformed, its social and political structures rearranged, and the ways people make their living sharply altered. The resistance is immense, often leading to unrest or civil war. It cannot be undertaken while paying close attention to human rights or without major departures from democracy. It runs into detours when those who rule use the state for personal enrichment instead of nation-building, but the threat that this will happen comes with initiating the process and cannot be avoided.

This is a scary argument. It says peacebuilding will not work, at least not often, so improvements in societal security will often be temporary. There are various responses to this charge and the earlier ones. Perhaps today's peacebuilding efforts are more sophisticated than earlier Western nation-building, at least about what works and what does not. It is known that democracy is not built in a day. People are more sensitive to different conceptions of human rights. Some allowances are made for the necessities of state-building. In the end peacebuilding must be done by the peoples involved; outsiders only help. In short, people can do a better job now.

Furthermore, peacebuilding responds to real needs that people have and can therefore develop a durable popularity. It is attempted after people have seen the worst that can happen. Earlier Western nation-building was attempted when the peoples involved were optimistic about how their new nations and governments would work out, but the failures that eventually led to today's peacebuilding have had a more sobering effect. Finally, state- and nation-building could have been so costly and difficult in the past because outsiders usually resisted it, wanting to control the territory, people, and resources for themselves. If outsiders are determined to help instead, the process could be far less difficult, with more rapid progress and a higher rate of success.

SOURCES AND OTHER USEFUL READINGS

The Reychler conception is laid out in the opening chapter of Luc Reychler and Thania Paffenholz, *Peace-Building*. Anyone wanting to follow up the reference to Jesse James and trace some of the peacebuilding difficulties after the U.S. Civil War should read T. J. Stiles, *Jesse James*.

Many interesting publications focus on peacebuilding in general. *Peacebuilding as Politics*, edited by Elizabeth M. Cousens and Chetan Kumar, elaborates on the political dimension of all peacebuilding efforts. See also *Peacekeeping and Conflict Resolution,* edited by Thomas Woodhouse and Oliver Ramsbotham. The case for peacebuilding as best done from the ground up, working with citizens, is presented in John Paul Lederach, *Preparing for Peace.* The role of IGO administration in peacebuilding is examined in a special January-March 2004 issue of *Global Governance.*

On the role of nongovernmental organizations in peacebuilding, see, for example, *NGOs at the Table,* edited by Nari Fitzduff and Cheyane Church; Pamela Aall, "NGOs, Conflict Management, and Peacekeeping"; Benjamin Gidron, Stanley N. Katz, and Yeheskel Hasenfeld, *Mobilizing for Peace*; and Ann M. Florini, *The Third Force.* The larger subject of global civil society has attracted so much attention that its development is now chronicled in a yearbook series entitled *Global Civil Society.*

The case against peacebuilding as ethnocentric, even imperialist, and unlikely to ever be successful is laid out in Roland Paris, "Peacebuilding and the Limits of Liberal Internationalism," and his "Wilson's Ghost." The liberal internationalism he is attacking is presented in a case study in Mark Peceny and William Stanley, "Liberal Social Reconstruction and the Resolution of Civil Wars in Central America." To get a sense of the range of peacebuilding activities that are operating today, see, for example, *Searching for Peace in Asia Pacific,* edited by Annelies Heijmans, Nicola Simmonds, and Hans van de Veen; and *Searching for Peace in Europe and Eurasia,* edited by Paul Van Tongeren, Hans van de Veen, and Juliette Verhoeven.

There has been a surge of interest in the difficulties and necessities involved in reforming the security sector as part of peacebuilding. See, for instance, Robert M. Perito, *Where Is the Lone Ranger When We Need Him?*; Michael Rose, "Military Aspects of Peacekeeping"; Annika Hansen, "From Congo to Kosovo"; Jane Chanaa, "Security Sector Reform"; Charles T. Call and William Stanley, "Protecting the People"; and Thomas G. Weiss, *Military-Civilian Interactions.* On the culture clash and organizational friction between IGOs or NGOs and military peacekeeping forces, see *Aspects of Peacekeeping,* edited by D. S. Gordon and F. H. Toase; Christopher Dandeker and James Gow, "Military Culture and Strategic Peacekeeping"; and Andrew Harris and Peter Dombrowski, "Military Collaboration with Humanitarian Organizations in Complex Emergencies."

On the impact of the classic security dilemma in ethnic and other internal conflicts, see Barry R. Posen, "The Security Dilemma and Ethnic Conflict"; *Civil Wars, Insecurity, and Intervention,* edited by Barbara F. Walter and Jack Snyder; the theoretical discussion in David A. Lake and Donald Rothchild, "Containing Fear"; and, for a different view, Paul Roe, "Former Yugoslavia."

Regarding the impact of humanitarian considerations, see Thomas G. Weiss, "The Humanitarian Impulse"; and Kurt Mills, "Neo-Humanitarianism." Much of this humanitarian concern is related to rising pressure to enhance human rights. A good start on this topic is Edward A. Kolodziej, *A Force Profonde*.

Shepard Forman and Stewart Patrick's *Good Intentions* and Stewart Patrick's "The Check Is in the Mail" provide chapter and verse on the gap between the aid promised for peacebuilding and the aid delivered.

CHAPTER 13

Conclusion

Economics was long referred to as the "dismal science" and at some point during the Cold War suggestions were made that, with conflict and war in mind, the dismal science in current times is international politics. In concluding a book on war in international politics it is gratifying to be able to reemphasize that wars are down. A full-fledged war between two or more great powers in the international system has not broken out for many years, and only one dispute between great powers today contains a distinct possibility of a war in the future—the U.S.-China disagreement about Taiwan. The general level of cooperation and comity among the great powers is high in comparison with many past eras. The number of outright wars between governments has shrunk to a low level, even though the number of states recognized by the United Nations (UN) has risen considerably. The number of civil wars has also declined in the past decade, and the total number of casualties in wars seems to have declined to a notable degree. No dismal science there.

Under the pressure provided by the existence of warfare, international politics has been steadily changing, albeit at a stately pace. War has gradually become a problem to be confronted, not just endured, and a wide range of solutions, most of them fairly beneficent, have emerged in theory and practice. Some of this stems from a rising concern not only for the interests of states but also the interests of people. Furthermore, both the study and practice of international politics have proven flexible enough to embrace this concern. Thus one of the changes in international politics is that a preoccupation with maintaining sovereignty is slowly yielding ground to concern about internal wars, sometimes even those in small countries far away. Another is that war is no longer a pro forma agenda item in world affairs. That is, one of those things everyone is officially against as long as no one tried to do something about it. It is now a serious problem taken seriously.

Have some of the strategies outlined in this book been at least partly responsible for the drop in interstate war and intrastate fighting? It is hard to know for sure, but it is a reasonable possibility. What is clear is that more attention is being paid to the problem of war and more effort is going into getting it under control than ever before in the history of international politics. Nothing dismal about that.

The next most important developments include the sturdy enlargement of peacebuilding efforts. This is striking given the fact that those efforts are elaborate and complex, as well as expansive and optimistic in their objectives. In addition, these efforts bring together, however uneasily at times, the resources of international organizations, national governments, and international civil society. Contemporary efforts to deal with war now have broader and deeper roots. Another important development is the multiplication of international community interventions of all sorts into internal conflicts. A surge in interventions took place after the Cold War ended, and then the inevitable morning-after reaction emerged against having overdone it, only to be followed by a renewed rise in interventions under the auspices of international organizations. That is an impressive display of staying power.

Furthermore, a sharp drop was seen in the level of casualties and destruction in the course of fighting a war that is acceptable to many people in the leading nations in the world. The decline applies not only to the casualties that one's own forces might suffer but also to those they can inflict. The American armed forces, preparing to invade Iraq in 2003, were aware that holding down casualties on both sides, and avoiding civilian losses in lives and property, was an imperative for success in sustaining or gaining support for the war in the United States and elsewhere. The Russians know that the Chechens do not enjoy a broad base of support in much of the world but that Russia does not either, because its ways of fighting the war with the Chechens are so indiscriminately violent.

Numerous failures and shortcomings also can be reported. International organizations and governments are apt to take serious steps to deal with a particular conflict much later than is desirable, for several reasons. Analysts have suggested that conflicts often have to reach the point of a hurtful stalemate, after much death and destruction have been perpetrated, before the participants will proceed seriously to negotiations. The reaction in the international system to serious fighting usually arrives at the point of deciding to really do something only when the level of irritation with the fighting is high and, in retrospect, well beyond when active concern should have taken hold.

The various strategies have their flaws and failure is a repeated occurrence, not just a vague possibility, for each one of them. However, a robust consistent deterrence of war by a true collective actor, such as the UN Security Council or the North Atlantic Treaty Organization (NATO), does not exist, most likely because no consistently effective, forcible, response by such actors is available to threats of war. The slow-motion reaction to the situation in the Darfur region of the Sudan is too often what results. Contrast this with the international reaction to the emergence of a new Ebola virus, severe acute respiratory syndrome (SARS) epidemic, or the avian influenza or how rapidly the management of the international economic system has been mobilized to deal with a serious breakdown in a country such as Brazil, Mexico, or Indonesia.

This makes it more disturbing that multilateralism has been under a significant assault in recent years from the United States. Without vigorous American participation it is unlikely that the credibility and feasibility of international reactions to potential and actual outbreaks of fighting can continue to grow. Serious concern arose in 2005 in some quarters about the prospects for European integration because of the rejection by some countries of the proposed constitution for the European Union.

If the trends on wars are down, then perhaps there is no reason to worry. Alas, other trends are not so comforting. One is the slow but steadily detectable preparations in China and the United States for a possible future confrontation and war. China's military modernization is continuing rapidly and it is based, more than anything else, on preparing for a possible war with the United States. Meanwhile, the United States has shifted the central focus of its national security strategy to East Asia, is altering the general deployments of its forces abroad accordingly, and is knitting together a web of contacts in Asia that look much like plans to resurrect the containment doctrine, focused this time on China. All this is taking place despite the vast and beneficial U.S.-Chinese interactions that are so often reported in the media, the rising interdependence of the two societies, and the retreat in both countries from the antagonism each displayed toward the other on a variety of matters.

Another trend is the growing use of advanced technology to make wars less painful. This is being done primarily by crippling the enemy's command and communications structure, logistics, and transportation. It is a deliberate effort to make war more tolerable, for both sides. One possible outcome would be that the willingness to use force to suppress outbreaks of fighting will rise because using force will become less painful. That would presumably enhance the management of violent conflict in international politics.

Another possible outcome would move in a different direction. What if advanced technology is fast turning war into a much more usable tool of statecraft? That might begin to cut back on the rejection of war as a policy instrument. If the use of force would become more acceptable for system management by, or on behalf of, the international community, why wouldn't it become more attractive for individual governments as a tool?

Yet another possibility, and the one that is currently most widely discussed, is that advanced technology will continue to enlarge the possible harm that terrorists, or single individuals, can do to even the most powerful of countries. When it comes to the potential use by terrorists or other small groups of weapons of mass destruction, harm on the scale of a war can occur without a war.

What these possibilities suggest is that the decline in the incidence and destructiveness of warfare will not necessarily continue indefinitely. Periods of decline in war have existed before, followed by a return to warfare on a notable scale. As noted earlier in this book, a number of analysts think contemporary East Asia is a potential replay of Europe in the late nineteenth and early twentieth centuries—phenomenal national development in a number of countries culminating in a period of ferocious military struggle.

The concept of managing peace and security at both the global and regional levels needs continued development so as to provide the best possible chance of continuing to shrink the incidence and relevance of war in modern life. It also seems necessary to pursue peace and security on at least three levels simultaneously, keeping in mind that security on one level can be sought and even achieved while doing considerable harm to security on another. The result is a different but real kind of security dilemma. At the systemic level, a much more developed sense exists that the global and regional international system must be, and can be, managed for purposes of security. For avoiding, halting, and suppressing wars, governments have gradually assembled an array of management resources out of the ongoing byplay between theory and practice. This has been done in a pragmatic fashion in keeping with the constraints imposed by the preoccupation with autonomy and sovereignty, which is the core component of state security. States have been well served in this regard. That preoccupation has slowly yielded to the necessity for a degree of system management and the mounting pressure for more action to enhance societal security. As long as wars among states remain rare, priority must be given to building on the progress already made in enhancing the security of individuals and societies from the threats posed by internal warfare.

The right balance is yet to be found among the three levels, judging by the limitations of each of the strategies examined in this book, but significant progress has been made. Ultimately, the objective must be to do far better in the twenty-first century with regard to war than in the calamitous twentieth century. People and governments must never go through something like it again.

actors Participants in international politics that have a significant capacity to take action of importance to other participants. The most significant actors are governments and some of their major units (such as the U.S. Department of Defense). Other prominent actors are international organizations, peoples (such as the Palestinians), major corporations, and occasionally a particularly prominent and distinguished individual (such as Indian leader Mahatma Gandhi) (p. 3).

adjudication Reaching decisions, or settling issues, by using a formal legal process. In international politics that would include having an issue decided by an international tribunal, such as the world court (p. 177).

anarchy In international politics, a situation in which, politically, there is no supreme authority or government. The international system is anarchical because, for the most part, no system of government or supreme body of law consistently and reliably governs the behavior of the main actors—the states (p. 2).

arbitration Turning an issue over to a third party to make a decision that will be binding on the parties to the dispute. This is seldom used in international politics, particularly on important issues (p. 177).

arms control Individual or cooperative steps by governments to limit or reduce the costs and other harmful consequences of the continued existence of arms. Arms control seeks to avoid unauthorized uses of weapons, limit arms races, eliminate unusually destructive weapons, prevent environmental damage from weapons, control proliferation of selected kinds of weapons, and so on. The emphasis on limiting the consequences of arms instead of eliminating them distinguishes arms control from disarmament (p. 85).

autonomy The condition of being self-controlled, not answering to any superior authority, in most or all of one's activities or in a clearly designated and important sphere of activity. In international politics states claim broad autonomy, restricted mainly when they give their consent. Autonomy is very attractive, a major objective of political activity, particularly in international politics and in many civil conflicts (pp. 2, 3).

best alternative to a negotiated agreement (BATNA) A term in the Roger Fisher approach to negotiations identifying the alternative against which each party will evaluate a proposed settlement of a dispute. When its BATNA is better than the proposed settlement, a party should reject the settlement. Therefore, a negotiator must keep his own and the opponent's BATNA in mind in crafting a possible agreement (p. 181).

biological weapons Weapons that inflict harm on people, animals, or plants by using organisms or toxins created by organisms. These weapons may be lethal, damaging, or incapacitating (p. 94).

bipolarity A term, realist in character, developed in the Cold War to describe the international distribution of power in that era and in similar international systems. That is, two great powers are clearly much more powerful than any others. The power of each is primarily contained, or balanced, by the power of the other. The bipolar distribution is the dominant determinant of political-security relations in that system (p. 49).

blitzkrieg A German term—lightning war—for the style of fighting German troops used in the early years of World War II. Armored units with close air support penetrated enemy lines and ranged widely to disrupt the opposing forces, producing rapid victories (p. 67).

chemical weapons Primarily weapons that use poisonous gases to kill, damage, or incapacitate. They can be used against people, plants, and animals (p. 94).

CNN effect The determination of whether an issue, problem, or other situation in international politics receives serious attention by how it is covered in the major news media. The claim is made that key mass media, by how they cover the news, often determine the agenda in international politics and thus whether action is taken on particular matters. Whether this is true is a subject of debate (p. 240).

coercive diplomacy Use of threats of harm by an international politics actor to shape the behavior of other actors. The concept encompasses both deterrence and compellence (p. 77).

common security A term highlighted by Soviet leader Mikhail S. Gorbachev and others in asserting that true security among nations can be achieved only collectively and not through individual efforts of states to gain security for themselves (p. 162).

complex multilateralism Carrying ordinary multilateralism to a higher, more involved, level of community by having a general principle (or principles) apply equally to all member nations, building a higher sense of community among the members, and practicing diffuse reciprocity among them. The West developed numerous examples of this during the Cold War, all of which are still operating (p. 154).

democratic peace theory The assertion that democratic governments almost never go to war with each other, plus one or more explanations for this that refer, in some way, to their being democracies. That is, the nature of the governments is considered responsible for the phenomenon. The main implication is that spreading democracy is a major way, perhaps the ultimate way, to promote peace (p. 99).

diffuse reciprocity A willingness to reach an agreement without getting all that one believes is properly due because the rest can be gained from future interactions that the agreement will facilitate. For example, instead of insisting on my share now, I compromise to make an agreement possible in the belief that I will do better later, at least partly because others appreciate the sacrifice I am making (p. 157).

direct deterrence When an actor seeks to keep from being attacked by threatening a potential attacker with a serious military response, either in mounting a defense or in retaliation (pp. 79, 80).

distribution of power The relative power of the major states in an international system, with power typically calculated primarily in military terms. Many analysts and officials see the distribution of power as the key to how states relate to each other; it shapes much of their behavior (p. 37).

doctrine of the offensive The view that victory on the battlefield would go to the forces that attacked in the most resolute and determined way, pressing forward against all obstacles. Associated with French military thinking in particular, prior to and early in World War I (p. 66).

escalation Expansion of a conflict to a higher level of intensity—from verbal insults to fighting, from limited to more extensive fighting, and so on. The term came into wide use during the Cold War in discussions of deterrence and arms control. Escalation may be deliberately generated or emerge in an unplanned, nondeliberate way. Many approaches to security seek to prevent, or potentially reverse, instances of conflict escalation (p. 86).

ethnic cleansing The practice of violently homogenizing a region ethnically by driving out, or killing, members of unwanted ethnic groups. It was used by several groups in the 1990s as Yugoslavia disintegrated. The term came to be widely applied to ethnically rooted warfare over territory and is now often associated with genocide (p. 217).

extended deterrence An effort by a government or governments to deter an attack on another country by threatening force in response either as retaliation or in defense of that country. As a promise to bear serious costs on behalf of another without being initially attacked oneself, extended deterrence is difficult to make credible so it can be a complex activity to undertake (pp. 79, 80).

failed states States that have not established, or have lost, the ability to effectively rule their territories and societies. The failure may be evident in successful secessions, widespread secession efforts, a breakdown in law and order, lack of legitimacy in the eyes of the citizens, a deterioration in performance of standard government functions, and so on (p. 47).

first-strike capability The ability to attack so effectively that no serious military response can be made. In deterrence theory, having a first-strike capability negates an opponent's deterrence. A deterrer must avoid letting the opponent gain this capability or deterrence could fail, while a potential attacker sees acquiring such a capability as ideal (pp. 80, 84).

flexible response A deterrence strategy in which an attack at any level is to be met with a stout, hopefully successful, military response at that level denying the opponent his objective. The goal is to deter an attack or, if one occurs, escalation to a higher level of violence by being able to fight successfully at every level. This was popular in the United States in the 1960s and was revived in the 1980s and again in the twenty-first century (pp. 82, 91).

free riding Achievement of a desired goal largely through the efforts of others while avoiding much effort oneself. In an alliance, for example, this would mean leaving the fighting to achieve the common objective largely or entirely to others while sharing in the benefits of the victory (p. 5).

global security management system An arrangement for deliberately taking steps to create and maintain a reasonably safe and secure global international system. The system could include norms and rules of behavior, international institutions, a great-power concert, controls over weapons proliferation, and so on (p. 86).

great-power concert An agreement among the most powerful members of an international system to act collectively to manage the system, usually to restrain competition among themselves and prevent serious disturbances in the system by other members. The arrangement can be informal or officially established by treaty and embodied in an international organization (such as the United Nations Security Council) (p. 109).

hard power A relatively recent term for distinguishing military power from important "soft" forms of power. Hard power is the ability to physically coerce others and the associated ability to coerce them by threats of force. In a realist view, hard power is central to the conduct of international politics (p. 38).

hegemon An actor with far more power, particularly hard power, than any other actor or probable coalition in an international system. Usually a hegemon is a single government, but it could also be an overwhelmingly powerful and highly cooperative group of governments. The United States is currently considered a hegemon in the global system and several regional systems (p. 41).

hegemonic stability The stability and security provided for an international system, directly and indirectly, by a hegemon. The hegemon is well placed to deter challenges to its position, restrain fighting or other destabilizing behavior by others, and foster extensive cooperation and other forms of system management. With confidence in system stability and security, other members may cooperate more widely, reducing rivalries and conflicts. The implication, however, is that once a hegemon weakens, system management becomes less effective and confidence in it lessens. Therefore competition and rivalry will grow, with declining security and stability that can culminate in warfare (pp. 43, 171).

high-context culture Raymond Cohen's model of societies, in which negotiations (and mediation) cannot be conducted in a problem-focused, narrowly rational fashion. Instead, attention must be paid to proper negotiating behavior that is, in turn, linked to broader social norms on being polite, paying proper respect, allowing others to save face, and the like. This often means playing down confrontation, avoiding expressions of open disagreement, refraining from open haggling, and so on (p. 191).

horizontal proliferation In arms control and security, the spreading of particular weapons systems (such as weapons of mass destruction) to additional governments or other actors. Major arms control efforts have been devoted to preventing horizontal proliferation (pp. 80, 95).

hot lines Communication links between governments constantly available for immediate use in the event of, or to prevent, serious crises. First developed for use between the United States and Soviet Union during the Cold War (p. 86).

humanitarian impulse The concept that there is a rising and spreading concern for the welfare of human beings in the contemporary era. This impulse is activated by instances of grievous harm, particularly outright physical harm, being inflicted and can lead to great pressure for direct action by the observers or action by others—governments, international organizations—to end the harm and assist those harmed (p. 219).

hurtful stalemate A situation in a conflict when the parties have reached a stalemate: Neither is likely to give up, they can continue inflicting suffering on each other, and they are tired of the suffering. Analysts have suggested that under these conditions the parties are most likely to negotiate seriously, mediation is most likely to be welcomed and work effectively, and other outside intervention to end a conflict is most likely to be successful (p. 196).

hydrogen weapons Weapons based on inducing the process of fusion of hydrogen atoms, which releases enormous energy in various forms. Fusion is the basic process in stars (p. 94).

integration The development by a set of governments and societies of such a high level of community, collective decision making, and collective governance that, in important ways and on many important matters, they no longer operate independently. They either make decisions on those matters together or closely coordinate their separate decision making. As a result, they eliminate international politics, as traditionally conceived, among themselves. This can be sought for various purposes, particularly to enhance peace and security (p.163).

intergovernmental organizations (IGOs) Organizations formed by governments, that are then the members, to carry out various tasks. Found in all areas of international politics, some function relatively independently of the members. In others, the main decisions and actions are taken by the member governments either individually or collectively. Examples include the United Nations, International Monetary Fund, and Association of Southeast Asian Nations (p. 154).

international civil society A term for the growing network of nongovernmental organizations that act, domestically and internationally, to promote the best interest, as they see it, of the world community. It derives from the concept of civil society—the dense web of private networks and activities present in successful democracies that makes them vigorous and powerful political communities and societies. Analysts see international civil society as making a similar contribution in the international political system (p. 236).

international diplomatic culture The existence of such a culture is suggested to explain how diplomats may transcend the cultures in which they were raised. They may be socialized by advanced education, training, experience, and service overseas into a cosmopolitan culture of diplomats and other international affairs specialists and practitioners. The fear that negotiations can be distorted by cultural differences would not apply when they were involved (p. 191).

leviathan Thomas Hobbes argued that without a powerful central authority over society, a leviathan, people engage in selfish behavior leading to violent conflict, producing insecurity and a dismal existence. Lack of a leviathan is cited to explain why, under anarchy, international politics has been competitive and violent—that is, why it is so Hobbesian. In turn, this explains why a hegemon can produce peace and security (p. 46).

low-context culture The opposite of the high-context culture model. The low culture approves of moving negotiations into clashing proposals and bargaining relatively quickly. It also endorses confrontation, strong expressions of disagreement, open bargaining, and haggling over compromises as part of an aggressive, pragmatic search for a deal that resolves or shelves an issue. This captures much of what a Western negotiating style often displays (p. 191).

massive retaliation A strategy for nuclear deterrence pursued in the 1950s by the US government and typically adopted by governments when they have small nuclear arsenals and confront other nuclear weapons states. Prompt and massive nuclear retaliation is threatened in response to a direct attack or relatively quickly in response to an attack on a friendly or allied nation (p. 90).

mediation Efforts by an outside party to facilitate negotiation by the parties to a conflict so as to either suspend or resolve it. Mediation in international politics can be conducted by many different kinds of actors and can include a wide variety of activities (pp. 177, 192).

Multiple Independently Targeted Reentry Vehicles (MIRVs) The technical name for several warheads carried on a single ballistic missile that can be aimed at individual, widely separated targets. MIRVing allows a single missile to destroy numerous targets in a short time, which is ideal for a first-strike attack. A MIRVed missile is also an ideal target for a first-strike attack because destroying it destroys a number of missiles at once. Both make MIRVed missiles potentially destabilizing because they invite launching attacks, so strategic arms control measures thus have put special emphasis on reducing these kinds of missiles and warheads (p. 92).

multipolarity The distribution of power when three or more major states are roughly equivalent in power, unlike a bipolar or unipolar (hegemonic) power distribution. Some analysts believe multipolarity promotes state security by leading to coalitions to prevent a single dominant power from emerging to threaten everyone. Others see it as prone to generating conflict and war and thus harmful to security on all three levels (p. 49).

mutual assured destruction (MAD) A term applied to both a strategy and a strategic relationship during the Cold War. In a MAD strategic relationship the hostile parties are capable of destroying each other either by attacking or in retaliation for being attacked, and this is the basis for their security relationship. (Nonhostile states may be able to destroy each other without this dominating their security relations.) A MAD strategy seeks to prevent a nuclear war by deliberately keeping both parties vulnerable to destruction. It requires negating efforts by either side to escape from MAD (p. 83).

nation A large group that feels strongly that it is alike in important ways, such as ethnicity, history, language, culture, and shared territory. A nation resists being absorbed completely into a larger society and culture, and when pieces of it are located in different states it may seek to coalesce into a single community (p. 3).

nationalism A passionate commitment to one's nation, often including a belief that it is superior to other groups. Nationalism is usually strongly supportive of a nation's government and state or, when they do not exist, in support of creating them. As such it has been the most powerful force in international politics since its emergence in revolutionary France in 1792–1815, affecting the creation of nation-states, the dissolution of empires and other states, and the conduct of many wars (p. 3).

nation-state Technically, a state closely identified with a particular nation that is the dominant component of its population. However, the term is widely used in international politics to refer to those governmental units generally recognized as sovereign independent members of the international system, even though many contain multiple nations within their borders and may even be reflections of nondominant nations (p. 3).

negotiation The exchange of views between parties to a conflict, usually reiterated over a period of time, with the intent of developing a jointly accepted solution. Usually negotiation involves direct meetings between representatives of the parties at some point, and often these are when the crucial interactions take place (p. 177).

nongovernmental organizations (NGOs) Organizations established and operated to take direct action in, or otherwise have an impact on, international politics but in which governments are not members. (Normally, the members are also not business entities.) NGOs may operate domestically, seeking to affect foreign policy making and implementation, or across national boundaries to affect other societies, or transnationally. They have become increasingly visible and important in recent decades (p. 154).

nuclear proliferation The spread of nuclear weapons to additional governments (horizontal proliferation) or an increase in the total numbers of the weapons held by a particular government (vertical proliferation). Since the Cold War, vertical proliferation of nuclear weapons has halted or been significantly reversed in half of the nuclear armed states, while horizontal proliferation has continued slowly in the face of strong international opposition (p. 86).

oligopoly Domination and management of an economic sector and its market by a small number of cooperating firms, allowing them to relax their competition and advance their interests, often at the expense of other firms and the customers the sector serves. An oligopoly may exist in international economic sectors, and the use of cooperation to ease the burden of competition is analogous to the action of forming and operating a great-power concert (p. 113).

peacebuilding The effort to create the basis for an effective political system, society, and economy that can meet citizen needs, to prevent future outbreaks of civil war in a country where that has been a serious problem. Peacebuilding involves assistance, advice, training, and at times initial administration of the country by external elements—intergovernmental organizations, nongovernmental organizations, and national governments (p. 257).

peace enforcement The use of force or the threat of force by outsiders to compel the parties to a conflict to behave in accordance with an agreement the parties have adopted to cease fighting (p. 230).

peace imposition The use of force or the threat of force by outsiders to compel the parties to a conflict to cease fighting even though one or more of them would prefer to continue fighting and to force those who made gains via the fighting to abandon them (p. 231).

peacekeeping The use of outside forces to assist parties to a conflict that have agreed to stop fighting to live up to their agreement. This may include such activities as providing buffer forces, maintaining neutral zones, investigating incidents, promoting negotiations between the parties, and maintaining order and security (p. 209).

people A group that feels the members have fundamental things in common. When the group is large enough it is typically called a nation. When it is small it may be referred to as a tribe or ethnic group. Membership in a people is frequently a core element in an individual's personal identity (p. 3).

pluralistic security community In international politics, a group of states and societies that have developed a community and interrelationships to the extent that it is hard for the members to imagine going to war with each other. Thus they have no fear of war in their relations. This community is pluralistic because member states and societies remain separate and independent, not integrated in a single society and political system (p. 158).

preemptive attack An attack in anticipation of being attacked. An actor expects to be attacked and decides to initiate the conflict by inflicting the first blow, often in hopes of spoiling or sharply reducing the attack it anticipated. During the Cold War, great concern arose that, with survival at risk, in a crisis the superpowers or other nuclear armed states would turn to preemptive attacks, eroding the effectiveness of deterrence (p. 83).

preventive diplomacy The effort by outsiders, particularly intergovernmental organizations, to intervene in a conflict situation, in international politics or a domestic dispute, before it has become so intense as to lead to fighting. Some analysts have proposed that such interventions include the use of force, when necessary, to forestall a war. This would sharply enhance the international management of peace and security but is such a radical step it has not been readily undertaken (pp. 196, 224, 240).

preventive war A war initiated by an actor because it believes that some time in the future it will be attacked and wishes to deal with the threat before it reaches that point. This differs from a preemptive attack because no immediate preparations for an attack have been made by the target. One U.S. justification for attacking Iraq in 2003 was that, left alone, Iraq would eventually take steps that would threaten the United States and its allies in the Middle East (p. 51).

rational decision approach A way to analyze decision making that assumes the decision maker is rational; that is, will assess ways of dealing with a situation by comparing them in terms of their anticipated costs and benefits, risks, and chances of success and will select a course of action that offers the best payoff. This approach can be used to explain the decisions of leaders and governments, or it can be used to offer advice on what the decisions should be or how they should be made (p. 182).

realism The name of one of the most influential schools of thought about international politics. In the realist view, anarchy and the competition of states in international politics inevitably produce insecurity, particularly among the most powerful states, and inhibit cooperation. They are ultimately responsible for the problem of war. Thus cooperative approaches to the problem of insecurity and war will not work over the long run and states should conduct their affairs accordingly (p. 2).

Revolution in Military Affairs (RMA) The label for the impact on military effectiveness, when properly utilized, of three interrelated changes: a vast improvement in reconnaissance and surveillance capabilities, the information revolution, and steadily improving accuracy in weapons systems. The RMA has greatly enhanced the relative military power of the United States and a few other governments in the past two decades (p. 70).

rule of law A well-established legal system that operates properly and to which everyone in society is ultimately responsible, particularly government officials. An effective legal system coordinates expectations, allowing much greater cooperation among people, and provides a greatly enhanced sense of security. Thus one target of peacebuilding efforts is the establishment or reinstallation of rule of law (p. 268).

scarcity Lack of sufficient amounts of valuable things to meet everyone's needs and desires. In international politics, governments and their societies are inevitably at odds over the distribution of power, status, wealth, resources, and other things that are never sufficiently available to meet the demand for them (p. 4).

security dilemma The situation that results when efforts by a government to build up its military strength to enhance its security provokes fears in other governments about their security, leading them to build up their military strength. As a result, everyone remains concerned about security after having made a greater effort, and because they made a greater effort, to enhance it. Security dilemmas also are involved when steps to enhance security at one level produce reductions in security at another (p. 4).

societal security Security for citizens of a state. In international politics this includes security for citizens from harm inflicted by outsiders and security from harm to them that could be inflicted by their state while dealing with outsiders. Increasingly it also includes security from harm inflicted by the state or other citizens when the society is improperly operated, because the actual and potential effects of badly operated societies have become a concern in international politics and, if they become sufficiently disturbing, may lead to international intervention (p. 8).

soft power In contrast to the power to coerce, this is the power to influence and persuade. Sources of such power include prestige, moral authority, respect, effective leadership in building cooperative endeavors, experience in managing interactions, agile and creative use of international organizations, and the like. Soft power is seen as increasingly important with growing interdependence, particularly by liberalist analysts (p. 38).

sovereign A legal status of being the dominant authority over a defined territory and the people who reside there. The status is primarily secured for a government by its being recognized as such by other sovereign units (pp. 2, 3).

sphere of influence An area of dominance created around a state that is considerably more powerful than its neighbors and which a state with a strong power projection capability can create even some distance away from its immediate neighborhood. Within its sphere of influence the dominant state expects to exercise considerable influence over other governments' decisions and to exclude other powerful states from having major influence there (p. 118).

stability-instability paradox The concern, raised in the Cold War, that effective mutual nuclear deterrence to preclude a nuclear war would leave the superpowers feeling free to fight at lower levels without fear of escalation. Stability at the highest level would produce instability at lower levels. This kind of analysis can be extended to other situations. For instance, during the Cold War superpower avoidance of direct warfare led them to vigorously support client states that then carried their own competition to greater levels, including wars (pp. 80, 101).

state A political and administrative entity that controls a specific territory and the people residing there. It is recognized by other states as being in control and deserving of treatment as a state. In a legal sense, states are the preeminent actors in international politics; their governments are the preeminent actors in a political sense (p. 2).

state security The physical safety and survival of a state and its government in the face of possible threats from outside or inside, including retention of its ability to operate as an autonomous actor in international politics (p. 7).

state-making Historically, the process through which states as centralized accumulations of power and authority were constructed, often over strong opposition from lower level units of society and from external contenders for rule over the territories involved. State-making was typically a long and violent process. Analysts stress that in much of the world, particularly Africa, the process is ongoing and continues to be violent (p. 287).

Strategic Arms Limitation Talks (SALT) The series of superpower negotiations during the 1970s designed to bring the nuclear arms race under some control, stabilize mutual nuclear deterrence, and reduce chances of nuclear war from accidents, misperceptions, nuclear proliferation, and other developments. Progress was limited, but the talks were important for helping turn Cold War deterrence into a degree of global security management and providing experience on détente that was later useful in the steps that ended the Cold War (pp. 80, 95).

strategic surprise An unanticipated development that has fundamental implications for a competitive relationship in international politics. In military terms, it could be a surprise attack that virtually determines the outcome of a war between states (Adolf Hitler's blitzkrieg attack on France). In political terms, it could be the sudden collapse of a major ally of one side in a hostile relationship (the collapse of the Soviet Union for North Korea) or the sudden shift of a major ally toward neutrality or hostility (the shift in relations with Iran for the United States because of the Iranian revolution) (p. 63).

strategy A plan for achieving a specified objective, typically when significant obstacles or opposition must be overcome for success (p. 39).

structural realism A version of the realist approach developed in the 1970s and 1980s that focuses on the system level to explain much of international politics. This includes seeing anarchy and system structure as crucial in determining how much of international politics operates, playing down the role of factors at other levels of analysis (p. 40).

systemic security The security of an international system, in terms of such things as the stability of its power distribution structure, the effectiveness of system security management arrangements, the likelihood of great-power or systemwide wars, the frequency of disruptions in the system that can produce warfare, and the incidence of intense conflicts among states that might turn into warfare (p. 7).

systemic wars Wars that involve all the great powers and normally are the ultimate determinant of the future structure and management of the system. The stakes are enormous and the most powerful governments are deeply involved. As a result, systemic wars are long and destructive. Often the fighting involves a series of wars before a decisive result is achieved, so a systemic war may be spread over several decades (p. 28).

Track II diplomacy The practice of using interactions among people who are not officials, drawn from the parties to a serious conflict, to contribute to developing a peaceful, negotiated settlement. Participants may include ordinary citizens, experts, retired officials, and people close to officials. Activities range from bridge building across hostilities, to establishing cooperative projects and habits of interaction, to considering possible peace proposals and unofficially floating ideas for a settlement (p. 193).

two-level game A model of international negotiations that sees negotiators as participating in a bargaining game against each other in designing a possible agreement and then engaging in another bargaining game with people they represent over what sort of agreement is acceptable. Requirements for success in one game shape what is needed to be successful in the other, greatly complicating the conduct of negotiations (p. 185).

unacceptable damage The term for, in the abstract, what must be credibly threatened to deter an opponent from attacking. The prospective damage must be unacceptably high to him so that he chooses not to attack. Because what constitutes unacceptable damage varies with the opponent, the situation, what is at stake, and so on, this is a concept hard to put into specific terms (p. 80).

vertical proliferation The expansion of existing arsenals of weapons of mass destruction. It stands in contrast with horizontal proliferation, in which the weapons are spreading to additional governments (pp. 80, 95).

Aall, Pamela. "NGOs, Conflict Management, and Peacekeeping," in *Peacekeeping and Conflict Resolution,* ed. Tom Woodhouse and Oliver Ramsbotham. London, England: Frank Cass, 2000, 121–141.

Adler, Emanuel, and Michael Barnett, eds. *Security Communities.* Cambridge, England: Cambridge University Press, 1998.

Allen, Dana H. "NATO's Balkan Interventions," *Adelphi Papers,* No. 347. London, England: International Institute for Strategic Studies, 2002.

Bercovitch, Jacob, ed. *Resolving International Conflicts: The Theory and Practice of Mediation.* Boulder, Colo.: Lynne Rienner, 1996.

Betts, Rickard K., ed. *Conflict after the Cold War: Arguments on Causes of War and Peace,* updated 2nd ed. New York: Pearson, Longman, 2005.

Biermann, Wolfgang, and Martin Vadset. *UN Peacekeeping in Trouble: Lessons Learned from the Former Yugoslavia.* Aldershop, England: Ashgate Publishing, 1998.

Biersteker, Thomas J. "State, Sovereignty, and Territory," in *Handbook of International Relations,* ed. Walter Carlsnaes, Thomas Risse, and Beth A. Simmons. Thousand Oaks, Calif.: SAGE Publications, 2001, 157–176.

Blair, Bruce G. "Keeping Presidents in the Nuclear Dark" (Episode #1: The Case of the Missing "Permissive Action Links"), Bruce Blair's Nuclear Column, February 14, 2004, Center for Defense Information, available at www.cdi.org.

Bloch, Ivan. *The Future of War.* New York: Doubleday and McClure, 1899.

Boutros-Ghali, Boutros. *An Agenda for Peace,* 2nd ed. N.Y.: United Nations Department of Public Information, 1995.

Boutros-Ghali, Boutros. "Empowering the United Nations," *Foreign Affairs* (Winter 1992–1993): 89–102.

Brown, Michael, Sean M. Lynn-Jones, and Steven E. Miller, eds. *The Perils of Anarchy: Contemporary Realism and International Security: An International Security Reader.* Cambridge, Mass.: MIT Press, 1995.

Buzan, Barry. *People, States, and Fear: An Agenda for International Security Studies in the Post–Cold War Era.* London, England: Harvester Wheatsheaf, 1991.

Buzan Barry, Ole Waever, and Japp de Wilde. *Security: A New Framework for Analysis.* Boulder, Colo.: Lynne Rienner, 1997.

Byman, Daniel, and Stephen Van Evera. "Why They Fight: Hypotheses on the Causes of Contemporary Deadly Conflict," *Security Studies* 7 (Spring 1998): 1–50.

Cahill, Kevin M., ed. *Preventive Diplomacy: Stopping Wars before They Start,* rev. ed. New York: Routledge, 2000.

Call, Charles T., and William Stanley. "Protecting the People: Public Security Choices after Civil Wars," *Global Governance* 7 (April-June 2001): 151–172.

Caplan, Richard. "A New Trusteeship? The International Administration of War-Torn Territories," *Adelphi Papers,* No. 341. London, England: International Institute for Strategic Studies, 2002.

Carpenter, Ted Galen, and Doug Bandow. *The Korean Conundrum: America's Troubled Relations with North and South Korea.* New York: Palgrave Macmillan, 2004.

Chanaa, Jane. "Security Sector Reform: Issues, Challenges, and Prospects," *Adelphi Papers,* No. 344. London, England: International Institute for Strategic Studies, 2002.

Chyrssochoou, Dimitris N. *Theorizing European Integration.* Thousand Oaks, Calif.: SAGE Publications, 2001.

Cirincione, Joseph, ed. *Repairing the Regime: Preventing the Spread of Weapons of Mass Destruction.* New York: Routledge, 2000.

Claude, Inis. *Swords into Plowshares,* 4th ed. New York: Random House, 1971.

Cohen, Raymond. "Language and Conflict Resolution: The Limits of English," *International Studies Review* 3 (Spring 2001): 25–51.

Cohen, Raymond. *Negotiating across Cultures,* rev. ed. Washington, D.C.: United States Institute of Peace Press, 1997.

Cordesman, Anthony H. *The Iran-Iraq War and Western Security.* London, England: Janes, 1987.

Cordesman, Anthony H. *The Iraq War: Strategy, Tactics, and Military Lessons.* Washington, D.C.: Center for Strategic and International Studies Press, 2003.

Cortright, David. "Incentive Strategies for Preventing Conflict," in *The Price of Peace: Incentives and International Conflict of Peace: Incentives and International Conflict Resolution,* ed. David Cortright. Lanham, Md.: Roman and Littlefield, 1997.

Cortright, David, ed. *The Price of Peace: Incentives and International Conflict Resolution.* Lanham, Md.: Rowman and Littlefield, 1997.

Cousens, Elizabeth M., and Charles K. Cater. *Toward Peace in Bosnia: Implementing the Dayton Accords.* Boulder, Colo.: Lynne Rienner, 2001.

Cousens, Elizabeth M., and Chetan Kumar, eds. *Peacebuilding as Politics: Cultivating Peace in Fragile Societies.*Boulder, Colo.: Lynner Rienner, 2001.

Crocker, Chester A., Fen Osler Hampson, and Pamela Aall, eds. *Herding Cats: Multiparty Mediation in a Complex World.* Washington, D.C.: United States Institute of Peace Press, 1999.

Crocker, Chester A., Fen Osler Hampson, and Pamela Aall, eds. *Managing Global Chaos: Sources of and Responses to International Conflict.* Washington, D.C.: United States Institute of Peace Press, 1996.

Crocker, Chester A., Fen Osler Hampson, and Pamela Aall. *Taming Intractable Conflicts: Mediation in the Hardest Cases.* Washington, D.C.: United States Institute of Peace Press, 2004.

Crocker, Chester A., Fen Osler Hampson, and Pamela Aall, eds. *Turbulent Peace: the Challenges of Managing International Conflict.* Washington, D.C.: United States Institute of Peace Press, 2001.

Cronin, Bruce. *Community under Anarchy: Transnational Identity and the Evolution of Cooperation* New York: Columbia University Press, 1999.

Daalder, Ivo H. *Getting to Dayton: The Making of America's Bosnia Policy.* Washington, D.C.: Brookings Institution Press, 2000.

Daalder, Ivo H., and Michael E. O'Hanlon. *Winning Ugly: NATO's War to Save Kosovo.* Washington, D.C.: Brookings Institution Press, 2000.

Dandeker, Christopher, and James Gow. "Military Culture and Strategic Peacekeeping," *Small Wars and Insurgencies* 10 (Autumn 2000): 58–79.

Daniel, Donald C. F., and Bradd C. Hayes. *Coercive Inducement and the Containment of International Crises.* Washington, D.C.: United States Institute of Peace Press, 1999.

Daniel, Donald C. F., and Bradd C. Hayes, eds. *Beyond Traditional Peacekeeping.* New York: St. Martin's Press, 1995.

Deutsch, Karl W., Sidney A. Burrell, and Robert A. Kann. *Political Community and the North Atlantic Area.* Princeton: Princeton University Press, 1957.

Diehl, Paul F. "Forks in the Road: Theoretical and Policy Concerns for 21st Century Peacekeeping," *Global Society* 14 no. 3 (2000): 337–360.

Diehl, Paul F. *International Peacekeeping.* Baltimore: Johns Hopkins University Press, 1994.

Dinan, Desmond. *Ever Closer Union: An Introduction to European Integration,* 3rd ed. Boulder, Colo.: Lynne Rienner, 2005.

Dougherty, James E., and Robert L. Pfaltzgraff Jr. *Contending Theories of International Relations: A Comprehensive Survey,* 5th ed. New York: Longman, 2001.

Downs, George W., ed. *Collective Security beyond the Cold War.* Ann Arbor: University of Michigan Press, 1994.

Doyle, Michael. *Ways of War and Peace: Realism, Liberalism, and Socialism.* New York: W. W. Norton, 1997.

Duffey, Tamara. "Cultural Issues in Contemporary Peacekeeping," in *Peacekeeping and Conflict Resolution,* ed. Tom Woodhouse and Oliver Ramsbotham. London, England: Frank Cass, 2000, 142–168.

Durch, William J., ed. *The Evolution of UN Peacekeeping.* New York: St. Martin's Press, 1993.

Evan, William M., ed. *War and Peace in an Age of Terrorism.* Boston: Pearson Education, 2006.

Fisher, Roger, Andrea S. Schneider, Elizabeth Borgwardt, and Brian Ganson. *Coping with International Conflict: A Systemic Approach to Influence in International Negotiation.* Upper Saddle River, N.J.: Prentice Hall, 1997.

Fisher, Roger, William Ury, and Bruce Patton. *Getting to Yes: Negotiating Agreement without Giving In,* 2nd ed. New York: Penguin Books, 1991.

Fitzduff, Nari, and Cheyanne Church, eds. *NGOs at the Table: Strategies for Influencing Policies in Areas of Conflict.* Lanham, Md.: Rowman and Littlefield, 2004.

Florini, Ann M. *The Third Force: The Rise of Transnational Civil Society.* Washington, D.C.: Carnegie Endowment for International Peace, 2000.

Forman, Shepard, and Stewart Patrick. *Good Intentions: Pledges of Aid for Postconflict Recovery.* Boulder, Colo.: Lynne Rienner, 2000.

Freedman, Lawrence. *The Evolution of Nuclear Strategy.* New York: St. Martin's Press, 1981.

Freedman, Lawrence, ed. *Strategic Coercion: Concepts and Cases.* New York: Oxford University Press, 1998.

Freedman, Lawrence, and Efraim Karsh. *The Gulf Conflict 1990–1991: Diplomacy and War in the New World Order.* Princeton: Princeton University Press, 1993.

Gaddis, John Lewis. "Great Illusions, the Long Peace, and the Future of the International System," in *The Long Postwar Peace: Contending Explanations and Projections,* ed. Charles W. Kegley Jr. New York: HarperCollins, 1991, 22–55.

Galtung, Johan. *Peace by Peaceful Means: Peace and Conflict, Development and Civilization.* Thousand Oaks, Calif.: SAGE Publications, 1996.

Garwin, Richard. *Nonlethal Technologies: Progress and Prospects.* New York: Council on Foreign Relations Press, 1999.

Ghobarah, Hazen, Paul Huth, and Bruce Russett. "Civil Wars Kill and Maim People—Long after the Shooting Stops," *American Political Science Review* 97 (May 2003): 189–202.

Gidron, Benjamin, Stanley N. Katz, and Yeheskel Hasenfeld. *Mobilizing for Peace: Conflict Resolution in Northern Ireland, Israel/Palestine, and South Africa.* Oxford, England: Oxford University Press, 2002.

Gilady, Lilach, and Bruce Russett. "Peacemaking and Conflict Resolution," in *Handbook of International Relations,* ed. Walter Carlsnaes, Thomas Risse, and Beth A. Simmons. Thousand Oaks, Calif.: SAGE Publications, 2001, 392–408.

Gill, Bates, and James Reilly. "Sovereignty, Intervention, and Peacekeeping: the View from Beijing," *Survival* 42 (Autumn 2000): 41–59.

Gilpin, Robert. *War and Change in World Politics.* New York: Cambridge University Press, 1981.

Global Civil Society. London, England: Oxford University Press, 2003 and other years.

Global Governance 10 (January-March 2004).

Goldblat, Josef. *Arms Control: The New Guide to Negotiations and Agreements,* 2nd ed. Thousand Oaks, Calif.: SAGE Publications, 2002.

Goodby, James E. "Conflict in Europe: The Case of Yugoslavia," in *Regional Conflicts: The Challenge to U.S.-Russian Cooperation,* ed. James E. Goodby. New York: Oxford University Press, 1995, 157–187.

Gordon, D. S., and F. H. Toase, eds. *Aspects of Peacekeeping.* London, England: Frank Cass, 2001.

Gurr, Ted Robert. "Ethnic Warfare on the Wane," *Foreign Affairs* 79 (May-June 2000): 52–64.

Gurr, Ted Robert. *Minorities at Risk: A Global View of Ethnopolitical Conflicts.* Washington, D.C.: United States Institute of Peace Press, 1993.

Gurr, Ted Robert. "Minorities, Nationalists, and Ethnopolitical Conflict," in *Managing Global Chaos: Sources and Responses to International Conflict,* ed. Chester A. Crocker and Fen Osler Hampson. Washington, D.C.: United States Institute of Peace Press, 1996, 53–77.

Gurr, Ted Robert. *People versus States: Minorities at Risk in the New Century.* Washington, D.C.: United States Institute of Peace Press, 2000.

Haass, Richard N. *Intervention: The Use of American Military Force in the Post-Cold War World.* Washington, D.C.: Carnegie Endowment for International Peace, 1994.

Halberstam, David. *War in a Time of Peace: Bush, Clinton, and the Generals.* New York: Touchstone, 2001.

Hampson, Fen Osler. *Nurturing Peace: Why Peace Settlements Succeed or Fail.* Washington, D.C.: United States Institute of Peace Press, 1996.

Hancock, Landon E. "To Act or Wait: A Two-Stage View of Ripeness," *International Studies Perspectives* 2 (May 2001): 195–205.

Hansen, Annika S. "From Congo to Kosovo: Civilian Police in Peace Operations," *Adelphi Papers,* No. 343. London, England: International Institute for Strategic Studies, 2002.

Harbom, Lotta. *States in Armed Conflict 2003.* Uppsala: Uppsala University, Department of Peace and Conflict Research, 2004.

Harris, Andrew, and Peter Dombrowski. "Military Collaboration with Humanitarian Organizations in Complex Emergencies," *Global Governance* 8 (April-June 2002): 155–178.

Hartzell, Caroline, Mathew Hoddie, and Donald Rothchild. "Stabilizing the Peace after Civil War: An Investigation of Some Key Variables," *International Organization* 55 (Winter 2001): 183–208.

Herrmann, David G. *The Arming of Europe and the Making of the First World War.* Princeton: Princeton University Press, 1996.

Heijmans, Annelies, Nicola Simmonds, and Hans van de Veen, eds. *Searching for Peace in Asia Pacific: An Overview of Conflict Prevention and Peacebuilding Activities.* Boulder, Colo.: Lynne Rienner, 2004.

Holbrooke, Richard C. *To End a War.* New York: Random House, 1998.

Holsti, Kalevi J. *Peace and War: Armed Conflicts and International Order 1648–1989.* New York: Cambridge University Press, 1991.

Hopmann, P. Terrence. "Bargaining and Problem Solving: Two Perspectives on International Negotiation," in *Turbulent Peace: The Challenges of Managing International Conflict,* ed. Chester A. Crocker, Fen Osler Hampson, and Pamela Aall. Washington, D.C.: United States Institute of Peace Press, 2002, 445–468.

Howard, Michael. *War in European History.* Oxford, England: Oxford University Press, 1976.

Ikenberry, John G. *After Victory: Institutions, Strategic Restraint, and the Building of Order after Major Wars.* Princeton: Princeton University Press, 2001.

International Institute for Strategic Studies. *Armed Conflict Database.* London, England: Europa Publications, updated regularly.

International Institute for Strategic Studies. *The Military Balance.* London: International Institute for Strategic Studies, published annually.

Jacoby, Wade. *The Enlargement of the European Union and NATO.* Cambridge, England: Cambridge University Press, 2004.

Jakobsen, Peter Viggo. *Western Use of Coercive Diplomacy after the Cold War.* New York: St. Martin's Press, 1998.

Jervis, Robert. "From Balance to Concert: A Study of International Security Cooperation," *World Politics* 18, no. 1 (1985): 58–79.

Jervis, Robert. *The Meaning of the Nuclear Revolution: Statecraft and the Prospect of Armageddon.* Ithaca: Cornell University Press, 1989.

Jett, Dennis C. *Why Peacekeeping Fails.* New York: St. Martin's Press, 1999.

Kagan, Robert. "How We Will Fight China," *Atlantic,* May-June 2005, 49–51, 54–55, 58, 60, 62, 64.

Kaiser, David. *Politics and War: European Conflict from Philip II to Hitler,* Cambridge, Mass.: Harvard University Press, 2000.

Kartchner, Kerry M. *Negotiating START: Strategic Arms Reduction Talks and the Quest for Strategic Stability.* New Brunswick, N.J.: Transaction, 1992.

Kaufmann, Chaim D. "When All Else Fails: Evaluating Population Transfers and Partition as Solutions to Ethnic Conflict," in *Civil Wars, Insecurity, and Intervention,* ed. Barbara F. Walter and Jack Snyder. New York: Columbia University Press, 1999, 221–260.

Keaney, Thomas A., and Eliot A. Cohen. *Gulf War Air Power Survey Summary Report.* Washington, D.C.: Government Printing Office, 1993.

Kegley, Charles W. Jr., and Gregory A. Raymond. *A Multipolar Peace.* New York: St. Martin's Press, 1994.

Keohane, Robert O. *After Hegemony: Cooperation and Discord in the World Political Economy.* Princeton: Princeton University Press, 1984.

Kissinger, Henry A. *White House Years.* Boston: Little Brown, 1979.

Kissinger, Henry A. *Years of Upheaval.* Boston: Little Brown, 1982.

Knock, Thomas J. *To End All Wars: Woodrow Wilson and the Quest for a New World Order.* Princeton: Princeton University Press, 1992.

Knorr, Klaus, and Patrick M. Morgan. *Strategic Military Surprise.* New Brunswick, N.J.: Transaction Books, 1983.

Kolodziej, Edward A. *A Force Profonde: The Power, Politics, and Promise of Human Rights.* Philadelphia: University of Pennsylvania Press, 2003.

Krasner, Stephen D. *Sovereignty: Organized Hypocrisy.* Princeton: Princeton University Press, 1999.

Krasner, Stephen D., ed. *International Regimes.* Ithaca: Cornell University Press, 1983.

Kriesberg, Louis. *Constructive Conflicts: From Escalation to Resolution,* 2nd ed. Lanham, Md.: Rowman and Littlefield, 2003.

Kugler, Jacek, and Douglas Lemke. *Parity and War.* Ann Arbor: University of Michigan Press, 1996.

Kupchan, Charles A., and Clifford A. Kupchan. "Concerts, Collective Security, and the Future of Europe," *International Security* 16, no. 1 (1991): 114–161.

Lake, David A., and Donald Rothchild. "Containing Fear: The Origins and Management of Ethnic Conflict," *International Security* 21 (Fall 1996): 41–75.

Lambeth, Benjamin S. *NATO's Air War For Kosovo: A Strategic and Operational Assessment.* Santa Monica: RAND, 2001.

Langewiesche, William. "Peace Is Hell," *Atlantic Monthly,* October 2001.

Larsen, Jeffrey A., ed. *Arms Control: Cooperative Security in a Changing Environment.* Boulder, Colo.: Lynne Rienner, 2002.

Layne, Christopher. "The Unipolar Illusion: Why New Great Powers Will Arise," *International Security* 17 (Spring 1993): 86–124

Lederach, John Paul. *Preparing for Peace: Conflict Transformation across Cultures.* Syracuse: Syracuse University Press, 1995

Lenin, Vladimir I. *Imperialism.* New York: International Press, 1939.

Levy, Jack S. "The Causes of War and the Conditions of Peace," in *Annual Review of Political Science,* vol. 1, ed. Nelson W. Polsby. Palo Alto, Calif.: Annual Reviews, 1998, 139–165.

Levy, Jack S. "Theories of Interstate and Intrastate War: A Levels-of-Analysis Approach," in *Turbulent Peace: The Challenges of Managing International Conflict,* ed. Chester A Crocker, Fen Osler Hampson, and Pamela Aall. Washington, D.C.: United States Institute of Peace Press, 2001, 3–27.

Levy, Jack S. "War and Peace," in *Handbook of International Relations,* ed. Walter Carlsnaes, Thomas Risse, and Beth A. Simmons. Thousand Oaks, Calif.: SAGE Publications, 2001, 350–368.

Lewis, David P. *The Road to Europe: History, Institutions, and Prospects of European Integration, 1945–1993.* New York: Peter Lang, 1993.

Lund, Michael. S. *Preventing Violent Conflicts: A Strategy for Preventive Diplomacy.* Washington, D.C.: United States Institute of Peace Press, 1996.

Luttwak, Edward N. "Give War a Chance," *Foreign Affairs* 78 (July-August 1999): 36–44.

Luttwak, Edward N. "The Curse of Inconclusive Intervention," in *Turbulent Peace: The Challenges of Managing International Conflict,* ed. Chester A. Crocker, Fen Osler Hampson, and Pamela Aall. Washington, D.C.: United States Institute for Peace Press, 2004, 265–272.

Malone, David M., ed. *The UN Security Council: From the Cold War to the 21st Century.* Boulder, Colo.: Lynne Rienner, 2004.

Mearsheimer, John J. *The Tragedy of Great Power Politics.* New York: W. W. Norton, 2001.

Miller, Benjamin. "Between Hot War and Cold Peace: States, Nations, and Great Powers." Manuscript.

Miller, Lynn H. "The Idea and Reality of Collective Security," *Global Governance* 5, no. 3 (1999): 303–332.

Miller, Steven E., ed. *Military Strategy and the Origins of the First World War: An International Security Reader.* Princeton: Princeton University Press, 1985.

Mills, Kurt. "Neo-Humanitarianism: The Role of International Humanitarian Norms and Organizations in Contemporary Conflict," *Global Governance* 11 (April-June 2005): 161–183.

Mirbagheri, Farid. *Cyprus and International Peacekeeping.* London, England: Hurst and Company, 1998.

Modelski, George. "Long Cycles and Global War," in *Handbook of War Studies,* ed. Manus I. Midlarsky. Ann Arbor: University of Michigan Press, 1989, 23–54.

Modelski, George. "Long Cycles of World Leadership," in *Contending Approaches to World System Analysis,* ed. William R. Thompson. Beverly Hills, Calif.: SAGE Publications, 1983.

Morgan, Patrick M. *Deterrence Now.* Cambridge, England: Cambridge University Press, 2003.

Morgan, Patrick M. "Multilateralism and Security: Prospects in Europe," in *Multilateralism Matters: The Theory and Praxis of an Institutional Form,* ed. John G. Ruggie. New York: Columbia University Press, 1993.

Morgenthau, Hans J. *Politics among Nations.* New York: Knopf, 1994.

Mueller, John. "A New Concert of Europe," *Foreign Policy* (Winter 1989-1990): 3–16.

Mueller, John. *Retreat from Doomsday: The Obsolescence of Major War.* New York: Basic Books, 1989.

Muller, Harold. "Security Cooperation," in *Handbook of International Relations,* ed. Walter Carlsnaes, Thomas Risse, and Beth A. Simmons. Thousand Oaks, Calif.: SAGE Publications, 2002, 369–391.

Nye, Joseph S., Jr. *Bound to Lead: The Changing Nature of American Power.* New York: Basic Books, 1990.

Nye, Joseph S., Jr. "Soft Power and Conflict Management in the Information Age," in *Turbulent Peace: The Challenges of Managing International Conflict,* ed. Chester A. Crocker, Fen Osler Hampson, and Pamela Aall. Washington, D.C.: United States Institute of Peace Press, 2001, 353–363.

Nye, Joseph S., Jr. *Understanding International Conflicts: An Introduction to Theory and History,* 3rd ed. New York: Longman, 2000.

Oberdorfer, Don. *The Two Koreas: A Contemporary History.* Reading, Mass.: Addison-Wesley, 1997.

Organski, A. F. K., and Jacek Kugler. *The War Ledger.* Chicago: University of Chicago, 1980.

Oye, Kenneth A., ed. *Cooperation under Anarchy.* Princeton: Princeton University Press, 1986.

Paris, Roland. "Peacebuilding and the Limits of Liberal Internationalism," *International Security* 22 (Fall 1997): 54–89.

Paris, Roland. "Wilson's Ghost: The Faulty Assumptions of Postconflict Peacebuilding," in *Turbulent Peace: The Challenges of Managing International Conflict,* ed. Chester A. Crocker, Fen Osler Hampson, and Pamela Aall. Washington, D.C.: United States Institute of Peace Press, 2001, 765–784.

Patrick, Stewart. "The Check Is in the Mail: Improving the Delivery and Coordination of Postconflict Assistance," *Global Governance* 6 (January-March 2000): 61–94.

Paul, T. V., James J. Wirtz, and Michael Fortmann, eds. *Balance of Power: Theory and Practice in the 21st Century.* Stanford: Stanford University Press, 2004.

Payne, Keith B. *The Fallacies of Cold War Deterrence and a New Direction.* Lexington: University Press of Kentucky, 2001.

Peceny, Mark, and William Stanley. "Liberal Social Reconstruction and the Resolution of Civil Wars in Central America," *International Organization* 55 (Winter 2001): 149–182.

Perito, Robert M. *Where Is the Lone Ranger When We Need Him? America's Search for a Postconflict Stability Force.* Washington, D.C.: United States Institute of Peace Press, 2004.

Persico, Joseph E. *Eleventh Month, Eleventh Day, Eleventh Hour: Armistice Day 1918, World War I, and Its Violent Climax.* New York: Random House, 2004.

Posen, Barry R. "The Security Dilemma and Ethnic Conflict," *Survival* 35, no. 1 (1993): 27–47.

Posen, Barry R. *The Sources of Military Doctrine: France, Britain, and Germany between the World Wars.* Ithaca: Cornell University Press, 1984.

Rasler, Karen A., and William R. Thompson. *War and State Making: The Shaping of Global Powers.* Boston: Unwin Hyman, 1989.

Ray, James Lee. *Democracy and International Conflict: An Evaluation of the Democratic Peace Proposition.* Columbia: University of South Carolina Press, 1995.

Ray, James Lee. "Does Democracy Cause Peace?" in *Annual Review of Political Science,* vol. 1, ed. Nelson W. Polsby. Palo Alto, Calif.: Annual Reviews, 1998, 27–46.

Reusse, Eberhard. *The Ills of Aid.* Chicago: University of Chicago Press 2002.

Reychler, Luc, and Thania Paffenholz. *Peace-Building: A Field Guide.* Boulder, Colo.: Lynne Rienner, 2001.

Roberts, Adam. "The Use of Force," in *The UN Security Council: From the Cold War to the 21st Century,* ed. David M. Malone. Boulder, Colo.: Lynne Rienner, 2004, 133–152.

Roe, Paul. "Former Yugoslavia: The Security Dilemma That Never Was?" *European Journal of International Relations* 6 (September 2000): 373–393.

Rose, Michael. "Military Aspects of Peacekeeping: Lessons Learned from Bosnia: A Commander's Perspective," in *UN Peacekeeping in Trouble: Lessons Learned from the Former Yugoslavia,* ed. Wolfgang Biermann and Martin Vadset. Aldershot, England: Ashgate Publishing, 1998.

Ruchhaus, Robert. *Explaining NATO Enlargement.* London, England: Frank Cass, 2000.

Ruggie, John G. *Multilateralism Matters: The Theory and Praxis of an Institutional Form.* New York: Columbia University Press, 1993.

Russett, Bruce. *Grasping the Democratic Peace: Principles for a Post–Cold War World.* Princeton: Princeton University Press, 1993.

Schwartz, Stephen I. *Atomic Audit: The Costs and Consequences of U.S. Nuclear Weapons Since 1940.* Washington, D.C.: Brookings Institution Press, 1998.

Sigal, Leon V. *Disarming Strangers: Nuclear Diplomacy with North Korea.* Princeton: Princeton University Press, 1998.

Singer, J. David. "The Levels of Analysis Problem in International Relations," in *The International System: Theoretical Essays,* ed. Klaus Knorr and Sidney Verba. Princeton: Princeton University Press, 1961.

Singer, J. David, and Melvin Small. *Resort to Arms: International and Civil Wars, 1816–1980.* Beverly Hills, Calif.: SAGE Publications, 1982.

Singer, J. David, and Melvin Small. *The Wages of War, 1816–1965: A Statistical Handbook.* New York: Wiley, 1972.

SIPRI Yearbook. Oxford, England, and Stockholm, Sweden: Oxford University Press, published annually.

Snyder, Jack L. *The Ideology of the Offensive: Military Decision Making and the Disasters of 1914.* Ithaca: Cornell University Press, 1984.

Snyder, Jack, and Robert Jervis. "Civil War and the Security Dilemma," in *Civil Wars, Insecurity, and Intervention*, ed. Barbara F. Walter and Jack Snyder. New York: Columbia University Press, 1999, 15–37.

Starkey, Brigid, Mark A. Boyer, and Jonathan Wilkenfeld. *Negotiating a Complex World: An Introduction to International Negotiation*, 2nd ed. Lanham, Md.: Rowman and Littlefield, 2005.

Stedman, Stephan John, Donald Rothchild, and Elizabeth M. Cousens, eds. *Ending Civil Wars: The Implementation of Peace Agreements*. Boulder, Colo.: Lynne Rienner, 2002.

Stiles, T. J. *Jesse James: Last Rebel of the Civil War*. New York: Knopf, 2002.

Stremlau, John. *People in Peril: Human Rights, Humanitarian Action, and Preventing Deadly Conflicts*. New York: Carnegie Corporation of New York, 1998.

Stueck, William. *The Korean War: An International History*. Princeton: Princeton University Press, 1995.

Tarriff, Terry, Stuart Croft, Lucy James, and Patrick M. Morgan. *Security Studies Today*. Cambridge, England: Polity Press, 1999.

Tilly, Charles. *Coercion, Capital, and European States*. Cambridge, Mass.: Basil Blackwell, 1990.

Tilly, Charles. "War Making and State Making as Organized Crime," in *Bringing the State Back In*, ed. Peter Evans, Dietrich Rueschmeyer, and Theda Skocpol. Cambridge, England: Cambridge University Press, 1985.

Toland, John. *The Rising Sun: The Rise and Fall of the Japanese Empire*. New York: Random House, 1970.

Traub, James. "Peacekeeping," *New York Times Magazine*, April 11, 2004.

Tuchman, Barbara. *The Guns of August*. New York: Macmillan, 1962; New York: Ballantine Books, reissued 1994.

Van Tongeren, Paul, Hans van de Veen, and Juliette Verhoeven, eds. *Searching for Peace in Europe and Eurasia: An Overview of Conflict Prevention and Peacebuilding Activities*. Boulder, Colo.: Lynne Rienner, 2002.

Vasquez, John A. "The Deterrence Myth: Nuclear Weapons and the Prevention of Nuclear War," in *The Long Postwar Peace: Contending Explanations and Projections*, ed. Charles A. Kegley Jr. New York: HarperCollins, 1991, 205–223.

Vasquez, John A. *The Power of Power Politics: A Critique*. New Brunswick, N.J.: Rutgers University Press, 1983.

Vasquez, John A. *The War Puzzle*. Cambridge, England: Cambridge University Press, 1993.

Viotti, Paul R., and Mark V. Kaupi. *International Relations Theory: Realism, Pluralism, Globalism*, 3rd ed. Boston: Allyn and Bacon, 1999.

Wallensteen, Peter. *Understanding Conflict Resolution: War, Peace, and the Global System*. Thousand Oaks, Calif.: SAGE Publications, 2002.

Wallensteen, Peter, ed. *Preventing Violent Conflicts.* Uppsala: Uppsala University, Department of Peace and Conflict Research, 1998.

Walt, Stephen M. *Revolution and War.* Ithaca: Cornell University Press, 1996.

Walter, Barbara. "The Critical Barrier to Civil War Settlement," *International Organization* 51, no. 3 (Summer 1997): 335–364.

Walter, Barbara F., and Jack Snyder, eds. *Civil Wars, Insecurity, and Intervention.* New York: Columbia University Press, 1999.

Waltz, Kenneth N. *Man, the State, and War.* New York: Columbia University Press, 1959.

Waltz, Kenneth N. *Theory of International Politics.* New York: Random House, 1979.

Weiss, Thomas G. "The Humanitarian Impulse," in *The UN Security Council: From the Cold War to the 21st Century,* ed. David M. Malone. Boulder, Colo.: Lynne Rienner, 2004, 37–54.

Weiss, Thomas G. *Military–Civilian Interactions: Humanitarian Crises and the Responsibility to Protect,* 2nd ed. Lanham, Md.: Rowman and Littlefield, 2005.

Weiss, Thomas G., and Laurse S. Hayes Holgate. "Opportunities and Obstacles for Collective Security after the Cold War," in *Building a New Global Order: Emerging Trends in International Security,* ed. David Dewitt, David Haglund, and John Kirten. New York: Oxford University Press, 1994, 258–283.

Whitman, Jim, ed. *Peacekeeping and the UN Agencies.* London: Frank Cass, 1999.

Williams, Abiodun. *Preventing War: The United Nations and Macedonia.* Lanham, Md.: Rowman and Littlefield, 2000.

Wit, Joes S., Daniel B. Poneman, and Robert L. Gallucci. *Going Critical: The First North Korean Nuclear Crisis.* Washington, D.C.: Brookings Institution Press, 2004.

Wohlforth, William, C. "The Stability of a Unipolar World," *International Security* 24 (Summer 1999): 5–41.

Woodhouse, Tom, and Oliver Ramsbotham, eds. *Peacekeeping and Conflict Resolution.* London: Frank Cass, 2000.

Zartman, I. William. "Dynamics and Constraints in Negotiations in Internal Conflicts," in *Elusive Peace: Negotiating an End to Civil Wars,* ed. I. William Zartman. Washington, D.C.: Brookings Institution Press, 1995, 3–29.

Zartman, I. William. *Ripe for Resolution: Conflict and Intervention in Africa.* New York: Oxford University Press, 1989.

Zartman, I. William, ed. *The 50% Solution.* New York: Doubleday Anchor, 1976.

Zartman, I. William, ed. *The Negotiation Process: Theories and Applications.* Beverly Hills, Calif.: SAGE Publications, 1978.

Ziring, Lawrence, Jack C. Plano, and Roy Alton. *International Relations: A Political Dictionary,* 5th ed. Santa Barbara, Calif.: ABC-Clio, 1995.